Mastering Tableau 2021

Third Edition

Implement advanced business intelligence techniques
and analytics with Tableau

Marleen Meier
David Baldwin

BIRMINGHAM - MUMBAI

Mastering Tableau 2021
Third Edition

Producer: Tushar Gupta
Acquisition Editor – Peer Reviews: Divya Mudaliar
Content Development Editor: Edward Doxey
Technical Editor: Gaurav Gavas
Project Editor: Parvathy Nair
Proofreader: Safis Editing
Indexer: Manju Arasan
Presentation Designer: Ganesh Bhadwalkar

First published: May 2021

Production reference: 1270521

Published by Packt Publishing Ltd.
Livery Place
35 Livery Street
Birmingham B3 2PB, UK.

ISBN 978-1-80056-164-9

www.packt.com

Foreword

Hello, I'm Kate Strachnyi, founder of DATAcated®, and I am extremely passionate about data visualization and storytelling. In 2013, I made a career shift from risk management and regulatory compliance into the world of data analytics, and Tableau played a significant role in my professional journey. As I jumped into data analytics, I was provided with access to Tableau Desktop, along with various sets of data. My task was to derive insights and design visuals to support and communicate those insights. It was love at first sight. Tableau's intuitive layout made it easy for me to connect data sources and extract information, and I was able to build my first dashboard within minutes of obtaining access to the tool. From that point on, I was hooked on data visualization.

In this book, *Mastering Tableau 2021 - Third Edition*, Marleen Meier and David Baldwin take the reader on a journey that teaches the advanced offerings of Tableau 2021 and empowers them to tackle various data challenges. The book starts with the basics, by connecting Tableau to data and performing various data preparation activities, before going into more advanced features, such as Level of Detail calculations and data densification. The authors deftly illustrate Tableau's ability to create various charts with just a few clicks or by dragging and dropping fields into the view, which speeds up the visualization process and lets the user focus purely on the stories within the data. The authors take this a step further by demonstrating how basic visualizations can be evolved beyond their basic functionality. The book goes on to demonstrate a spectrum of advanced topics, including geo-spatial visualizations, time series visualizations, implementing Python and R functionality, and more!

My personal passion lies in using visual design best practices to tell impactful data stories. Meier and Baldwin make it simple to customize data visualizations and dashboards in a way that drives data-informed decision making, with a focus on formatting and design customization. This book considers the steps that we can take, such as reducing clutter, improving formatting, and using color intelligently, that can help tell more effective stories with data. Meier and Baldwin take the reader through the process of applying these steps in Tableau, discussing design theory, color rules, and other dos and don'ts of data visualization that will help focus your audience's attention.

In addition to designing useful dashboards, the book covers methods for improving the performance of those dashboards. The authors address various aspects of performance, with the intent of empowering the reader with techniques to create workbooks that load quickly and respond to end user interaction. With the end user in mind, Meier and Baldwin also provide extended use cases that take the reader through the thought process of analyzing queries, generating insights, and creating useful self-service dashboards. In doing so, the book helps you create visualizations to empower users (whether that might be your boss, a colleague, or a customer) to dig into data themselves, as opposed to waiting on IT or data teams to present it to them.

Kate Strachnyi
DATAcated®

Contributors

About the authors

Marleen Meier has been working in the field of data science since 2013. Her experience includes Tableau training, producing proofs of concept, and implementing and enabling projects, as well as quantitative analysis, machine learning and artificial intelligence. In 2018, she was a speaker at the Tableau conference, where she showcased an anomaly detection model using neural networks, visualized in Tableau. In February 2019, her first book in this series was published.

Writing this book has been such a rewarding journey and would never have been possible without the Packt team. I want to thank Tushar Gupta, Parvathy Nair, and Ravi Mistry for your encouragement, guidance, and great work relationships – a special thanks to Edward Doxey, my editor, for your attention to detail and for always pushing me to do better. Thank you!

David Baldwin has provided consulting in the business intelligence sector for 21 years. His experience includes Tableau training and consulting, developing BI solutions, project management, technical writing, and the web and graphic design. His vertical experience includes corporate, government, higher education, and non-profit. As a Tableau trainer and consultant, David enjoys serving a variety of clients throughout the USA. Tableau provides David with a platform that collates his broad experience into a skill set that can service a diverse client base.

Many people provided invaluable support in the writing of this book. Although I cannot name everyone, I would like to draw special attention to my wife, Kara, and my children, Brent and Brooke, for their unfailing support. Also, my colleagues at Teknion Data Solutions exemplify world-class technical expertise and always challenge me to do my best.

About the reviewer

Ravi Mistry is a Tableau Zen Master and Ambassador, and a data visualization specialist. A lapsed economist, he enables folks to make sense of data through analytics and visualization. When he's not following his hometown football team, Ipswich Town, Ravi is a keen enthusiast in contemporary technology, as well as TV, film, and media.

Table of Contents

Preface

Tableau is one of the leading business intelligence (BI) tools used to solve data analysis challenges. With this book, you will master Tableau's features and offerings in various paradigms of the BI domain.

Updated with fresh topics and the newest Tableau Server features, including relationships, Quick Level of Detail (LOD) expressions, Einstein Discovery, and more, this book covers essential Tableau concepts and advanced functionalities. Leveraging Tableau Hyper files and using Prep Builder, you'll be able to perform data preparation and handling easily. You'll gear up to perform complex joins, spatial joins, unions, and data blending tasks using practical examples. Following this, you'll learn how to use data densification, and consider how to use Tableau extensions to help you with calculations, mapping, and visual design. You'll cover advanced use cases such as self-service analysis, time series analysis, and geo-spatial analysis, before moving on to improving dashboard performance and connecting to Tableau Server with expert-level examples. Finally, you'll connect to and implement Python and R within Tableau, to achieve things that are impossible with Tableau's native functionalities alone.

By the end of this Tableau book, you'll have mastered the advanced offerings of Tableau 2021 and be able to tackle common and advanced BI challenges.

Who this book is for

This book is designed for business analysts, BI professionals, and data analysts who want to master Tableau to solve a range of data science and BI problems. The book is ideal if you have a good understanding of Tableau and want to take your skills to the next level.

What this book covers

Chapter 1, Getting Up to Speed – A Review of the Basics, takes you through the basic and essential Tableau concepts needed to get you started.

Chapter 2, All About Data – Getting Your Data Ready, introduces the Tableau data-handling engine, after which we will dive into knowledge-discovery process models, as well as data mining. Last but not least, we will talk about data cleaning.

Chapter 3, Tableau Prep Builder, discusses Tableau Prep Builder, a new member of the Tableau family, and how it can benefit your workflows.

Chapter 4, All About Data – Joins, Blends, and Data Structures, considers the big question that Tableau users face on a daily basis: should I blend, join, or union my data? We will also discuss relationships, join calculations, and spatial joins, which are fairly new features in Tableau.

Chapter 5, Table Calculations, covers functions and table calculations in the process flow and explains why table calculations are still relevant now that LOD calculations are available.

Chapter 6, All About Data – Data Densification, Cubes, and Big Data, discusses data densification and how we can display more granular data than the given granularity of the dataset. We will then move on to cubes and big data, and how to deal with it in Tableau.

Chapter 7, Level of Detail Calculations, helps you understand how to use LODs in such a way that you won't want to live without them any longer, by building a variety of playgrounds to experiment with. We will then combine LOD calculations with table calculations, sets, and parameters to maximize their potential.

Chapter 8, Beyond the Basic Chart Types, introduces some widely used chart types, demonstrating how to extend their usefulness, along with some more unique chart types, all beyond the "Show Me" section. Tableau extensions, a new feature, are explained too, with a couple of examples.

Chapter 9, Mapping, covers Tableau's mapping capabilities using custom polygons, heatmaps, and layered maps, and looks at extending Tableau mapping with other technologies, such as Web Map Services and Mapbox.

Chapter 10, Tableau for Presentations, shows how the user can make use of Tableau for presentation purposes. Tableau is typically thought of as a BI and analytics platform; however, it can be, and often is, used as a presentation tool. In this chapter, you will get some insight into tips and tricks to make the most of this element of Tableau.

Chapter 11, Visualization Best Practices and Dashboard Design, takes you through different formatting techniques and design rules to maximize the aesthetics and utility of your Tableau visualizations.

Chapter 12, Advanced Analytics, will help you test your knowledge using three use cases, which incorporate elements of self-service analytics, time series analytics, and geo-spatial analytics.

Chapter 13, Improving Performance, addresses various aspects of performance on Tableau with the intent of empowering you with techniques to create workbooks that load quickly and respond snappily to end user interaction.

Chapter 14, Interacting with Tableau Server/Online, covers the Tableau Server architecture and its different offerings and functionalities. We will go through the process of publishing, editing, and maintaining your visualizations on Tableau Server.

Chapter 15, Programming Tool Integration, shows how to integrate Tableau with R and Python, in order to implement advanced models such as regression analysis, sentiment analysis, and more in your Tableau projects.

To get the most out of this book

A basic knowledge of Tableau is required. You will need a Tableau license, or to sign up for the 14-day free trial version of Tableau. Readers are also expected to have a basic knowledge of R/RStudio and Python in order to make the most of the final chapter.

Download the example code files

The code bundle for the book is hosted on GitHub at `https://github.com/PacktPublishing/Mastering-Tableau-2021`. We also have other code bundles from our rich catalog of books and videos available at `https://github.com/PacktPublishing/`. Check them out!

Download the color images

We also provide a PDF file that has color images of the screenshots/diagrams used in this book. You can download it here: `https://static.packt-cdn.com/downloads/9781800561649_ColorImages.pdf`.

Conventions used

There are a number of text conventions used throughout this book.

CodeInText: Indicates code words in text, database table names, folder names, filenames, file extensions, pathnames, dummy URLs, user input, and Twitter handles. For example: "We can configure webpack using the webpack.config.js file"

A block of code is set as follows:

```
SCRIPT_REAL("
from numpy import random as rd
mu, sigma = _arg2, _arg3
return (rd.normal(mu, sigma, _arg1[0])).tolist()
",
SIZE(), [mu], [sigma]
)
```

Any command-line input or output is written as follows:

```
pip install tabpy
```

Bold: Indicates a new term, an important word, or words that you see on the screen, for example, in menus or dialog boxes, also appear in the text like this. For example: "To start R within a Windows environment, navigate to **Start | Programs | R x64 4.0.3**."

 Warnings or important notes appear like this.

 Tips and tricks appear like this.

Get in touch

Feedback from our readers is always welcome.

General feedback: Email feedback@packtpub.com, and mention the book's title in the subject of your message. If you have questions about any aspect of this book, please email us at questions@packtpub.com.

Errata: Although we have taken every care to ensure the accuracy of our content, mistakes do happen. If you have found a mistake in this book we would be grateful if you would report this to us. Please visit, http://www.packtpub.com/submit-errata, selecting your book, clicking on the Errata Submission Form link, and entering the details.

Piracy: If you come across any illegal copies of our works in any form on the Internet, we would be grateful if you would provide us with the location address or website name. Please contact us at copyright@packtpub.com with a link to the material.

If you are interested in becoming an author: If there is a topic that you have expertise in and you are interested in either writing or contributing to a book, please visit http://authors.packtpub.com.

Reviews

Please leave a review. Once you have read and used this book, why not leave a review on the site that you purchased it from? Potential readers can then see and use your unbiased opinion to make purchase decisions, we at Packt can understand what you think about our products, and our authors can see your feedback on their book. Thank you!

For more information about Packt, please visit packtpub.com.

1

Getting Up to Speed – A Review of the Basics

Tableau is one of the leading tools used to solve **business intelligence (BI)** and analytics challenges. With this book, you will master Tableau's features and offerings in various paradigms of the BI domain. As an update to the successful *Mastering Tableau* series, this book covers essential Tableau concepts, data preparation, and calculations with Tableau, all the way up to machine learning use cases.

This edition comes with new datasets, more examples of how to improve dashboard performance, and the most up-to-date know-how on data visualizations, Tableau Server, and Tableau Prep Builder. This new edition will also explore Tableau's connections with Python and R, Tableau extensions, joins, and unions, and last but not least, three new use cases of powerful self-service analytics, time series analytics, and geo-spatial analytics in order to implement the learned content. By the end of this book, you'll have mastered the advanced offerings of Tableau and its latest updates, up to Tableau version 2021.

Those who are fairly new to Tableau should find this chapter helpful in getting up to speed quickly; however, since this book targets advanced topics, relatively little time is spent considering the basics. For a more thorough consideration of fundamental topics, consider *Learning Tableau, Fourth Edition*, written by Joshua Milligan and published by Packt Publishing.

In this chapter, we'll discuss the following topics:

- Creating worksheets and dashboards
- Connecting Tableau to your data
- Measure Names and Measure Values
- Three essential Tableau concepts
- Exporting data to other devices

Now, let's get started by exploring worksheet and dashboard creation in Tableau.

Creating worksheets and dashboards

At the heart of Tableau are **worksheets** and **dashboards**. Worksheets contain individual visualizations and dashboards contain one or more worksheets. Additionally, worksheets and dashboards may be combined into **stories** to communicate particular insights to the end user through a presentation environment. Lastly, all worksheets, dashboards, and stories are organized in **workbooks** that can be accessed using Tableau Desktop, Server, Reader, or the Tableau mobile app.

At this point, I would like to introduce you to **Tableau Public** (`https://public.tableau.com`). At times you might need some inspiration, or you might want to replicate a dashboard created by another Tableau user. In this case, Tableau Public will be your place to go! It is a web-based collection of dashboards and works like LinkedIn for the Tableau community. You can create your own profile—registration is free—and share all the dashboards you've created, that you think the world shouldn't miss out on. The best part, however, is that you can download all of them, open them in your own version of Tableau, and start learning and replicating. Even without your own profile or registration, it is possible to download dashboards.

In this section, we'll consider how to create worksheets and dashboards. Our intention here is to communicate the basics, but we'll also provide some insight that may prove helpful to more seasoned Tableau users.

Creating worksheets

Before creating a worksheet, we'll need to create a visualization to populate it with. At the most fundamental level, a visualization in Tableau is created by placing one or more **fields** on one or more **shelves**. As an example, note that the visualization created in the following diagram is generated by placing the **Number of Records** field on the **Text** shelf on the **Marks** card:

Figure 1.1: The Marks card

Having considered some basic theory, in the next subsection you will get the chance to follow along in your own Tableau workbook. Let's go!

Creating a visualization

Now, let's explore the basics of creating a visualization using an exercise:

1. Navigate to https://public.tableau.com/profile/marleen.meier to locate and download the workbook associated with this chapter.

2. Open the file by double-clicking on the downloaded workbook.

3. In the workbook, find and select the tab labeled **Fundamentals of Visualizations**:

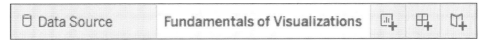

Figure 1.2: Navigating worksheet tabs

4. Locate **Sport** within the **Dimensions** portion of the **Data** pane, which can be found on the left-hand side of the **Fundamentals of Visualizations** sheet:

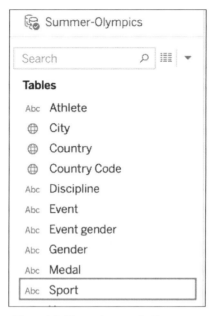

Figure 1.3: Dimensions on the Data pane

5. Drag **Sport** to **Color** on the **Marks** card:

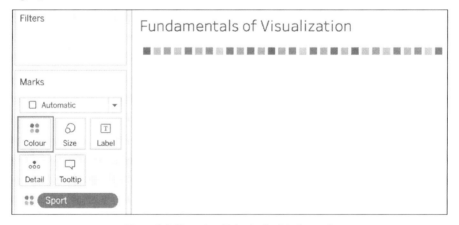

Figure 1.4: Dragging Color to the Marks card

6. Click on **Color** on the **Marks** card and then on **Edit Colors...** to adjust the colors of your visualization as desired. This will allow you to edit the colors used in your visualization, and **Transparency** and **Border** effects:

Figure 1.5: Edit Colors...

7. Now see what happens if you move **Sport** to the **Size**, **Label**, **Detail**, **Columns**, and **Rows** shelves. After placing **Sport** on each shelf, you can click on each shelf individually to access additional options.

8. Drop other fields on various shelves to continue exploring Tableau's behavior. One example could be, on an empty canvas, dragging **Year** to the **Columns** shelf, **Number of Records** to the **Rows** shelf, and **Medal** to **Color** on the **Marks** card. You will now see the number of medals per medal type over time:

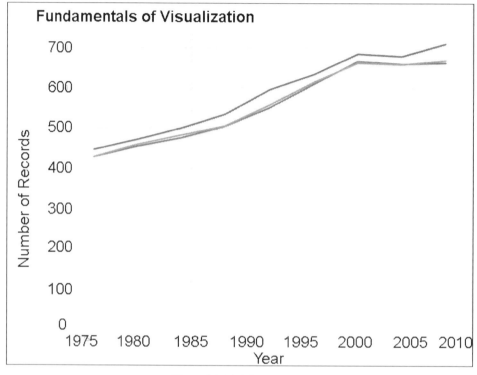

Figure 1.6: Medals over time

9. Did you come up with any interesting visualizations? Feel free to share them on Tableau Public. Add the tag #MasteringTableau if you want other readers of this book to find them—sharing is caring!

As you explore Tableau's behavior by dragging and dropping different fields onto different shelves, you'll notice that Tableau responds with default behaviors. These defaults, however, can be overridden, which we'll explore next.

Beyond the default behavior

In the preceding exercise, *Creating a visualization*, we can notice that the **Marks** card reads **Automatic**. This means that Tableau is providing the default view. The default view can be easily overridden by choosing a different selection from the drop-down menu:

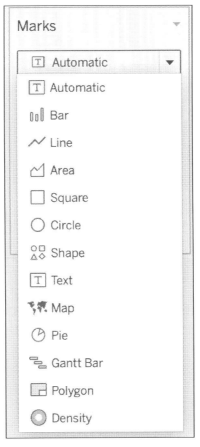

Figure 1.7: The Marks card drop-down menu

By changing these settings on the **Marks** card, we can adjust the format in which your data will be displayed.

Another type of default behavior can be observed when dragging a field onto a shelf. For example, dragging and dropping a measure onto a shelf will typically result in the SUM() aggregation, which will sum up all the values to the highest level of aggregation. If no dimension is present, it will be the sum of all values. If a dimension is present on the **Marks** card, for example, this same dimension will serve as the highest level of aggregation. We will see an example of this behavior later in this section.

In Windows, you can override this default behavior by right-clicking and dragging a pill from the **Data** pane and dropping it onto a shelf. Tableau will respond with a dialog box with possible options:

Figure 1.8: Changing the default aggregation

If you are working on macOS, you can right-click on the pill after you've dragged it to its location and then adjust the default behavior by changing the measure. This works on Windows as well. Another option is to right-click on the field while it is still in the **Data** pane on your left-hand side and select **Default Properties | Aggregation**.

Now, let's walk through an exercise where we'll override another default behavior on the **Marks** card:

1. In the workbook associated with this chapter, navigate to the **Overriding Defaults** worksheet.

2. Right-click and drag **Year** from the data pane to the **Columns** shelf:

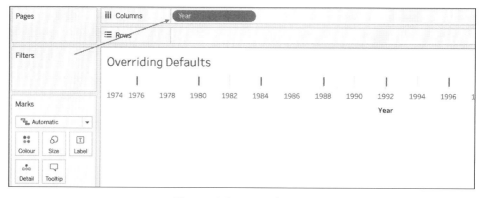

Figure 1.9: Year to Columns

3. Place **Number of Records** on the **Rows** shelf (which is automatically aggregated to **SUM(Number of Records)** and **Sport** on the **Detail** shelf.

4. Click on the dropdown on the **Marks** card and select **Area**:

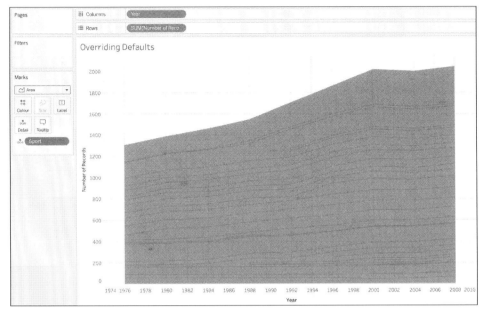

Figure 1.10: Area chart

In *Figure 1.10*, we can see the **Number of Records** over time (**Year**), where each line represents one type of **Sport**. We chose to visualize this in a stacked area chart.

Sorting and nested sorting

Now that you are familiar with the basics of dragging and dropping pills and are aware of Tableau's default behavior, the next thing most users want to do is to sort the data to draw first conclusions, regarding, for example, minimum and maximum values.

Navigate to the **Nested Sorting** tab and try to sort the countries by the amount of medals won but separately for gold, silver, and bronze.

Did it work for you? In Tableau, sorting and nested sorting can be done by simply clicking on the icon next to each column name:

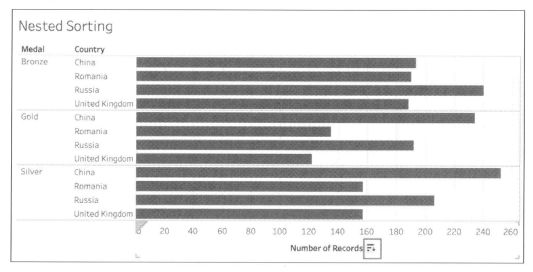

Figure 1.11: Sorting

To double-check the way of sorting, click on the arrow next to a given field, in this case, **Country**, and select **Sort**:

Figure 1.12: Sort settings

From the dropdown, select **Nested** and the desired **Field Name** as well as the **Aggregation** type:

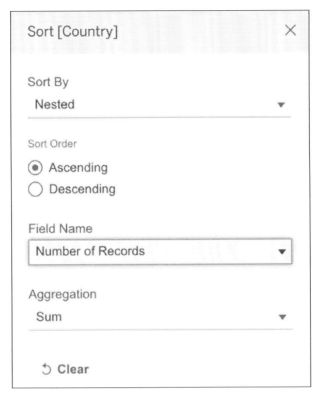

Figure 1.13: Nested Sort

After having completed and understood **Sort** and **Nested Sort**, you will immediately be able to add value to your dashboards by presenting values in the most logical way. Now we can move on to the next topic, the different default chart types Tableau comes with: **Show Me**.

Show Me

Show Me can help people new to Tableau to create the visualization they are looking for, such as bar charts, histograms, and area charts. It allows the Tableau author to create visualizations from inputted data at the click of a button. To understand how it works, let's refer to the following screenshot, which again makes use of the **Overriding Defaults** worksheet. This view can be accessed by clicking the **Show Me** button in the upper-right corner of any Tableau sheet:

Figure 1.14: Show Me

Now let's look at the following aspects that are highlighted in the preceding screenshot:

- **A**: Selected fields in the **Data** pane
- **B**: Fields deployed in the view, that is, pills
- **C**: The recommended view, highlighted in the **Show Me** panel
- **D**: Help text that communicates the requirements for creating the recommended view or any selection choice over which the cursor is placed

Every icon in **Show Me** that isn't grayed out represents a visualization that can be created simply by clicking on it. For example, in the preceding screenshot, *Figure 1.14*, the Tableau author may choose to click on the area chart icon to create an area chart based on the selected and deployed fields.

Show Me options are highlighted based on two criteria: the selected fields in the **Data** pane and the fields deployed in the view.

Show Me may be effectively used for the following reasons:

- **Efficiency**: The proficient Tableau author already knows how to create the basic visualization types. Show Me automates these basic types and thus may be used for quicker production.

- **Inspiration**: Determining an effective way to visualize a dataset can be challenging. Show Me can help with this challenge by allowing the Tableau author to quickly consider various options.

- **Education**: An inexperienced Tableau author may access **Show Me** to better understand how various visualizations are created. By reading the help text displayed at the bottom of Show Me and changing pill placement accordingly, much can be learned.

These three reasons demonstrate the strong capabilities that **Show Me** provides for worksheet creation; however, be careful not to use it as a crutch. If you click on the various options without understanding how each visualization is created, you're not only shortchanging the educational process, but you may generate results that aren't well understood and could lead to detrimental business decisions.

Once you are happy with the results and confident that the selected visualization puts enough emphasis on your data story, your worksheet is ready for the next round of development. We've looked at some basic visualization creation and configuration techniques, so let's now look at how to group multiple worksheets into a dashboard.

Creating dashboards

Although, as stated earlier in this section, a dashboard contains one or more worksheets, dashboards are much more than static presentations. They're an essential part of Tableau's interactivity. In this section, we'll populate a dashboard with worksheets and then deploy actions for interactivity.

Let's begin by building a dashboard.

Building a dashboard

The following are the steps for building a dashboard:

1. In the workbook for this chapter, navigate to the **Building a Dashboard** tab.

2. In the **Dashboard** pane, located on the left side of the *Figure 1.15*, double-click on each of the following worksheets (in the order in which they are listed) to add them to the dashboard pane: **Count of Disciplines**, **Attendees**, **Medals**, and **Medal Shapes**:

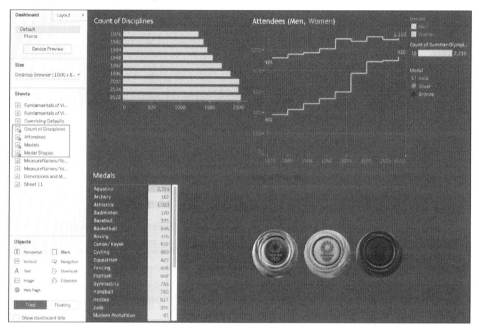

Figure 1.15: Creating a dashboard

3. In the bottom-right corner of the dashboard, click in the blank area (indicated by an arrow in *Figure 1.16*) to select a **container**. Containers are a selection of sheets that auto-adjust to fit next to/underneath each other on your dashboard:

Figure 1.16: Deleting a container

4. After clicking in the blank area, you should see a blue border around the filter and the legends. This indicates that the vertical container is selected. Select the vertical container handle and delete it.

5. A selected container can also be dragged to a different location on the dashboard, replacing an existing sheet or sharing space. Note the gray shading in *Figure 1.17*, which communicates where the selection will be placed. Drag the **Attendees** worksheet by selecting and holding the handle and put it on top of the **Count of Disciplines** worksheet in order to swap the two:

Figure 1.17: Moving worksheets

 The gray shading provided by Tableau when dragging elements, such as worksheets and containers, onto a dashboard helpfully communicates where the element will be placed. Take your time and observe carefully when placing an element on a dashboard or the results may be unexpected.

6. Note the **Floating** and **Tiled** buttons at the bottom left, next to your dashboard, as well as under the handle dropdown. If you select **Floating** instead of **Tiled**, your worksheets will not auto-adjust anymore and will be "floating" around the dashboard instead. This is a free form of worksheet arrangement on a dashboard, which is a powerful functionality, especially combined with transparent backgrounds. Note that floating can also be achieved by selecting it from the **More Options** dropdown on the right-hand side of every sheet in the dashboard:

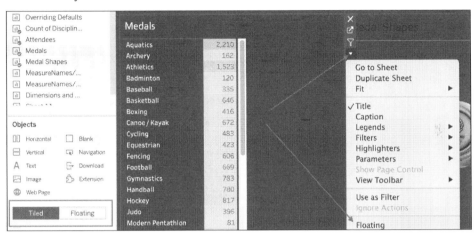

Figure 1.18: Tiled and Floating

7. Now, you can format the dashboard as desired. The following tips may prove helpful:

   - Adjust the sizes of the elements on the screen by hovering over the edges between each element and then clicking and dragging. Drag the edges of containers to adjust the size of each worksheet.

   - Make an element floating, as shown in *Figure 1.18*.

   - Create horizontal and vertical containers by dragging **Horizontal** and **Vertical** from the **Objects** pane onto the dashboard. Other objects, such as **Text**, **Image**, and **Blank**, can be added to containers too.

- Display the dashboard title by selecting **Dashboard** in the top pane, then **Show Title**. Double-click the title itself to adjust:

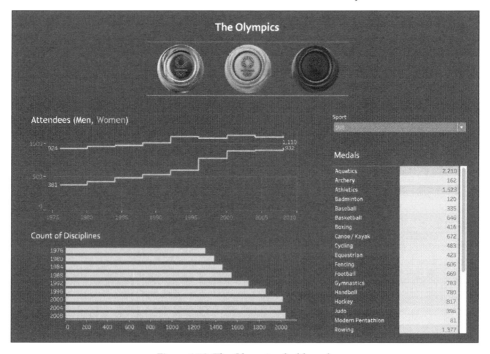

Figure 1.19: The Olympics dashboard

As you can see, you have just created your first dashboard. All worksheets are in place now. In the next part, we will add filter functionality to make the dashboard more interactive and meaningful.

Adding interactivity to a dashboard

One of the primary benefits of Tableau is the interactivity it provides the end user. Dashboards aren't simply for viewing; they're meant for interaction. In this exercise, we'll add interactivity to the dashboard that was created in the previous exercise:

1. Select the **Medals** sheet on the dashboard and click on the drop-down arrow on the right-hand side, which will open a menu as shown in *Figure 1.20*. From there, select **Filters**, then **Sport**:

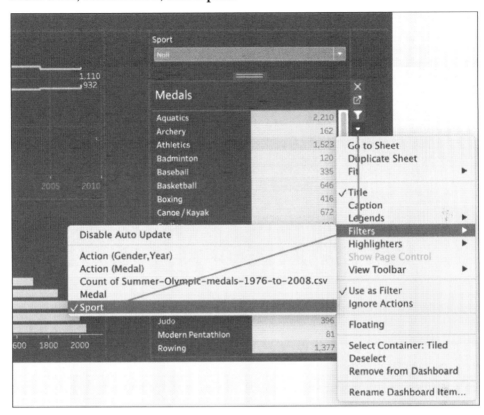

Figure 1.20: Adding a filter

2. Now select the newly created filter, **Sport**, click again on the drop-down options arrow, and select **Multiple Values (dropdown)** as well as **Apply to Worksheets | All Using This Data Source**, as shown in *Figure 1.21*:

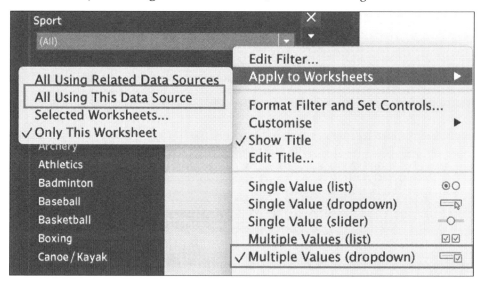

Figure 1.21: Filter settings

3. Lastly, place the filter above the **Medals** sheet by clicking and dragging it.

4. To use the images of the medals as a filter for the other worksheets on the dashboard pane, click the **Use as Filter** icon located at the top-right corner of the **Medals Shapes** worksheet:

Figure 1.22: The Use as Filter option

5. Alternatively, navigate to **Dashboard | Actions**. In the dialog box, click **Add Action | Filter** and create a filter, as shown:

Figure 1.23: Adding a filter action

From here on in, you are good to go and use filters and action filters. In *Chapter 13, Improving Performance*, this topic will be discussed in more detail.

Having completed the preceding dashboard exercise, you should now be able to click on various objects on the dashboard to observe the interactivity. To learn some more advanced dashboard techniques, be sure to check out *Chapter 11, Visualization Best Practices and Dashboard Design*.

To conclude, you have learned how to put existing worksheets, as tiled or floating objects, on a dashboard. You have changed the dashboard layout by dragging and dropping, as well as by using containers, filters, and action filters. Each of these core activities will be repeated multiple more times throughout the book, so feel free to come back to this chapter and repeat the exercise steps whenever needed!

Next, you will learn how to connect your own data to Tableau and work with it.

Connecting Tableau to your data

At the time of writing, Tableau's data connection menu includes more than 70 different connection types. And that's somewhat of an understatement since some of those types contain multiple options. For example, **Other Files** includes 34 options. Of course, we won't cover the details for every connection type, but we will cover the basics.

Upon opening a new instance of Tableau Desktop, you'll notice a link in the top-left corner of the workspace. Clicking on that link will enable you to connect to the data. Alternatively, you can click on the **New Data Source** icon on the toolbar:

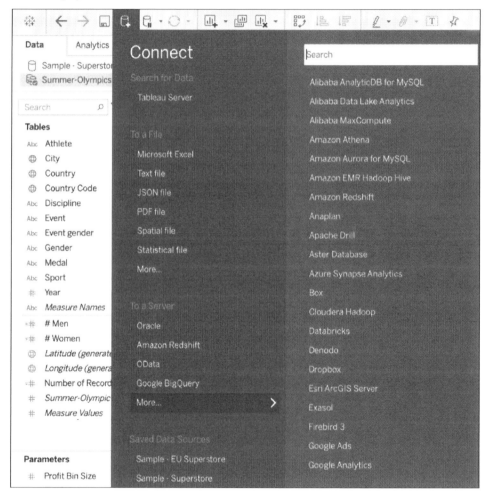

Figure 1.24: Connecting to data

Although in future chapters we'll connect to other data sources, here we'll limit the discussion to connecting to Microsoft Excel and text files.

Connecting to a file

Let's see how you can connect to a file, using Excel as an example:

1. In a new instance of Tableau, navigate to **Data | New Data Source | Excel** to connect to the sample `Superstore` dataset that installs with Tableau Desktop (it should be located on your hard drive under **My Tableau Repository | Data sources**).

2. Double-click on the **Orders** sheet.

3. Click on the **New Worksheet** tab, as shown in *Figure 1.25*:

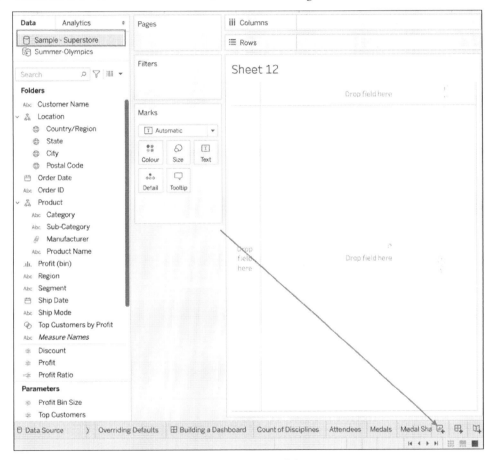

Figure 1.25: New worksheet

4. Rename the newly created tab to `First Worksheet` by right-clicking and selecting **Rename**.

5. Place **Discount** on the **Text** shelf in the **Marks** card.

6. Double-click on **Profit** and **Sales**:

Figure 1.26: First worksheet

7. You've just created your first worksheet!

If you want to connect to a `.csv` file, you could use the **Text file** option, as shown in *Figure 1.24*. I encourage you to try that option, as well as **Access files** if applicable for you. Later in this book, in *Chapter 12, Advanced Analytics*, we will also connect to spatial files.

In this section, we learned how to connect to files. We'll continue with another important connection type in the next section: Tableau Server.

Connecting to Tableau Server

Connecting to Tableau Server is perhaps the single most important server connection type to consider, since it's frequently used to provide a better level of performance than may otherwise be possible. Additionally, connecting to Tableau Server enables the author to receive not only data, but information regarding how that data is to be interpreted — for example, whether a given field should be considered a measure or a dimension. We'll discuss the difference between these terms in the *Dimensions and measures* section later in the chapter.

The following are the steps for connecting to Tableau Server:

1. To complete this exercise, access to an instance of Tableau Server is necessary. If you don't have access to Tableau Server, consider installing a trial version on your local computer.

2. In the workbook associated with this chapter, navigate to the **Connecting to Tableau Server** worksheet.

3. Right-click on the Superstore data source and select **Publish to Server...**:

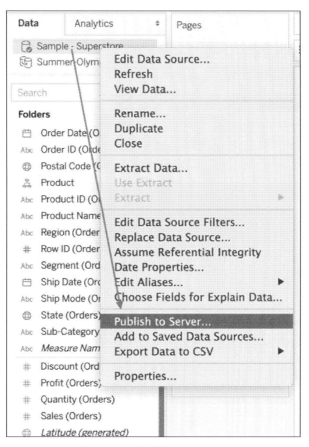

Figure 1.27: Publish to Server...

4. Log in to **Tableau Server** and follow the prompts to complete the publication of the data source.

5. Open a new instance of Tableau Desktop and select **Data | New Data Source | Tableau Server**, then search for the Superstore dataset you just published and connect.

Having completed the preceding two exercises, let's discuss the most germane point, that is, **metadata**. Metadata is often defined as *data about the data*. In the preceding case, the data source name, default aggregation, and default number formatting are all examples of consistency across multiple authors. If you were to change a field name, for example, then publish the data source to Tableau Server, the new field name would remain, since Tableau remembers changes made to the metadata. This is important, for example, if your company has a policy regarding the use of decimal points when displaying currency; that policy will be easily adhered to if all Tableau authors start building workbooks by pointing to data sources where all formatting has been predefined.

Later on in this book, we will connect to other server types, like Google BigQuery, but the handling of all servers is pretty much the same and very straightforward. If you still have questions, you can always check out `https://help.tableau.com/current/pro/desktop/en-us/exampleconnections_overview.htm`.

Now, our last missing piece regarding connections is saved data sources. Please follow along with the next section to understand those as well.

Connecting to saved data sources

Connecting to a saved data source on a local machine is very similar to connecting to a data source published on Tableau Server. Metadata definitions associated with the local data source are preserved just as they are on Tableau Server. Of course, since the data source is local instead of remote, the publication process is different.

Let's explore the following steps to create a local data connection using an example:

1. In the workbook associated with this chapter, navigate to the **First Worksheet** tab.

2. In the **Data** pane, right-click on the Superstore data source and select **Add to Saved Data Sources**.

3. Using the resulting dialog box, save the data source as Superstore in **My Tableau Repository | Data sources**, which is located on your hard drive.

4. Click on the **Go to Start** icon located in the top-left part of your screen and observe the newly saved data source:

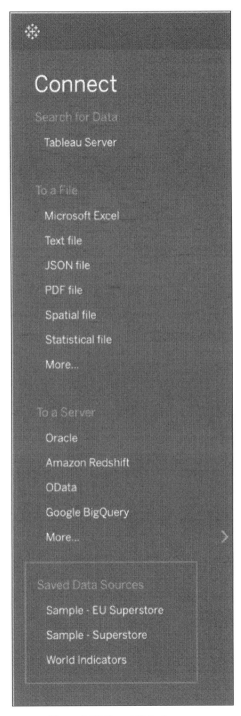

Figure 1.28: Saved Data Sources

You can save a local data source that points to a published data source on Tableau Server. First, connect to a published data source on Tableau Server. Then, right-click on the data source in your workspace and choose **Add to Saved Data Sources**. Now you can connect to Tableau Server directly from your start page!

Now that we've learned how to connect to files, Tableau Server, and saved data sources, we will continue our journey and dive into more details regarding **Measure Names** and **Measure Values**.

Measure Names and Measure Values

I've observed the following scenario frequently: a new Tableau author creates a worksheet and drags a measure to the **Text** shelf. The author does this in order to create another row to display a second measure but doesn't know how. They drag the second measure to various places on the view and get results that seem entirely unpredictable. The experience is very frustrating for the author since it's so easy to accomplish this in Microsoft Excel! The good news is that it's also easy to accomplish this in Tableau. It just requires a different approach.

Measure Names and **Measure Values** are generated fields in Tableau. They don't exist in the underlying data, but they're indispensable for creating many kinds of views. As may be guessed from its placement in the **Data** pane and its name, **Measure Names** is a dimension whose members are made up of the names of each measure in the underlying dataset. **Measure Values** contains the numbers or values of each measure in the dataset.

In this section, we'll watch what happens when these generated fields are used independently, then observe how they work elegantly together to create a view. Let's explore this with an exercise:

1. In the workbook associated with this chapter, navigate to the **MeasureNames/Values** worksheet and make sure that the Olympics data source is selected.

2. Drag **Measure Values** to the **Text** shelf and observe the results:

Figure 1.29: Measure Values

3. Clear the worksheet by clicking on the **Clear Sheet** icon on the toolbar:

Figure 1.30: Clear Sheet

4. Now, drag **Measure Names** to the **Rows** shelf and observe that the view merely displays no **Measure Values**.

5. Drag **Measure Values** to the **Text** shelf. Note the list of measures and associated values:

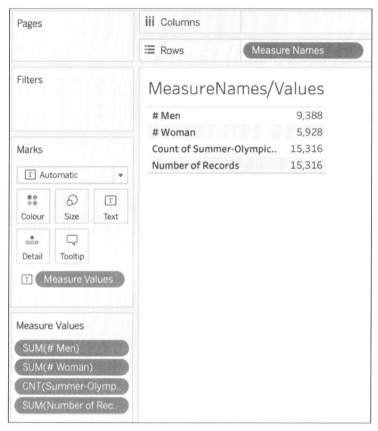

Figure 1.31: List of Measure Values

Perhaps the relationship between **Measure Names** and **Measure Values** is best explained by an analogy. Consider several pairs of socks and a partitioned sock drawer. *Step 2* is the equivalent of throwing the socks into a pile. The results are, well, disorganized. *Step 4* is the equivalent of an empty sock drawer with partitions. The partitions are all in place but where are the socks? *Step 5* is a partitioned drawer full of nicely organized socks. Measure Names is like the partitioned sock drawer. Measure Values is like the socks.

Independent of one another, they aren't of much use. Used together, they can be applied in many different ways.

Measure Names and Measure Values shortcuts

Tableau provides various shortcuts to quickly create the desired visualization. If you're new to the software, this shortcut behavior may not seem intuitive. But with a little practice and a few pointers, you'll quickly gain an understanding of it. Let's use the following exercise to explore how you can use a shortcut to rapidly deploy `Measure Names` and `Measure Values`:

1. In the workbook associated with this chapter, navigate to the **MeasureNames/Values ShrtCts** worksheet.

2. Drag **# Women** onto **Text** in the **Marks** card.

3. Drag **# Men** directly on top of **# Women** in the view (**Show Me** appears):

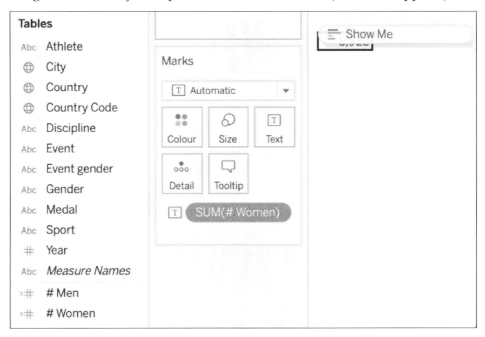

Figure 1.32: Show Me and Measures

4. Observe the results, including the appearance of the **Measure Values** shelf, and the deployment of **Measure Names** on the **Rows** and **Filters** shelves and **Measure Values** on the **Text** shelf:

Figure 1.33: Measure Values appearance

Several things happened in *Step 2* of this exercise. After placing the # Men number on top of the # Women number in the view, Tableau did the following:

1. Deployed Measure Names on the **Filters** shelf:

    - Open the Measure Names filter by right-clicking and hit **Edit**. Observe that only # Men and # Women are selected. This limits the view to display only those two measures.

2. Deployed Measure Names on the **Rows** shelf:

    - Measure Names is acting like a partitioned container, that is, like the sock drawer in the analogy. Because of the filter, the only rows that display are for # Men and # Women.

3. Displayed the **Measure Values** shelf:

   - The **Measure Values** shelf is somewhat redundant. Although it clearly shows the measures that display in the view, it essentially acts as an easy way to access the filter. You can simply drag measures on and off of the **Measure Values** shelf to adjust the filter and thus display/hide additional Measure Values. You can also change the order within the **Measure Values** shelf to change the order of the measures in the view.

4. Deployed Measure Values on the **Text** shelf:

   - Measure Values is simply defining the numbers that will display for each row—in this case, the numbers associated with # Men and # Women.

If the visualization has an axis, the shortcut to deploy **Measure Names** and **Measure Values** requires the placement of a second measure on top of the axis of an initial measure. In *Figure 1.34*, **Year** is located on the **Columns** shelf and **Number of Records** on the **Rows** shelf. Note that the screenshot has been taken while **# Women** has been placed on top of the *y*-axis:

Figure 1.34: Axis shortcut

The resulting worksheet can be seen in *Figure 1.35*. Note that **Measure Names** has been placed on **Color** to better see which line has been added:

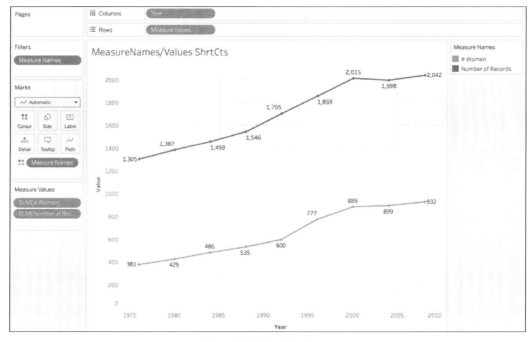

Figure 1.35: Two-line chart

The preceding section gave us a better understanding of **Measure Names** and **Measure Values**. You will come across those concepts more in your Tableau career, but now that you've successfully mastered the basics, let's move on to three other concepts that will be beneficial for your learning curve.

Three essential Tableau concepts

An important step on the road to mastering Tableau involves three essential concepts. In this section, we'll discuss each of them:

- Dimensions and measures
- Row-level, aggregate-level, and table-level calculations
- Continuous and discrete

We'll start by defining **dimensions** and **measures**.

Dimensions and measures

Tableau categorizes every field from an underlying data source as either a **dimension** or a **measure**. A dimension is qualitative or, to use another word, categorical. A measure is quantitative or aggregable. A measure is usually a number but may be an aggregated, non-numeric field, such as MAX (Date). A dimension is usually a text, Boolean, or date field, but may also be a number, such as Number of Records. Dimensions provide meaning to numbers by slicing those numbers into separate parts/categories. Measures without dimensions are mostly meaningless.

Let's look at an example to understand better:

1. In the workbook associated with this chapter, navigate to the **Dimensions and Measures** worksheet.

2. Drag **Number of Records** to the **Rows** shelf. The result is mostly meaningless. The **Number of Records** measure is **15,316**, but without the context supplied by slicing the measure with one or more dimensions, there is really no way to understand what it means:

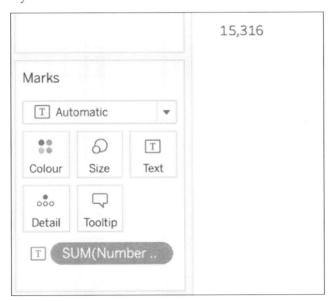

Figure 1.36: Worksheet without context

3. Place **Country** and **Year** on the **Columns** shelf:

Figure 1.37: Dimensions and Measures

As shown in *Figure 1.37, Step 3* brings meaning. Placing **Country** and **Year** on the **Columns** shelf provides context, which imparts meaning to the visualization.

Row-level, aggregate-level, and table-level calculations

There are three levels of calculations in Tableau: *row*, *aggregate*, and *table*. To understand how these three levels function, it's important to understand the Tableau processes. We'll do so with an example that considers the Number of Records and Quantity fields from the Superstore dataset.

Consider the following calculation types, calculated fields, and queries. A comparison to the commonly used language SQL will give us a better understanding of how to interpret Tableau calculations. Note that the SQL is slightly simplified for the sake of this example.

Let's take a deeper look at the three levels of calculations and consider the example in the following table:

Calculation type	Calculated field in Tableau	Query passed to data source

Row level	`Number of Records/Quantity`	`SELECT SUM(Number of Records / Quantity)`
		
		`FROM Orders`

Aggregate level	`Sum([Number of Records])/ Sum(Quantity)`	`SELECT SUM([Number of Records]),`
		
		`SUM(Quantity) FROM [Orders]`

Table level	`WINDOW_AVG(Sum([Number of Records])/Sum(Quantity))`	`SELECT SUM([Number of Records]),`
		
		`SUM(Quantity) FROM [Orders]`

For the row- and aggregate-level calculations, the computation is actually completed by the data source engine, as Tableau is an in-memory tool. Tableau merely displays the results. This, however, isn't the case for the table-level calculation. Although the query passed to the data source for the table-level calculation is identical to the query for the aggregate-level calculation, Tableau performs additional computations on the returned results. Let's explore this further with an exercise using the same calculated fields.

Let's look at the following steps and begin our exercise:

1. In the workbook associated with this chapter, navigate to the **Row_Agg_Tbl** worksheet.

2. Select **Analysis | Create Calculated Field** to create the following calculated fields. Note that each must be created separately; that is, it isn't possible in this context to create a single calculated field that contains all three calculations:

    - Name the first calculation `Lev – Row` and enter the following code: `[Number of Records]/[Quantity]`.

    - Next, name the second calculation `Lev – Agg` and enter the following code: `SUM ([Number of Records])/SUM (Quantity)`.

    - Lastly, name the third calculation `Lev – Tab` and enter `WINDOW_AVG ([Lev - Agg])`.

3. In the **Data** pane, right-click on the three calculated fields you just created and select **Default Properties | Number format**.

4. In the resulting dialog box, select **Percentage** and click **OK**.

5. Place **Order Date** on the **Columns** shelf.

6. Place **Measure Names** on the **Rows** shelf, and **Measure Values** on **Text** on the **Marks** card.

7. Exclude all values except for **Lev - Row**, **Lev - Agg**, and **Lev – Tab** by dragging them off the **Measure Values** shelf or removing them from the **Measure Names** filter:

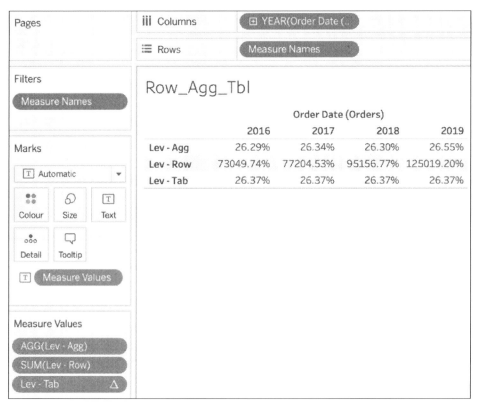

Figure 1.38: Level of calculations

- **Lev - Agg** is an aggregate-level calculation. The computation is completed by the data source engine. The sum of [Number of Records] is divided by the sum of [Quantity]. The results of the calculation are likely useful for the Tableau author.

- **Lev - Row** is a row-level calculation. The computation is completed by the data source engine. [Number of Records] is divided by [Quantity] for each row of the underlying data. The results are then summed across all rows. Of course, in this case, the row-level calculation doesn't provide useful results; however, since a new Tableau author may mistakenly create a row-level calculation when an aggregate-level calculation is what's really needed, the example is included here.

- **Lev - Tab** is a table calculation. Some of the computation is completed by the data source engine, that is, the aggregation. Tableau completes additional computation on the results returned from the data source engine based on the dimensions and level of detail in the data displayed in the sheet. Specifically, the results of **Lev – Agg** are summed and then divided by the number of members in the dimension. For the preceding example, this is:

$$\frac{26.29\% + 26.34\% + 26.30\% + 26.55\%}{4}$$

Once again, the results in this case aren't particularly helpful but do demonstrate knowledge that the budding Tableau author should possess.

Continuous and discrete

Continuous and discrete aren't concepts that are unique to Tableau. Indeed, both can be observed in many arenas. Consider the following example:

Figure 1.39: Continuous and discrete

The preceding diagram is of two rivers: *River-Left* and *River-Right*. Water is flowing in River-Left. River-Right is composed of ice cubes. Could you theoretically sort the ice cubes in River-Right? Yes! Is there any way to sort the water in River-Left? In other words, could you take buckets of water from the bottom of the river, cart those buckets upstream and pour the water back into River-Left and thereby say, I have sorted the water in the river? No. The H_2O in River-Left is in a continuous form, that is, water. The H_2O in River-Right is in a discrete form, that is, ice.

Having considered continuous and discrete examples in nature, let's turn our attention back to Tableau. Continuous and discrete in Tableau can be more clearly understood with the following seven considerations:

1. Continuous is green. Discrete is blue:

    • Select any field in the **Data** pane or place any field on a shelf and you'll note that it's either green or blue. Also, the icons associated with fields are either green or blue.

2. Continuous is always `numeric`. Discrete may be a `string`.

3. Continuous and discrete aren't synonymous with dimension and measure:

    • It's common for new Tableau authors to conflate continuous with measure and discrete with dimension. They aren't synonymous. A measure may be either discrete or continuous. Also, a dimension, if it's a number, may be discrete or continuous. To prove this point, right-click on any numeric or date field in Tableau and note that you can convert it:

Figure 1.40: Converting between discrete and continuous

4. Discrete values can be sorted. Continuous values can't:

   • Sortable/not sortable behavior is most easily observed with dates, as shown in the following example:

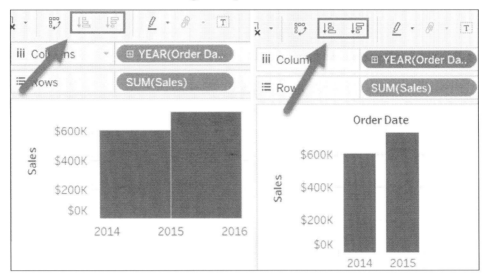

Figure 1.41: Left: continuous (not sortable). Right: discrete (sortable)

5. Continuous colors are gradients. Discrete colors are distinct:

   • The following example shows **Profit** as continuous and then as discrete. Note the difference in how colors are rendered. The left portion of the screenshot demonstrates the continuous results in gradients, and the right portion demonstrates the discrete results in distinctly colored categories:

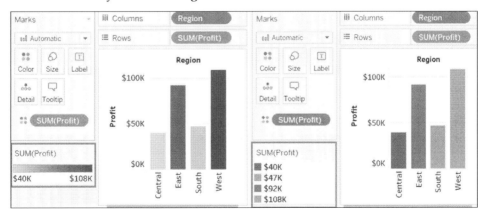

Figure 1.42: Profit as continuous (left) and discrete (right)

6. Continuous pills can be placed to the right of discrete pills, but not to the left because the discrete pills define the aggregation level:

   - The Tableau author is able to place **Region** to the right of **Year** when **Year** is discrete.

   - The Tableau author is unable to place **Region** to the right of **Year** when **Year** is continuous.

7. Continuous creates axes. Discrete creates headers:

   - Note in the left portion of the following screenshot that **Year(Order Date)** is continuous and the **Year of Order Date** axis is selected. Since **Year of Order Date** is an axis, the entire *x*-plane is selected. In the right portion, however, **Year(Order Date)** is discrete and **2014** is selected. Since 2014 is a header only, it's selected and not the entire *x*-plane:

Figure 1.43: Continuous (left) and discrete (right) dates

Congratulations, you just mastered three important concepts in Tableau: measures and dimensions, the level of calculations, and discrete and continuous values. With this knowledge alone, you will be able to create your first dashboards. I want to highly encourage you to do so; the learning curve when playing around with these tools will be very steep, and you will gain confidence quickly with practice! It will also help you to follow along in the upcoming chapters.

To conclude the basics, we will cover the export of dashboards to other devices next. Even if you don't feel ready to do so yet, it will round up the basic Tableau Desktop tour and will provide the raw diamond as a whole. We can then continue improving all bits and pieces in future chapters!

Exporting data to other devices

Once a dashboard looks as it's expected to, the developer has different choices for sharing the work. An upload to Tableau Server is the most likely option. The end user might not look at the results on just a laptop; they could use a tablet or cellphone, too.

Exporting data to a mobile phone

While developing a dashboard, Tableau Creator has the option to take a look at **Device Designer** or **Device Preview**. You can find it here:

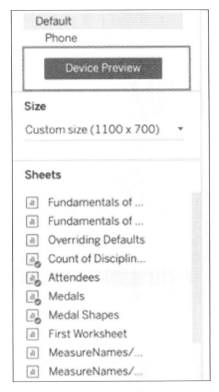

Figure 1.44: Device Preview

Tableau comes with default phone settings. If needed, those defaults can be adjusted by clicking on **Phone** and then on the three dots. Once you're in the **Device Designer** mode, select a **Device type** option and you'll get choices of the most common models:

Figure 1.45: Device type set to Phone

Please be aware that you can only use the sheets that are in the default layout of your dashboard. If you want to add a default layout for a tablet, for example, go into **Device Designer** mode, select **Tablet**, and move the content in a way that means the sheets you want to see on your tablet are within the device frame. Satisfied? Then add the new layout (highlighted with a red box in *Figure 1.46*) to the workbook. It will appear under the **Default** one in the top-left area:

Figure 1.46: Add Tablet Layout

The user can now select the design needed whenever opening a workbook from Tableau Server.

Not only can your projects be viewed conveniently on a mobile device, but you can also work on them on the go using Tableau Mobile! We'll cover this in the next section.

Tableau Mobile

In order to support flexible working, Tableau has created an app that can be downloaded in the App Store or from Google Play, called **Tableau Mobile**. Once installed on your phone and/or tablet, you will get an option to connect the app to Tableau Server or Tableau Online. Go ahead and publish the dashboard we created in this chapter, *The Olympics*, to either of those two instances. If you have questions regarding the publishing, please see *Chapter 14, Interacting with Tableau Server/Online*, for further instructions.

At the bottom of your landing page, click **Explore** to see all the views you just published. Click on the **Building a Dashboard** view and see your previously created dashboard, **The Olympics**:

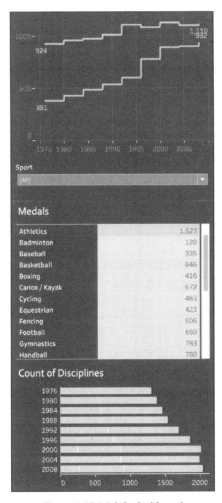

Figure 1.47: Mobile dashboard

And the best part is yet to come. The dashboard is fully interactive, so try the drop-down filter or the medals filter. Also, try to click on a mark and select **Keep Only**. By clicking on the workbook icon at the top right, the first icon from the left, all the other sheets you created will be visible, making it possible to switch between sheets:

Figure 1.48: Sheet selection

Now, if you click the three dots at the top right, even more options will appear, such as **Revert**, **Alert**, **Subscribe**, and so on. To learn more about the different options that are also available on Tableau Server, see *Chapter 14, Interacting with Tableau Server/ Online*. For now, we can conclude that Tableau Mobile makes it easy to check your favorite dashboards wherever you are.

Summary

In this chapter, we covered the basics of Tableau. We began with some basic terminology, then we looked at the basics of creating worksheets and dashboards. We focused on default behavior, how to override that behavior, and we considered some best practices. Then, we reviewed the fundamental principles of Measure Names and Measure Values. After that, we explored three essential Tableau concepts: dimensions and measures; row-, aggregate-, and table-level calculations; and the concepts of continuous and discrete. Of particular importance is understanding that row- and aggregate-level calculations are computed by the data source engine, while table-level calculations are handled by Tableau. Finally, we saw how to adjust your dashboard for other devices, such as a cellphone or tablet and Tableau Mobile in action.

In the next chapter, we'll continue our Tableau exploration by looking at data. We'll consider how data is prepared using Tableau's data handling engine, Hyper, and explore some useful data preparation models and techniques.

2
All About Data – Getting Your Data Ready

Ever asked yourself whether your data is clean enough to be analyzed? It's likely that everyone who works with data has, which is why this chapter is dedicated to getting your data ready for analysis, otherwise known as data cleaning.

The first part of this chapter is theory-oriented and does not include exercises. A careful reading of this information is encouraged, since it provides a foundation for greater insight. The latter portion of the chapter provides various exercises specifically focused on data preparation.

Now let's dive into this fascinating topic with the goal of enriching our understanding and becoming ever-better data stewards.

In this chapter, we will discuss the following topics:

- Understanding Hyper
- Data mining and knowledge discovery process models
- CRISP-DM
- Focusing on data preparation
- Surveying data
- Cleaning messy data

Since Tableau Desktop 10.5 has been on the market for some time, you may already have heard of Hyper. Regardless of whether you have or not, continue reading for a primer on this useful tool!

Understanding Hyper

In this section, we will explore Tableau's data-handling engine, and how it enables structured yet organic data mining processes in enterprises. Since the release of Tableau 10.5, we can now make use of Hyper, a high-performing database, allowing us to query source data faster than ever before. Hyper is Tableau's data-handling engine, which is usually not well understood by even advanced developers, because it's not an overt part of day-to-day activities; however, if you want to truly grasp how to prepare data for Tableau, this understanding is crucial.

Hyper originally started as a research project at the University of Munich in 2008. In 2016, it was acquired by Tableau and appointed as the dedicated data engine group of Tableau, maintaining its base and employees in Munich. Initially in 10.5, Hyper replaced the earlier data-handling engine only for extracts. It is still true that live connections are not touched by Hyper, but Tableau Prep Builder now runs on the Hyper engine too, with more use cases to follow.

What makes Hyper so fast? Let's have a look under the hood!

The Tableau data-handling engine

The vision shared by the founders of Hyper was to create a high-performing, next-generation database; one system, one state, no trade-offs, and no delays. And it worked—today, Hyper can serve general database purposes, data ingestion, and analytics at the same time.

Memory prices have decreased exponentially. If we go back in time to 1996, 1 GB of data could cost $45,000 in production costs. Today, much more than that can be found on every phone, or even on a smartwatch, costing as little $2 to produce. The same goes for CPUs; transistor counts increased according to Moore's law, while other features stagnated. Memory is cheap but processing still needs to be improved.

 Moore's Law is the observation made by Intel co-founder Gordon Moore that the number of transistors on a chip doubles every two years while the costs are halved. In 1965, Gordon Moore noticed that the number of transistors per square inch on integrated circuits had doubled every two years since their invention. Information on Moore's Law can be found on Investopedia at https://www.investopedia.com/terms/m/mooreslaw.asp.

While experimenting with Hyper, the founders measured that handwritten C code is faster than any existing database engine, so they came up with the idea to transform Tableau Queries into LLVM code and optimize it simultaneously, all behind the scenes, so the Tableau user won't notice it. This translation and optimization comes at a cost; traditional database engines can start executing code immediately. Tableau needs to first translate queries into code, optimize that code, then compile it into machine code, after which it can be executed. So the big question is, is it still faster? As proven by many tests on Tableau Public and other workbooks, the answer is yes!

Furthermore, if there is a query estimated to be faster if executed without the compilation to machine code, Tableau has its own **virtual machine** (**VM**) in which the query will be executed right away. And next to this, Hyper can utilize 99% of available CPUs, whereas other paralyzed processes can only utilize 29% of available CPUs. This is due to the unique and innovative technique of morsel-driven parallelization.

For those of you that want to know more about morsel-driven parallelization, a paper, which later on served as a baseline for the Hyper engine, can be found at https://15721.courses.cs.cmu.edu/spring2016/papers/p743-leis.pdf.

If you want to know more about the Hyper engine, I can highly recommend the following video at https://youtu.be/h2av4CX0k6s.

Hyper parallelizes three steps of traditional data warehousing operations:

- Transactions and **Continuous Data Ingestion (Online Transaction Processing, or OLTP)**
- **Analytics (Online Analytical Processing, or OLAP)**
- **Beyond Relational (Online Beyond Relational Processing, or OBRP)**

Executing those steps simultaneously makes it more efficient and more performant, as opposed to traditional systems where those three steps are separated and executed one after the other.

To sum up, Hyper is a highly specialized database engine that allows us as users to get the best out of our queries. If you recall, in *Chapter 1*, *Getting Up to Speed – A Review of the Basics*, we already saw that every change on a sheet or dashboard, including drag and drop pills, filters, and calculated fields, among others, are translated into queries. Those queries are pretty much SQL-lookalikes, however, in Tableau we call the querying engine VizQL.

VizQL, another hidden gem in your Tableau Desktop, is responsible for visualizing data into chart format and is fully executed in memory. The advantage is that no additional space on the database site is required here. VizQL is generated when a user places a field on a shelf. VizQL is then translated into SQL, MDX, or **Tableau Query Language (TQL)**, and passed to the backend data source with a driver. Two aspects of the VizQL module are of primary importance:

- VizQL allows you to change field attributions on the fly
- VizQL enables table calculations

We'll discuss these two aspects in more detail in the following sections.

Changing field attribution

In this section, we'll demonstrate how changing a worksheet's field attribution will allow you more flexibility in your dashboard creation.

Let's look at the World Happiness Report. Please navigate to the workbook associated with this chapter on `https://public.tableau.com/profile/marleen.meier` and open the `Score per country` sheet. We create the following worksheet by placing **AVG(Happiness Score)** and **Country** on the **Columns** and **Rows** shelves respectively. **AVG(Happiness Score)** is, of course, treated as a measure in this case. Lastly, sort the countries by their happiness score, highest to lowest.

Let's take a look at this in the following screenshot:

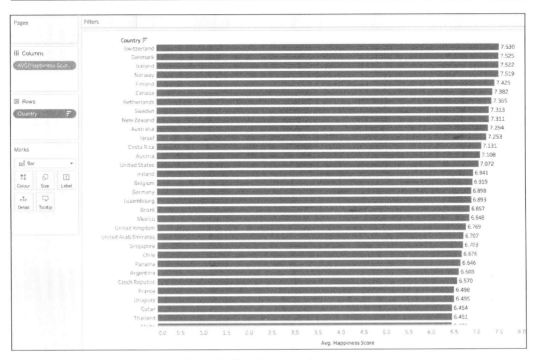

Figure 2.1: Happiness score by country

Next, please create a second worksheet called Score/Rank to analyze the scores relative to the ranks by using **Happiness Score** on **Rows** and **Happiness Rank** on **Columns**. Both pills should be continuous, hence green-colored.

In order to accomplish this, the user defines **Happiness Rank** as a **Dimension**, as shown in the following screenshot:

Figure 2.2: Ranking score per country

Please note that **Columns** and **Rows** have been moved to the left for better readability. This can be achieved by dragging and dropping the shelves.

In order to add steps to your visualization, click on **Path** in the **Marks Card** and select the second option, **Step**.

You can view the code generated by Tableau that is passed to the data source with the performance recorder, which is accessible through **Help**, then **Settings and Performance**, and then **Start Performance Recording**. See *Chapter 13, Improving Performance*, for additional details.

Studying the SQL generated by VizQL to create the preceding visualization is particularly insightful:

```
SELECT ['Happiness Report$'].[Happiness.Rank] AS [Happiness.Rank],
AVG(['Happiness Report$'].[Happiness.Score]) AS [avg:Happiness.
Score:ok] FROM
[dbo].['Happiness Report$'] ['Happiness Report$'] GROUP BY ['Happiness
Report$'].[Happiness.Rank]"
```

The GROUP BY clause clearly communicates that Happiness Rank is treated as a dimension because grouping is only possible on dimensions. The takeaway is to note that VizQL enables the analyst to change the SQL code input by changing a field from measure to dimension rather than the source metadata. This on-the-fly ability enables creative exploration of the data that's not possible with other tools, and avoids lengthy exercises attempting to define all possible uses for each field.

The previous section taught us how we can manipulate data types in Tableau itself without touching the data source and its metadata itself. In the next section, we will take a closer look at table calculations.

Table calculation

In this section, we will explore how VizQL's table calculations can be used to add data to a dashboard without adding any data to the data source.

In the following example, which can be viewed by opening **Sheet 4** on this chapter's workbook, note that **Freedom** on the vertical axis is set to **Quick Table Calculation** and **Moving Average**. Calculating a **Moving Average**, **Running Total**, or other such comparison calculations can be quite challenging to accomplish in a data source. Not only must a data architect consider what comparison calculations to include in the data source, but they must also determine the dimensions for which these calculations are relevant.

VizQL greatly simplifies such challenges using table calculations, as seen in the following screenshot:

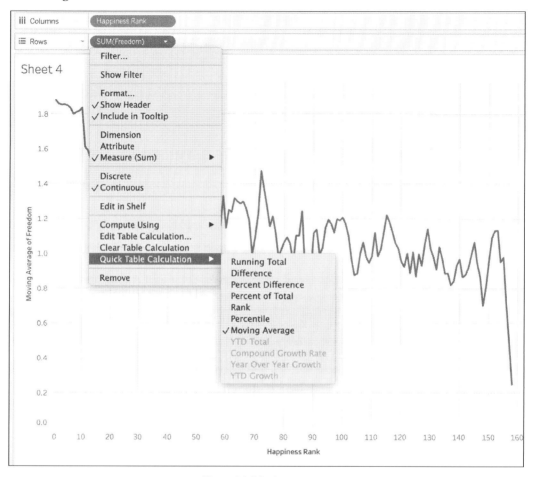

Figure 2.3: Moving average

Taking a look at the relevant portion of SQL generated by the preceding worksheet shows that the table calculation is not performed by the data source. Instead, it is performed in Tableau by the VizQL module.

The following is the SQL query:

```
SELECT SUM([Happiness Report$].[Freedom]) AS [sum:Freedom:ok],
[Happiness Report$].[Happiness.Rank] AS [Happiness.Rank]
FROM [dbo].[Happiness Report$] [Happiness Report$] GROUP BY ['Happiness
Report$'].[Happiness.Score]
```

To reiterate, nothing in the preceding call to the data source generates the moving average. Only an aggregated total is returned, and Tableau calculates the moving average with VizQL.

Hyper takeaways

This overview of the Tableau data-handling engine demonstrates a flexible approach to interfacing with data. Knowledge of the data-handling engine is helpful if you want to understand the parameters for Tableau data readiness. Two major takeaways from this section are as follows:

- It is not necessary to explicitly define data types and roles for optimal Tableau usage.
- Comparison calculations such as moving averages and running totals can be addressed by table calculations in Tableau and thus do not need to be calculated in advance.

The knowledge of these two takeaways can reduce data preparation and data modeling efforts, and thus helps us streamline the overall data mining life cycle. Don't worry too much about data types and data that can be calculated based on the fields you have in your database. Tableau can do all the work for you in this respect. In the next section, we will discuss what you should consider from a data source perspective.

Data mining and knowledge discovery process models

Data modeling, data preparation, database design, data architecture—the question that arises is, how do these and other similar terms fit together? This is no easy question to answer! Terms may be used interchangeably in some contexts and be quite distinct in others. Also, understanding the interconnectivity of any technical jargon can be challenging.

In the data world, data mining and knowledge discovery process models attempt to consistently define terms and contextually position and define the various data sub-disciplines. Since the early 1990s, various models have been proposed.

Survey of the process models

In the following table, we can see a comparison of blueprints for conducting a data mining project with three data processing models, all of which are used to discover patterns and relationships in data in order to help make better business decisions.

 The following list is adapted from *A Survey of Knowledge Discovery and Data Mining Process Models* by Lukasz A. Kurgan and Petr Musilek, and published in *The Knowledge Engineering Review*, Volume 21, Issue 1, March 2006.

Later on, we will see how Tableau comes into play and makes this process easier and faster for us.

	KDD	CRISP-DM	SEMMA
Phase I	Selection	Business understanding	Sample
Phase II	Pre-processing	Data understanding	Explore
Phase III	Transformation	Data preparation	Modify
Phase IV	Data mining	Modeling	Model
Phase V	Interpretation/ evaluation	Evaluation	Assess
Phase VI	Consolidate knowledge	Deployment	-

Since **CRISP-DM** is used by four to five times the number of people as the closest competing model (**SEMMA**), it is the model we will consider in this chapter. For more information, see `http://www.kdnuggets.com/2014/10/crisp-dm-top-methodology-analytics-data-mining-data-science-projects.html`.

The important takeaway is that each of these models grapples with the same problems, particularly concerning the understanding, preparing, modeling, and interpreting of data.

CRISP-DM

Cross Industry Standard Process for Data Mining (CRISP-DM) was created between 1996 and 2000 as a result of a consortium including SPSS, Teradata, Daimler AG, NCR Corporation, and OHRA. It divides the process of data mining into six major phases, as shown in the CRISP-DM reference model in the preceding comparison table.

This model provides a bird's-eye view of a data-mining project life cycle. The sequence of the phases are not rigid; jumping back and forth from phase to phase is allowed and expected. Data mining does not cease upon the completion of a particular project. Instead, it exists as long as the business exists, and should be constantly revisited to answer new questions as they arise.

In the next section, we will consider each of the six phases that comprise CRISP-DM and explore how Tableau can be used throughout the life cycle. We will particularly focus on the data preparation phase, as that is the phase encompassing data cleaning, the focus of this chapter. By considering the following steps, you will be able to understand in more detail what a full data mining process circle looks like under CRISP-DM. This framework can be used to make your workflow in Tableau more efficient by working according to an established model.

CRISP-DM phases

In the following sections, we will briefly define each of the six CRISP-DM phases and include high-level information on how Tableau might be used.

Phase I – business understanding:

- This phase determines the business objectives and corresponding data mining goals. It also assesses risks, costs, and contingencies, and culminates in a project plan.
- Tableau is a natural fit for presenting information to enhance business understanding.

Phase II – data understanding:

- This phase begins with an initial data collection exercise. The data is then explored to discover early insights and identify data quality issues.
- Once the data is collected into one or more relational data sources, Tableau can be used to effectively explore the data and enhance data understanding.

Phase III – data preparation:

- This phase includes data selection, cleaning, construction, merging, and formatting.
- Tableau can be effectively used to identify the preparation tasks that need to occur; that is, Tableau can be used to quickly identify the data selection, cleaning, merging, and so on, that should be addressed. Additionally, Tableau can sometimes be used to do actual data preparation. We will walk through examples in the next section.

As Tableau has evolved, functionality has been introduced to do more and more of the actual data preparation work as well as the visualization. For example, Tableau Prep Builder is a standalone product that ships with Tableau Desktop and is dedicated to data prep tasks. We will cover Tableau Prep Builder in *Chapter 3, Tableau Prep Builder*.

Phase IV – modeling:

- In this phase, data modeling methods and techniques are considered and implemented in one or more data sources. It is important to choose an approach that works well with Tableau; for example, as discussed in *Chapter 6, All About Data – Data Densification, Cubes, and Big Data*, Tableau works better with relational data sources than with cubes.

- Tableau has some limited data modeling capabilities, such as pivoting datasets through the data source page.

Phase V – evaluation:

- The evaluation phase considers the results; do they meet the business goals with which we started the data mining process? Test the model on another dataset, for example, from another day or on a production dataset, and determine whether it works as well in the workplace as it did in your tests.

- Tableau is an excellent fit for considering the results during this phase, as it is easy to change the input dataset as long as the metadata layer remains the same — for example, the column header stays the same.

Phase VI – deployment:

- This phase should begin with a carefully considered plan to ensure a smooth rollout. The plan should include ongoing monitoring and maintenance to ensure continued streamlined access to quality data. Although the phase officially ends with a final report and accompanying review, the data mining process, as stated earlier, continues for the life of the business. Therefore, this phase will always lead to the previous five phases.

- Tableau should certainly be considered a part of the deployment phase. Not only is it an excellent vehicle for delivering end-user reporting; it can also be used to report on the data mining process itself. For instance, Tableau can be used to report on the performance of the overall data delivery system and thus be an asset for ongoing monitoring and maintenance.

- Tableau Server is the best fit for *Phase VI*. We will discuss this separate Tableau product in *Chapter 14*, *Interacting with Tableau Server/Online*.

Now that we have learned what a full data mining circle looks like (and looked like pre-Tableau) and understood that every step can be executed in Tableau, we can see how it makes sense that data people celebrate Tableau Software products.

 The phrase "data people" is especially memorable after listening to the song written for the 2019 Las Vegas Tableau Conference, at `https://youtu.be/UBrH7MXf-Q4`.

Tableau makes data mining so much easier and efficient, and the replication of steps is also easier than it was before, without Tableau. In the next section, we will take a look at a practical example to explore the content we've just learned with some hands-on examples.

Focusing on data preparation

As discussed earlier, Tableau can be used effectively throughout the CRISP-DM phases. Unfortunately, a single chapter is not sufficient to thoroughly explore how Tableau can be used in each phase. Indeed, such a thorough exploration may be worthy of an entire book! Our focus, therefore, will be directed to data preparation, since that phase has historically accounted for up to 60% of the data mining effort. Our goal will be to learn how Tableau can be used to streamline that effort.

Surveying data

Tableau can be a very effective tool for simply surveying data. Sometimes in the survey process, you may discover ways to clean the data or populate incomplete data based on existing fields. Sometimes, regretfully, there are simply not enough pieces of the puzzle to put together an entire dataset. In such cases, Tableau can be useful to communicate exactly what the gaps are, and this, in turn, may incentivize the organization to more fully populate the underlying data.

In this exercise, we will explore how to use Tableau to quickly discover the percentage of null values for each field in a dataset. Next, we'll explore how the data might be extrapolated from existing fields to fill in the gaps.

Establishing null values

The following are the steps for surveying the data:

1. If you haven't done so just yet, navigate to `https://public.tableau.com/profile/marleen.meier` to locate and download the workbook associated with this chapter.

2. Navigate to the worksheet entitled **Surveying & Exploring Data**.

3. Drag **Region** and **Country** to the **Rows** shelf. Observe that in some cases the **Region** field has **Null** values for some countries:

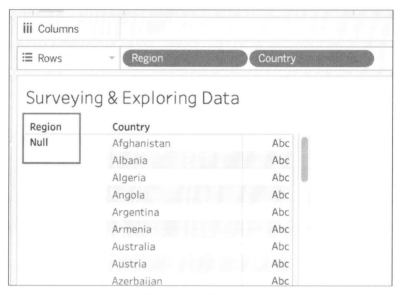

Figure 2.4: Null regions

4. Right-click and **Edit** the parameter entitled **Select Field**. Note that the **Data Type** is set to **Integer** and we can observe a list that contains an entry for each field name in the dataset:

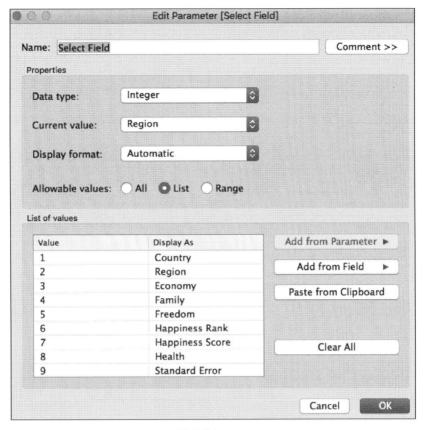

Figure 2.5: Editing a parameter

5. In the **Data** pane, right-click on the parameter we just created and select **Show Parameter Control**.

6. Create a calculated field entitled % Populated and write the following calculation:

```
SUM([Number of Records]) / TOTAL(SUM([Number of Records]))
```

7. In the **Data** pane, right-click on % **Populated** and select **Default Properties | Number Format...**:

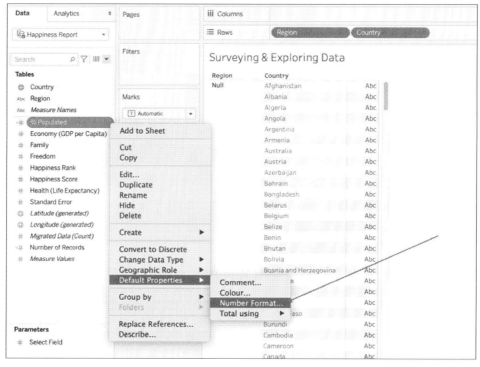

Figure 2.6: Adjusting default properties

8. In the resulting dialog box, choose **Percentage**.

9. Create a calculated field entitled Null & Populated and add the following code. Note that the complete case statement is fairly lengthy but is also repetitive.

 In cases requiring a lengthy but repetitive calculation, consider using Excel to more quickly and accurately write the code. By using Excel's CONCATENATE function, you may be able to save time and avoid typos.

In the following code block, the code lines represent only a percentage of the total but should be sufficient to enable you to produce the whole:

```
CASE [Select Field]
WHEN 1 THEN IF ISNULL ([Country]) THEN 'Null Values' ELSE
'Populated Values' END
WHEN 2 THEN IF ISNULL ([Region]) THEN 'Null Values' ELSE
```

```
'Populated Values' END
WHEN 3 THEN IF ISNULL ([Economy (GDP per Capita)]) THEN 'Null
Values' ELSE
'Populated Values' END
WHEN 4 THEN IF ISNULL ([Family]) THEN 'Null Values' ELSE
'Populated Values' END
WHEN 5 THEN IF ISNULL ([Freedom]) THEN 'Null Values' ELSE
'Populated Values' END
WHEN 6 THEN IF ISNULL ([Happiness Rank]) THEN 'Null Values' ELSE
'Populated Values' END
WHEN 7 THEN IF ISNULL ([Happiness Score]) THEN 'Null Values'
ELSE
'Populated Values' END
WHEN 8 THEN IF ISNULL ([Health (Life Expectancy)]) THEN 'Null
Values' ELSE
'Populated Values' END
WHEN 9 THEN IF ISNULL ([Standard Error]) THEN 'Null Values' ELSE
'Populated Values' END
END
```

10. Remove **Region** and **Country** from the **Rows** shelf.

11. Place **Null & Populated** on the **Rows** and **Color** shelves and % **Populate** on the **Columns** and **Label** shelves:

Figure 2.7: Populated values

12. Change the colors to red for **Null Values** and green for **Populated Values** if desired. You can do so by clicking on **Color** in the **Marks** card and **Edit Colors**.

13. Click on the arrow in the upper right corner of the **Select Field** parameter on your sheet and select **Single Value List**.

14. Select various choices in the **Select Field** parameter and note that some fields have a high percentage of null values. For example, in the following diagram, 32.98% of records do not have a value for **Region**:

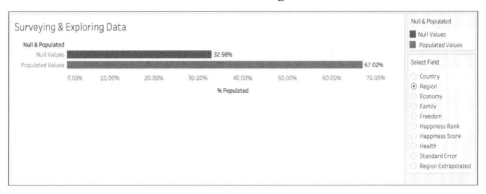

Figure 2.8: Comparing null and populated values

Building on this exercise, let's explore how we might clean and extrapolate data from existing data using the same dataset.

Extrapolating data

This exercise will expand on the previous exercise by cleaning existing data and populating some of the missing data from known information. We will assume that we know which country belongs to which region. We'll use that knowledge to fix errors in the Region field and also to fill in the gaps using Tableau:

1. Starting from where the previous exercise ended, create a calculated field entitled Region Extrapolated with the following code block:

```
CASE [Country]
WHEN 'Afghanistan' THEN 'Southern Asia'
WHEN 'Albania' THEN 'Central and Eastern Europe'
WHEN 'Algeria' THEN 'Middle East and Northern Africa'
WHEN 'Angola' THEN 'Sub-Saharan Africa'
WHEN 'Argentina' THEN 'Latin America and Caribbean'
WHEN 'Armenia' THEN 'Central and Eastern Europe'
WHEN 'Australia' THEN 'Australia and New Zealand'
WHEN 'Austria' THEN 'Western Europe'
```

```
//complete the case statement with the remaining fields in the
data set
END
```

To speed up the tedious creation of a long calculated field, you could download the data to an Excel file and create the calculated field by concatenating the separate parts, as shown here:

SUM		fx =B2&" "&C2&A4&C2&" "&D2&" "&C2&B4&C2		
	A	B	C	D	E
1					
2		WHEN	'	THEN	
3					
4	Afghanistan	Southern Asia	&C2		
5	Albania	Central and Eastern Europe	WHEN 'Albania' THEN 'Central and Eastern Europe'		
6	Algeria	Middle East and Northern Af	WHEN 'Algeria' THEN 'Middle East and Northern Africa'		
7	Angola	Sub-Saharan Africa	WHEN 'Angola' THEN 'Sub-Saharan Africa'		
8	Argentina	Latin America and Caribbear	WHEN 'Argentina' THEN 'Latin America and Caribbean'		
9	Armenia	Central and Eastern Europe	WHEN 'Armenia' THEN 'Central and Eastern Europe'		
10	Australia	Australia and New Zealand	WHEN 'Australia' THEN 'Australia and New Zealand'		
11	Austria	Western Europe	WHEN 'Austria' THEN 'Western Europe'		
12	Azerbaijan	Central and Eastern Europe	WHEN 'Azerbaijan' THEN 'Central and Eastern Europe'		
13	Bahrain	Middle East and Northern Af	WHEN 'Bahrain' THEN 'Middle East and Northern Africa'		
14	Bangladesh	Southern Asia	WHEN 'Bangladesh' THEN 'Southern Asia'		
15	Belarus	Central and Eastern Europe	WHEN 'Belarus' THEN 'Central and Eastern Europe'		
16	Belgium	Western Europe	WHEN 'Belgium' THEN 'Western Europe'		
17	Belize	Latin America and Caribbear	WHEN 'Belize' THEN 'Latin America and Caribbean'		
18	Benin	Sub-Saharan Africa	WHEN 'Benin' THEN 'Sub-Saharan Africa'		
19	Bhutan	Southern Asia	WHEN 'Bhutan' THEN 'Southern Asia'		
20	Bolivia	Latin America and Caribbear	WHEN 'Bolivia' THEN 'Latin America and Caribbean'		
21	Bosnia and Herzegovina	Central and Eastern Europe	WHEN 'Bosnia and Herzegovina' THEN 'Central and Eastern Europe'		
22	Botswana	Sub-Saharan Africa	WHEN 'Botswana' THEN 'Sub-Saharan Africa'		
23	Brazil	Latin America and Caribbear	WHEN 'Brazil' THEN 'Latin America and Caribbean'		
24	Bulgaria	Central and Eastern Europe	WHEN 'Bulgaria' THEN 'Central and Eastern Europe'		
25	Burkina Faso	Sub-Saharan Africa	WHEN 'Burkina Faso' THEN 'Sub-Saharan Africa'		
26	Burundi	Sub-Saharan Africa	WHEN 'Burundi' THEN 'Sub-Saharan Africa'		
27	Cambodia	Southeastern Asia	WHEN 'Cambodia' THEN 'Southeastern Asia'		
28	Cameroon	Sub-Saharan Africa	WHEN 'Cameroon' THEN 'Sub-Saharan Africa'		
29	Canada	North America	WHEN 'Canada' THEN 'North America'		

Figure 2.9: Compiling a calculation in Excel

You can then copy them from Excel into Tableau. However, for this exercise, I have created a backup field called Backup, which can be found in the Tableau Workbook associated with this chapter, which contains the full calculation needed for the Region Extrapolated field. Use this at your convenience. The **Solutions** dashboard also contains all of the countries. You can therefore copy the Region Extrapolated field from that file too.

2. Add a **Region Extrapolated** option to the **Select Field** parameter:

Figure 2.10: Adding Region Extrapolated to parameter

3. Add the following code to the **Null & Populated** calculated field:

```
WHEN 10 THEN IF ISNULL ([Region Extrapolated]) THEN 'Null
Values' ELSE
'Populated Values' END
```

4. Note that the **Region Extrapolated** field is now fully populated:

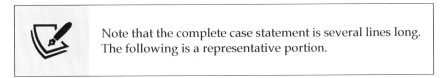

Figure 2.11: Fully populated Region Extrapolated field

Now let's consider some of the specifics from the previous exercises:

- Let's look at the following code block:

> Note that the complete case statement is several lines long. The following is a representative portion.

```
CASE [% Populated]
WHEN 1 THEN IF ISNULL ([Country]) THEN 'Null Values' ELSE
'Populated Values' END
...
```

This case statement is a row-level calculation that considers each field in the dataset and determines which rows are populated and which are not. For example, in the representative line of the preceding code, every row of the Country field is evaluated for nulls. The reason for this is that a calculated field will add a new column to the existing data — only in Tableau, not in the data source itself — and every row will get a value. These values can be N/A or null values.

- The following code is the equivalent of the quick table calculation Percent of Total:

```
SUM([Number of Records]) / TOTAL(SUM([Number of Records]))
```

In conjunction with the `Null & Populated` calculated field, it allows us to see what percentage of our fields are actually populated with values.

 It's a good idea to get into the habit of writing table calculations from scratch, even if an equivalent quick table calculation is available. This will help you more clearly understand the table calculations.

- The following CASE statement is an example of how you might use one or more fields to extrapolate what another field should be:

```
CASE [Country]
WHEN 'Afghanistan' THEN 'Southern Asia'
... END
```

For example, the `Region` field in the dataset had a large percentage of null values, and even the existing data had errors. Based on our knowledge of the business (that is, which country belongs to which region) we were able to use the `Country` field to achieve 100% population of the dataset with accurate information.

Nulls are a part of almost every extensive real dataset. Understanding how many nulls are present in each field can be vital to ensuring that you provide accurate business intelligence. It may be acceptable to tolerate some null values when the final results will not be substantially impacted, but too many nulls may invalidate results. However, as demonstrated here, in some cases one or more fields can be used to extrapolate the values that should be entered into an underpopulated or erroneously populated field.

As demonstrated in this section, Tableau gives you the ability to effectively communicate to your data team which values are missing, which are erroneous, and how possible workarounds can be invaluable to the overall data mining effort. Next, we will look into data that is a bit messier and not in a nice column format. Don't worry, Tableau has us covered.

Cleaning messy data

The United States government provides helpful documentation for various bureaucratic processes. For example, the **Department of Health and Human Services (HSS)** provides lists of ICD-9 codes, otherwise known as International Statistical Classification of Diseases and Related Health Problems codes. Unfortunately, these codes are not always in easily accessible formats.

As an example, let's consider an actual HHS document known as R756OTN, which can be found at `https://www.cms.gov/Regulations-and-Guidance/Guidance/Transmittals/downloads/R756OTN.pdf`.

Cleaning the data

Navigate to the `Cleaning the Data` worksheet in this workbook and execute the following steps:

1. Within the **Data** pane, select the **R756OTN Raw** data source:

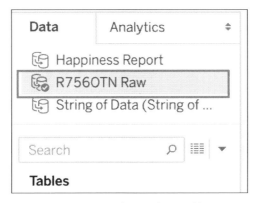

Figure 2.12: Selecting the raw file

2. Drag **Diagnosis** to the **Rows** shelf and choose **Add all members**. Note the junk data that occurs in some rows:

Figure 2.13: Adding Diagnosis to Rows

3. Create a calculated field named DX with the following code:

```
SPLIT( [Diagnosis], "", 1 )
```

4. Create a calculated field named Null Hunting with the following code:

```
INT(MID([DX],2,1))
```

5. In the **Data** pane, drag Null Hunting from **Measures** to **Dimensions**.

6. Drag **Diagnosis**, **DX**, and **Null Hunting** to the **Rows** shelf. Observe that **Null** is returned when the second character in the **Diagnosis** field is not numeric:

Figure 2.14: Ordering fields on Rows

7. Create a calculated field named `Exclude from ICD codes` containing the following code:

```
ISNULL([Null Hunting])
```

8. Clear the sheet of all fields, as demonstrated in *Chapter 1, Getting Up to Speed – a Review of the Basics*, and set the **Marks** card to **Shape**.

9. Place **Exclude from ICD Codes** on the **Rows**, **Color**, and **Shape** shelves, and then place **DX** on the **Rows** shelf. Observe the rows labeled as **True**:

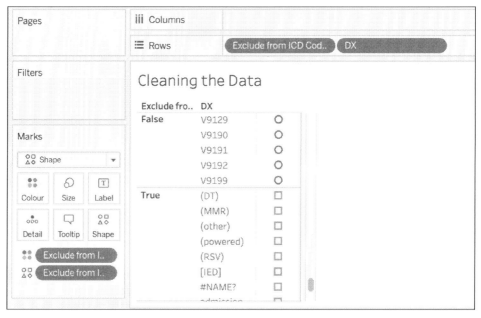

Figure 2.15: Excluding junk data

10. In order to exclude the junk data (that is, those rows where Exclude from ICD Codes equates to TRUE), place Exclude from ICD Codes on the **Filter** shelf and deselect **True**.

11. Create a calculated field named Diagnosis Text containing the following code:

```
REPLACE([Diagnosis],[DX] + "","")
```

12. Place **Diagnosis Text** on the **Rows** shelf after **DX**. Also, remove **Exclude from ICD Codes** from the **Rows** shelf and the **Marks Card**, and set the mark type to **Automatic**:

Figure 2.16: Observing the cleaned data

Now that we've completed the exercise, let's take a moment to consider the code we have used:

- The SPLIT function was introduced in Tableau 9.0:

    ```
    SPLIT([Diagnosis], "", 1 )
    ```

    As described in Tableau's help documentation about the function, the function does the following:

    > *Returns a substring from a string, as determined by the delimiter extracting the characters from the beginning or end of the string.*

    This function can also be called directly in the **Data Source** tab when clicking on a column header and selecting **Split**. To extract characters from the end of the string, the token number (that is, the number at the end of the function) must be negative.

- Consider the following code, which we used to create the `Null Hunting` field:

```
INT(MID([DX],2,1))
```

The use of `MID` is quite straightforward, and is much the same as the corresponding function in Excel. The use of `INT` in this case, however, may be confusing. Casting an alpha character with an `INT` function will result in Tableau returning `Null`. This satisfactorily fulfills our purpose, since we simply need to discover those rows not starting with an integer by locating the nulls.

- `ISNULL` is a Boolean function that simply returns `TRUE` in the case of `Null`:

```
ISNULL([Null Hunting])
```

- The `REPLACE` function was used while creating the `Diagnosis Text` field:

```
REPLACE([Diagnosis],[DX] + "","")
```

This calculated field uses the ICD-9 codes isolated in `DX` to remove those same codes from the `Diagnosis` field and thus provides a fairly clean description. Note the phrase *fairly clean*. The rows that were removed were initially associated with longer descriptions that thus included a carriage return. The resulting additional rows are what we removed in this exercise. Therefore, the longer descriptions are truncated in this solution using the `replace` calculation.

The final output for this exercise could be to export the data from Tableau as an additional source of data. This data could then be used by Tableau and other tools for future reporting needs. For example, the `DX` field could be useful in data blending.

Does Tableau offer a better approach that might solve the issue of truncated data associated with the preceding solution? Yes! Let's turn our attention to the next exercise, where we will consider regular expression functions.

Extracting data

Although, as shown in the previous exercise, *Cleaning the data*, the SPLIT function can be useful for cleaning data, regular expression functions are far more powerful and represent a broadening of the scope from Tableau's traditional focus on visualization and analytics to also include data cleaning capabilities. Let's look at an example that requires us to deal with some pretty messy data in Tableau. Our objective will be to extract phone numbers.

The following are the steps:

1. If you have not already done so, please download the **Chapter 2** workbook from https://public.tableau.com/profile/marleen.meier and open it in Tableau.

2. Select the **Extracting the Data** tab.

3. In the **Data** pane, select the **String of Data** data source and drag the **String of Data** field to the **Rows** shelf. Observe the challenges associated with extracting the phone numbers:

Figure 2.17: Extracting data from a messy data format

4. Access the underlying data by clicking the **View data** button and copy several rows:

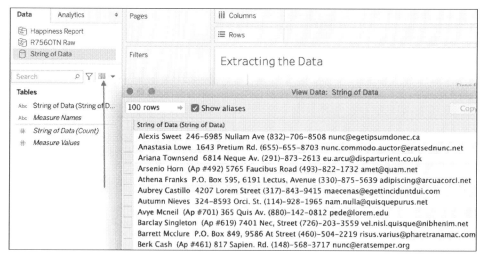

Figure 2.18: Accessing underlying data

5. Navigate to `http://regexpal.com/` and paste the data into the pane labeled **Test String**; that is, the second pane:

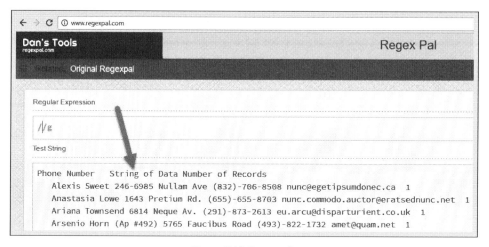

Figure 2.19: Regexpal

6. In the first pane (the one labeled **Regular Expression**), type the following:

    `\([0-9]{3}\)-[0-9]{3}-[0-9]{4}`

7. Return to Tableau and create a calculated field called `Phone Number` with the following code block. Note the regular expression nested in the calculated field:

```
REGEXP_EXTRACT([String of Data (String of Data)],'(\([0-9]{3}\)-
[0-9]{3}-[0-9]{4})')
```

8. Place **Phone Number** on the **Rows** shelf, and observe the result:

Figure 2.20: Extracting data final view

Now let's consider some of the specifics from the preceding exercise in more detail:

- Consider the following code block:

```
REGEXP_EXTRACT([String of Data],'()')
```

The expression pattern is purposely excluded here as it will be covered in detail later. The `'()'` code acts as a placeholder for the expression pattern. The `REGEXP_EXTRACT` function used in this example is described in Tableau's help documentation as follows:

> *Returns a substring of the given string that matches the capturing group within the regular expression pattern.*

- Note that as of the time of writing, the Tableau documentation does not communicate how to ensure that the pattern input section of the function is properly delimited. For this example, be sure to include '()' around the pattern input section to avoid a null output.

- Nesting within a calculated field that is itself nested within a VizQL query can affect performance (if there are too many levels of nesting/aggregation).

- There are numerous regular expression websites that allow you to enter your own code and help you out, so to speak, by providing immediate feedback based on sample data that you provide. `http://regexpal.com/` is only one of those sites, so search as desired to find one that meets your needs!

- Now, consider the expression:

```
\([0-9]{3}\)-[0-9]{3}-[0-9]{4}
```

In this context, the \ indicates that the next character should not be treated as special but as literal. For our example, we are literally looking for an open parenthesis. [0-9] simply declares that we are looking for one or more digits. Alternatively, consider \d to achieve the same results. The {3} designates that we are looking for three consecutive digits.

As with the opening parenthesis at the beginning of the pattern, the \ character designates the closing parentheses as a literal. The - is a literal that specifically looks for a hyphen. The rest of the expression pattern should be decipherable based on the preceding information.

After reviewing this exercise, you may be curious about how to return just the email address. According to `http://www.regular-expressions.info/email.html`, the regular expression for email addresses adhering to the RFC 5322 standard is as follows:

```
(?:[a-z0-9!#$%&'*+/=?^_`{|}~-]+(?:\.[a-z0-9!#$%&'*+/=?^_`{|}~-
]+)*|"(?:[\x01-\x08\x0b\x0c\x0e-\x1f\x21\x23-\x5b\x5d-
\x7f]|\\[\x01-\x09\x0b\x0c\x0e-\x7f])*")@(?:(?:[a-z0-9](?:[a-z0-9-
]*[a-z0-9])?\.)+[a-z0-9](?:[a-z0-9-]*[a-
z0-9])?|\[(?:(?:25[0-5]|2[0-4][0-9]|[01]?[0-9][0-9]?)\.){3}(?:25[0-
5]|2[0-4][0-9]|[01]?[0-9][0-9]?|[a-z0-9-]*[a-z0-9]:(?:[\x01-
\x08\x0b\x0c\x0e-\x1f\x21-\x5a\x53-\x7f]|\\[\x01-\x09\x0b\x0c\x0e-
\x7f])+)\])
```

 Emails do not always adhere to RFC 5322 standards, so additional work may be required to truly clean email address data.

Although I won't attempt a detailed explanation of this code, you can read all about it at `http://www.regular-expressions.info/email.html`, which is a great resource for learning more about regular expressions. Also, YouTube has several helpful regular expression tutorials.

The final output for this exercise should probably be used to enhance existing source data. **Data dumps** such as this example do not belong in data warehouses; however, even important and necessary data can be hidden in such dumps, and Tableau can be effectively used to extract it.

Summary

We began this chapter with a discussion of the Tableau data-handling engine. This illustrated the flexibility Tableau provides in working with data. The data-handling engine is important to understand in order to ensure that your data mining efforts are intelligently focused. Otherwise, your effort may be wasted on activities not relevant to Tableau.

Next, we discussed data mining and knowledge discovery process models, with an emphasis on CRISP-DM. The purpose of this discussion was to get an appropriate bird's-eye view of the scope of the entire data mining effort. Tableau authors (and certainly end users) can become so focused on the reporting produced in the deployment phase that they end up forgetting or short-changing the other phases, particularly data preparation.

Our last focus in this chapter was on the phase that can be the most time-consuming and labor-intensive, namely data preparation. We considered using Tableau for surveying and also cleaning data. The data cleaning capabilities represented by the regular expression functions are particularly intriguing, and are worth further investigation.

Having completed our first data-centric discussion, we'll continue with *Chapter 3, Tableau Prep Builder*, looking at one of the newer features Tableau has brought to the market. Tableau Prep Builder is a dedicated data pre-processing interface that is able to reduce the amount of time you need for pre-processing even more. We'll take a look at cleaning, merging, filtering, joins, and the other functionality Tableau Prep Builder has to offer.

3
Tableau Prep Builder

Tableau Prep Builder was introduced with version 2018.1 of Tableau Desktop, but what can we use Tableau Prep Builder (henceforth referred to in this chapter as *Prep*) for? The core purpose of the tool is data preparation. The good news is, Prep is fully compatible with Tableau Desktop, and also with Tableau Server. That means you can execute jobs in Prep to clean your data with the click of a button. Additionally, Prep is as visual as its big brother, Tableau Desktop, meaning that you can see every step of data preparation in a fully visual format.

Therefore, let's dive into the **Graphical User Interface (GUI)** and be amazed by another high-end product, which will allow you to get initial data insights, enabling you to decide faster if your dataset is worth analysis. Prep will pave the way for an even smoother Tableau Desktop experience.

In this chapter, the following topics will be discussed:

- Connecting to data
- The Tableau Prep Builder GUI
- Prepping data
- Additional options with Tableau Prep Builder
- Exporting data

In order to get started, we need to load data. How to do so in Prep will be described in the following section.

Connecting to data

If you are familiar with Tableau Desktop, Tableau Prep Builder will be an easy game for you. The handling and interfaces are very similar, and connecting to data, if the connector is available in Prep, works all the same whether it's a text file, a database, or an extract. At first sight, you might not even notice a difference between the Tableau Prep Builder the Tableau Desktop GUIs, which provides the handy advantage that you can start prepping right away.

To get started, begin by opening Tableau Prep Builder:

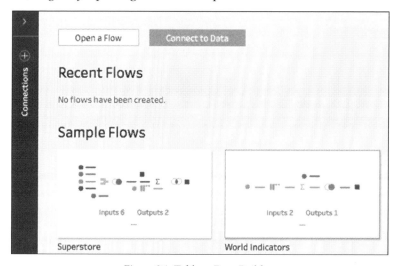

Figure 3.1: Tableau Prep Builder

From here, click on the **+** in order to open a file. After doing so, the following screen will appear:

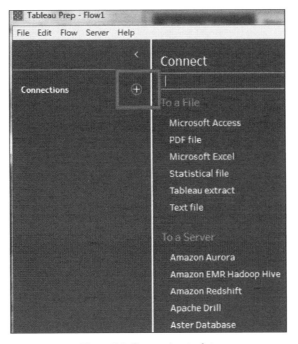

Figure 3.2: Connecting to data

From the preceding screenshot, we can see that you can choose the type of data you want to connect to in the search bar. Just as in Tableau, the repertoire of Tableau Prep Builder includes multiple databases.

Now let's connect to a dataset with a practical exercise. For this exercise, we need the following dataset: `https://www.kaggle.com/airbnb/boston`. Please download `calendar.csv`, `listings.csv`, and `reviews.csv`. Alternatively, download them from the workbook associated with this chapter on Tableau Public: `https://public. tableau.com/profile/marleen.meier`.

First, we are going to start with the `calendar.csv` file. Add it to the empty Prep canvas by making a connection with a text file, followed by the selection of your `.csv` file. You will now see the following screen:

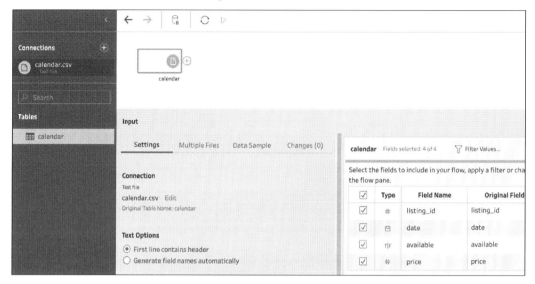

Figure 3.3: Input data

Congratulations—you've just made your first Tableau Prep Builder connection. Here, you can manipulate and visualize your connected dataset as required!

In the following section, I will describe the GUI in more detail.

The Tableau Prep Builder GUI

User experience is an important topic, not only when you build a dashboard but also when you use other aspects of Tableau. One of the biggest selling points of Tableau is and has always been the ease of using the GUI, and is only one of the reasons Tableau is a much-loved tool by its customers.

The Tableau Prep Builder GUI has two important canvases to look at. Right after you have connected data to Tableau Prep Builder, the workspace will split into several parts:

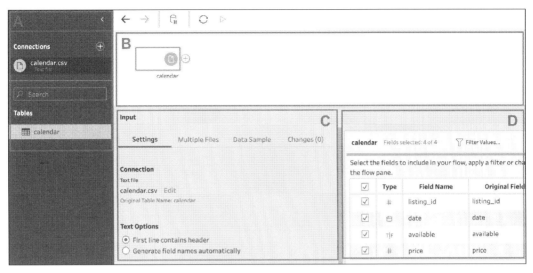

Figure 3.4: Prep workspace sections

Let's look at what we can see from the preceding screenshot:

- **A**: The connection pane, showing you the input files available at the location selected.

- **B**: The flow pane, which shows your current Prep flow. This always starts with an input step.

- **C**: The input pane settings, which give you several options to configure your input.

- **D**: The input pane samples, showing the fields you moved to the connection pane, including sample values.

In the input pane (the section marked with **C**), you can use the wildcard union (multiple files) function to add multiple files from the same directory. Also, you can limit the sample set that Tableau Prep Builder will print in order to increase performance. In the input pane samples (the section marked with **D**) you can select and deselect the fields you want to import and change their data types. The data type options are, for example, strings, dates, or numbers.

The second GUI is the profile pane. Once you've selected the input data needed, click on the + in the flow pane and select **Add: Clean Step**. Now the profile pane will appear:

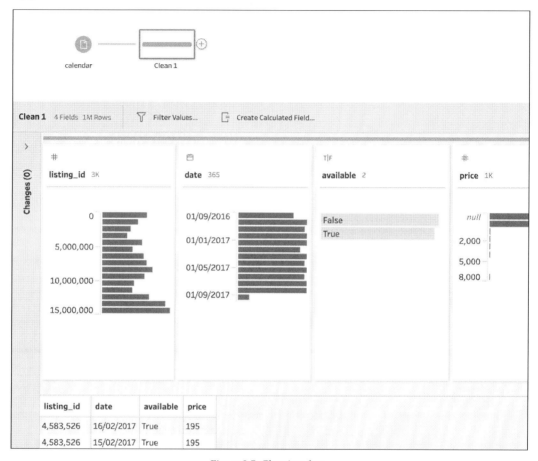

Figure 3.5: Cleaning data

In the preceding screenshot, the profile pane shows every column from the data source in two sections. The upper sections show aggregates. For example, column 2, **date**, shows the number of rows per date in a small histogram. The columns can all be sorted by clicking on the sort icon (a mini bar-chart that appears when your mouse is hovering over a column) next to the column name and by selecting one item. Let's take, for example, **True**, in **available** (column 3). All related features will be highlighted:

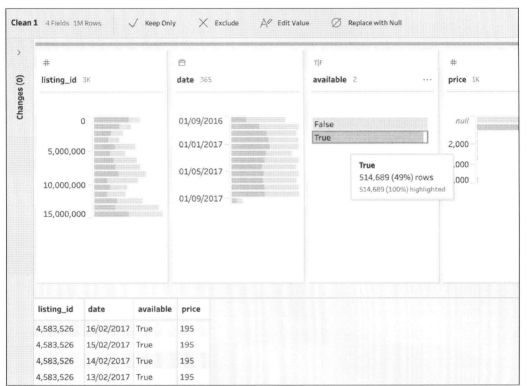

Figure 3.6: Visual filtering

This gives you the chance to get some insights into the data before we even start to clean it up. In the following screenshot, each row is shown as it is in the data source in the lower part of the profile pane:

Figure 3.7: Data overview

So far we have seen that, after loading data in Prep, visual filters can be applied by clicking on a field or bar in one of the columns. The lower pane will always show the data source of the selection made at the row level. Next, we will continue by adding more data sources.

Getting to know Tableau Prep Builder

Let's start with a practical example.

Next to the `calendar.csv` file, connect to the following files:

- `listings.csv`
- `reviews.csv`

Now, drag them onto the flow pane:

Figure 3.8: Multiple tables input

Can you answer the following questions?

- How many listings use the word "beach" in their description?
- What is the percentage of condominiums that are marked with "exact location"?
- On which day were the most reviews entered?

Without a tool like Tableau Prep Builder, it is much more difficult to find the solution to these types of questions. Prep makes our data analytics journey much faster and easier and that is exactly the reason why I encourage you to spend the additional time and learn Prep as well as Tableau Desktop!

Solutions can be found in the workbook associated with this chapter at the following link: `https://public.tableau.com/profile/marleen.meier`.

Here you see, as an example, I used the sort function on **date** in order to answer the third question: *On which day were the most reviews entered?*

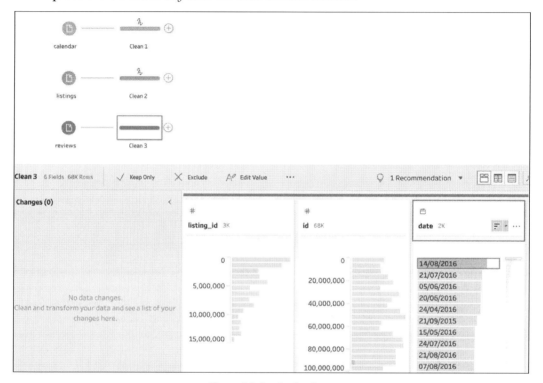

Figure 3.9: Sorting by date

As you can see, sorting this field ordered the dates by number of entries, thus making it very simple to answer the question, *on which day were the most reviews entered?* After the first few clicks, it already starts to feel natural, doesn't it?

 All the changes you made to the dataset can be traced back on the left side of the profile pane. But don't forget to add a proper name to each step: this will make it much easier for others, and yourself, to understand your process.

So, let's continue on to the cleaning features of Tableau Prep Builder.

Prepping data

Tableau Prep Builder comes with lots of different features. Sometimes you might use many different tools to prepare your dataset in order to get it in a shape you desire. Other times you might just run an aggregation (one feature) and be done. It really depends on the dataset itself and the expected output. The fact is, the closer your Prep output data is to what you need for your Tableau Desktop visualization, the more efficiently VizQL will run on Tableau Desktop. Fewer queries in Tableau Desktop means faster generation of dashboards.

To me, the best part about Tableau Prep Builder is that it can handle a huge amount of data. Sometimes I even use it for datasets I don't want to visualize in Tableau Desktop, just to get a quick overview of, for example, how many rows contain a specific word, how many columns are needed, what happens to the date range if I filter a particular value, and so on! Within a few minutes I have insights that would have taken me much more time to get with database queries or Excel functions. I hope that by the end of this chapter you will be able to cut your time spent data prepping in half (at least). We will divide the prepping features into five subcategories: cleaning, unions and joins, aggregating, pivoting, and scripting. Let's start with cleaning data!

Cleaning data

We have seen the following canvas before in the *The Tableau Prep Builder GUI* section. To create the cleaning step, the user can simply click on **+** next to the input and select **Add: Clean Step**. During the cleaning step, multiple operations can be performed, such as filtering or creating a calculated field. Also note the recommendations Tableau Prep Builder gives you:

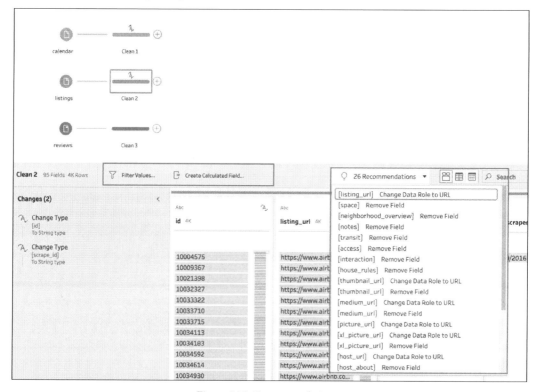

Figure 3.10: Recommendations

Tableau Prep Builder analyzes the column content and proposes changes that might fit the data. The column listing_url for example is being recognized as a webpage and therefore Prep recommends you change it to the data role URL. The second, third, and several more recommendations after listing_url are to remove certain columns. This is probably the case because the column does not contain any data or contains only a small amount of data. The list goes on.

This feature can be very useful, especially for unfamiliar datasets. My way of working would be, look at the recommendations, check if they make sense, and execute the change—or not. Don't blindly trust these recommendations, but they can point out data flaws you might have missed otherwise.

Data is often messy, involving null values, typos from manual entries, different formatting, changes in another system, and so on. As a consequence, you will have to sort out the mess before you can get reliable results from an analysis or a dashboard. This section will show you how to clean data on a column level.

Once a value is selected within your clean step, you have the option to **Keep Only**, **Exclude**, **Edit Value**, or **Replace with Null**:

Figure 3.11: Quick access

None of these changes will change the data source itself. Prep is like an in-between step, or a filter between the original data source and your Tableau Desktop. Excluding a value, as highlighted in *Figure 3.11*, will only remove it from Tableau Prep Builder. However, if used later on as input for Tableau Desktop, there won't be an option to add that specific value back in. This option will remain in Tableau Prep Builder only.

Another slightly hidden option is to click on the ellipses (**...**) next to the column headers (as shown in *Figure 3.12*) and select **Clean**:

Figure 3.12: More options

This **Clean** functionality operates based on the data type of the column. In the preceding screenshot, the data type is a string (indicated by the **Abc** icon). For other data types, the option will be grayed out since **Clean** is only available for strings. The option allows you to make use of eight more cleaning features:

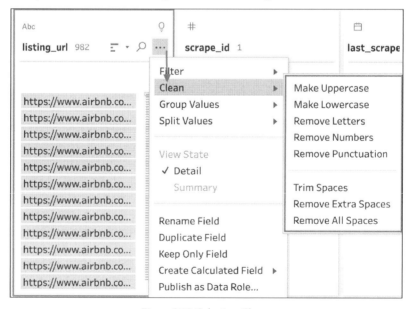

Figure 3.13: Selecting Clean

The data type can be changed just above each column header; you will find a symbol above the column name, which can be changed by clicking on it, just like in Tableau Desktop:

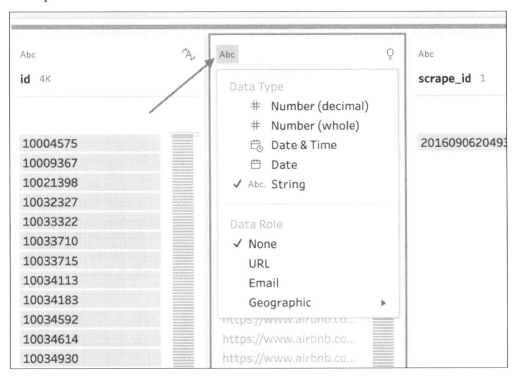

Figure 3.14: Changing Data Type

This comes in handy in case Prep misinterprets the data type of a column. A wrongly assigned data type can have effects on the calculation you perform on them and how Tableau Desktop would visualize the column.

In the upcoming section, we will practice combining multiple datasets. You might want to combine for example order data with shipment data (using join) or append 2020 sales data to your 2019 sales dataset (using union). To find out how, read on!

Unions and joins

We will now join the three datasets, so that we may analyze and visualize them together. The nature of the three datasets (listings.csv, reviews.csv, and calendar.csv) require a join but not a union. However, I will still walk you through the steps of a union in order for you to know when you need it!

Adding unions

A union in Tableau is the appending of data to an existing dataset. Imagine you have two Excel files. Both have the exact same header, but one contains data from 2019, the other data from 2020. If you union the 2020 data to the 2019 data, you append the rows of the 2020 files to add them underneath the rows of the 2019 files. To perform a union, both datasets need to have almost the same layout/header. Why almost? You will see in the following exercise:

1. To begin this exercise, your Prep flow pane should look like this:

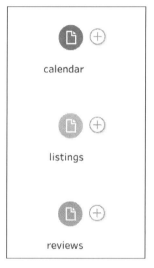

Figure 3.15: Flow pane

2. Add a clean step by clicking the **+** next to the **listings** dataset.

 You can change the color of each step according to your preferences by right-clicking on a step and selecting **Edit Color**.

3. Select the column **host_identity_verified** and filter on **True**:

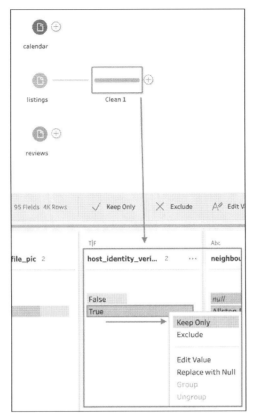

Figure 3.16: Filtering on True

4. Now, create a calculated field, called **DatasetA_ID,** containing just a string, 'A':

Figure 3.17: Creating a calculated field

5. Create a second cleaning step from the same listings data and filter this time on **False** in the **host_identity_verified** column:

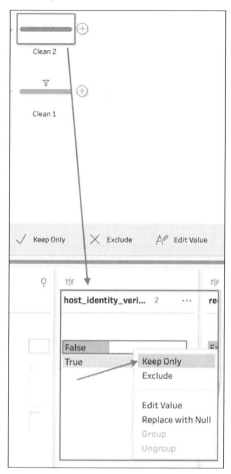

Figure 3.18: Filtering on False

6. Create a calculated field **DatasetB_ID** containing just a string 'B', using the same process shown in *Figure 3.17*. Renaming the steps by right-clicking and hitting **Rename** helps to keep track of the applied changes. Your flow should look like the following:

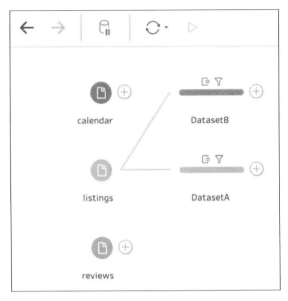

Figure 3.19: Visual flow

7. You have now created two datasets that can be combined using a union, without changing the original data. Union the two by either selecting **Union** after clicking on the **+** next to the step **DatasetA** or by dragging one step over the other (**DatasetB** over **DatasetA** or vice versa):

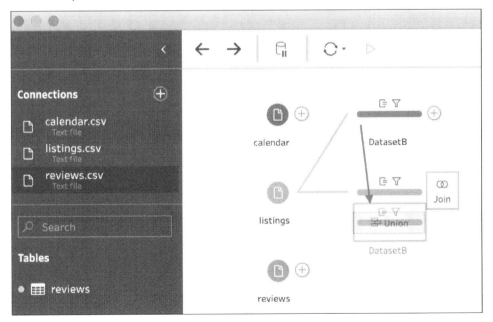

Figure 3.20: Union

8. Check whether all fields match by clicking on the step **Union 1** and looking at the input details in the bottom left of the screen:

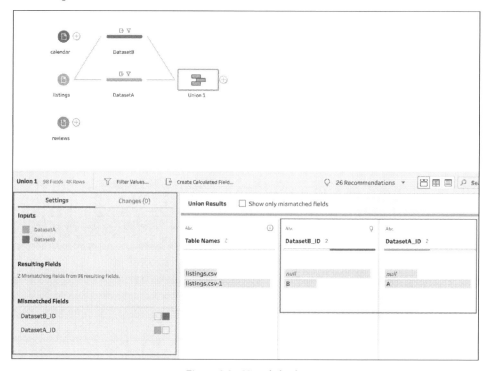

Figure 3.21: Visual check

9. In the preceding screenshot, you can see that on the left, you have information about the union. From top to bottom: the **Inputs** and their respective colors (these are the same as in the flow pane), the **Resulting Fields**, showing 2 mismatching fields, and finally, the mismatched fields themselves: **DatasetA_ID** and **DatasetB_ID**. The colors next to each mismatched field show that our **DatasetB_ID** field does not exist in **DatasetA**, and the **DatasetA_ID** field does not exist in **DatasetB**.

10. In this case, we know that those columns can be appended even despite the different naming conventions. A better name for both fields would have been **Dataset_ID** (you can go a few steps back and try this out). Prep will not show any mismatches then. But for us here, we can go ahead and drag and drop one field on top of the other to merge them and thereby give Prep the permission to view them as one column:

Figure 3.22: Merge

11. See how the **Resulting Fields** now show 0 mismatches, and how both dataset colors are now represented in the bar underneath the column header:

Figure 3.23: Color coding

12. Rename by selecting and right-clicking the union step from **Union 1** to **listings2**, and add a description by selecting and right-clicking the union step and hit **Add Description** if you like—all the extra effort you make now will help you later with replication, documentation, and explanation.

Congratulations, your first union was a success. We first split the original listings dataset in two and then combined them again to one. Stacking data with the same layout on top of each other, as we've done here, is a typical task for unions.

Adding joins

Now, we will continue to work in the same flow pane and focus on a join. As a quick refresher, a join appends data horizontally. As a rule of thumb, unions increase the number of rows, joins change the number of columns.

1. Drag **listings2** onto **reviews** until the **Join** option appears.

Figure 3.24: Join

2. Select **listing_id** from **reviews** and **id** from **listings2** for your join. Please note that you can change the join type by clicking on the Venn diagram under **Join Type**:

Figure 3.25: Visual check join

What the preceding overview tells us is that all 68,275 rows of the **reviews** dataset were matched to a row in the **listing2** dataset. However, we do have 756 mismatches from the **listing2** dataset. Our total **Join Result** is therefore 68,275 rows. But it is likely that not all listings have reviews and therefore we can safely assume that our join worked as expected.

3. Another check could be to change the join to a full outer join and dive deeper into the data later in Tableau Desktop. In order to get to a full outer join, simply click on the outer edge of the two circles:

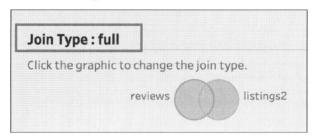

Figure 3.26: Full join

4. If you want to check immediate results, simply right-click on, for example, the join symbol (represented by the Venn diagram icon, as shown in the following screenshot), and you'll be able to check the data in Tableau Desktop by selecting **Preview in Tableau Desktop**:

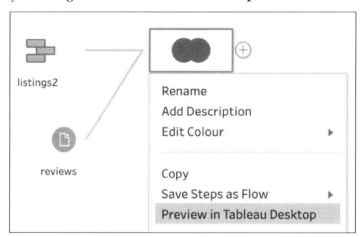

Figure 3.27: Preview

5. We can also rename the step; let's change our join's name to **lis&rev**.

By now, we've seen how to clean data, and how to use unions and joins. The union part taught us how to append data vertically or underneath each other. The join part allowed us to combine data horizontally or next to each other. More specifically, we were able to combine the listings with their respective reviews. Instead of having two datasets, we have created one that allows us to look up a listing review, and in the same row, view all the data regarding the listing itself, like type of listing, number of bedrooms, whether it has an ocean view, and so on.

Let's continue next with the aggregation step.

Aggregating

An aggregation is used when you want to change the granularity of your data. In our dataset, we have one row per review. However, we want to see if hosts that have been in the Airbnb business in Boston longer have more reviews compared to hosts that started more recently. In order to do so we need to get an aggregated number of reviews per year that the host started offering listings. The field **host_since** will give us helpful information as well as the field **reviewer_id**. For the latter we will count the distinct reviewers that left reviews. Let's do it!

Our current flow pane looks like this:

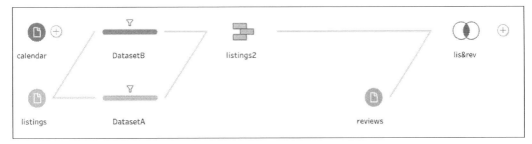

Figure 3.28: Flow pane

To aggregate the amount of reviews, please take the following steps:

1. First, click on the **+** sign next to the **lis&rev** and choose **Aggregate**:

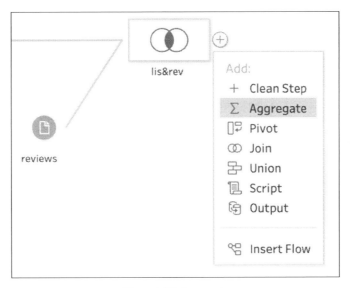

Figure 3.29: Aggregate

2. This will open a window entitled **Aggregate 1**. Our goal is to see how many people reviewed accommodation per year from when the host started offering listings; therefore, take the following actions.

    a. Using the search field in the **Additional Fields** pane, as indicated by the arrow on the left in *Figure 3.30*, add the **host_since** field to **Grouped Fields** by dragging and dropping.

    b. Add the **reviewer_id** to **Aggregated Fields**, also by dragging and dropping. Note that the default aggregation is **SUM**, as indicated by the arrow on the right:

Figure 3.30: Aggregated fields

3. Change the **reviewer_id** aggregation by clicking on **SUM under Aggregated Fields**, and change it to **Count Distinct**:

Figure 3.31: Count Distinct

4. This will change the default aggregation, **Sum** (where every review is counted), to **Count Distinct**, which counts the distinct reviewer ID aggregation. This will allow us to focus on how many different reviewers left reviews. This is just an arbitrary choice; feel free to try out the other aggregations and see how the data changes.

Let's have a look at the Tableau Desktop preview by right-clicking on the **Aggregate** step on our flow pane and selecting **Preview in Tableau Desktop**:

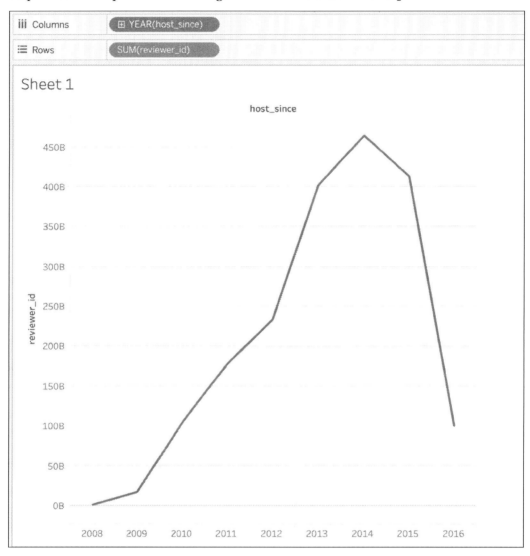

Figure 3.32: Host chart

In the preceding screenshot, we can see the distinct count of reviews per **host_since** date. Of course, in this specific example, Tableau Desktop could also count the reviews per **host_since** date if those were the only fields dragged onto the view without the help of Tableau Prep Builder. But a benefit of aggregating prior to importing the data into Tableau Desktop is that you have less data to import; hence, it's possible to achieve better performance. If you want to continue analyzing the dataset in either Tableau Prep Builder or Tableau Desktop, you can now ask further questions, such as the following:

- Which type of accommodation has the highest discount for staying a week rather than a day?
- Is there a correlation between the size of the accommodation and the monthly price?
- How many hosts (as a percentage) have more than one listing?

Good luck and happy dashboard building!

We finish this section here and look back at a graph consisting of only 9 datapoints, which we created by aggregating the almost 64,000 rows of **review_id** data by year that the host started offering the listing. The graph tells a story; 64,000 individual rows of data don't. That is why it is so important to always reduce your data, and aggregate it if possible. In the next section we will talk about another important feature: pivoting.

Pivoting

Do you recognize a situation where you drag and drop your fields onto your Tableau Desktop row and column shelves but somehow the visualization doesn't do what you want? Chances are that you have to turn your data, or better, pivot it. If data that you expect to be in one column, spread over multiple rows, appears in multiple columns instead, it's a case for pivoting. The following example will showcase a need for pivoting.

For our pivot example, we will make use of another dataset. You can find it at `https://public.tableau.com/profile/marleen.meier`. The dataset is very simple and looks like this:

Day	Blue	Green	Yellow
1	3	4	3
2	4	7	4
3	3	5	2
4	2	6	3
5	3	5	2

Figure 3.33: Excel input

It has three different colors that were observed on five different days, x amount of times. This data is a typical example of when pivoting is helpful to tidy up the data because multiple columns have the same purpose—**B**, **C**, and **D** are all observations. If you wanted to visualize this table, it could look like the following:

Figure 3.34: Pivot I

But you might be wondering, since the color scheme already indicates which color has been observed, wouldn't it be better to put all three lines in one graph? Separate lines per color, within one line-chart? Let's accomplish this!

Begin by connecting the **PivotDataSet** to Tableau Prep Builder, then follow these steps to pivot the data:

1. From Prep, connect to the just created Excel file and add the **PivotDataSet** to the flow pane, click on the + next to the input data step, and select **Pivot**. A new step called **Pivot 1** will appear:

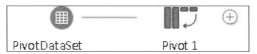

Figure 3.35: Adding a Pivot step

2. Click on the **Pivot 1** step in the flow pane, and *Figure 3.36* will appear at the bottom of your Prep window. Select all three colors from the **Fields** pane shown in **Step I**, and drag them onto the **Pivoted Fields** pane, as shown in **Step II**:

Figure 3.36: Pivot steps

3. Now, have a look at the **Pivot Results** pane, as shown in **Step III** of the preceding screenshot, and rename **Pivot1 Names** to Colors and **Pivot1 Values** to Observations by right-clicking and selecting **Rename**. And voilá, we now have a clean table, called **Clean 1** by default:

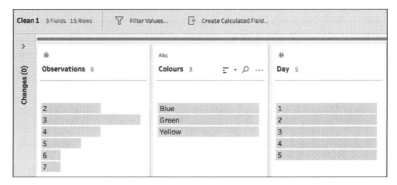

Figure 3.37: Pivot results

4. Remember our problem from the beginning? Our line chart can now be created in a different way, as shown in *Figure 3.38*. Note that **Colors** is a dimension now and the **Observations** are their own field, compared to before when they were located under the column header of each color:

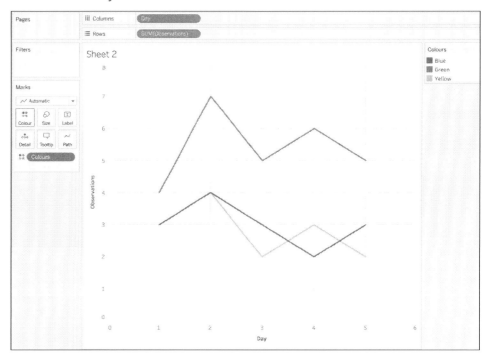

Figure 3.38: Pivoted line chart

This is a simple use case for pivoting, but the technique here can be transferred to any other dataset.

As a quick tip: Tableau Prep Builder has a built-in feature recommendation. Whenever you see a light-bulb at the upper-right corner of a column, check it out and see if this recommendation applies to your needs:

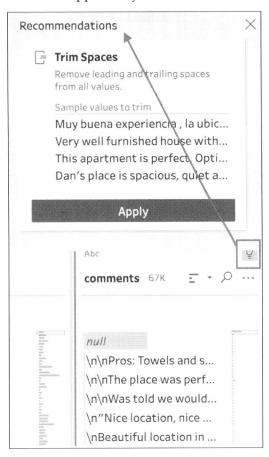

Figure 3.39: Trim spaces

In this case, Tableau recommends us to remove all leading and trailing spaces, which is exactly what we need! As demonstrated here, it's always worth it to check the recommendations.

Perfect, you are all set with the main Prep functionality. However, you might be wondering what you are supposed to do if you require any further preparation. No problem, Prep has you covered. Scripting is the newest addition to Prep and the most powerful of all; it is virtually limitless! Continue reading to explore Prep's scripting feature.

Scripting

The script functionality that we will discuss next is one of the more recently added features to Tableau. We will discuss it next because a programming language like Python or R gives you endless flexibility. If you ever reach the boundaries of Prep's offerings you can fall back on scripting and write your own code to do exactly what you want.

In order to make use of it, you have to connect to Python (or R, if using), outside of Tableau first. The following steps are based on the instructions from `https://help.tableau.com/current/prep/en-us/prep_scripts_TabPy.htm` for Python or `https://help.tableau.com/current/prep/en-us/prep_scripts._R.htm` for R.

For this exercise we will be using the Boston Airbnb dataset, more specifically the calendar table. Download this dataset from `https://www.kaggle.com/airbnb/boston` and connect to the `calendar` table in Tableau Prep Builder:

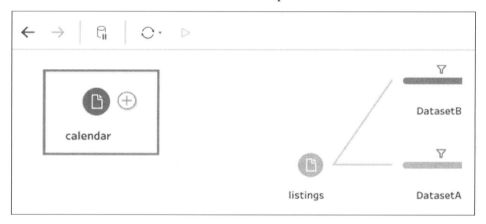

Figure 3.40: Calendar dataset

Now, let's take a step back and connect Python to Tableau Prep Builder:

1. Download and install Python from `python.org` (or download and install R from `https://www.r-project.org/`).

2. Download and install `tabpy` by executing the following command in your terminal or on the command line:

   ```
   pip install tabpy
   ```

3. Alternatively, if using R, open R and execute:

   ```
   install.packages("Rserve", , "http://rforge.net")
   ```

4. Open tabpy on the command line/terminal by entering the following command:

```
tabpy
```

Or, in the R GUI, type:

```
library(Rserve)
Rserve()
```

5. Back in Tableau Prep Builder, click on the **+** on the right-hand side of the calendar table and add a **Clean Step**.

6. Add a calculated field called **PythonTest** (use **RTest** instead if you've chosen to experiment with R) with a string value "Test":

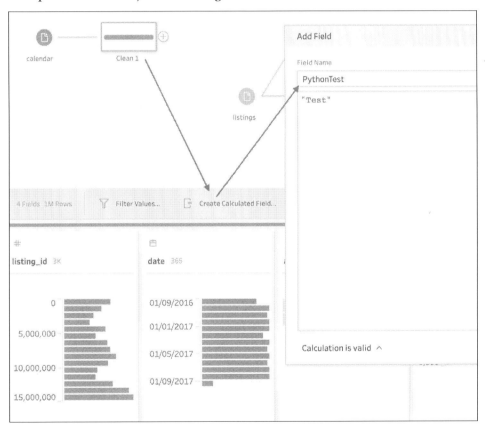

Figure 3.41: Python test

7. Now, click on the + on the right-hand side of the **Clean 1** step and add **Script**.

> By selecting the **Script** step, the **Settings** pane at the bottom (see *Figure 3.41*) will give you an option to connect to Rserve or TabPy. Rserve is the Tableau server for R and TabPy is the Tableau server for Python.

8. Choose your connection type by selecting **Rserve** or **Tableau Python (TabPy) Server**. Connect Tableau Prep Builder to tabpy by using **localhost** and **Port 9004** (if using R, connect to Rserve by selecting it under **Connection type** and using **localhost** and **Port 6311** in the same popup):

> If using an SSL-encrypted Rserve server, **Port 4912** is the default port.

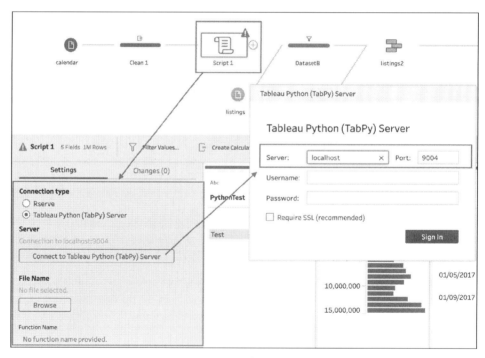

Figure 3.42: TabPy Server

9. Next, if experimenting with Python, create a `.py` file containing the following code:

    ```
    def ChangeString(df):
        df['PythonTest'] = 'Python'
    return df
    ```

    Alternatively, create a `.R` file containing the following code:

    ```
    Get ChangeString<- add_column(
    .data,
    .before = 'Test'
    .after = 'R') {
    Return (data.frame ())
    }
    ```

10. The script we just created is written to change an existing column in Prep and rename every row from Test to Python or R, depending on which language you've chosen.

11. We'll continue with the Python script. Back in Tableau Prep Builder, browse for the `.py` file we just created and add the function name to the Tableau Prep Builder interface. I called the file `PrepTableau.py` and the function name is **ChangeString**, as defined in the preceding step:

Figure 3.43: Adding a function

12. Run the flow and observe that the **PythonTest** column has changed from **Test** to **Python**:

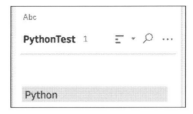

Figure 3.44: PythonTest

Our little experiment worked! And even though we used a very simplistic example, it shows that the scripting feature works, and you can just follow your creativity with what else you might be able to do by using scripting. Examples include everything from calculating an inverse normal distribution to machine learning with sentiment analysis or clustering.

You might have noticed that we did not import pandas in the script itself, but still used a pandas DataFrame. This is due to the fact that the pandas import comes with tabpy. You can see this in your command line/terminal after opening tabpy:

```
ut_schema(df)\nresult_schema_output = get_output_schema_13fba4e2991a40c4b6826d7676030f98(pd.DataFrame(_arg1))\nreturn result_schem
a_output.to_dict(orient=\'split\') if isinstance(result_schema_output, pd.DataFrame) else result_schema_output'}'...
2020-08-01 10:39:29 [INFO] (base_handler.py:base_handler:121): function to evaluate=def _user_script(tabpy, _arg1):
    import pandas as pd
    def get_output_schema():
        return 'fd4196a3-2f56-4d84-b391-a03cc841bb9c'
    def prep_string():
        return ['prep_string_type']
    def prep_bool():
        return ['prep_bool_type']
    def prep_int():
        return ['prep_int_type']
    def prep_decimal():
        return ['prep_decimal_type']
    def prep_date():
        return ['prep_date_type']
    def prep_datetime():
        return ['prep_datetime_type']
    def AddColumn(df):
        df["PythonScriptTest"] = 'PythonInput'
        return df
    def get_output_schema_13fba4e2991a40c4b6826d7676030f98(df = pd.DataFrame()):
        import inspect
        if len(inspect.getfullargspec(get_output_schema).args) == 0:
            return get_output_schema()
        else:
            return get_output_schema(df)
    result_schema_output = get_output_schema_13fba4e2991a40c4b6826d7676030f98(pd.DataFrame(_arg1))
    return result_schema_output.to_dict(orient='split') if isinstance(result_schema_output, pd.DataFrame) else result_schema_output
```

Figure 3.45: Importing pandas on the command line

If you want to use other libraries in your script, you can install them by using pip install on your command line/terminal. You only have to restart tabpy afterward and you will be able to use them too. Remember, always open tabpy on the terminal/command line first or else Tableau Prep Builder can't execute the script.

At the time of writing, Tableau Prep Builder does not support a script as input yet—you could however use a dummy `.csv` file as a workaround and add a script to the flow immediately after it.

Additional options with Tableau Prep Builder

This section will discuss some smaller stand-alone but very powerful features. Some of you might have been using Prep already since the very first release. With each release and each additional user and given feedback, Tableau was able to create a priority list of features that stakeholders—like you and I—really wished to see. The upcoming topics are some of the best examples. None of these features were present in the initial release but have made the product so much better, more valuable, and more complete. You are able now to save part of your flow and reuse it, write back your data to an external database, refresh parts of your dataset, and schedule flows with the Tableau Data Management add-on. Let's take a closer look and start with the 'insert flow' in flow function.

Insert flow

An option in Tableau Prep Builder is to add an existing flow to your own flow. For example, say someone already worked on the Boston Airbnb dataset and created a flow of the highlighted steps only:

Figure 3.46: Save to File

You could save the steps you wish to insert into your flow by right-clicking and selecting **Save to File**, as shown in *Figure 3.46*. These steps can be inserted back into your flow by right-clicking on the canvas, selecting **Insert Flow**, and browsing your .tfl files for the previously downloaded file:

Figure 3.47: Insert Flow

After inserting the file containing the steps you previously downloaded, the result will look like this:

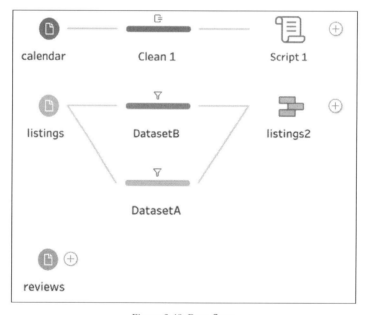

Figure 3.48: Prep flow

This functionality is very convenient to share work and reuse already created steps. Next we will look into another functionality that will allow you to refresh the data used in your Prep flow: the incremental refresh.

Incremental refresh

Tableau Prep Builder 2020.2 saw the introduction of the incremental refresh feature. After completing a flow and adding an output you can decide if you want a full or incremental refresh, and which field you want to use as an indicator. Imagine you have a dataset of infections per day of a particular disease. By every end of the day, you want to add the new data, which comes from a health ministry database, to your dataset. So, what are you going to do?

Typically, you would load the whole dataset, all of it, after the newest datapoints were added. But nothing changes about the datapoints older than that day; they will remain the same and you loaded them before already. Therefore, it is a waste of resources to reload the whole dataset. An incremental refresh will only load new datapoints and add them to the existing data, which has been built up over many days. You can imagine how much time and effort this will save. It is a much more sustainable way to keep your data up to date than a full refresh.

We are going to look at an example in the following workflow. It is important that the **Output** is there:

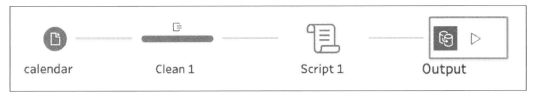

Figure 3.49: Incremental refresh

To add the incremental refresh, take the following steps:

1. Click on the **calendar** input table and scroll down the **Settings** tab until you see the **Set up Incremental Refresh** option. Then, click the **Enable** toggle:

Figure 3.50: Set up Incremental Refresh

2. After you click on the **Enable** box, a dropdown will appear. This dropdown contains all fields that Tableau Prep Builder finds useful as an indicator for a data refresh. In our case, **date** is the perfect field to use since as soon as a new date is added to the original data source, the refresh will start:

Figure 3.51: Select a refresh field

3. Tableau Prep Builder will also ask you for the output field that will represent the date column in the output. In our case it is still **date**:

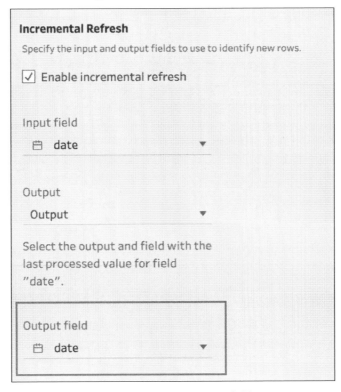

Figure 3.52: Select an output field

4. After everything is set up, click on the **Output** step again and note how you can now select the type of refresh, full or incremental, you prefer for this flow by clicking on the drop-down menu on the **Run Flow** option:

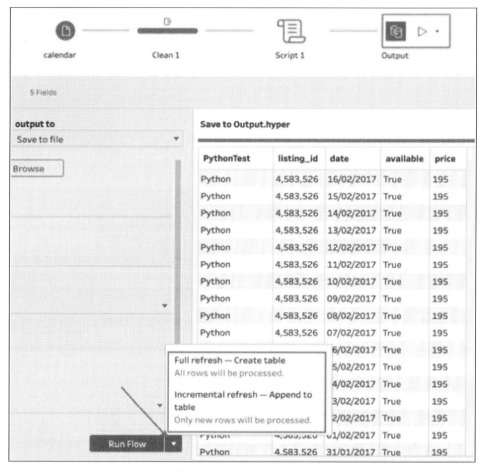

Figure 3.53: Refresh options

You just learned how to set up your data refresh—full as well as incremental. This will help you with the sustainable usage of compute resources and to always have your data up to date. Next we will introduce another Tableau feature that unfortunately does not ship with the normal license but is definitely worth investigating—Tableau Prep Conductor.

Tableau Prep Conductor

With **Tableau Prep Conductor** you can publish your Prep flows to Tableau Server, schedule them to run at a certain time, and always have refreshed data. The conductor is available in the Tableau Data Management add-on and doesn't ship with Tableau Desktop nor Tableau Prep Builder.

 For more information, please check `https://www.tableau.com/products/add-ons/data-management`.

Exporting data

Last, but not least, we may want to export our data. We have seen before that a right-click on a symbol in the flow pane offers the possibility to preview the data in Tableau Desktop:

1. If you want a flow to run according to a schedule or save it to a location, it's best to use **Add | Output**:

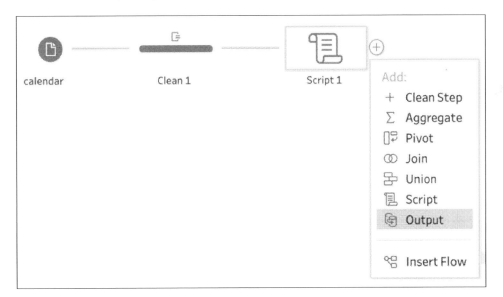

Figure 3.54: Output

2. After you do this, the following screen will appear:

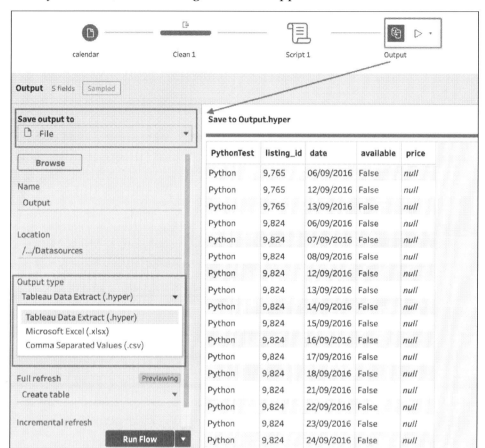

Figure 3.55: Save to file

3. The user now has the option to save the data to a file, and also to save it in Hyper file format as `.hyper`, as `.xlsx` (new in Tableau 2021.1), or as a `.csv` file.

4. Another option is to publish the newly generated data source directly to Tableau Server and make it available for other users. For this option, select **Publish as a data source** instead of **Save to File** from the dropdown.

5. A third option to save Prep output was been added in Tableau 2020.3: writing the resulting data to an external database. If you want to do so, select the option **Database table** from the dropdown. At the time of writing, seven databases are compatible with the write back functionality, but more will likely be added based on user demand:

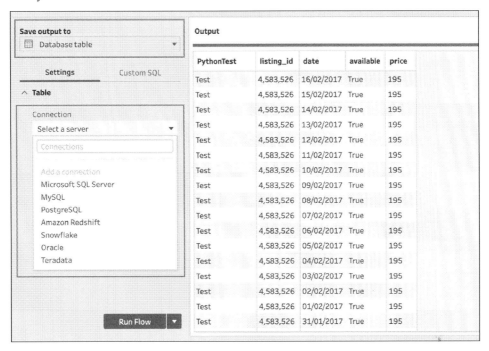

Figure 3.56: Save to external database

This section has shown us how to save our work or even more so, the output of our Prep flows. To me, the ability to save output to an external database is the best new feature, because it is the easiest way to share my output in a structured and organized way with others. So not only I, but also other users, can work with the prepped data, saving additional work. The flow can then be reused not only by me, but by anyone.

Summary

We started this chapter with an introduction to Tableau Prep Builder. We looked at the GUI and how we can connect data to it. After that, we did some exercises regarding data preparation. This can be divided into five parts: data cleaning, unions and joins, aggregating, pivoting, and scripting. We also considered several additional options to improve the usefulness of your data, including inserting steps from other flows, and incremental refreshes. To round out this chapter on Tableau Prep Builder, we looked at exporting data. Here, we saw that the new dataset can be saved as a file or data extract, written back to an external database, or pushed directly to Tableau Server.

Just like Tableau Desktop, Tableau Prep Builder is very much self-explanatory and highly visual. Colors, symbols, and highlights make it easy to get used to this extract, transform, and load tool, which is invaluable for preparing your data before manipulating it on the main Tableau interface!

In the next chapter, we'll continue our exploration of data in Tableau. We'll explore how to prepare data for Tableau by looking at joins, blends, and data structures.

4

All About Data – Joins, Blends, and Data Structures

Connecting Tableau to data often means more than connecting to a single table in a single data **source**. You may need to use Tableau to join multiple tables from a single data source. For this purpose, we can use joins, which combine a dataset row with another dataset's row if a given key value matches. You can also join tables from disparate data sources or union data with a similar metadata structure.

Sometimes, you may need to merge data that does not share a common row-level key, meaning if you were to match two datasets on a row level like in a join, you would duplicate data because the row data in one dataset is of much greater detail (for example, cities) than the other dataset (which might contain countries). In such cases, you will need to blend the data. This functionality allows you to, for example, show the count of cities per country without changing the city dataset to a country level.

Also, you may find instances when it is necessary to create multiple connections to a single data source in order to pivot the data in different ways. This is possible by manipulating the data structure, which can help you achieve data analysis from different angles, using the same dataset. It may be required in order to discover answers to questions that are difficult or simply not possible with a single data structure.

In this chapter, we will discuss the following topics:

- Relationships
- Joins
- Unions
- Blends
- Understanding data structures

In version 2020.2, Tableau added functionality that will you allow you to join or blend without specifying one of the two methods in particular. It is called **relationships**. We will start this chapter off by explaining this new feature before we look into the details of joins, blends, and more.

Relationships

Although this chapter will primarily focus on joins, blends, and manipulation of data structures, let's begin with an introduction to **relationships**: a new functionality since Tableau 2020.2, and one that the Tableau community has been waiting for a long time. It is the new default option in the data canvas; therefore, we will first look into **relationships**, which belong on the **logical layer of the data model,** before diving deeper into the join and union functionalities that operate on the **physical layer.**

 To read all about the physical and logical layers of Tableau's data model, visit the Tableau help pages: `https://help.tableau.com/current/online/en-us/datasource_datamodel.htm`.

For now, you can think of the logical layer as more generic, where the specifics are dependent on each view, whereas the physical layer dives deeper, starting from the data source pane.

In the following screenshot, you can see the data source canvas, with two datasets combined in a relationship on the left-hand side, and the same datasets combined using a **join** on the right-hand side. Please note that relationships only show a line between the tables (**DimProduct** and **DimProductSubcategory**), whereas joins indicate the type of join by two circles:

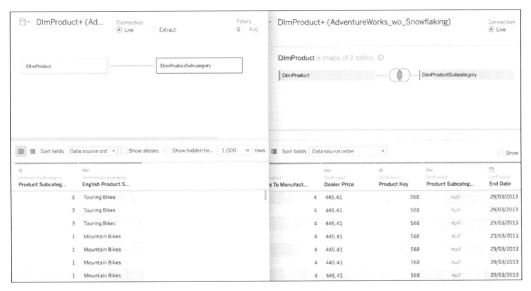

Figure 4.1: Relationships and joins on the data source canvas

A key difference is that the preview of the data, at the bottom, will show only data from the selected table in relationships, compared to all data when using joins. This makes sense because the granularity of data can change in relationships, depending on the fields you are using in your dashboard. Joins however have a fixed level of granularity, which is defined by the type of join and join clauses you choose.

Relationships are the default for Tableau Desktop 2020.2 and higher. However, if you still want to make use of the join functionality, you can drag a dataset into the data source canvas, click on the drop-down arrow, and select **Open…**:

This will open the dataset as you used to see it in the data pane in Tableau in versions before 2020.2 and you will be able to use joins the old way, as we will describe in the *Joins* section.

The line between two datasets in a relationship (based on the logical layer) is called a **noodle**. Tableau detects a relationship as soon as you drag in the second data source to the data source canvas, but you can add more key columns or remove and adjust them if needed, by clicking on the noodle itself:

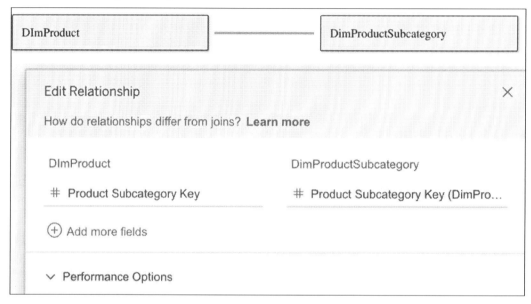

Figure 4.2: Relationships

If you open older dashboards in Tableau 2020.2 or later versions, you will see that the joined data will be shown as **Migrated**. This is intentional. Just click on the migrated data source and Tableau will switch from the logical to the physical layer, meaning you will see the join-based data source canvas instead of the relationship canvas.

Looking at the worksheet, you will notice differences as well. In *Figure 4.3* you will see that in the new relationships layout (left), the columns are divided by table name first and then split into **Dimensions** and **Measures** per data source, while in a join (right), the columns are divided into dimensions and measures and split by table name:

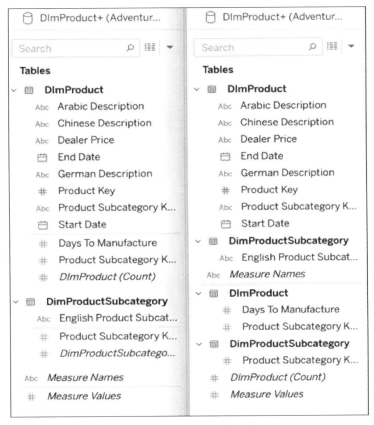

Figure 4.3: New and old Tableau layout

To conclude on relationships, the new data source layout makes it a lot easier to combine datasets and you don't have to decide upfront if you want to join or blend. People that are used to the old data source pane might have to get used to the new flexibility a bit, but for new Tableau users, it will be much easier to work with different datasets from the start. Nevertheless, we will still cover joins next, especially because the functionality is still part of Tableau in the physical layer.

Joins

This book assumes basic knowledge of joins, specifically inner, left-outer, right-outer, and full-outer joins. If you are not familiar with the basics of joins, consider taking W3Schools' SQL tutorial at `https://www.w3schools.com/sql/default.asp`. The basics are not difficult, so it won't take you long to get up to speed.

The terms **simple join** and **complex join** mean different things in different contexts. For our purposes, we will consider a simple join to be a single join between two tables. Every other instance of joining will be considered complex.

The following screenshot shows a star schema, as an example of a complex join:

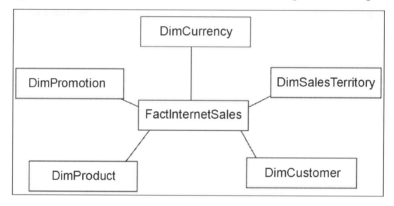

Figure 4.4: Star schema

A **star schema** consists of a fact table (represented by **FactInternetSales** in *Figure 4.4*) that references one or more dimension tables (**DimCurrency**, **DimSalesTerritory**, **DimCustomer**, **DimProduct**, and **DimPromotion**). The fact table typically contains measures, whereas the dimension tables, as the name suggests, contain dimensions. Star schemas are an important part of data warehousing since their structure is optimal for reporting.

The star schema pictured is based on the **AdventureWorks** data warehouse for MS SQL Server 2014.

 Access to the database, at `https://github.com/Microsoft/sql-server-samples/releases/tag/adventureworks`, may prove helpful when working through some of the exercises in this chapter.

The workbook associated with this chapter does not include the whole SQL Server database but just an extract. Also, to keep the file size of the workbook small, the extract has been filtered to only include data for the United Kingdom.

One feature Tableau has that is less visible to us developers is join culling, which Tableau makes use of every time multiple datasets are joined. To better understand what Tableau does to your data when joining multiple tables, let's explore join culling.

Join culling

The following screenshot is a representation of the star schema graphic shown in *Figure 4.4* on the Tableau data source page using joins:

Figure 4.5: Join culling

The preceding screenshot communicates an inner join between the fact table, **FactInternetSales**, and various dimension tables. **FactInternetSales** and **DimSalesTerritory** are connected through an inner join on the common key, **SalesTerritoryKey**.

In order to better understand what just has been described, we will continue with a join culling exercise. We will look at the SQL queries generated by Tableau when building a simple view using these two tables, which will show us what Tableau does under the hood while we simply drag and drop.

Note that Tableau always de-normalizes or flattens extracts; that is, no joins are included in our AdventureWorks extract that ships with the Tableau workbook for this chapter. If you still want to see the SQL join queries and you don't have access to the database or the data files on GitHub, you can download the data from the Tableau workbook and put it in separate Excel sheets yourself. You can then join the tables in the manner shown in *Figure 4.4*.

As shown in the following screenshot, you can separate the data based on the table structure in the worksheets:

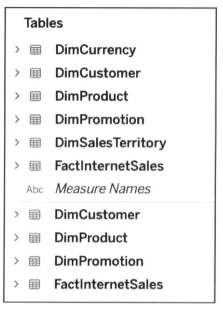

Figure 4.6: Tables

Open the tables and place the columns into separate files:

0	0	2294.99	2294.99	1	10	363	2	10	11422	20130203	########	1	98		
DimCurrency		DimCustomer		DimPromotion		DimProduct		FactInternetSales		DimSalesTeritory		FactInternetSalesPartII		DimProductSubcategory	

Figure 4.7: Separate input data

Once you have done so, please follow these steps:

1. Locate and download the workbook associated with this chapter from https://public.tableau.com/profile/marleen.meier/.

2. Select the **Join Culling** worksheet and click on the **AdventureWorks_Join_Culling** data source.

3. Drag **Sales Territory Country** to the **Rows** shelf and place **SalesAmount** on the **Text** shelf:

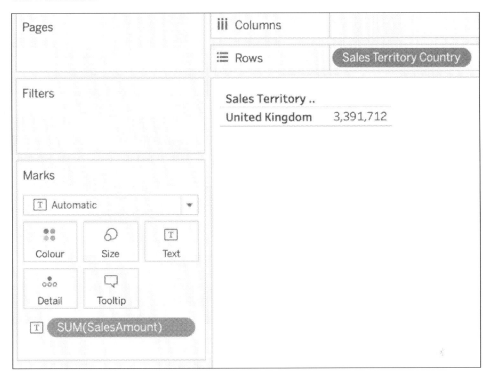

Figure 4.8: Sales amount

4. From the menu, select **Help**, then **Settings and Performance**, and then **Start Performance Recording**:

Figure 4.9: Start Performance Recording

5. Press *F5* on your keyboard to refresh the view.

6. Stop the recording with **Help**, then **Settings and Performance**, and finally **Stop Performance Recording**.

7. In the resulting **Performance Summary** dashboard, drag the time slider to **0.0000** and select **Executing Query**. Now you see the SQL generated by Tableau:

Figure 4.10: Performance recording

So far, we have connected Tableau to our dataset, then we created a very simple worksheet, showing us the number of sales for the United Kingdom. But, in order for Tableau to show the country and the sales amount, it needs to get data from two different tables: **DimSalesTerritory** and **FactInternetSales**. The performance recording in *Figure 4.10* shows how long each step of building the dashboard took and which query was sent to the database. That query is exactly what we are interested in, to see what is going on behind the scenes. Let's look at it in detail:

```
SELECT "DimSalesTerritory"."SalesTerritoryCountry" AS
"SalesTerritoryCountry", "FactInternetSales"."SalesAmount" AS
"SalesAmount"
FROM "TableauTemp"."FactInternetSales$" "FactInternetSales"
INNER JOIN "TableauTemp"."DimSalesTerritory$" "DimSalesTerritory" ON
("FactInternetSales"."SalesTerritoryKey" = "DimSalesTerritory"."SalesTe
rritoryKey")
GROUP BY 1, 2
```

Note that a single inner join was generated, between `FactInternetSales` and `DimSalesTerritory`. Despite the presence of a complex join—meaning that multiple tables are being joined—Tableau only generated the SQL necessary to create the view. In other words, it only created one out of a number of possible joins. This is **join culling** in action.

In Tableau, join culling assumes tables in the database have referential integrity; that is, a join between the fact table and a dimension table does not require joins to other dimension tables. Join culling ensures that if a query requires only data from one table, other joined tables will not be referenced. The end result is better performance. Next, we'll consider another concept in Tableau that affects how datasets are joined: snowflaking.

Snowflaking

Let's make one small change to the star schema and add the **DimProductSubcategory** dimension. In the workbook provided with this chapter, the worksheet is entitled **Joins w/ Snowflaking**. Viewing the joins presupposes that you have connected to a database as opposed to using the extracted data sources provided with the workbook.

Let's look at the changes made in the following screenshot:

Figure 4.11: Snowflaking

Note that there is no common key between **FactInternetSales** and **DimProductSubcategory**. The only way to join this additional table is to connect it to **DimProduct**, so we want to understand what Tableau is doing in this case and if this will have any complications for our dashboard building.

Let's repeat the steps listed in the *Join culling* section to observe the underlying SQL and consider the results in the following code block:

1. Select the **Join w/ Snowflaking** worksheet and click on the **AdventureWorks_w_Snowflaking** data source

2. Drag **Sales Territory Country** to the **Rows** shelf and place **SalesAmount** on the **Text** shelf

3. From the menu, select **Help**, then **Settings and Performance**, and then **Start Performance Recording**

4. Press *F5* on your keyboard to refresh the view

5. Stop the recording with **Help**, then **Settings and Performance**, and finally **Stop Performance Recording**

6. In the resulting **Performance Summary** dashboard, drag the time slider to **0.0000** and select **Executing Query**

Now you should see the SQL generated by Tableau:

```
SELECT "DimSalesTerritory"."SalesTerritoryCountry" AS
"SalesTerritoryCountry", "FactInternetSales"."SalesAmount" AS
"SalesAmount"
FROM "TableauTemp"."FactInternetSales" "FactInternetSales" INNER JOIN
"TableauTemp"."DimProduct" "DimProduct" ON ("FactInternetSales"."Produc
tKey" = "DimProduct"."ProductKey")
INNER JOIN "TableauTemp"."DimSalesTerritory" "DimSalesTerritory" ON
("FactInternetSales"."SalesTerritoryKey" = "DimSalesTerritory"."SalesTe
rritoryKey")
WHERE (NOT ("DimProduct"."ProductSubcategoryKey" IS NULL)) GROUP BY 1,
2
```

Although our view does not require the **DimProduct** table, an additional join was generated for the **DimProduct** table. Additionally, a WHERE clause was included. What's going on?

The additional inner join was created because of **snowflaking**. Snowflaking normalizes a dimension table by moving attributes into one or more additional tables that are joined on a foreign key. As a result of the snowflaking, Tableau is limited in its ability to exercise join culling, and the resulting query is less efficient. The same is true for any secondary join.

A materialized view is the result of a query that is physically stored in a database. It differs from a view in that a view requires the associated query to be run every time it needs to be accessed.

The important points to remember from this section are as follows:

- Using secondary joins limits Tableau's ability to employ join culling. This results in less efficient queries to the underlying data source.

- Creating an extract materializes all joins. Thus even if secondary joins are used when connecting to the data source, any extract from that data source will be denormalized or flattened. This means that any query to an extract will not include joins and may thus perform better. Therefore, in the case of complex joins, try to use extracts where possible to improve performance.

Now that the technical details have been discussed, let's take a look at joins in dashboards themselves.

Join calculations

In Tableau, it is also possible to join two files based on a calculation. You would use this functionality to resolve mismatches between two data sources. The calculated join can be accessed in the dropdown of each join.

See the following screenshot:

Figure 4.12: Create Join Calculation...

As an example, imagine a dataset that contains one column for **First Name**, and another column for **Last Name**. You want to join it to a second dataset that has one column called **Name**, containing the first and last name. One option to join those two datasets is to create a **Join Calculation** like the following in the first dataset:

```
[First Name] + ' ' + [Last Name]
```

Now, select the **Name** column in the second dataset and your keys should be matching!

If you want to know more about calculated joins, please check the Tableau Help pages: https://help.tableau.com/current/pro/desktop/en-us/joining_tables. htm#use-calculations-to-resolve-mismatches-between-fields-in-a-join.

Spatial joins

In Tableau 2018.2, **spatial joins** were added. What this means is that you can join spatial fields from Esri shapefiles, KML, GeoJSON, MapInfo tables, Tableau extracts, and SQL Server. Imagine two datasets, one about the location of basins, indicated by a spatial field, and a second dataset containing the locations of waterfowl sightings, also in a spatial column. Tableau allows you to join the two, which is very hard to do otherwise because most programs don't support spatial data.

In order to join on spatial columns, you have to select the **Intersects** field from the **Join** dropdown:

Figure 4.13: Intersects

For more information on joining spatial files in Tableau, read the following resources from Tableau:

- `https://help.tableau.com/current/pro/desktop/en-us/maps_spatial_join.htm`
- `https://www.tableau.com/about/blog/2018/8/perform-advanced-spatial-analysis-spatial-join-now-available-tableau-92166`

Alternatively to a horizontal join, you might need a vertical join, also called a **union**. A typical union use case is visualizing data that is stored in multiple files or tables over time. You might have a daily report, in which the column structure is the same but collected as a new file every day, stored in a monthly or yearly folder.

Combining those files gives so much more insight than a single one at a time! You will be able to analyze trends and changes from day to day or maybe year to day. So, we will continue with an in-depth explanation of unions in Tableau next.

Unions

Sometimes you might want to analyze data with the same metadata structure, which is stored in different files, for example, sales data from multiple years, or different months, or countries. Instead of copying and pasting the data, you can union it. We already touched upon this topic in *Chapter 3, Tableau Prep Builder*, but a union is basically where Tableau will append new rows of data to existing columns with the same header. Let's consider how to create a union, by taking the following steps:

1. Create the union by dragging and dropping **FactInternetSalesPartII** from the left pane on top of **FactInternetSales** in the data source pane, until the word **Union** appears, a sign that when dropping the data now, the data will be used for a union:

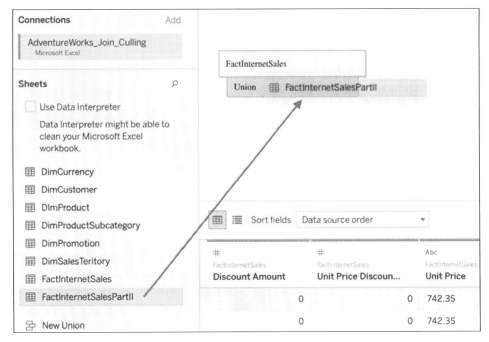

Figure 4.14: Union

2. Alternatively, right-click on the primary dataset and select **Convert to Union…**:

Figure 4.15: Convert to Union…

3. In the following popup (*Figure 4.16*), the user has the option to select all the data tables that should be part of the union individually by drag and drop, or use a **Wildcard** union that includes all tables in a certain directory based on the naming convention—a * represents any character. **FactInternetSales*** will include any file that starts with FactInternetSales:

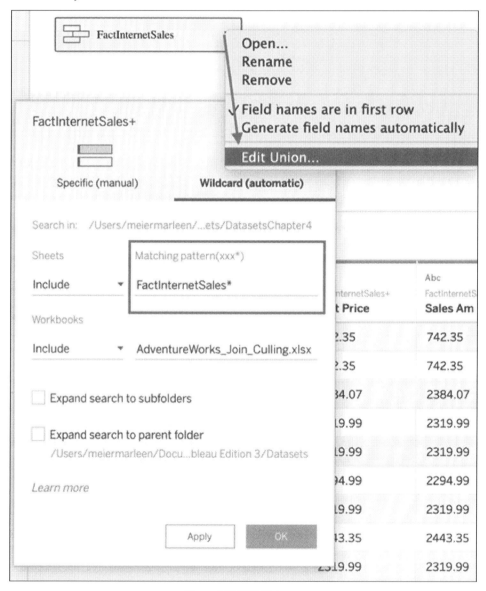

Figure 4.16: Edit Union...

Unions are used to combine data that is very similar and can be appended underneath each other. They are most often used for multiple data files where each has a different date stamp, or a different region, or a different manager, and so forth. By using a union, you want to make the dataset more complete. We saw that Tableau allows unions by drag and drop, as well as right-clicking on the initial data source. We also talked about unions that combine one or more other datasets, using drag and drop or wildcards. *Figure 4.17* presents a typical union example:

Dataset A

Date	Name	Sales
10-18-2020	Spencer	$100
10-18-2020	Maggie	$200
10-18-2020	Ruth	$150

Dataset B

Date	Name	Sales
10-19-2020	Spencer	$50
10-19-2020	Maggie	$125
10-19-2020	Ruth	$80
10-19-2020	Niti	$500

Union A & B

Date	Name	Sales
10-18-2020	Spencer	$100
10-18-2020	Maggie	$200
10-18-2020	Ruth	$150
10-19-2020	Spencer	$50
10-19-2020	Maggie	$125
10-19-2020	Ruth	$80
10-19-2020	Niti	$500

Figure 4.17: Union

Let's look at the aspects we need to remember:

- Unions append data in creating additional rows.
- A union should contain datasets that have many common columns.
- Unions should only be used for same-structured data stored across multiple data sources.
- Keep an eye on performance when using unions. With each additional dataset in the union, you will increase the complexity of Tableau's VizQL.

Since you just became a union expert, it's time to move on to the next feature Tableau offers: **blending**! Blending helps you to combine datasets that have a different level of granularity. Think *one-to-many* relationships between datasets. One dataset has a unique key per row, the other has multiple rows per key. In order to avoid duplicating rows in the first-mentioned dataset, Tableau came up with blending, long before relationships were part of the software package.

Blends

Relationships make data blending a little less needed and it can be seen as legacy functionality. But for the sake of completeness and for older Tableau versions (below 2020.2) let's consider a summary of data blending in the following sections. In a nutshell, data blending allows you to merge multiple, disparate data sources into a single view. Understanding the following four points will give you a grasp on the main points regarding data blending:

- Data blending is typically used to merge data from multiple data sources. Although as of Tableau 10, joins are possible between multiple data sources, there are still cases when data blending is the only possible option to merge data from two or more sources. In the following sections, we will see a practical example that demonstrates such a case.

- Data blending requires a shared dimension. A date dimension is often a good candidate for blending multiple data sources.

- Data blending aggregates and then matches. On the other hand, joining matches and then aggregates.

- Data blending does not enable dimensions from a secondary data source. Attempting to use dimensions from a secondary data source will result in a * or null in the view. There is an exception to this rule, which we will discuss later, in the *Adding secondary dimensions* section.

Now that we've introduced relationships, joins, and unions, I would like to shift your focus a bit to data structures within your workbook. You might have set up the perfect join or union, start dragging and dropping fields onto your workbook canvas, use a filter, use a calculated field, and then receive some unexpected results. Tableau is behaving just not the way you like it. Why might that be?! The order of operation here is key. It is essential to know when which filter will be applied and how this affects your data. Therefore, next in line: order of operations.

Exploring the order of operations

Isn't a data blend the same thing as a left join? This is a question that new Tableau authors often ask. The answer, of course, is no, but let's explore the differences. The following example is simple, even lighthearted, but does demonstrate serious consequences that can result from incorrect aggregation resulting from an erroneous join.

In this example, we will explore in which order aggregation happens in Tableau. This will help you understand how to more effectively use blends and joins.

One day, in the near future, you may move to fulfill a lifelong desire to open a brick and mortar store. Let's assume that you will open a clothing store specializing in pants and shirts. Because of the fastidious tendencies you developed as a result of years of working with data, you are planning to keep everything quite separate, that is, you plan to normalize your business. As evidenced by the following diagram, the pants and shirts you sell in your store will be quite separated:

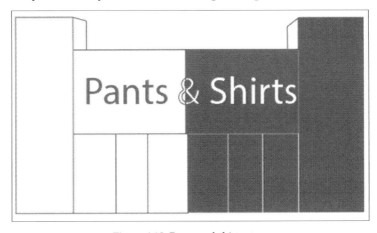

Figure 4.18: Pants and shirts store

You also intend to keep your data stored in separate tables, although these tables will exist in the same data source.

Let's view the segregation of the data in the following screenshot:

Pants Table			Shirt Table	
Salesperson	Pants Amount		Sales Associate	Shirt Amount
Tanya	100		Tanya	50
Zhang	100		Zhang	50
Tanya	100		Tanya	50
Zhang	100		Zhang	50

Figure 4.19: Pants and shirts tables

In these tables, two people are listed: **Tanya** and **Zhang**. In one table, these people are members of the **Salesperson** dimension, and in the other, they are members of the **Sales Associate** dimension. Furthermore, **Tanya** and **Zhang** both sold $200 in pants and $100 in shirts. Let's explore different ways Tableau could connect to this data to better understand joining and data blending.

When we look at the spreadsheets associated with this exercise, you will notice additional columns. These columns will be used in a later exercise.

Please take the following steps:

1. In the workbook associated with this chapter, right-click on the **Pants** data source and look at the data by clicking **View data**. Do the same for the **Shirts** data source.

2. Open the **Join** data source by right-clicking on it and selecting **Edit Data Source**, and observe the join between the **Pants** and **Shirts** tables using **Salesperson/Sales Associate** as the common key:

Figure 4.20: Join

3. On the **Pants** worksheet, select the **Pants** data source and place **Salesperson** on the **Rows** shelf and **Pants Amount** on the **Text** shelf:

Figure 4.21: Setting up the worksheet

4. On the **Shirts** worksheet, select the **Shirts** data source and place **Sales Associate** on the **Rows** shelf and **Shirt Amount** on the **Text** shelf:

Figure 4.22: Shirts

5. On the **Join** worksheet, select the **Join** data source and place **Salesperson** on the **Rows** shelf. Next, double-click **Pants Amount** and **Shirt Amount** to place both on the view:

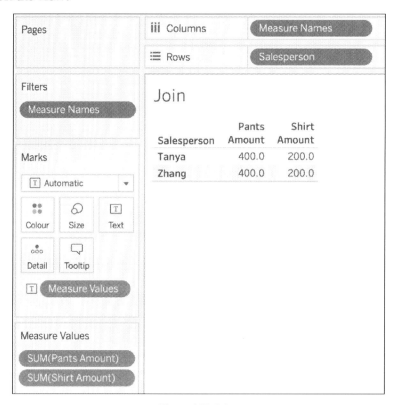

Figure 4.23: Join

6. On the **Blend – Pants Primary** worksheet, select the **Pants** data source and place **Salesperson** on the **Rows** shelf and **Pants Amount** on the **Text** shelf:

Figure 4.24: Blend pants

7. Stay on the same worksheet and select the **Shirts** data source from the data source pane on the left and double-click on **Shirt Amount**. Click **OK** if an error message pops up.

8. Select **Data** then **Edit Blend Relationships…**:

Figure 4.25: Edit Blend Relationships...

9. In the resulting dialog box, click on the **Custom** radio button as shown in *Figure 4.26*, then click **Add...**.

10. In the left column, select **Sales Associate**, and in the right column, select **Salesperson**. The left column represents data from the **Primary data source** and the right column represents all the data available in the **Secondary data source**, as shown in *Figure 4.26*.

11. Remove all other links if any and click **OK**. The results in the dialog box should match what is displayed in the following screenshot:

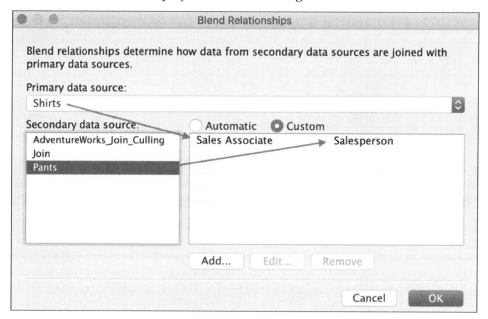

Figure 4.26: Blend Relationships

A little recap on what we have done so far: we are working with three data sources: **Pants**, **Shirts**, and **Join**, where **Join** consists of **Pants** and **Shirts**. We have also created a blend with **Pants** being the primary data source and we connected them by using **Salesperson** and **Sales Associate** as keys.

Don't get confused by the name **Blend Relationships**. This has nothing to do with the logical layer **Relationships**. It is just the name of the pop-up window.

Going back to the exercise, continue with the following steps.

12. On the **Blend – Shirts Primary** worksheet, select the **Shirts** data source and place **Sales Associate** on the **Rows** shelf and **Shirt Amount** on the **Text** shelf:

Figure 4.27: Blend Shirts – Primary

13. On the same workbook, select the **Pants** data source and double-click **Pants Amount** in order to add it to the view:

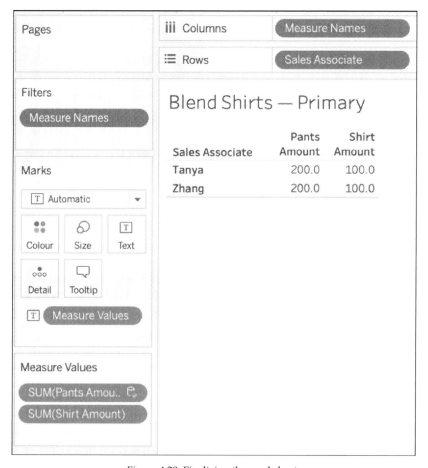

Figure 4.28: Finalizing the worksheet

14. Place all five worksheets on a dashboard. Format and arrange as desired. Now let's compare the results between the five worksheets in the following screenshot:

Pants		Shirts	
Salesperson		Sales Assoc..	
Tanya	200	Tanya	100
Zhang	200	Zhang	100

Join			
Salesperson	Pants Amount	Shirt Amount	
Tanya	400.0	200.0	
Zhang	400.0	200.0	

Blend Pants - Primary		Blend Shirts — Primary	
Salesperson		Sales Asociate	
Tanya	200	Tanya	100
Zhang	200	Zhang	100

Figure 4.29: Comparison

In the preceding screenshot, the **Join** worksheet has double the expected results. Why? Because a join first matches on the common key (in this case, **Salesperson/ Sales Associate**) and then aggregates the results. The more matches found on a common key, the worse the problem will become. If multiple matches are found on a common key, the results will grow exponentially. Two matches will result in squared results, three matches will result in cubed results, and so forth. This exponential effect is represented graphically in the following screenshot:

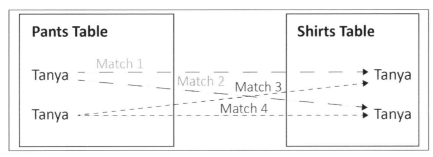

Figure 4.30: Join

On the other hand, the blend functioned more efficiently but before the blend could function properly, we had to edit the data relationship so that Tableau could connect the two data sources using the **Salesperson** and **Sales Associate** fields. If the two fields had been identically named (for example, Salesperson), Tableau would have automatically provided an option to blend between the data sources using those fields.

The results for the **Blend Pants – Primary** and **Blend Shirts – Primary** worksheets are correct. There is no exponential effect. Why? Because data blending first aggregates the results from both data sources, and then matches the results on a common dimension.

In this case, it is **Salesperson/Sales Associate**, as demonstrated in the following screenshot:

Figure 4.31: Blending results

What we saw in this exercise is that joins can change the data structure, so be careful when using them and be very aware of which columns are a suitable key. Also, do checks before and after joining your data, which can be as easy as counting rows and checking if this is the expected result.

Blending has advantages and disadvantages; adding dimensions, for example, is not that straightforward. But we will explore more details regarding secondary dimensions in the next section.

Adding secondary dimensions

Data blending, although very useful for connecting disparate data sources, has limitations. The most important limitation to be aware of is that data blending does not enable dimensions from a secondary data source. There is an exception to this limitation; that is, there is one way you can add a dimension from a secondary data source. Let's explore further.

There are other fields besides **Salesperson/Sales Associate** and **Shirt Amount/ Pants Amount** in the data sources. We will reference those fields in this exercise:

1. In the workbook associated with this chapter, select the **Adding Secondary Dimensions** worksheet.

2. Select the **Shirts** data source.

3. Add a relationship between the **Shirts** and **Pants** data sources for **Material Type**, taking the following steps:

    1. Select **Data** then **Edit Relationships**.

    2. Ensure that **Shirts** is the primary data source and **Pants** is the secondary data source.

    3. Select the **Custom** radio button.

    4. Click **Add...**:

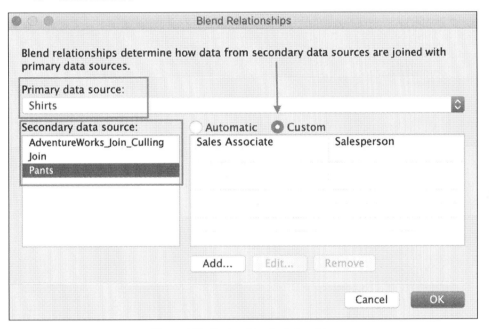

Figure 4.32: Custom blend relationships

4. Select **Material Type** in both the left and right columns:

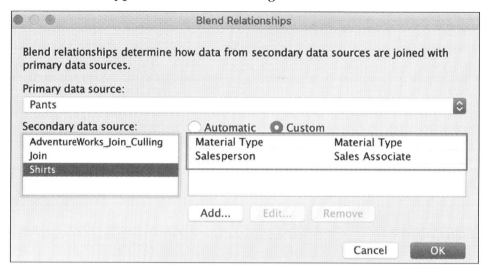

Figure 4.33: Custom blend relationships

5. Click **OK** to return to the view.

6. Place **Material Type** on the **Rows** shelf.

7. Select the **Pants** data source and make sure that the chain-link icon next to **Material Type** in the **Data** pane is activated and that the chain-link icon next to **Salesperson** is deactivated. If the icon is a gray, broken chain-link, it is not activated. If it is an orange, connected chain-link, it is activated:

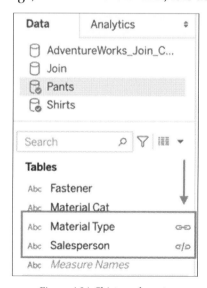

Figure 4.34: Shirts and pants

8. Place **Material Cat** *before* **Material Type**, and **Fastener** *after* **Material Type** on the **Rows** shelf as follows:

Figure 4.35: Secondary dimensions

Material Cat is a dimension from a secondary data source. Data blending does not enable dimensions from a secondary data source. Why does it work in this case? There are a few reasons:

- There is a one-to-many relationship between **Material Cat** and **Material Type**; that is, each member of the **Material Type** dimension is matched with one and only one member of the **Material Cat** dimension.

- The view is blended on **Material Type**, not **Material Cat**. This is important because **Material Type** is at a lower level of granularity than **Material Cat**. Attempting to blend the view on **Material Cat** will not enable **Material Type** as a secondary dimension.

- Every member of the **Material Type** dimension within the primary data source also exists in the secondary data source.

Fastener is also a dimension from the secondary data source. In *Figure 4.35*, it displays * in one of the cells, thus demonstrating that **Fastener** is not working as a dimension should; that is, it is not slicing the data, as discussed in *Chapter 1, Getting Up to Speed – A Review of the Basics*. The reason an asterisk displays is that there are multiple fastener types associated with **Wool**. **Button** and **Velcro** display because **Acrylic** and **Polyester** each have only one fastener type in the underlying data.

If you use blending, make sure that your main reason is to combine measures and that you don't need the dimensions on a detailed level. It is very useful to know this before you create a dashboard, in order to prepare accordingly. Maybe your data needs extra prepping (check *Chapter 3, Tableau Prep Builder*) because neither a join nor a blend can bring you the expected data structure. Or maybe you can make use of scaffolding, a technique that uses a helper data source—we will discuss this in the next section.

Introducing scaffolding

Scaffolding is a technique that introduces a second data source through blending for the purpose of reshaping and/or extending the initial data source. Scaffolding enables capabilities that extend Tableau to meet visualization and analytical needs that may otherwise be very difficult or altogether impossible. Joe Mako, who pioneered scaffolding in Tableau, tells a story in which he used the technique to recreate a dashboard using four worksheets. The original dashboard, which did not use scaffolding, required 80 worksheets painstakingly aligned pixel by pixel.

Among the many possibilities that scaffolding enables is extending Tableau's forecasting functionality. Tableau's native forecasting capabilities are sometimes criticized for lacking sophistication. Scaffolding can be used to meet this criticism.

The following are the steps:

1. In the workbook associated with this chapter, select the **Scaffolding** worksheet and connect to the **World Indicators** data source.

2. Using Excel or a text editor, create a Records dataset. The following two-row table represents the Records dataset in its entirety:

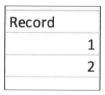

Figure 4.36: Excel file

3. Connect Tableau to the dataset.

4. To be expedient, consider copying the dataset directly from Excel by using *Ctrl + C* and pasting it directly into Tableau with *Ctrl + V*.

5. Create a **Start Date** parameter in Tableau, with the settings seen in the following screenshot. In particular, notice the highlighted sections in the screenshot by which you can set the desired display format:

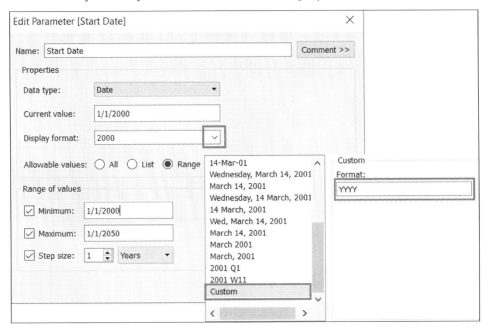

Figure 4.37: Display format

6. Create another parameter named **End Date** with identical settings.

7. In the **Data** pane, right-click on the **Start Date** and **End Date** parameters you just created and select **Show Parameter**:

Figure 4.38: Show Parameter

8. Set the start and end dates as desired, for example, 2000–2024:

Figure 4.39: Start and end dates

9. Select the **Records** data source and create a calculated field called Date with the following code:

```
IIF([Records]=1,[Start Date],[End Date])
```

10. Place the **Date** field on the **Rows** shelf.

11. Right-click on the **Date** field on the **Rows** shelf and select **Show Missing Values**. Note that all the dates between the start and end date settings now display:

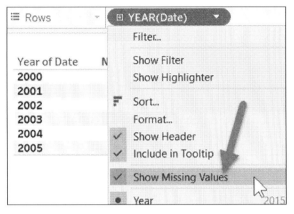

Figure 4.40: Show Missing Values

12. Create a parameter named **Select Country A** with the settings shown in the following screenshot. In particular, note that the list of countries was added with the **Add from Field** button:

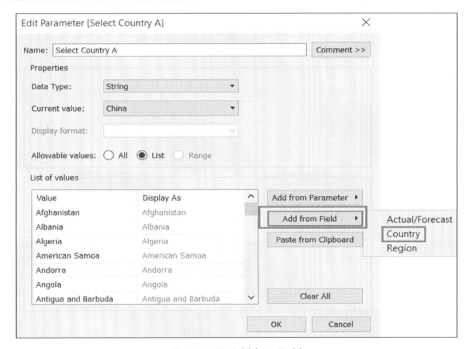

Figure 4.41: Add from Field

13. Create another parameter named **Select Country B** with identical settings.

14. Create a parameter named **Select Country A Forecast** with the settings given in the following screenshot. In particular, notice the sections by which you can set the desired display format:

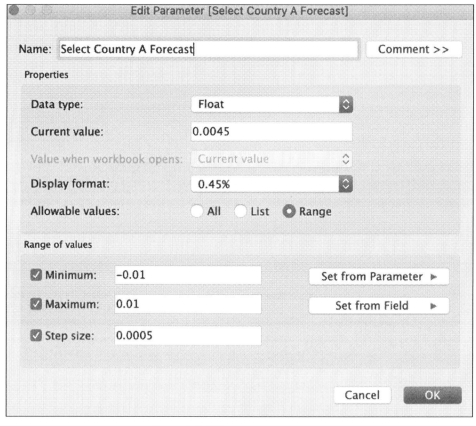

Figure 4.42: Edit parameter

15. Create another parameter named **Select Country B Forecast** with identical settings.

16. In the **Data** pane, right-click on the four parameters you just created (**Select Country A**, **Select Country B**, **Select Country A Forecast**, and **Select Country B Forecast**) and select **Show Parameter**:

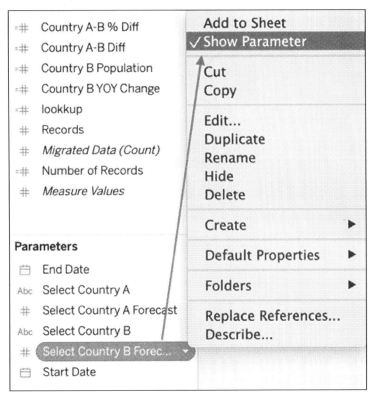

Figure 4.43: Show Parameter

17. Make sure that the **Date** field in the **World Indicators** data source has the orange chain-link icon deployed. This indicates it's used as a linking field:

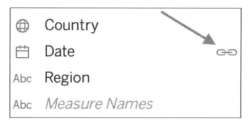

Figure 4.44: Link

18. Within the **World Indicators** dataset, create the following calculated fields:

Calculated field name	Calculated field code
Country A Population	`IIF([Country] = [Select Country A],[Population Total],NULL)`
Country B Population	`IIF([Country] = [Select Country B],[Population Total],NULL)`

19. Within the **Records** dataset, create the following calculated fields:

Calculated field name	Calculated field code
Actual/Forecast	`IIF(ISNULL(AVG([World Indicators].[Population Total])),"Forecast","Actual")`

Country A Population	`IF [Actual/Forecast] = "Actual" THEN SUM([World Indicators].[Country A Population]) ELSE PREVIOUS_VALUE(0)`
	
	 `*[Select Country A Forecast] + PREVIOUS_VALUE(0)`
	
	 `END`

Country A YOY Change	`([Country A Population] - LOOKUP([Country A Population], -1)) /`
	
	 `ABS(LOOKUP([Country A Population], -1))`

Country B Population	IF [Actual/Forecast] = "Actual" THEN SUM([World Indicators].[Country B Population]) ELSE PREVIOUS_VALUE(0) *[Select Country B Forecast] + PREVIOUS_ VALUE(0) END
Country B YOY Change	([Country B Population] - LOOKUP([Country B Population], -1)) / ABS(LOOKUP([Country B Population], -1))
Country A-B Diff	[Country A Population] - [Country B Population]
Country A-B % Diff	[Country A-B Diff]/[Country A Population]

20. Within the **Data** pane, right-click on **Country A YOY Change**, **Country B YOY Change**, and **Country A-B % Diff** and select **Default Properties | Number format...** to change the default number format to **Percentage**, as shown in the following screenshot:

Figure 4.45: Default Properties

21. With the **Records** data source selected, place the **Actual/Forecast**, **Measure Values**, and **Measure Names** fields on the **Color**, **Text**, and **Columns** shelves, respectively:

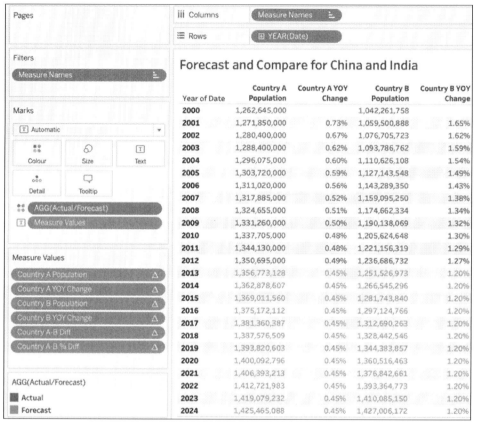

Figure 4.46: Forecast setup

22. Adjust the **Measure Values** shelf so that the fields that display are identical to the following screenshot. Also, ensure that **Compute Using** for each of these fields is set to **Table (down)**:

Figure 4.47: Compute Using

So, what have we achieved so far? We basically created a duplicated data structure that allows us to compare two countries in two separate columns, even though the data is in one column in the original dataset. This setup allows us to ask more advanced questions.

To demonstrate this, let's ask, "*When will India's population overtake China's?*" You can set the parameters as desired—I chose 0.45% and 1.20% as the average yearly growth rates, but feel free to choose any parameter you think works best for a country. In *Figure 4.48* you see that with a growth rate of 0.45% and 1.20% for China and India, respectively, India will have more inhabitants than China by 2024. You can observe this by looking at the columns **Country A Population** and **Country B Population**. Everything in orange is a forecast, while everything in blue is actual data from our dataset:

Forecast and Compare for China and India

Year of Date	Country A Population	Country A YOY Change	Country B Population	Country B YOY Change	Country A-B Diff	Country A-B % Diff
2000	1,262,645,000		1,042,261,758		220,383,242	17.45%
2001	1,271,850,000	0.73%	1,059,500,888	1.65%	212,349,112	16.70%
2002	1,280,400,000	0.67%	1,076,705,723	1.62%	203,694,277	15.91%
2003	1,288,400,000	0.62%	1,093,786,762	1.59%	194,613,238	15.11%
2004	1,296,075,000	0.60%	1,110,626,108	1.54%	185,448,892	14.31%
2005	1,303,720,000	0.59%	1,127,143,548	1.49%	176,576,452	13.54%
2006	1,311,020,000	0.56%	1,143,289,350	1.43%	167,730,650	12.79%
2007	1,317,885,000	0.52%	1,159,095,250	1.38%	158,789,750	12.05%
2008	1,324,655,000	0.51%	1,174,662,334	1.34%	149,992,666	11.32%
2009	1,331,260,000	0.50%	1,190,138,069	1.32%	141,121,931	10.60%
2010	1,337,705,000	0.48%	1,205,624,648	1.30%	132,080,352	9.87%
2011	1,344,130,000	0.48%	1,221,156,319	1.29%	122,973,681	9.15%
2012	1,350,695,000	0.49%	1,236,686,732	1.27%	114,008,268	8.44%
2013	1,356,773,128	0.45%	1,251,526,973	1.20%	105,246,155	7.76%
2014	1,362,878,607	0.45%	1,266,545,296	1.20%	96,333,310	7.07%
2015	1,369,011,560	0.45%	1,281,743,840	1.20%	87,267,720	6.37%
2016	1,375,172,112	0.45%	1,297,124,766	1.20%	78,047,346	5.68%
2017	1,381,360,387	0.45%	1,312,690,263	1.20%	68,670,124	4.97%
2018	1,387,576,509	0.45%	1,328,442,546	1.20%	59,133,962	4.26%
2019	1,393,820,603	0.45%	1,344,383,857	1.20%	49,436,746	3.55%
2020	1,400,092,796	0.45%	1,360,516,463	1.20%	39,576,332	2.83%
2021	1,406,393,213	0.45%	1,376,842,661	1.20%	29,550,552	2.10%
2022	1,412,721,983	0.45%	1,393,364,773	1.20%	19,357,210	1.37%
2023	1,419,079,232	0.45%	1,410,085,150	1.20%	8,994,081	0.63%
2024	1,425,465,088	0.45%	1,427,006,172	1.20%	-1,541,084	-0.11%

Select Country A: China
Select Country B: India
Start Date: 2000
End Date: 2024
Select Country A For...: 0.45%
Select Country B For...: 1.20%

Figure 4.48: Forecast dashboard

In reality, we are obviously already many years ahead; can you use this dashboard to figure out the actual average growth rate for China and India from 2012 to 2020 if I tell you that the population in 2020 was 1,439,323,776 in China and 1,380,004,385 in India? Share your results on Tableau Public with the tag #MasteringTableau!

One key to this exercise is data scaffolding. Data scaffolding produces data that doesn't exist in the data source. The **World Indicators** dataset only includes dates from 2000 to 2012 and obviously, the **Records** dataset does not contain any dates.

By using the **Start Date** and **End Date** parameters coupled with the calculated **Date** field, we were able to produce any set of dates desired. We had to blend the data, rather than join or union, in order to keep the original data source intact and create all additional data outside of the world indicators itself.

The actual data scaffolding occurred upon selecting **Show Missing Values** from the **Date** field dropdown after it was placed on the **Rows** shelf. This allowed every year between **Start Date** and **End Date** to display even when there were no matching years in the underlying data. *Chapter 6, All About Data – Data Densification, Cubes, and Big Data*, will explore something very similar to data scaffolding, data densification, in more detail.

Let's look at a few of the calculated fields in more depth to better understand how the forecasting works in this exercise.

Calculated Field: `Actual/Forecast`:

```
IIF(ISNULL(AVG([World Indicators].[Population
Total])),"Forecast","Actual")
```

The preceding code determines whether data exists in the **World Indicators** dataset. If the date is after 2012, no data exists and thus Forecast is returned.

Calculated Field: `Country A Population`:

```
IF [Actual/Forecast] = "Actual" THEN SUM([World Indicators].[Country A
Population]) ELSE PREVIOUS_VALUE(0)
*[Select Country A Forecast] + PREVIOUS_VALUE(0) END
```

If forecasting is necessary to determine the value (that is, if the date is after 2012), the ELSE portion of this code is exercised. The PREVIOUS_VALUE function returns the value of the previous row and multiplies the results by the forecast and then adds the previous row.

Let's look at an example in the following table:

Previous Row Value (PRV)	1,000
Forecast (F)	0.01
PRV * F	10
Current Row Value	1,010

One important thing to note in the Country A Population calculated field is that the forecast is quite simple: multiply the previous population by a given forecast number and tally the results. Without changing the overall structure of the logic, this section of code could be modified with more sophisticated forecasting.

These exercises have shown that with a few other tricks and techniques, blending can be used to great effect in your data projects. Last but not least we will talk about data structures in general such that you will better understand why Tableau is doing what it is doing and how you can achieve your visualization goals.

Understanding data structures

The right data structure is not easily definable. True, there are ground rules. For instance, tall data is generally better than wide data. A wide dataset with lots of columns can be difficult to work with, whereas the same data structured in a tall format with fewer columns but more rows is usually easier to work with.

But this isn't always the case! Some business questions are more easily answered with wide data structures. And that's the crux of the matter. Business questions determine the right data structure. If one structure answers all questions, great! However, your questions may require multiple data structures. The pivot feature in Tableau helps you adjust data structures on the fly in order to answer different business questions.

Before beginning this exercise, make sure you understand the following points:

- Pivoting in Tableau is limited to Excel, text files, and Google Sheets, otherwise, you have to use Custom SQL or Tableau Prep
- A pivot in Tableau is referred to as *unpivot* in database terminology

As a business analyst for a hospital, you are connecting Tableau to a daily snapshot of patient data. You have two questions:

- How many events occur on any given date? For example, how many patients check in on a given day?
- How much time expires between events? For example, what is the average stay for those patients who are in the hospital for multiple days?

To answer these questions, take the following steps:

1. In the starter workbook associated with this chapter, select the **Time Frames** worksheet, and within the **Data** pane, select the **Patient_Snapshot** data source.
2. Click on the dropdown in the **Marks** card and select **Bar** as the chart type.

3. Right-click in the **Data** pane to create a parameter named **Select Time Frame** with the settings displayed in the following screenshot:

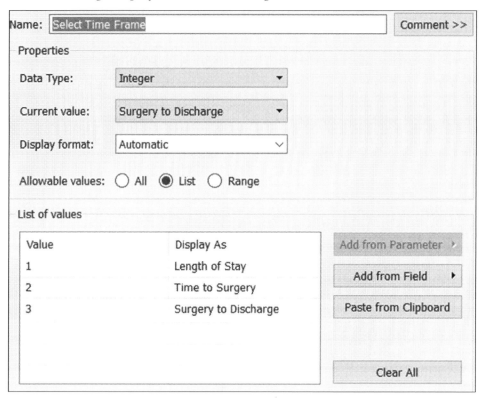

Figure 4.49: Parameter

4. Right-click on the parameter we just created and select **Show Parameter**.

5. Right-click in the **Data** pane to create a calculated field called Selected Time Frame with the following code:

```
CASE [Select Time Frame]
WHEN 1 THEN DATEDIFF('day',[Check-in Date],[Discharge Date])
WHEN 2 THEN DATEDIFF('day',[Surgery Date],[Discharge Date])
WHEN 3 THEN DATEDIFF('day',[Check-in Date],[Surgery Date])
END
```

6. Drag the following fields to the associated shelves and define them as directed:

Field name	Shelf directions
Patient Type	Drag to the **Filter** shelf and check **Inpatient**.
Check-in Date	Drag to the **Filter** shelf and select **Range of dates**. Also right-click on the resulting filter and select **Show Filter**.
Check-in Date	Right-click and drag to the **Columns** shelf and select **MDY**.
Selected Time Frame	Right-click and drag to the **Rows** shelf and select **AVG**.
Selected Time Frame	Right-click and drag to the **Color** shelf and select **AVG**. Set colors as desired.

After these actions, your worksheet should look like the following:

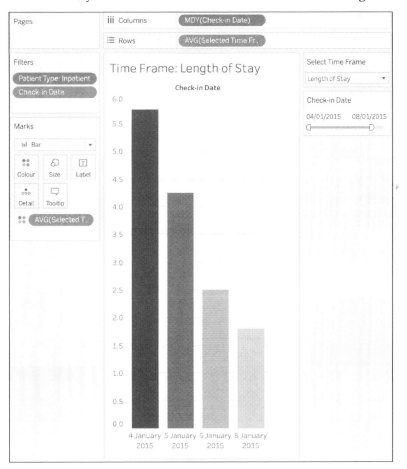

Figure 4.50: Initial dashboard

7. Right-click on the **Avg Selected Time Frame** axis and select **Edit Axis…**, as shown in the following figure. Then delete the title:

Figure 4.51: Edit Axis

8. Select **Worksheet | Show Title**. Edit the title by inserting the parameter `Select Time Frame`, as shown in the following screenshot:

Figure 4.52: Add parameter

The data structure was ideal for the first part of this exercise. You were probably able to create the visualization quickly. The only section of moderate interest was setting up the **Selected Time Frame** calculated field with the associated parameter.

This allows the end user to choose which time frame they would like to view:

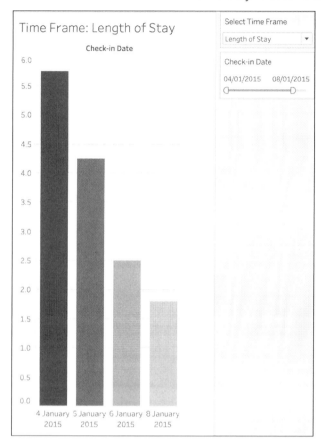

Figure 4.53: Dashboard

But what happens if you need to find out how many people were involved in a type of event per day?

This question is rather difficult to answer using the current data structure because we have one row per patient with multiple dates in that row. In *Figure 4.54* you can see the difference: the right-hand side is our current data structure and the left-hand side is the data structure that would make it easier to count events per day:

Patient	Event	Date		Patient	Event A Date	Event B Date	Event C Date
U	A	X		U	X	Y	Z
U	B	Y		V	Y	X	
U	C	Z					
V	A	Y					
V	B	X					

Figure 4.54: Patient data structure

Therefore, in the second part of this exercise, we'll try a different approach by pivoting the data:

1. In the starter workbook associated with this chapter, select the **Events Per Date** worksheet.

2. In the **Data** pane, right-click the **Patient_Snapshot** data source and choose **Duplicate**.

3. Rename the duplicate **Events**.

4. Right-click on the **Events** data source and choose **Edit Data Source...**:

Figure 4.55: Edit Data Source...

5. Review the highlighted areas of the following screenshot and take the following steps:

   a. Click on the **Manage metadata** icon

   b. Select all five of the date fields with *Shift* or *Ctrl* + click

c. Select the drop-down option for any of the selected fields and choose **Pivot**:

Figure 4.56: Pivot

6. The pivot will turn rows and columns around and we will get a data structure just like in *Figure 4.54* on the left-hand side. Rename the pivoted fields to **Event Type** and **Event Date**.

7. Select the **Events Per Date** worksheet and place the following fields on the associated shelves and define as directed:

Field name	Shelf directions
Event Date	Right-click and drag to the **Rows** shelf and select **MDY**
Event Type	Place after **Event Date** on the **Rows** shelf
Patient Type	Right-click and select **Show Filter**
Number of Records	Drag to **Columns** shelf

From this, your worksheet should look like the following:

Figure 4.57: Events per Date

The original data structure was not well suited for this exercise; however, after duplicating the data source and pivoting, the task to count events per day was quite simple since we were able to achieve this by using only three fields: **Event Date**, **Number of Records**, and **Event Type**. That's the main takeaway. If you find yourself struggling to create a visualization to answer a seemingly simple business question, consider pivoting.

Summary

We began this chapter with an introduction to relationships, followed by a discussion on complex joins, and discovered that, when possible, Tableau uses join culling to generate efficient queries to the data source. A secondary join, however, limits Tableau's ability to employ join culling. An extract results in a materialized, flattened view that eliminates the need for joins to be included in any queries. Unions come in handy if identically formatted data, stored in multiple sheets or data sources, needs to be appended.

Then, we reviewed data blending to clearly understand how it differs from joining. We discovered that the primary limitation in data blending is that no dimensions are allowed from a secondary source; however, we also discovered that there are exceptions to this rule. We also discussed scaffolding, which can make data blending surprisingly fruitful.

Finally, we discussed data structures and learned how pivoting can make difficult or impossible visualizations easy. Having completed our second data-centric discussion, in the next chapter, we will discuss table calculations as well as partitioning and addressing.

5
Table Calculations

The topic of table calculations in Tableau is so rich and deep that it alone could legitimately be the subject of an entire book. Exploring the various options that are available for each table calculation function and the various ways that table calculations can be applied is an interesting and rewarding endeavor. As you review the examples in this chapter, you will undoubtedly encounter techniques that you can apply in your day-to-day work; however, you may struggle to understand why some of these techniques work. This chapter has been written with the intent of providing ways of thinking about table calculations that will prove useful in your journey toward mastering this fascinating topic. Along the way, some practical examples will be considered as well.

I would like to draw your attention to the work of three individuals who helped to make this chapter possible. Joshua Milligan provided the idea of directional and non-directional as a taxonomy for considering how Tableau table calculation functions are applied. Of the dozens of blogs, forum posts, conference sessions, articles, and white papers reviewed for this chapter, Jonathan Drummy's blog post (`http://drawingwithnumbers.artisart.org/at-the-level-unlocking-the-mystery-part-1-ordinal-calcs/`), *At the Level – Unlocking the Mystery Part 1: Ordinal Calcs*, was the clearest and most insightful for understanding the various nuances of partitioning and addressing. Lastly, Joe Mako's unsurpassed understanding of the inner workings of Tableau and his willingness to share that insight through the Tableau forums was very helpful.

In this chapter, we will discuss the following topics:

- A definition and two questions
- Introducing functions
- Directional and non-directional table calculations
- Application of functions

Let's go into more detail and start this chapter off with a general definition of table calculations and two resulting questions, which we will answer by the end of this chapter.

A definition and two questions

As discussed in *Chapter 1, Getting Up to Speed – A Review of the Basics*, calculated fields can be categorized as either row-level, aggregate-level, or table-level. For row - and aggregate-level calculations, the underlying data source engine does most (if not all) of the computational work and Tableau merely visualizes the results. For table calculations, Tableau also relies on the underlying data source engine and the available RAM on your machine to execute computational tasks; however, after that work is completed and a dataset is returned, Tableau performs additional processing before rendering the results.

Let us look at the definition of table calculations, as follows:

> *A table calculation is a function performed on a cached dataset that has been generated as a result of a query from Tableau to the data source.*

Let's consider a couple of points regarding the dataset in cache mentioned in the preceding definition:

- This cache is not simply the returned results of a query. Tableau may adjust the returned results. We will consider this in *Chapter 6, All About Data – Data Densification, Cubes, and Big Data*; Tableau may expand the cache through data densification but usually, it is user-driven.

- It's important to consider how the cache is structured. Basically, the dataset in cache is the table used in your worksheet and, like all tables, is made up of rows and columns. This is particularly important for table calculations since a table calculation may be computed as it moves along the cache. Such a table calculation is *directional* (for an example, see *Figure 5.1*).

- Alternatively, a table calculation may be computed based on the entire cache with no directional consideration. These table calculations are *non-directional*. Directional and non-directional table calculations will be explored more fully in the *Directional and non-directional table calculations* section.

 Note that in the Tableau documentation, the dataset in cache is typically referred to as a partition. This chapter will often use both terms side by side for clarity.

The structure of this chapter was created with the intent of providing a simple schema for understanding table calculations. This is communicated through two questions:

- What is the function?
- How is the function applied?

These two questions are inexorably connected. You cannot reliably apply something until you know what it is. And you cannot get useful results from something until you correctly apply it. The *Introducing functions* section explores each unique table calculation function, and how each can be considered **directional** or **non-directional**. The *Application of functions* section explores how table calculations are applied to the view via partitioning and addressing dimensions.

Introducing functions

As discussed earlier in this chapter, it may be helpful to enhance your understanding of table calculations with the following two questions: what is the function and how is the function applied? We will begin by grouping each table calculation function to be directional or non-directional.

Tableau offers a wide range of table calculations, but if we narrow our consideration to unique groups of table calculation functions, we will discover that there are only 11.

The following table shows those 11 functions organized into two categories:

Directional Functions	Non-Directional Functions
LOOKUP	SCRIPT_STR
PREVIOUS VALUE	SIZE
RUNNING	TOTAL
WINDOW	
FIRST	
INDEX	
LAST	
RANK	

As mentioned in *A definition and two questions*, non-directional table calculation functions operate on the entire cache and thus are not computed based on movement through the cache. For example, the SIZE function doesn't change based on the value of a previous row in the cache. On the other hand, RUNNING_SUM does change based on previous rows in the cache and is therefore considered directional. In the following section, we'll see directional and non-directional table calculation functions in action.

Directional and non-directional table calculations

Let us have a closer look at directional and non-directional table calculations:

1. Navigate to https://public.tableau.com/profile/marleen.meier to locate and download the workbook associated with this chapter.

2. Navigate to the **Directional/Non-Directional** worksheet.

3. Create the calculated fields, as shown in the following table:

Name	Calculation	Notes
Lookup	LOOKUP(SUM([Sales]),-1)	Notice the -1 included in this calculation. This instructs Tableau to retrieve the value from the previous row.
Size	SIZE()	The SIZE function returns the number of rows in the partition. Therefore, as can be seen in the following screenshot, the size equals the total number of rows.
Window Sum	WINDOW_SUM(SUM([Sales]))	The Window sum functions (WINDOW_SUM(expression, [start, end]) can operate either directionally or non-directionally. Since this example does not include the [start, end] option, it operates non-directionally.
Window Sum w/ Start&End	WINDOW_SUM(SUM([Sales]),0,1)	This example of a window function is operating directionally, as can be seen by the inclusion of the [start, end] option.
Running Sum	RUNNING_SUM(SUM([Sales]))	By their nature, RUNNING functions operate directionally since they consider previous rows in order to compute.

4. Place **Category** and **Ship Mode** on the **Rows** shelf.

5. Double-click on **Sales**, **Lookup**, **Size**, **Window Sum**, **Window Sum w/ Start&End**, and **Running Sum** to populate the view as shown in the following screenshot:

Figure 5.1: Table calculation

6. The table in *Figure 5.1* shows you that the Size function and the Window Sum function are the only two non-directional functions. All others present a number depending on the direction. For example, Lookup moves down and prints the value prior to the actual field. You can change the direction by clicking on the triangle of any table calculation field and selecting **Edit Table Calculation**.

In answer to the question what is the function, we have considered a taxonomy composed of two categories: directional and non-directional. Now, we will move on to considering the table calculation functions individually. Regretfully, space does not allow us to explore all table calculations; however, to gain a working understanding, it should suffice to consider all but one of the unique groups of options. The four table calculations that begin with Script_ will be covered in *Chapter 15, Programming Tool Integration*.

Although some effort has been made to make the following exercises useful for real-world scenarios, each is focused on demonstrating table calculation functionality while considering how each interacts directionally or non-directionally with the dataset in cache (also known as the partition).

Exploring each unique table calculation function

The following exercises will show us each table calculation individually, based on an example.

Lookup and Total

The objectives of the following worksheet are to display those customers who made purchases in the last 2 days of 2013, and the associated absolute as well as relative sales of the month of December.

In the following table, LOOKUP behaves directionally whereas TOTAL is non-directional. This behavior is easy to notice in the results. Follow these steps in order to do so:

1. In the workbook associated with this chapter, navigate to the **Lookup/Total** worksheet.

2. Drag **Customer Name** and **Order Date** to the **Rows** shelf. Set **Order Date** to **Month/Day/Year** discrete by right-clicking and selecting **Day** as well as **Discrete**.

3. Place **Order Date** on the **Filters** shelf, choose to view only December 2013, and select **Month/Year** as the date format.

4. Create the following calculated fields:

Name	Calculation
Lookup Intervening Time	DATEDIFF('day',LOOKUP(Max([Order Date]),0), MAKEDATE(2013,12,31))
% Total Sales	SUM(Sales)/TOTAL(SUM([Sales]))

5. Right-click on % **Total Sales** and select **Default Properties | Number format** to set the number format to percentage with two decimal places.

6. Place **Lookup Intervening Time** on the **Filters** shelf and choose a range from 0 to 1.

7. Double-click on **Sales** and % **Total Sales** to place both fields on the view.

8. Format as desired:

Figure 5.2: Total Sales

Let's consider how the preceding worksheet functions:

- The filter on **Order Date** ensures that the dataset returned to Tableau only includes data from the month of December 2013.

- The **% Total Sales** SUM(Sales)/TOTAL(SUM([Sales])) includes the TOTAL(SUM([Sales])) calculated field, which returns the total sales for the entire dataset. Dividing SUM([Sales]) by this total returns the percentage of the total.

- **Lookup Intervening Time**: DATEDIFF('day',LOOKUP(Max([Order Date]),0), MAKEDATE(2013,12,31)) will return an integer that reflects the difference between the date returned by the LOOKUP function and **12/31/2013**. Note that the LOOKUP function has an offset of zero. This results in each row returning the date associated with that row. This differs from directional and non-directional table calculations, which include a LOOKUP function with an offset of -1, which caused each row in the view to return data associated with the previous row.

At first glance, you might think that you could simplify this workbook by removing **Lookup Intervening Time** from the **Filters** shelf and adjusting the filter on [Order Date] to display only the last two days of December. However, if you do this, % **Total Sales** will add up to 100% across all rows in the view, which would not satisfy the workbook's objectives. Think of **Lookup Intervening Time** as not filtering but hiding all but the last two days in December. This hiding ensures that the data necessary to calculate % **Total Sales** is in the dataset in cache/partition.

Previous Value

The objectives of the following worksheet are to return the aggregate value of sales for each year and set next year's sales goal. Note that two options have been provided for determining next year's sales goal in order to demonstrate how PREVIOUS_VALUE differs from LOOKUP. Also note that PREVIOUS_VALUE behaves directionally.

Let us have a look at the steps:

1. In the workbook associated with this chapter, navigate to the **Previous Value** worksheet.

2. Create the following calculated fields:

Name	Calculation
Next Year Goal Prv_Val	PREVIOUS_VALUE(SUM([Sales])) * 1.05
Next Year Goal Lkup	LOOKUP(SUM([Sales]),0) * 1.05

3. Place **Order Date** on the **Rows** shelf.

4. Double-click **Sales** and **Next Year Goal Prv_Val** to place each on the view.

5. Format as desired, or as seen in the following screenshot (by dragging the piles in **Measure Values**, the order will change accordingly in the view as seen in the following screenshot):

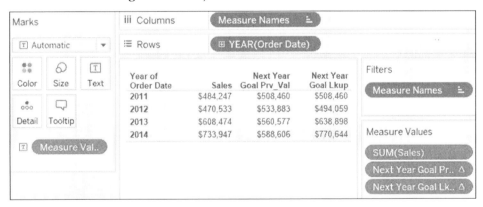

Figure 5.3: Next year

Let's consider how the preceding worksheet functions:

*   **Next Year Goal Prv_Val**: PREVIOUS_VALUE(SUM([Sales])) *1.05 is applied in this worksheet, which retrieves the results from each previous row and adds 5%. In other words, the goal is a steady-state growth rate of 5% per year over all years.

- **Next Year Goal Lkup**: `LOOKUP(SUM([Sales]),0) * 1.05` is also applied in this worksheet; this calculation adds 5% to the current year's sales. In other words, the goal for next year is for sales that are 5% greater than this year. Previous years are not considered.

To better understand this exercise, consider the values associated with **2014** in the preceding screenshot. **Next Year Goal Prv_Val** is calculated via **2013 Next Year Goal Prv_Val**; that is, **$560,577 * 1.05**. On the other hand, **Next Year Goal Lkup** is calculated via the **2014** sales; that is, **$733,947 * 1.05**.

Running

The objective of the following worksheet is to display the running minimum profit, running average profit, and running maximum profit compared with **SUM(Profit)** for each month in the dataset.

The following example demonstrates how the Running functions behave directionally:

1. In the workbook associated with this chapter, navigate to the **Running** worksheet.

2. Create the following calculated fields:

Name	Calculation
Running Min	`RUNNING_MIN(SUM([Profit]))`
Running Max	`RUNNING_MAX(SUM([Profit]))`
Running Avg	`RUNNING_AVG(SUM([Profit]))`

3. Place **Order Date** on the **Columns** shelf and set it to **Month/Year** continuous. Place **Measure Values** on the **Rows** shelf.

4. Remove all instances of measures from the **Measure Values** shelf except for **Running Min**, **Running Max**, **Running Avg**, and **Profit**.

5. Move **SUM(Profit)** from the **Measure Values** shelf to the **Rows** shelf. Right-click on **SUM(Profit)** and select **Dual Axis**.

6. Format as desired, or as seen in the following screenshot:

Figure 5.4: Running

Let's consider how the preceding worksheet functions:

- **Running Min**: RUNNING_MIN(SUM([Profit])) is visible in the preceding screenshot, which compares the current **SUM(Profit)** with the least **SUM(Profit)** recorded to that point in time. If the current **SUM(Profit)** is less than the least **SUM(Profit)** recorded to date, the current **SUM(Profit)** replaces the least **SUM(Profit)**.

- **Running Max**: RUNNING_MAX(SUM([Profit])) operates similarly to **Running Min**, except of course it looks for maximum values.

- **Running Avg**: RUNNING_AVG(SUM([Profit])) calculates the average **SUM(Profit)** based on every month to the current month.

Window

The objective of the following worksheet is to display a directional instance of a WINDOW function and a non-directional instance.

Please follow these steps:

1. In the workbook associated with this chapter, navigate to the **Window** worksheet.

2. Create the following calculated fields:

Name	Calculation
Win Avg Directional	WINDOW_AVG(SUM([Profit]),-2,0)
Win Avg Non-Directional	WINDOW_AVG(SUM([Profit]))

3. Place **Order Date** on the **Columns** shelf and set it to **Month/Year** continuous. Place **Measure Values** on the **Rows** shelf.

4. Remove all instances of measures from the **Measure Values** shelf except **Win Avg Directional**, **Win Avg Non-Directional**, and **Profit**.

5. From the **Data** pane, drag another instance of **Profit** to the **Rows** shelf. Right-click on the instance of **Profit** on the **Rows** shelf and select **Quick Table Calculation | Moving Average**. Right-click on the instance of **Profit** on the **Rows** shelf and select **Dual Axis**.

6. Right-click on the axis labeled **Moving Average of Profit** and select **Synchronize Axis**.

7. Format as desired, or as seen in the following screenshot:

Figure 5.5: Window

Let's consider how the preceding worksheet functions:

- **Win Avg Directional**: `Window_AVG(SUM([Profit]),-2,0)` has a start point of -2 and an end point of 0, which signifies that Tableau will create a point based on the average of the `SUM([Profit])` calculated on the current month and the previous two months. Changing the 0 to 2 would cause the average of each point to be calculated on the previous 2 months, the current month, and the next 2 months. Double-click on the instance of **Profit** on the **Rows** shelf to view the underlying code. (This is the instance of **Profit** that was changed into a table calculation by right-clicking and selecting **Quick Table Calculation | Moving Average**.) Note that the calculation is identical to the code created for **Win Avg Directional**. However, if you right-click on both pills and select **Edit Table Calculation**, you will notice that the resulting dialog boxes differ. The dialog box associated with **Profit** has more options, including the ability to change the previous and next values. Changing the previous and next values for **Win Avg Directional** requires adjusting the calculated field.

- **Win Avg Non-Directional**: WINDOW_AVG(SUM([Profit])) is associated with the horizontal line across the view. Note that it is not dependent on direction. Instead, it is a single value generated by the average of all aggregated **Profit** values in the dataset in cache/partition and will therefore be the same no matter the order of the data points.

First and Last

The objective of the following worksheet is to display the first and last instance of the best-selling item in the Superstore dataset. Notice how the following example demonstrates that the FIRST and LAST functions behave directionally.

Take the following steps:

1. In the workbook associated with this chapter, navigate to the **First/Last** worksheet

2. Create the following calculated fields:

Name	Calculation
First	FIRST()
Last	LAST()
First or Last	FIRST() = 0 OR LAST() = 0

3. Place **Product Name** on the **Filters** shelf, select the **Top** tab, and choose **Top 1** by **Sum** of **Sales**, as shown in the following screenshot:

Figure 5.6: Top filter

4. Place **First or Last** on the **Filters** shelf and select **True** in the resulting dialog box

5. Drag **Product Name**, **Order Date**, and **Row ID** to the **Rows** shelf

6. Set **Order Date** to **Month/Day/Year** discrete

7. Double-click on **Sales**, **First**, and **Last** to place each on the view

8. Right-click on **First**, **Last**, and **First or Last** and select **Compute Using |
   Table (down)**

9. Format as desired:

Figure 5.7: First and Last

Let's consider how the preceding worksheet functions:

- **First**: FIRST() starts at **0** and counts down to the last row of the dataset in
  cache. In the preceding screenshot, note that the first instance of **Canon
  imageCLASS** occurs on **05/24/13**. The fact that FIRST() ranges from 0 to **-4**
  communicates that there are five instances of **Canon imageCLASS** in the
  dataset in cache or within the window cache.

- **Last**: LAST() starts at the last row of the dataset in cache and counts down
  to 0. In the preceding screenshot, note that the last instance of **Canon
  imageCLASS** occurs on **11/18/14**. The fact that LAST() ranges from **4** to **0**
  communicates that there are five instances of **Canon imageCLASS** in the
  dataset in cache.

- **First or Last**: FIRST() = 0 OR LAST() = 0, when placed on the **Filters** shelf
  and set to **True**, hides all instances of matching rows except the first and last.

- The **Row ID** field is included in the view to make sure that the very first
  and last instances of **Canon imageCLASS** display. Otherwise, if there are
  multiple instances of **Canon imageCLASS** on the first or last date, sales
  numbers will reflect multiple values. It's important to set **Compute Using** to
  Table (down) for each table calculation in the view. **Compute Using** is the
  same as **Addressing**, which will be discussed in detail in the *Application of
  functions* section.

Index

The objective of the following worksheet is to list those states in the USA with over 50 postal codes represented in the underlying dataset.

Notice how the following example demonstrates that the INDEX function behaves directionally and can be seen as a count of rows:

1. In the workbook associated with this chapter, navigate to the **Index** worksheet.

2. Set the **Marks** card to **Circle**.

3. Place **State** on the **Rows** shelf and **Postal Code** on the **Detail** shelf.

4. Create a calculated field named **Index** with the code: INDEX(). Drag **Index** to the **Filters** shelf and select the **Range of values** filter. Choose to view only values that are 50 or greater by moving the slider to a minimum value of **50**.

5. Right-click on **Index** and select **Edit Table Calculation**. Select **Specific Dimensions** and check **Postal Code**:

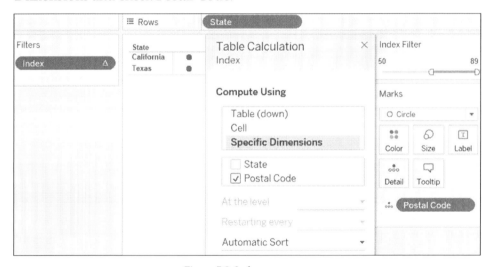

Figure 5.8: Index

6. Select **Analysis | Stack Marks | Off**, then review:

Figure 5.9: Final index

Let's consider how the preceding worksheet functions:

*   **Index**: INDEX( ) counts from 1 to *n*. As such, it behaves directionally. In this case, as a result of the partitioning and addressing settings, **Index** is counting postal codes. (Partitioning and addressing will be discussed in detail in the *Application of functions* section.) Setting the **Index** filter to display only values of 50 or more ensures that only those states with 50 or more postal codes in the partition/dataset in cache display.

Rank

The objective of the following worksheet is to display the top three selling items in each region. This example will demonstrate how RANK interacts directionally with the dataset in cache:

1. In the workbook associated with this chapter, navigate to the **Rank** worksheet.

2. Place **Product Name** on the **Filters** shelf, select the **Top** tab, and choose **Top 3** by **Sum** of **Sales**:

Figure 5.10: Filter

3. Place **Region** and **Product Name** on the **Rows** shelf and **Sales** on the **Columns** shelf.

4. Note that only two items display for each region:

Figure 5.11: Reviewing the top two items

5. Create a calculated field named **Rank** with the code Rank(SUM(Sales)). Drag **Rank** between **Region** and **Product Name** on the **Rows** shelf.

6. Note that before you can place **Rank** between the two pills on the **Rows** shelf, you have to cast it as discrete. One way to accomplish this is by placing **Rank** on the **Detail** shelf, right-clicking on the pill, and selecting **Discrete**.

7. Right-click on **Rank** and select **Compute Using | Product Name**.

8. Remove **Product Name** from the **Filters** shelf.

9. Press *Ctrl* (or press *Option* on Mac), and right-click and drag **Rank** from the **Rows** shelf to the **Filters** shelf. Pressing the *Ctrl* key while dragging a pill from one shelf to another will create a copy of that pill. Failing to press the *Ctrl* key will, of course, simply result in moving the pill. In the resulting dialog box, select **1**, **2**, and **3**.

10. Format as desired:

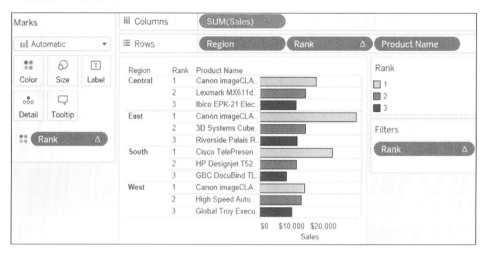

Figure 5.12: Rank

Let's consider how the preceding worksheet functions:

- If you followed the step-by-step instructions for this exercise, you will have noticed that after placing **Region** and **Product Name** on the **Rows** shelf and filtering to show only the top three product names, the resulting visualization only showed two products in each region. This is because the filter on **Product Name** showed the top three products overall, but it so happened that two out of the three were always present in each region. But we actually wanted to show the top three per region rather than overall. To fix this issue, we employed the Rank table calculation function.

- Let's understand how this works. Instead of writing the Rank(Sum(Sales)) function, the same code will be automatically generated by right-clicking on an instance of **Sales** on any shelf and selecting **Quick Table Calculation | Rank**. Note that **Rank** is counting the product names within each region. This demonstrates that the **Rank** table calculation operates directionally on the dataset in cache/partition.

Size

The objective of the following worksheet is to display all states with five or fewer cities in the **Superstore** dataset. This example will demonstrate how SIZE utilizes the entire partition/dataset in cache and is thus non-directional. We will also use the FIRST table calculation function, which is directional, in order to clean up the view.

Please follow along with the steps:

1. In the workbook associated with this chapter, navigate to the **Size** worksheet.
2. Set **Analysis | Stack Marks** to **Off**.
3. Create the following calculated fields:

Name	Calculation
Size	SIZE()
City Count	IF FIRST() = 0 THEN [Size] ELSE NULL END

4. Drag **State** to the **Rows** shelf, **City** to the **Detail** shelf, **City Count** to the **Text/Label** shelf, and **Size** to the **Detail** shelf.
5. Right-click on the **Size** filter and select **Compute Using | City**. Move **Size** from the **Marks** card to the **Filters** shelf.
6. In the resulting dialog box, select an **At most** value of **5**:

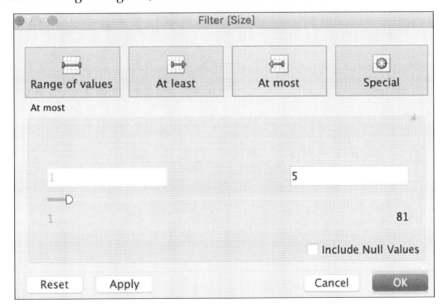

Figure 5.13: At most

7. On the **Marks** card, right-click on **City Count** and select **Edit Table Calculation**. Under **Nested Calculations**, select **City Count**.

8. Select **Compute Using | Specific Dimensions** and check **City**:

Figure 5.14: Specific Dimensions

9. Now use the dropdown under **Nested Calculations** again and select **Size**. Then, select **Compute Using | Specific Dimensions** and check **City**.

10. Observe the final view:

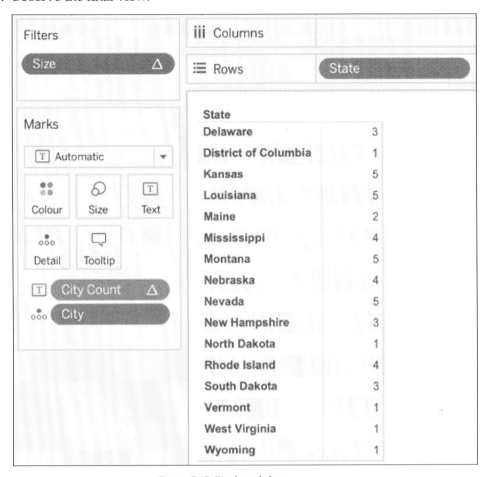

Figure 5.15: Final worksheet

Let's consider how the preceding worksheet functions:

- **Size**: `Size()` generates a single number, for example, 3 for Delaware, based on the partition/dataset in cache. That number can change depending on the partitioning and addressing settings, but does not change based on movement across the partition. As such, it behaves non-directionally.

- **City Count**: The `IF FIRST() = 0 THEN LOOKUP([Size],0) ELSE NULLEND` field is not strictly necessary. You could, instead, simply place **Size** on the **Text/Label** shelf. However, if you do so, you will note that the numbers in the view will look bold. This occurs because the numbers are actually repeated and then layered on top of each other. Utilizing `FIRST() = 0` causes only one set of numbers to display.

Perhaps the most difficult thing to grasp about this exercise is the use of partitioning and addressing. We will discuss partitioning and addressing in the *Application of functions* section. Note that the preceding exercise had an option for **Nested Calculations**, which is because the `Size` calculated field was referenced within the `City Count` calculated field.

Now that we have presented the different table calculations, we will see how they can be manipulated in the scope and direction of calculation.

Application of functions

So far, we have covered the first of our two major questions: *What is the function?* Now we will proceed to the next question: *How is the function applied?*

Let's try to understand that question via the following three options, which are all applications of the `INDEX` function:

One Application of INDEX()				Another Application...				...and Another			

Category	Consumer	Corporate	Home Office	Category	Consumer	Corporate	Home Office	Category	Consumer	Corporate	Home Office
Furniture	1	2	3	Furniture	1	1	1	Furniture	1	2	3
Office Sup..	1	2	3	Office Sup..	2	2	2	Office Sup..	4	5	6
Technology	1	2	3	Technology	3	3	3	Technology	7	8	9

The `INDEX` function is used in each of these three screenshots; however, it is applied differently in each. The first and second screenshots both display **1**, **2**, and **3**, but differ directionally. The third screenshot ranges from **1** to **9**. So, how is `INDEX` being applied in each case?

Answering this question can be confusing because Tableau uses different terminology. Within Tableau itself, the way a table calculation is applied may be referred to as running along, moving along, compute using, or **partitioning** and **addressing**. For our purposes, we will utilize the terms partitioning and addressing, which we will define here according to the Tableau documentation (`https://help.tableau.com/current/pro/desktop/en-us/calculations_tablecalculations.htm`):

> *The dimensions that define how to group the calculation, that is, define the scope of data it is performed on, are called partitioning fields. The table calculation is performed separately within each partition. The remaining dimensions, upon which the table calculation is performed, are called addressing fields, and determine the direction of the calculation.*

This basically means that the partition defines which fields are being used, for example, Segment. If you have three segments divided over three categories, you could look at each combination separately, or at all categories within one segment, or at all segments within one category. The way you look at it is what Tableau calls addressing.

If a table calculation is utilized in the view, you can right-click on it and select **Edit Table Calculation**. Upon doing so, you will see a dialog box that will allow you to choose specific dimensions. If a dimension is checked, it is addressed. If it is unchecked, it is partitioned.

See an example in the following figure:

Figure 5.16: Addressing and partitioning

Tableau provides many out-of-the-box partitioning and addressing settings, including **Table (down)**, **Table (across)**, **Pane (down)**, and **Cell**. We will reference these options occasionally but will not give a detailed review. This leads us to our first partitioning and addressing guideline:

Don't use the out-of-the-box partitioning and addressing settings provided by Tableau, including Table (across) and Pane (down). Force yourself to click Specific Dimensions and manually define the partitioning and addressing so that you clearly understand how every table calculation is applied.

There are a couple of caveats to the preceding guideline:

- There's an exception, which is **Cell**. It is not possible to address individual cells in a view using partitioning and addressing. Instead, it is necessary to use **Compute Using** as **Cell** or, within the **Table Calculation** dialog box, to select **Cell**. Surprisingly, addressing a table calculation along each cell can be useful. An example is provided in the workbook associated with this chapter, on the worksheet **Percent of Total**. There it is used to show 100% for each cell divided into two categories.

- If you set partitioning and addressing for a given table calculation and then add dimensions to the view, usually Tableau will not automatically adjust the partitioning and addressing settings; they are locked down. However, when using **Table (down)**, **Pane (across)**, and the like, Tableau will make automatic adjustments as dimensions are added to the view.

This leads us to our next guideline:

Place all needed dimensions on the desired shelves before setting partitioning and addressing for table calculations.

Following these guidelines will help ensure that you are always clear about how your table calculations are being applied.

Building a playground

Let's set up a simple playground environment to quickly and efficiently explore partitioning and addressing:

1. In the workbook associated with this chapter, navigate to the **Playground** worksheet.

2. Place **Category** on the **Rows** shelf and the **Index** calculation on the **Label** shelf.

3. The **Index** calculation is simply Index( ). Click on the drop-down menu associated with **Index** and select **Edit Table Calculation**. In the resulting dialog box, click **Specific Dimensions**.

4. Position the screen components optimally. See the following screenshot for one possible setup:

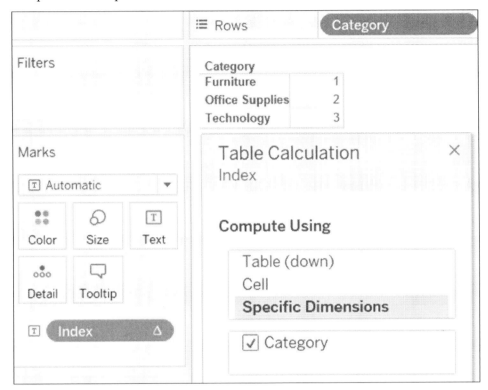

Figure 5.17: Building a playground

You can see in *Figure 5.17* that we created a worksheet displaying the three categories **Furniture**, **Office Supplies**, and **Technology**. By adding the **Index** field to the **Text** shelf we have the minimum requirement to use a table calculation, which is one dimension, one table calculation. Now we can change the compute used in the table calculation and can spot what changes in the visualization. Later on, we will explore more complex examples; however, always start easy and increase the level of complexity slowly to fully understand what is happening.

In the following pages, we will utilize our playground extensively and modify it as necessary. However, for the sake of efficiency, we will need to keep the focus of the playground and the accompanying discussion narrow. The discussion will be confined to dimensions on the **Rows** and **Columns** shelves and the INDEX function on the **Text** shelf.

We could explore different functions on various shelves and the different options that that affords. For instance, placing a date field on the **Pages** shelf will cause a table calculation that uses the TOTAL function to display an option to compute the total across all pages. Regretfully, exploring every possible nuance is simply not possible in one chapter but if you are interested in this topic, feel free to check out the Tableau help page for more content and examples: https://help.tableau.com/current/pro/desktop/en-us/functions_functions_tablecalculation.htm.

Partitioning and addressing with one dimension

Let's use our playground to start exploring partitioning and addressing with the simplest possible example:

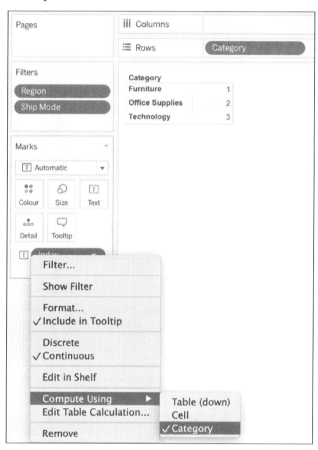

Figure 5.18: Compute Using | Category

In this simple example, addressing **Category** causes each member of the **Category** dimension to be counted. This demonstrates that addressing a dimension determines the direction of the calculation. In our example, we have the **Table Calculation Index**, but **Index** depends on partitioning and addressing as we learned before. **Category** serves as a partition in the **Rows** shelf. We split the data into three: **Furniture**, **Office Supplies**, **Technology**. Now we also say address **Category** for the **Table Calculation**. We did that by selecting **Category** from **Compute Using** (*Figure 5.18*). Now the **Table Calculation** will be applied to the categories and hence counts 1, 2, 3 categories.

If you were to select **Compute Using | Cell**, the partition into three categories would still remain in the view—you would still see **Furniture**, **Office Supplies**, **Technology**—but the counting would happen per cell and not for the whole **Category** dimension. Hence the **Index** will count 1, then move to the next cell and count 1, then the next cell and again count 1:

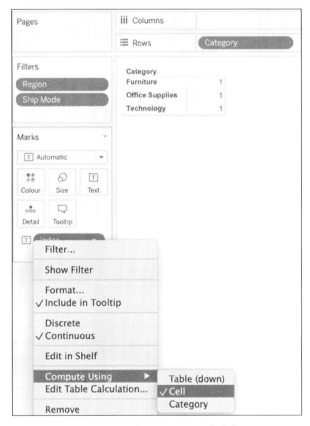

Figure 5.19: Compute Using | Cell

Now, let's consider partitioning and addressing with not one, but two dimensions.

Partitioning and addressing with two dimensions

Two additional options are made available when partitioning and addressing two or more dimensions: **At the level** and **Restarting every**. You can compare this scenario to the task of counting all countries per continent. In this scenario, **At the level** will be countries, since you are not counting streets or trees but countries. **Restarting** will be continents. After you are done counting countries for one continent, you start at 1 again for the next continent:

Figure 5.20: Two dimensions

Both **At the level** and **Restarting every** allow the author to choose dimensions from a drop-down menu. **At the level** allows the author to choose what level to increment at, and as the name suggests, **Restarting every** allows the author to choose which dimensions to restart on. The examples here will provide context for your understanding.

Note that **At the level** has one additional choice: **Deepest**. In this case, setting **At the level** to **Deepest** is the same as selecting **Ship Mode**. This leads us to our next guideline:

It is not necessary to choose the bottom dimension in the At the level drop-down menu. It is always identical to Deepest.

To recreate the iterations listed here, you will need to make some changes to the playground environment. In addition to **Category** on the **Rows** shelf and **Index** on the **Label** shelf, also place **Ship Mode** on the **Rows** shelf. We will not cover iterations that include one or more dimensions on the **Columns** shelf since the behavior of these possibilities is much the same.

As you consider and/or reproduce the following options, note that the **Addressing** order is important. For examples 3–5, **Category** is first on the addressing list. For options 6–8, **Ship Mode** is first on the list.

In the first example, configure the partitioning and addressing settings thus:

- **Partitioning**: **Category**
- **Addressing**: **Ship Mode**
- **At the level**: -
- **Restarting every**: -

This will produce the following visualization:

Category	Ship Mode	
Furniture	First Class	1
	Same Day	2
	Second Class	3
	Standard Class	4
Office Supplies	First Class	1
	Same Day	2
	Second Class	3
	Standard Class	4
Technology	First Class	1
	Same Day	2
	Second Class	3
	Standard Class	4

Figure 5.21: Example 1

Here, we count the **Ship Mode** per **Category**.

In the second example, configure the partitioning and addressing settings thus:

- **Partitioning**: **Ship Mode**
- **Addressing**: **Category**
- **At the level**: -
- **Restarting every**: -

This will produce the following visualization:

Category	Ship Mode	
Furniture	First Class	1
	Same Day	1
	Second Class	1
	Standard Class	1
Office Supplies	First Class	2
	Same Day	2
	Second Class	2
	Standard Class	2
Technology	First Class	3
	Same Day	3
	Second Class	3
	Standard Class	3

Figure 5.22: Example 2

In this example, we count the **Category** per **Ship Mode**.

In the third example, configure the partitioning and addressing settings thus:

- **Partitioning**: -
- **Addressing**: Category, Ship Mode
- **At the level**: Deepest
- **Restarting every**: None

This will produce the following visualization:

Category	Ship Mode	
Furniture	First Class	1
	Same Day	2
	Second Class	3
	Standard Class	4
Office Supplies	First Class	5
	Same Day	6
	Second Class	7
	Standard Class	8
Technology	First Class	9
	Same Day	10
	Second Class	11
	Standard Class	12

Figure 5.23: Example 3

This time, we count the **Category** and **Ship Mode** combination.

In the fourth example, configure the partitioning and addressing settings thus:

- **Partitioning**: -
- **Addressing**: Category, Ship Mode
- **At the level**: Deepest
- **Restarting every**: Category

This will produce the following visualization:

Category	Ship Mode	
Furniture	First Class	1
	Same Day	2
	Second Class	3
	Standard Class	4
Office Supplies	First Class	1
	Same Day	2
	Second Class	3
	Standard Class	4
Technology	First Class	1
	Same Day	2
	Second Class	3
	Standard Class	4

Figure 5.24: Example 4

Here, we count the combination **Category** and **Ship Mode** and restart counting at every new **Category**.

In the fifth example, configure the partitioning and addressing settings thus:

- **Partitioning**: -
- **Addressing**: Category, Ship Mode
- **At the level**: Category
- **Restarting every**: None

This will produce the following visualization:

Category	Ship Mode	
Furniture	First Class	1
	Same Day	1
	Second Class	1
	Standard Class	1
Office Supplies	First Class	2
	Same Day	2
	Second Class	2
	Standard Class	2
Technology	First Class	3
	Same Day	3
	Second Class	3
	Standard Class	3

Figure 5.25: Example 5

We count the combination **Category** and **Ship Mode** that appears at the **Category** level. Since the **Category** level is higher in the hierarchy than **Ship Mode**, we end up counting only one value per **Category**.

In the sixth example, configure the partitioning and addressing settings thus:

- **Partitioning**: -
- **Addressing**: Ship Mode, Category
- **At the level**: Deepest
- **Restarting every**: None

This will produce the following visualization:

Category	Ship Mode	
Furniture	First Class	1
	Same Day	4
	Second Class	7
	Standard Class	10
Office Supplies	First Class	2
	Same Day	5
	Second Class	8
	Standard Class	11
Technology	First Class	3
	Same Day	6
	Second Class	9
	Standard Class	12

Figure 5.26: Example 6

We count the combination **Ship Mode** and **Category** at the **Ship Mode** level; hence we count **First Class** and all the **Category** combinations with it before **Same Day** and its combinations with **Category**.

In the seventh example, configure the partitioning and addressing settings thus:

- **Partitioning**: -
- **Addressing**: **Ship Mode, Category**
- **At the level**: **Deepest**
- **Restarting every**: **Ship Mode**

This will produce the following visualization:

Category	Ship Mode	
Furniture	First Class	1
	Same Day	1
	Second Class	1
	Standard Class	1
Office Supplies	First Class	2
	Same Day	2
	Second Class	2
	Standard Class	2
Technology	First Class	3
	Same Day	3
	Second Class	3
	Standard Class	3

Figure 5.27: Example 7

We count the **Ship Mode** and **Category** combinations at the deepest level but we restart at every **Ship Mode**, therefore we count **First Class** and **Furniture**, **First Class** and **Office Supplies**, then **First Class** and **Technology**. Then we move on to **Same Day** and its combinations, restarting at 1 again.

In the eighth example, configure the partitioning and addressing settings thus:

- **Partitioning**: -
- **Addressing**: Ship Mode, Category
- **At the level**: Ship Mode
- **Restarting every**: None

This will produce the following visualization:

Category	Ship Mode	
Furniture	First Class	1
	Same Day	2
	Second Class	3
	Standard Class	4
Office Supplies	First Class	1
	Same Day	2
	Second Class	3
	Standard Class	4
Technology	First Class	1
	Same Day	2
	Second Class	3
	Standard Class	4

Figure 5.28: Example 8

We count the **Ship Mode** and **Category** combinations at the **Ship Mode** level.

Now, let's consider some of the possibilities presented here in more detail. Some of the options are identical. In fact, out of the nine options, only four are unique. Let's consider examples 1, 4, and 8, each of which have identical end results. Does this mean that each is truly identical? Options 1 and 4 are identical. Option 8, however, is slightly different. To understand this, note the description within the table calculation dialog box for option 8:

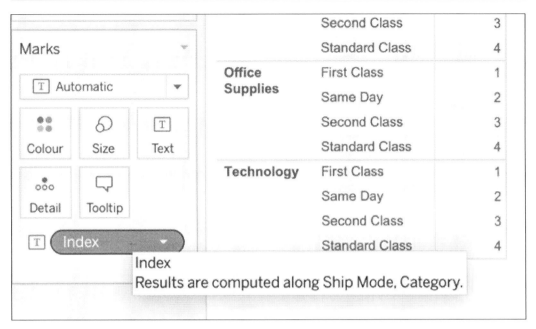

Figure 5.29: Index

The description in example 8 reads **Results are computed along Ship Mode, Category** (*Figure 5.29*). The text in the description box for example 1 is identical to that for example 4: **Results are computed along Ship Mode for Category**, which can be translated as partitioning **Category** and addressing **Ship Mode**. This translation is identical to the actual partitioning/addressing setup accomplished in example 1. Therefore, examples 1 and 4 are identical. But does the slight difference to example 8 mean there are practical differences? No!

Example 6 may seem confusing at first. Why has the odd numbering sequence occurred? Because the order in which the dimensions are addressed differs from the order of dimensions on the **Rows** shelf. The addressing order is **Ship Mode**, **Category**. The order on the **Rows** shelf is **Category**, **Ship Mode**. Simply reversing the position of **Category** and **Ship Mode** on the **Rows** shelf and noting the change in the number sequence should help dispel any confusion:

Figure 5.30: Switch dimensions

Is there any practical use for example 6? Yes. From time to time, it may be necessary to address dimensions in a different order than they are listed on a shelf. But this is not usually the case. This leads us to our next guideline:

When addressing multiple dimensions for a table calculation, the order of addressing will usually reflect the order of dimensions on the Rows and/or Columns shelves.

Partitioning and addressing with three dimensions

Let's add another dimension to our playground and reorder things slightly. Place **Category** and **Region** on the **Rows** shelf and **Ship Mode** on the **Columns** shelf. **Index** should remain on the **Label** shelf. Also add two filters. Filter **Region** to **East**, **South**, and **West**. Filter **Ship Mode** to **First Class**, **Second Class**, and **Standard Class**.

When partitioning and addressing three dimensions, the number of possible iterations jumps to 57; however, only 14 of these are unique. Here is a listing of those unique possibilities.

In the first example, configure the partitioning and addressing settings thus:

- **Partitioning**: **Category**, **Region**
- **Addressing**: **Ship Mode**
- **At the level**: -
- **Restarting every**: -

This will produce the following visualization:

		Ship Mode		
Category	**Region**	**First Class**	**Second Class**	**Standard Class**
Furniture	East	1	2	3
	South	1	2	3
	West	1	2	3
Office Supplies	East	1	2	3
	South	1	2	3
	West	1	2	3
Technology	East	1	2	3
	South	1	2	3
	West	1	2	3

Figure 5.31: Example 1

Here we count the different **Ship Modes** per **Category** and **Region** combinations.

In the second example, configure the partitioning and addressing settings thus:

- Partitioning: **Category**, **Ship Mode**
- Addressing: **Region**
- At the level: -
- Restarting every: -

This will produce the following visualization:

Category	Region	Ship Mode		
		First Class	Second Class	Standard Class
Furniture	East	1	1	1
	South	2	2	2
	West	3	3	3
Office Supplies	East	1	1	1
	South	2	2	2
	West	3	3	3
Technology	East	1	1	1
	South	2	2	2
	West	3	3	3

Figure 5.32: Example 2

Here we count the different **Regions** per **Category** and **Ship Mode** combinations.

In the third example, configure the partitioning and addressing settings thus:

- **Partitioning**: Category
- **Addressing**: Region, Ship Mode
- **At the level**: -
- **Restarting every**: -

This will produce the following visualization:

Category	Region	Ship Mode		
		First Class	**Second Class**	**Standard Class**
Furniture	East	1	1	1
	South	1	1	1
	West	1	1	1
Office Supplies	East	2	2	2
	South	2	2	2
	West	2	2	2
Technology	East	3	3	3
	South	3	3	3
	West	3	3	3

Figure 5.33: Example 3

Here we count the different **Categories** per **Region** and **Ship Mode** combinations.

In the fourth example, configure the partitioning and addressing settings thus:

- **Partitioning: Category**
- **Addressing: Region, Ship Mode**
- **At the level: Deepest**
- **Restarting every: None**

This will produce the following visualization:

Category	Region	Ship Mode		
		First Class	Second Class	Standard Class
Furniture	East	1	2	3
	South	4	5	6
	West	7	8	9
Office Supplies	East	1	2	3
	South	4	5	6
	West	7	8	9
Technology	East	1	2	3
	South	4	5	6
	West	7	8	9

Figure 5.34: Example 4

Here we count the different **Categories** per **Region** and **Ship Mode** combinations at the deepest level.

In the fifth example, configure the partitioning and addressing settings thus:

- **Partitioning**: Category
- **Addressing**: Ship Mode, Region
- **At the level**: Deepest
- **Restarting every**: None

This will produce the following visualization:

Category	Region	Ship Mode		
		First Class	**Second Class**	**Standard Class**
Furniture	East	1	4	7
	South	2	5	8
	West	3	6	9
Office Supplies	East	1	4	7
	South	2	5	8
	West	3	6	9
Technology	East	1	4	7
	South	2	5	8
	West	3	6	9

Figure 5.35: Example 5

Here we count the different **Categories** per **Ship Mode** and **Region** combinations at the deepest level.

In the sixth example, configure the partitioning and addressing settings thus:

- **Partitioning**: **Region**
- **Addressing**: **Category, Ship Mode**
- **At the level**: **Deepest**
- **Restarting every**: **None**

This will produce the following visualization:

Category	Region	Ship Mode		
		First Class	**Second Class**	**Standard Class**
Furniture	East	1	2	3
	South	1	2	3
	West	1	2	3
Office Supplies	East	4	5	6
	South	4	5	6
	West	4	5	6
Technology	East	7	8	9
	South	7	8	9
	West	7	8	9

Figure 5.36: Example 6

Here we count the different **Regions** per **Category** and **Ship Mode** combinations at the deepest level.

In the seventh example, configure the partitioning and addressing settings thus:

- **Partitioning**: Ship Mode
- **Addressing**: Category, Region
- **At the level**: Deepest
- **Restarting every**: None

This will produce the following visualization:

Category	Region	Ship Mode First Class	Second Class	Standard Class
Furniture	East	1	1	1
	South	2	2	2
	West	3	3	3
Office Supplies	East	4	4	4
	South	5	5	5
	West	6	6	6
Technology	East	7	7	7
	South	8	8	8
	West	9	9	9

Figure 5.37: Example 7

Here we count the different **Ship Modes** per **Category** and **Region** combinations at the deepest level.

In the eighth example, configure the partitioning and addressing settings thus:

- **Partitioning**: **Ship Mode**
- **Addressing**: **Region**, **Category**
- **At the level**: **Deepest**
- **Restarting every**: **None**

This will produce the following visualization:

Category	Region	Ship Mode		
		First Class	Second Class	Standard Class
Furniture	East	1	1	1
	South	4	4	4
	West	7	7	7
Office Supplies	East	2	2	2
	South	5	5	5
	West	8	8	8
Technology	East	3	3	3
	South	6	6	6
	West	9	9	9

Figure 5.38: Example 8

Here we count the different **Ship Modes** per **Region** and **Category** combinations at the deepest level.

In the ninth example, configure the partitioning and addressing settings thus:

- **Partitioning**: -
- **Addressing**: Category, Ship Mode, Region
- **At the level**: Deepest
- **Restarting every**: None

This will produce the following visualization:

Category	Region	Ship Mode		
		First Class	**Second Class**	**Standard Class**
Furniture	East	1	4	7
	South	2	5	8
	West	3	6	9
Office Supplies	East	10	13	16
	South	11	14	17
	West	12	15	18
Technology	East	19	22	25
	South	20	23	26
	West	21	24	27

Figure 5.39: Example 9

Here we count the **Category**, **Ship Mode**, and **Region** combinations at the deepest level.

In the tenth example, configure the partitioning and addressing settings thus:

- **Partitioning**: -
- **Addressing**: **Ship Mode**, **Category**, **Region**
- **At the level**: **Deepest**
- **Restarting every**: **None**

This will produce the following visualization:

Category	Region	Ship Mode		
		First Class	**Second Class**	**Standard Class**
Furniture	East	1	10	19
	South	2	11	20
	West	3	12	21
Office Supplies	East	4	13	22
	South	5	14	23
	West	6	15	24
Technology	East	7	16	25
	South	8	17	26
	West	9	18	27

Figure 5.40: Example 10

Here we count the **Ship Mode**, **Category**, and **Region** combinations at the deepest level.

In the eleventh example, configure the partitioning and addressing settings thus:

- **Partitioning**: -
- **Addressing**: **Ship Mode, Category, Region**
- **At the level**: **Category**
- **Restarting every**: **None**

This will produce the following visualization:

Category	Region	Ship Mode		
		First Class	**Second Class**	**Standard Class**
Furniture	East	1	4	7
	South	1	4	7
	West	1	4	7
Office Supplies	East	2	5	8
	South	2	5	8
	West	2	5	8
Technology	East	3	6	9
	South	3	6	9
	West	3	6	9

Figure 5.41: Example 11

Here we count the **Ship Mode**, **Category**, and **Region** combinations at the **Category** level.

In the twelfth example, configure the partitioning and addressing settings thus:

- **Partitioning**: -
- **Addressing**: Ship Mode, Region, Category
- **At the level**: Deepest
- **Restarting every**: None

This will produce the following visualization:

Category	Region	Ship Mode		
		First Class	**Second Class**	**Standard Class**
Furniture	East	1	10	19
	South	4	13	22
	West	7	16	25
Office Supplies	East	2	11	20
	South	5	14	23
	West	8	17	26
Technology	East	3	12	21
	South	6	15	24
	West	9	18	27

Figure 5.42: Example 12

Here we count the **Ship Mode**, **Region**, and **Category** combinations at the deepest level.

In the thirteenth example, configure the partitioning and addressing settings thus:

- **Partitioning**: -
- **Addressing**: **Ship Mode, Region, Category**
- **At the level**: **Deepest**
- **Restarting every**: **Ship Mode**

This will produce the following visualization:

Category	Region	Ship Mode		
		First Class	**Second Class**	**Standard Class**
Furniture	East	1	1	1
	South	4	4	4
	West	7	7	7
Office Supplies	East	2	2	2
	South	5	5	5
	West	8	8	8
Technology	East	3	3	3
	South	6	6	6
	West	9	9	9

Figure 5.43: Example 13

Here we count the **Ship Mode, Region**, and **Category** combinations at the deepest level.

In the fourteenth example, configure the partitioning and addressing settings thus:

- **Partitioning**: -
- **Addressing**: Region, Ship Mode, Category
- **At the level**: Deepest
- **Restarting every**: None

This will produce the following visualization:

Category	Region	Ship Mode		
		First Class	**Second Class**	**Standard Class**
Furniture	East	1	4	7
	South	10	13	16
	West	19	22	25
Office Supplies	East	2	5	8
	South	11	14	17
	West	20	23	26
Technology	East	3	6	9
	South	12	15	18
	West	21	24	27

Figure 5.44: Example 14

We will not address the various instances of these possibilities. Instead, the reader is encouraged to recreate these 14 possibilities in Tableau in order to solidify their understanding of partitioning and addressing. Even better, consider recreating all 57 possible iterations and working to understand how Tableau is producing each end result. The process may be tedious, but the resulting understanding is invaluable, allowing the user to understand the things that Tableau is doing in the background when computing.

Summary

In this chapter, we explored the inner workings of table calculations. We began by considering two questions:

- What is the function?
- How is the function applied?

As we explored these two questions, we surveyed each unique group of table calculation functions with the exception of the Script_ functions, which will be covered in more detail in *Chapter 15, Programming Tool Integration*. We also learned how to apply these functions to a view through partitioning and addressing, where partitioning can be seen as the scope and addressing as the direction of the calculation.

We have seen examples where we counted, for example, the scope as **Ship Mode**, and the order of counting was **Category** and **Region**. Therefore, we would start with the first **Category** and **Region** and set 1 for the **Ship Mode**. We would then continue with the next **Region** in that same **Category** and count 2 for the next **Ship Mode** and so on. The order of how dimensions are being addressed is important and yields different results.

Using the knowledge we've picked up in this chapter of addressing and partitioning, in the next chapter, we will explore data densification, cubes, and big data.

6

All About Data – Data Densification, Cubes, and Big Data

Many data-related questions that Tableau newbies have are not related to data preparation, joins, unions, data blending, or data structures. Some of those questions are as follows:

- I just created a table calculation and observed that the view displays numbers that don't exist in the underlying data. Why?

- We use **SAP Business Warehouse (SAP BW)** in my organization. What should I know about how Tableau works with cubes?

- How does Tableau work with big data?

This chapter will continue the data discussion from the previous chapters by addressing the topics these three preceding questions target, respectively: **data densification**, working with **cubes**, and Tableau and **big data**.

There are a few people who have worked diligently to provide resources that were very helpful while writing this chapter. Joe Mako has championed data densification—be sure to check out his video on Vimeo (`https://vimeo.com/107354333`) for a deep dive into this challenging topic. The Tableau Online Help (`https://help.tableau.com/current/pro/desktop/en-us/cubes.htm`) has an invaluable series of articles and accompanying workbooks for understanding the ins and outs of working with OLAP cubes, and lastly, the Tableau help pages also provide an excellent resource on Tableau and big data: `https://www.tableau.com/solutions/big-data`.

In this chapter, we will discuss the following topics:

- Using the OData connector
- Introducing data densification
- Domain completion
- Domain padding
- Working with cubes
- Tableau and big data

We will start this chapter by introducing the OData connector. It is a great way to practice data visualization because it allows you access to many different data sources. We will use it in the *Introducing data densification* section to access and manipulate the Chicago Crime dataset.

Using the OData connector

The exercises in this chapter can be followed along with by downloading the workbook associated with this chapter on `https://public.tableau.com/profile/marleen.meier` or by using the OData connector directly. The following steps explain how datasets from the web can be loaded directly into Tableau by using an OData endpoint:

1. Navigate to `https://data.cityofchicago.org/Public-Safety/Crimes-2020/qzdf-xmn8` and select the **More** icon (indicated by an ellipsis, …), followed by the **Access Data via OData** button:

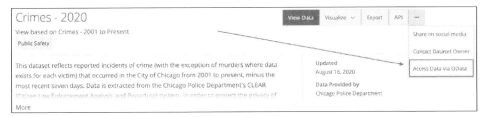

Figure 6.1: Chicago Data Portal

2. Copy the **OData Endpoint** value and open Tableau Desktop:

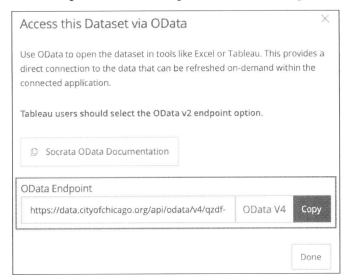

Figure 6.2: OData

3.   In the **Data Source** pane, search for OData, and select the **OData** option:

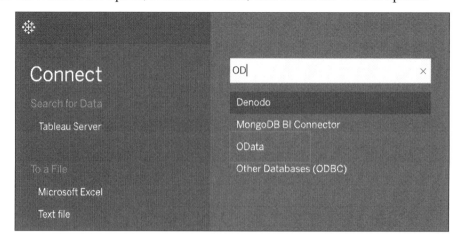

Figure 6.3: OData connector

4.   In the **Server** field, copy in the OData endpoint from the Chicago Crime website. Authentication is not necessary, so select **Sign In** to get started:

Figure 6.4: Server name

5.   Start building your dashboard!

Now that we have the data connection all set up, we can continue with our first real exercise about data densification. Knowing about data densification will help you to troubleshoot if you see unexpected data output in your dashboard and set up your visualization the right way to achieve your goals without having to troubleshoot at all.

Introducing data densification

Data densification is a largely undocumented aspect of Tableau that can be useful in many circumstances but can also be confusing when encountered unexpectedly. This section will provide information about data densification with the intent of dispelling confusion and providing the Tableau author with sufficient knowledge to use this feature to their advantage.

To begin understanding data densification, four terms should be defined: data densification, sparse data, domain completion, and domain padding. In addition to the definitions, each term will be discussed in detail by using examples to help improve understanding:

- **Data densification**: A behavior wherein Tableau displays marks in the view for which there is no corresponding underlying data

- **Sparse data**: An intersection of one or more dimensions and one measure for which there is no value

- **Domain completion**: The addition of marks on a sparsely populated view that cause all possible dimension/measure combinations to display results

- **Domain padding**: The addition of marks to the visualization through range-aware dimensions (that is, date and bin) even when there is no underlying data associated with those marks

The definitions should be clear now; let's continue with hands-on exercises.

Domain completion

There are two types of data densification: domain completion and domain padding. **Domain completion** is the more complex of the two and can be deployed cleverly to solve sparse data issues but may also appear unexpectedly and prove a challenge to address.

Grasping domain completion requires a good understanding of **dimensions** and **measures**—discrete and continuous—and **partitioning** and **addressing** within table calculations. The first two sets of terms, dimensions/measures and discrete/continuous, are discussed in *Chapter 1, Getting Up to Speed – A Review of the Basics*. The second set of terms, partitioning and addressing, was discussed in detail in *Chapter 5, Table Calculations*.

Now, let's consider how domain completion can be deployed, when it's helpful, and when it can be a problem.

Deploying domain completion

Domain completion can be activated in numerous and sometimes surprising and confusing ways. Adjusting the arrangement of pills on shelves, toggling dimensions between discrete and continuous, switching view types on the **Marks** card, adjusting partitioning, addressing, and other changes can impact domain completion activation. Although examples for every activation possibility will not be covered in this book, a review of typical domain completion scenarios should prove helpful.

Activating domain completion in a crosstab

The following steps will guide you through an example of domain completion.

Navigate to https://public.tableau.com/profile/marleen.meier to locate and download the workbook associated with this chapter or use the OData endpoint as described in the section *Using the OData connector*:

1. Navigate to the worksheet entitled DC - Crosstab.

2. Ensure that **Analysis | Table Layout | Show Empty Rows** and **Show Empty Columns** are both *deselected*.

3. In the Chicago Crime dataset, create a calculated field named **Index** with the code INDEX().

4. Add a **Location Description** filter to view only a few locations, for example, all the ones beginning with *AIRPORT*. Then place **Location Description** on the **Rows** shelf.

5. Place **Date** on the **Columns** shelf. Leave it at the year aggregation and change it to a discrete value. Note, as shown in the following screenshot, that the view is sparsely populated:

Figure 6.5: Crosstab

6. Place **Index** on the **Detail** shelf on the **Marks** card. Note that in the following screenshot the view now reflects domain completion, that is, the view is fully populated:

Figure 6.6: Crosstab II

7. Right-click on **YEAR(Date)** and select **Continuous**. Note that data densification is deactivated:

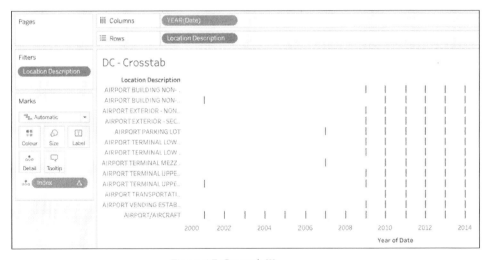

Figure 6.7: Crosstab III

8. Reset **YEAR(Date)** to **Discrete** and then right-click on **Index** and select **Edit Table Calculation**.

9. In the resulting dialog box, select **Specific Dimensions** and then observe the results for each of the following selections:

Select Specific Dimension	Data Densification Activated/Deactivated
`Location Description`	Activated
`Year of Date`	Activated
`Location Description` and `Year of Date`	Deactivated
No selection	Deactivated

The preceding exercise illustrates the following rule for deploying domain completion:

- Given a crosstab with discrete dimensions on the **Rows** and **Columns** shelves, utilizing a table calculation (in this case, the **Index** field) in which at least one dimension (but not all dimensions) is addressed activates domain completion

A key term in the preceding rule may have been confusing: addressed. Partitioning and addressing were covered in *Chapter 5, Table Calculations*, but will be defined again here to ensure understanding of this rule. Consider the following, from the Tableau documentation (`https://help.tableau.com/current/pro/desktop/en-us/calculations_tablecalculations.htm`):

> *The dimensions that define how to group the calculation, that is, that define the scope of the data it is performed on, are called* **partitioning fields**. *The table calculation is performed separately within each partition. The remaining dimensions, upon which the table calculation is performed, are called* **addressing fields**, *and determine the direction of the calculation.*

When editing a table calculation, you can choose to select/deselect specific dimensions. When a dimension is selected, that dimension is used to address the table calculation. When a dimension is not selected, the dimension is used to partition the table calculation. The following screenshot of a **Table Calculation** editing dialog box demonstrates addressing on **Location Description** and partitioning on **Year of Date**:

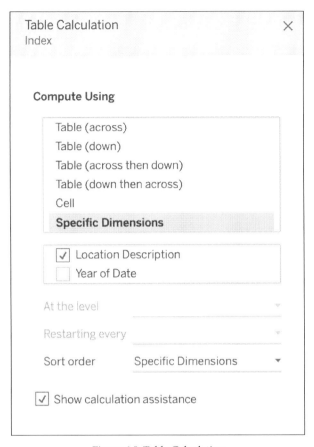

Figure 6.8: Table Calculation

We will now look at the remaining steps involved in activating domain completion in a crosstab:

1. Duplicate the worksheet from the previous exercise, **DC – Crosstab**. Name the new worksheet DC - Crosstab II.

2. Right-click on **Index** and select **Compute Using | Cell**. Note that the view is sparsely populated.

3. Select **Analysis | Table Layout | Show Empty Columns**. The view is now fully populated:

Figure 6.9: Crosstab

This exercise illustrates the following rules for deploying domain completion:

- Given a crosstab with discrete dimensions on the **Rows** and **Columns** shelves, selecting **Compute Using | Cell** deactivates domain completion

- Given a crosstab with discrete dimensions on the **Rows** and **Columns** shelves, selecting **Analysis | Table Layout | Show Empty Rows/Columns** activates domain completion

Setting **Compute Using** to **Cell** may raise a question: what about the other **Compute Using** options, such as **Table (across)** and **Table (down)**? These options are actually all variations of partitioning and addressing.

Activating domain completion through view types

We will now look into activating domain completion through view types.

1. Duplicate the worksheet from the previous exercise, **DC – Crosstab II**. Name the new worksheet DC - View Types.

2. Remove **Index** from the **Marks** view card and deselect **Analysis | Table Layout | Show Empty Columns**. The view is now sparsely populated.

3. Change the **Marks** type from **Automatic** to **Line**. The view is now fully populated with more marks:

Figure 6.10: View types

4. Choose each view type option on the **Marks** card and observe which view types activate domain completion and which do not.

The preceding exercise illustrates the following rule for deploying data completion:

- Given a view with discrete dimensions on the **Rows** and **Columns** shelves, selecting the **Line**, **Area**, and **Polygon** view types from the **Marks** view card activates domain completion

The usefulness of domain completion

Domain completion can be useful in many circumstances. In fact, you may have gleaned some uses from the previous exercises even though they were designed merely for illustration purposes. The following exercise demonstrates using domain completion to display no data for cells without a value in a sparsely populated view.

Labeling nulls

Let us look at the following steps to begin the exercise:

1. Duplicate the worksheet from the previous exercise, **DC – View Types**. Name the new worksheet DC - Labelling Nulls.

2. Adjust the duplicated worksheet so that the view type is set to **Text**. Also ensure that only **Location Description** and **Year** are deployed on the view. Be sure to leave **Location Description** on the **Filters** shelf so that a few locations are displayed.

3. Create a calculated field named **No Data** with the following code:

   ```
   IF ISNULL(COUNT([Case Number])) THEN 'No Data' ELSE 'Data' END
   ```

4. Place **Ward** and **No Data** on the **Text** shelf. Note that the text **No Data** does not display:

Figure 6.11: Labeling Nulls

5. Place **Index** on the **Detail** shelf. Note that the text **No Data** does display. The domain completion portion of the exercise is now complete but consider making the visualization more appealing by utilizing a shape:

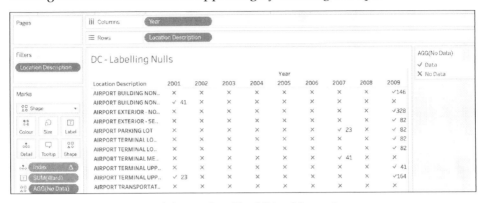

Figure 6.12: Labeling Nulls, with additional formatting

I hope this exercise has given you a practical example of how domain completion works. But what if you want to get rid of it altogether? We'll discuss this in the next section.

Removing unwanted domain completion

After being made aware of domain completion, a user will no longer be confused when unwanted marks display in the view. But knowing how to remove those unwanted marks from the display can be a challenge. The following exercise shows a scenario of undesired domain completion and how to address the problem. The goal of the exercise is to display each year that a given crime has been reported, with an accompanying filter to adjust the crimes that display based on the number of years data is available:

1. In the workbook associated with this chapter, navigate to the **DC - Year Count** worksheet.

2. Select the **Chicago Crime** dataset in the **Data** pane.

3. Optionally, in order to get the exact same view as in *Figure 6.13*, place **Description** on the **Filter** shelf and select **AGG PO HANDS NO/MIN INJURY.**

4. Place **Description** and **Date** on the **Rows** shelf, make **YEAR(Date)** discrete, and put **Ward** on the **Text** shelf. Format as desired. Note the missing value for 2001 as shown in the following screenshot:

Figure 6.13: Year Count

This is not an instance of data densification since the dataset actually has a row for 2001, despite the value for **Ward** being empty in that year. Therefore 2001 has a null value.

5. In order to remove the fields containing null values, click on the drop-down menu associated with **SUM(Ward)** and select **Filter**. In the resulting dialog box, select **Special | Non-null values**:

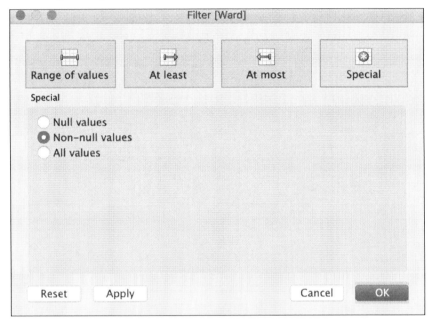

Figure 6.14: Filtering non-null values

6. Create a table calculation named **Year Count** with the following code:

    ```
    SIZE()
    ```

7. If you put the **Description** pill on the filters shelf in *step 3*, please remove it for the following steps.

8. Place a continuous instance of **Year Count** on the **Columns** shelf. Note that the resulting number, **6411**, represents every column in the view:

Figure 6.15: Year count

9. Right-click on **Year Count** and select **Compute Using | Date**. It appears as if the scenario discussed in *step 4* has returned. However, although the issue looks the same in the view, the underlying problem differs. **Year Count** is a table calculation and has caused domain completion. So this time we see one row for each year in the whole dataset, even though, for example, the combination of **$300 AND UNDER** and **2001** does not exist in the dataset. We see every year because of the table calculation **Year Count**:

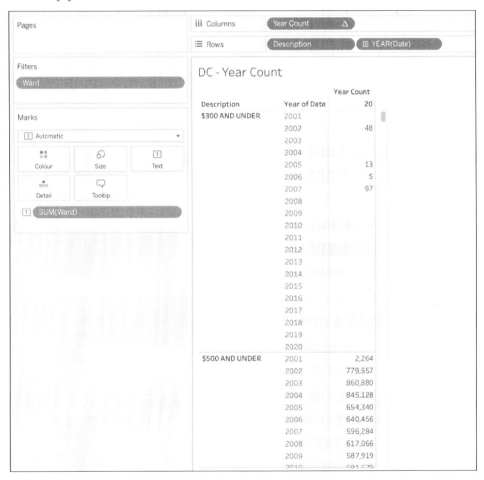

Figure 6.16: Year count domain completion

10. Right-click on **Year Count** and select **Edit Table Calculation**.

11. In the resulting dialog box, select **Specific Dimensions**. Make sure that **Description** and **Year of Date** are both checked and, by dragging and dropping, placed in the order shown in *Figure 6.17*. Leave **At the level** at **Deepest** and set **Restarting every** to **Description**. **Sort order** can remain as **Specific Dimensions** and if you check the **Show calculation assistance** box, you will see yellow highlighters in the viz, indicating the data points related to the selection:

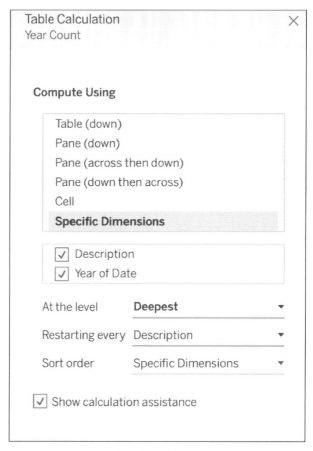

Figure 6.17: Specific Dimensions

12. If you have more than one value for **Year Count**, complete the exercise by moving **Year Count** from the **Columns** shelf to the **Filters** shelf. Format as desired (this allows you to filter on dimensions with the same number of rows in the partition):

Figure 6.18: Completing the Year Count worksheet

The formatting of the "This exercise demonstrates..." section is inconsistent throughout. Please make consistent.

The relevant section in the preceding rule for this exercise is "a table calculation in which at least one dimension is addressed (but not all dimensions) activates domain completion." The domain completion occurred when first deploying **Year Count**, which is a table calculation. Upon changing the addressing and partitioning of **Year Count** so that all dimensions were addressed (that is, no dimensions were partitioned), the issue was resolved.

Congratulations, you can cross domain completion off your "to learn" list. As mentioned in the introduction to this chapter, next in line is domain padding. You will want to know how to use domain padding because it helps you when working with dates and bins.

Domain padding

The second type of data densification is known as **domain padding**. It is fairly straightforward and, unlike domain completion, is discussed in the Tableau documentation. We will now consider how domain padding is deployed and when it's useful.

Deploying domain padding

You may recall that one of the ways to deploy domain completion is **Analysis | Table Layout | Show Empty Rows/Columns**. The same is true of domain padding, as is illustrated in the following exercise. This exercise demonstrates how to toggle domain padding on and off:

1. In the workbook associated with this chapter, select **Data | New Data Source** and connect to the **Sample Superstore** Excel workbook that ships with Tableau. It is located in **My Tableau Repository | Datasources+**.

2. In the resulting instance of the **Data Source** page, double-click on **Orders and Returns**. This will cause a relationship to be created on the field **Order ID**.

3. Name the data source **Superstore – Returns**.

4. Navigate to the worksheet entitled **DP – Show Missing Values** and select the **Superstore – Returns** data source that was just created.

5. Place **Ship Mode** and **State** on the **Rows** shelf. Next, place **Region** on the **Filters** shelf and select **West**. Lastly, put **SUM(Sales)** on the **Text** shelf. Note that, for example, **Wyoming** only appears for **Standard Class** shipping mode:

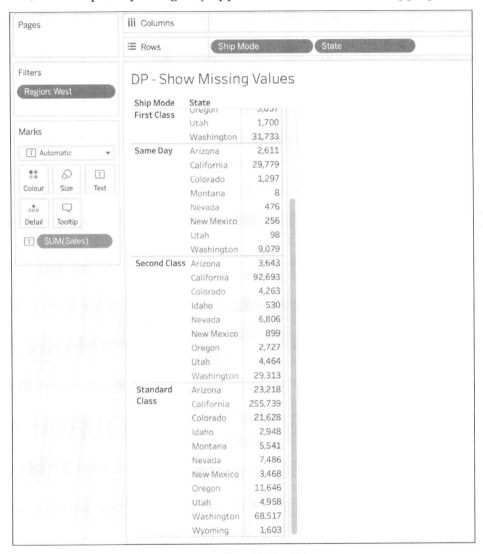

Figure 6.19: Show Missing Values

6.   Select **Analysis | Table Layout | Show Empty Rows**:

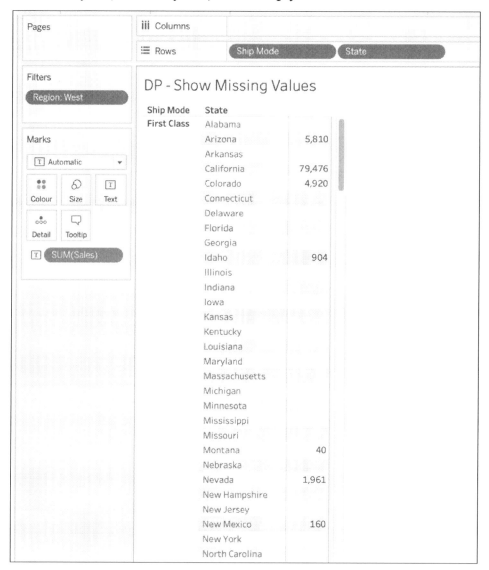

Figure 6.20: Show Missing Values II

And you can see domain padding in action. All states are showing now, even the ones that were filtered by **Region: West**. Now, the filter simply removes the sales amount but does show all possible states.

It was necessary to point to a live data source, such as the instance of **Superstore** that ships with Tableau, because using an extract would not, in this case, activate domain padding even if **Analysis | Table Layout | Show Empty Rows** was selected. The functionality gets lost as soon as you activate an extract.

The usefulness of domain padding

Domain padding is often useful when working with dates with gaps. Such gaps occur when some dates have associated values and some dates do not. As shown in the following example, returns do not occur every day in the Superstore dataset. Since a visualization that displays dates with gaps could be confusing, it might be helpful to fill in those gaps.

Using domain padding to fill in date gaps

We will now try to fill in date gaps:

1. In the workbook associated with this chapter, navigate to the worksheet entitled **DP – Filling Date Gaps**.

2. Select the **Superstore – Returns** data source that was created in the previous exercise.

3. Place a discrete instance of **MDY(Order Date)** on the **Columns** shelf and place **Sales** on the **Rows** shelf. Note that every mark in the view is equally spaced regardless of the length of time between dates:

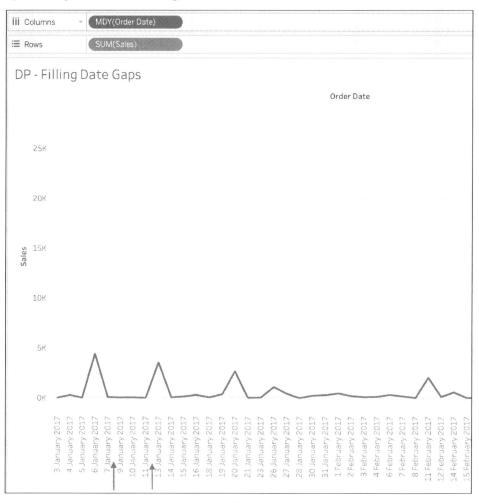

Figure 6.21: Filling Date Gaps

4. Right-click on **MDY(Order Date)** and select **Show Missing Values**.

5. Right-click on **SUM(Sales)** on the **Rows** shelf and select **Format**. In the resulting format window, choose the **Pane** tab and select **Marks: Show at Default Value**:

Figure 6.22: Filling Date Gaps II

Note that the distance between marks is now based on the length of time between dates. All dates with no value are displayed with **Sales** values of zero.

Problems of domain padding

Since domain padding can be toggled on or off through specific commands in Tableau (that is, **Show Missing Values** and **Show Empty Rows/Columns**), it's typically not a problem. There are a few scenarios, however, when domain padding may cause confusion, one of which is covered in the following example.

From a domain-padded visualization to a crosstab

Let's have a look at creating a crosstab from a domain-padded visualization:

1. In the workbook associated with this chapter, navigate to the worksheet entitled **DP – From Viz to Crosstab**.

2. Select the **Superstore – Returns** data source.

3. Right-click on **Discount** in the data pane and select **Create | Bins**. In the resulting dialog box, choose a bin size of **0.05**.

4. Place the newly created **Discount (bin)** dimension on the **Columns** shelf.

5. Right-click on **Discount (bin)** and ensure that **Show Missing Values** is selected.

6. Right-click and drag the **Discount** field from the **Data** pane to the **Rows** shelf. Select **CNT** as the measure. Note that some of the bins have no values. For example, as shown in the following screenshot, the **0.35** bin has no associated value:

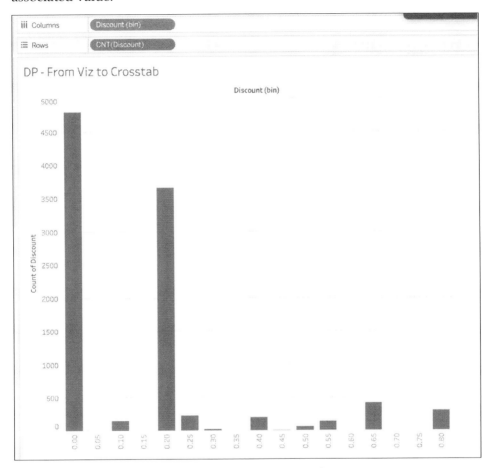

Figure 6.23: From Viz to Crosstab

7. Duplicate the sheet as a crosstab by right-clicking on the worksheet tab and selecting **Duplicate as Crosstab**. Note that **Show Missing Values** is still activated:

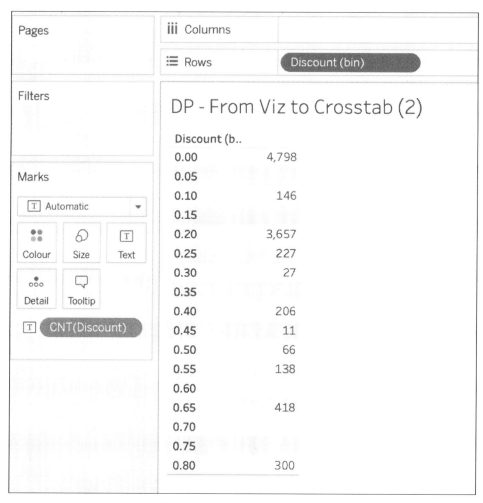

Figure 6.24: From Viz to Crosstab II

8. Complete the exercise by right-clicking on **Discount (bin)** and deselecting **Show Missing Values**:

Figure 6.25: From Viz to Crosstab III

Utilizing **Show Missing Values** for bins or dates is often helpful in a visualization but may not be helpful in a crosstab view. This is especially true if there are many rows or columns without values.

A special case of data densification will appear with cubes. That's why we will discuss this next. Even if you don't work with cubes now, I would recommend you follow along now to have a full picture of data densification in Tableau.

Working with cubes

For the most part, Tableau's behavior is uniform across data sources. For example, the experience of working with an Access database and an Oracle database is very similar. Of course, different data sources will have their nuances but, in general, Tableau attempts to make working with different data sources a seamless experience. However, working with cubes (that is, multidimensional data sources) is quite different. Major differences include the inability to alias, create calculated fields on dimensions, create groups or hierarchies, change aggregation types, and generate extracts.

 As of the time of writing, the central cube-related article is located at `https://onlinehelp.tableau.com/current/pro/desktop/en-us/cubes.htm`.

The preceding article provides detailed information and is worth studying in detail if you work with cubes. Provided with the article are many links and examples on how to reproduce typical Tableau behavior when working in a cube environment.

Although the Tableau Online Help provides many workarounds for these shortcomings, in this section, we want to mention the topic of using data blending to work more effectively with cubes.

In order to complete the following cube-related exercises, you must have access to **Microsoft Analysis Services** with an instance of the **AdventureWorks** cube (AdventureWorks is the sample cube that ships with Microsoft Analysis Services). Detailed instructions for installing SQL Server, Analysis Services, and the accompanying AdventureWorks cube are available at MSDN (`https://docs.microsoft.com/en-us/sql/samples/adventureworks-install-configure?view=sql-server-ver15&tabs=ssms`). A search engine query on `hh403424` will also return the link to these instructions.

Data blending for continuous months

Typically, a cube includes one or more date hierarchies. When Tableau is connected to a cube, the members of a date hierarchy that display in the **Data** pane behave like strings. Thus, Tableau's built-in hierarchy capabilities that are usually available when working with dates in relational data sources are not available. This limitation can be partially overcome by coding **Multidimensional Expressions (MDX)** queries in Tableau, but to achieve all the Tableau date capabilities, a data blend is necessary.

We will now look into data blending and cubes:

1. In the workbook associated with this chapter, navigate to the worksheet entitled **Cube – Continuous Days**.

2. Connect to the AdventureWorks data source through **Data | New Data Source | Microsoft SQL Server** (refer to the introduction to this section, *Working with cubes*, to learn how to install Analysis Services and the AdventureWorks cube).

3. In the dimension portion of the **Data** pane, expand **Date** and locate the **Date** field.

4. Note that different versions of the AdventureWorks cube have slightly different naming conventions. So, don't worry too much about the naming convention in the figures.

5. Right-click on **Date** and select **Change Data Type | Date**. Drag **Date** to the **Columns** shelf, and place **Internet Sales Amount** on the **Rows** shelf:

Figure 6.26: From Viz to Crosstab IV

The current viz looks a bit overwhelming. We have lots of data points and can't really see the difference between days. Let's continue by aggregating the data to a single value per month.

6. Select the worksheet entitled **Cube – Preparing Dates**.

7. Expand **Date** and then **Calendar**, and lastly **Date.Calendar**:

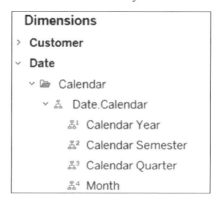

Figure 6.27: Dimensions

8. Drag **Calendar Year** and **Month** to the **Rows** shelf. Also, drag **Internet Sales Amount** to the **Text** shelf. Note that including **Internet Sales Amount** forces every month to display.

9. Select **Worksheet | Export | Crosstab to Excel**.

10. Adjust the Excel spreadsheet to look like the following screenshot. Be sure to replace the **Internet Sales Amount** column with a column named **Blended Month**, which should include first-of-the-month date information for each row, for example, **06/01/2011**. Also, copy and paste **Calendar Year** so that every cell is populated:

	A	B	C	D
1	Calendar Year	Month	Blended Month	
2	CY 2010	December 2010	12/1/2010	
3	CY 2011	January 2011	1/1/2011	
4	CY 2011	February 2011	2/1/2011	
5	CY 2011	March 2011	3/1/2011	
6	CY 2011	April 2011	4/1/2011	
7	CY 2011	May 2011	5/1/2011	
8	CY 2011	June 2011	6/1/2011	
9	CY 2011	July 2011	7/1/2011	
10	CY 2011	August 2011	8/1/2011	

Figure 6.28: Copying data to Excel

11. Save the Excel spreadsheet as AWDates.xlsx.

12. In Tableau, select the worksheet entitled **Cube – Continuous Months**.

13. Select the AdventureWorks (`AdventureWorksMultiDimensional`) dataset and drag **Internet Sales Amount** to the **Rows** shelf.

14. Add `AWDates.xlsx` as a new dataset.

15. Select **Data | Edit Data Relationships** and set the relationships so that **Date. Date.Calendar.Calendar Year** blends to **Calendar Year** and **Date.Date. Calendar.Month** blends to **Month**:

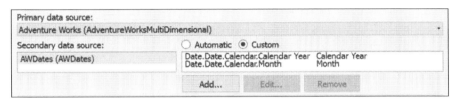

Figure 6.29: Blend relationships

16. In the **Data** pane, select the **AWDates** data source and blend on **Calendar Year** and **Month** by clicking the gray broken chainlink icons.

17. Right-click and drag **Blended Month** to the **Columns** shelf and select **Month continuous**:

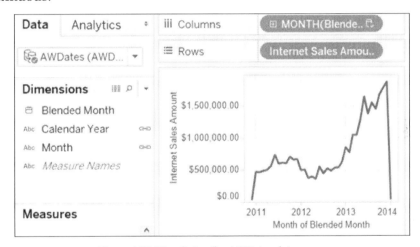

Figure 6.30: Visualizing the AWDates data source

In *steps 1-5*, we demonstrated a simple way to create a view with a continuous date when connected to a cube. No MDX code was necessary. However, these same steps also reveal the shortcomings of working with a cube, including that many of the choices normally available for dates in Tableau are not accessible. This is a problem that cannot be overcome by restructuring the cube or writing MDX code.

The remaining steps in the exercise demonstrate how this problem can be overcome through data blending. Although the data blend created in the exercise only provides month-level granularity, it would not be difficult to include day-level granularity. The end result is a demonstration that the date capabilities normally expected in Tableau can be made available when connected to a cube. Furthermore, if the blended data source remains small, the impact on performance should be negligible.

The last missing piece for working with cubes is the data blending for hierarchies, aliasing, and grouping. Follow along with the steps in the next section to understand how Tableau handles those for you.

Data blending for hierarchies, aliasing, and grouping

MDX can be used to provide some of the functionality normally available in Tableau that is otherwise missing when connected to a cube. For example, although you cannot create groups in Tableau when accessing a cube data source, MDX can be passed to the cube by using a calculated member to create groups. Instructions for how to do this are provided here: https://help.tableau.com/current/pro/desktop/en-us/cubes.htm. Similarly, it is possible to use MDX to create hierarchies or to alias dimension members, but that requires knowledge of MDX that most Tableau authors do not possess.

This exercise will demonstrate how to use data blending to accomplish hierarchies, aliasing, and grouping when accessing a cube:

1. Create an Excel spreadsheet named **Aliasing**, with the following data:

Group	Hemispheres
Europe	Eastern Hemisphere
North America	Western Hemisphere
Pacific	Eastern Hemisphere

2. In the workbook associated with this chapter, navigate to the **Cube – Hierarchy** worksheet.

3. If you have not already added the AdventureWorks dataset, connect through **Data | New Data Source | Microsoft Analysis Services** (see the introduction to this section, *Working with cubes*, to learn how to install Analysis Services and the AdventureWorks cube).

4. Select the AdventureWorks dataset and place **Internet Sales Amount** on the **Text** shelf.

5. Add the newly created Excel spreadsheet, **Aliasing**, as a data source.

6. In the **Aliasing** source, blend on **Group** by clicking the gray broken chainlink icon next to the field **Group**:

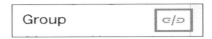

Figure 6.31: Blend

7. Create a hierarchy on **Group** and **Hemispheres** by selecting both in the **Data** pane, right-clicking, and selecting **Hierarchy | Create Hierarchy**. Name the hierarchy as desired.

8. Make **Hemispheres** the first dimension in the hierarchy by dragging it above **Group**:

Figure 6.32: Hierarchy

9. Place **Hemispheres** and **Group** on the **Rows** shelf:

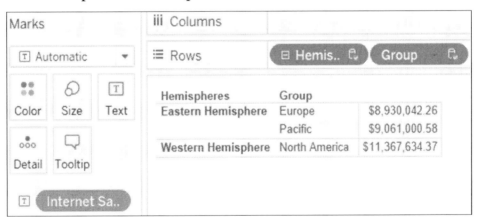

Figure 6.33: Hemispheres

10. Create a worksheet called **Cube – Aliasing and Grouping**.

11. Select the AdventureWorks dataset and place **Internet Sales Amount** on the **Text** shelf.

12. Select the **Aliasing** dataset, right-click on **Group**, and select **Duplicate**. Name the duplicate field Regional Groups.

13. Right-click on **Regional Groups** and select **Aliases**. Adjust the aliasing so that Europe is aliased as **EMEA**, Pacific is aliased as **AsiaPac**, and **North America** is left unchanged.

14. Blend on **Group** by clicking the gray broken chainlink icon.

15. Place **Hemispheres** and **Regional Groups** on the **Rows** shelf:

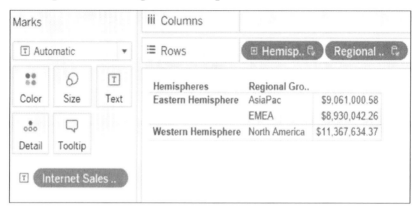

Figure 6.34: Hemispheres II

Typically, dimensions are not enabled for secondary data sources in a data blend; however, in the preceding case, since the secondary data source is blended on **Group** and there is a one-to-many relationship between **Hemispheres** and **Group**, both of these fields can be used as dimensions in the view. Nonetheless, for unrestricted use of dimensions, always use the primary data source.

One point of interest in the preceding exercise is the necessity of creating **Regional Groups** in the secondary data source by duplicating **Group**. This was required to successfully alias the dimension members. Attempting to alias members directly within **Group** breaks the data blend, as shown in the following screenshot:

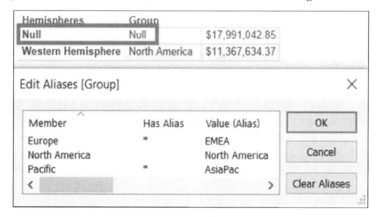

Figure 6.35: Null value

This section has shown how we can leverage cube data sources for hierarchies, using fields of different data sources within the cube. We needed to duplicate the **Group** field to be able to alias it but other than that we were able to prove that aliasing and grouping are possible with cubes. An example could be that you have products stored in one dimension of the cube database and countries in the other. Tableau will allow you to combine them with grouping.

Are cubes here to stay? Maybe not. The advent of big data solutions and the continued evolution of the **Relational Database Management System (RDBMS)** may make cubes obsolete. Cubes pre-aggregate data, which can make certain analytic and reporting needs very quick; however, as RDBMS and big data solutions become faster, easier to query, and more sophisticated, the pre-aggregation paradigm may become obsolete. Some argue that cubes are already obsolete. Also, cubes have serious drawbacks, including a lack of performance advantage for non-aggregated data (which is typical at lower levels of granularity), challenges with more complex analytic needs, difficulty mastering the MDX language, and the fact that many BI vendors do not cater to cubes. This last point is true of Tableau. Although Tableau can be used with cubes, there are challenges to overcome. In contrast, the topic we will discuss next, working with big data, is very straightforward.

Tableau and big data

Perhaps the first challenge of big data is defining it adequately. It's a term so widely used as to be almost meaningless. For example, some may refer to data exceeding 1,048,576 rows as big data (which is the row limit in Excel 2010 and 2013) while others would only apply the term to datasets in the multiple petabyte range. Definitions found on Wikipedia (`https://en.wikipedia.org/wiki/Big_data`) and Webopedia (`https://www.webopedia.com/TERM/B/big_data.html`) are so broad as to encompass both of these examples. True, it is probably simplistic to consider data that merely exceeds Excel's row limitation as big data; nevertheless, from the perspective of an individual for whom Excel is the traditional data-processing application, the preceding definitions fit.

Rather than try to provide an adequately narrow definition of what is essentially a buzzword, this section will primarily focus on one aspect of big data: massively parallel processing. However, before we begin, let's consider a couple of housekeeping items. First, when I have been asked about Tableau and big data, the intent of the question has invariably been about Tableau's performance when working with large datasets. Since *Chapter 13, Improving Performance*, is dedicated to Tableau's performance, this section will not address performance thoroughly. Second, for the user who works predominately or exclusively with Excel, exceeding the row limit is a real problem for which a solution may prove helpful. We'll cover this next.

Addressing Excel's row limitation

As mentioned in the section *Tableau and big data*, exceeding Excel's row limitation should not be considered big data. Nevertheless, that limitation can be an issue, and telling a Tableau author to use a database is often not helpful. A Tableau author may indeed want to utilize a database but may not have direct access. For example, the data that resides in the database may be exported through a web application and then imported into an Excel workbook that Tableau utilizes as a data source. If this process is performed weekly or monthly and each import involves 10,000+ rows, it won't be long before the Excel row limit is hit. In the next exercise, we will see one strategy for addressing this issue.

Note that this exercise is Windows-centric, but similar tasks can be implemented in a macOS environment. Follow the steps to learn more about how to work around Excel's row limitation:

1. In the workbook associated with this chapter, navigate to the dashboard entitled **Excel Row Limit**. That dashboard includes a link (`https://github.com/PacktPublishing/Mastering-Tableau-2021`) to GitHub where you can find the files necessary to complete this exercise.

2. Download the files, and open `Spreadsheet_2` in Excel or a text editor and remove the header, that is, the first row. Save the spreadsheet as a `.csv` file.

3. Place copies of the two files, `Spreadsheet_1` and `Spreadsheet_2`, in a new directory.

4. Open Command Prompt. This can be quickly done by pressing *Windows + R* and then entering `cmd`.

5. In Command Prompt, type the following, then press *Enter*:

    ```
    cd [filepath to the newly created directory]
    ```

    An example file path might look something like the following:

    ```
    C:\Users\MarleenMeier\Desktop\New_Directory
    ```

6. In Command Prompt, enter the following, then press *Enter*:

    ```
    for %f in (*.csv) do type "%f" >> output.csv
    ```

    Note that the resulting `.csv` file (that is, `output.csv`) will not open successfully in Excel but, as shown in the following steps, it can be used as a data source in Tableau.

7. In Tableau, press *Ctrl + D* to open a new data source, and in the resulting window, select **Text file**:

Figure 6.36: Text file data

8. Connect to the output.csv data source.

9. Place **Number of Records** on the **Text** shelf and observe that the total equals the number of rows in Spreadsheet_1 plus the number of rows in Spreadsheet_2:

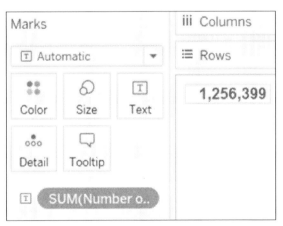

Figure 6.37: Number of records

This exercise could also be replaced by Tableau's built-in union function, which appends the same structured tables automatically. This has been described in detail in *Chapter 4, All About Data – Joins, Blends, and Data Structures.*

The scheduling of wildcard unions through the command line is available in Tableau Prep. You can find documentation about it here: `https://onlinehelp.tableau.com/current/prep/en-us/prep_save_share.htm#commandline`.

Talking about big data goes hand in hand with parallel processing. To make it easier for you to understand big data platforms and hence how you can build high-performing dashboards, we will take a quick turn into the world of massively parallel processing.

Massively parallel processing

Big data may be semi-structured or unstructured. The **massively parallel processing (MPP)** architecture structures big data to enable easy querying for reporting and analytic purposes. MPP systems are sometimes referred to as *shared-nothing systems*. This means that data is partitioned across many servers (otherwise known as **nodes**) and each server processes queries locally.

Let's explore MPP in detail using the following diagram as a point of reference:

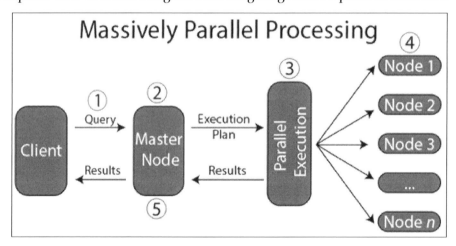

Figure 6.38: MPP

Please see the following explanation of the diagram:

1. The process begins with the **Client** issuing a query that is then passed to the **Master Node**.

2. The **Master Node** contains information, such as the data dictionary and session information, that it uses to generate an execution plan designed to retrieve the needed information from each underlying **Node**.

3. **Parallel Execution** represents the implementation of the execution plan generated by the **Master Node**.

4. Each underlying **Node** executes the unique query it has received and then passes the results to the **Master Node**. Each **Node** is actually a standalone server with its own RAM, disk space, and operating system.

5. The **Master Node** assembles the results, which are then passed to the **Client**.

On the plus side, MPP systems are easily scalable. Once the initial architecture is set up, adding additional hard drive space and processing power can be as easy as adding additional servers. On the downside, MPP systems can be costly to implement—requiring thousands or even tens of thousands of servers, along with associated failover requirements and highly skilled, costly labor for support.

For Tableau and working with big data, it is very important to know the partitions that your IT team has put in place for parallel processing. It could be, for example, the year, month, and day column. If you use those columns that are also used as partitions in the database, your Tableau dashboard will perform so much better than trying to query on a random field in the dataset. So, first put filters in place—preferably partitions. Then build your dashboard on a subset of the data. Once you are all done, load the data you need and check the performance again. More information regarding performance is given in *Chapter 13, Improving Performance*.

As a result of the expense, many organizations opt for a cloud-based solution, such as Amazon Redshift or Google BigQuery. Amazon Redshift uses an MPP system, while Google BigQuery uses tree architecture, which is a little different but still takes advantage of MPP techniques.

Building a visualization with Google BigQuery

One big data solution is BigQuery, next to many others. For this section of the book, we have chosen BigQuery just because readers can test it for free as long as you have a Gmail account. Secondly, you don't have to install anything, which makes it a good platform for an exercise in this book.

In order to build a visualization with Google BigQuery, you will need to first set up access to BigQuery. The following exercise will point you in the right direction. Once you have set up access to BigQuery, you will be able to connect to the BigQuery sample datasets. In the remainder of the exercise, you will build a visualization while connected to BigQuery.

Assuming you have a good internet connection, the performance will likely exceed what you experience when working with a local copy of an extracted data source of a similar size.

Let's have a look at how we can use Google BigQuery in our Tableau dashboard:

1. Log into your Google account, navigate to `https://cloud.google.com/bigquery/`, and follow the provided instructions to try **BigQuery** for free.

2. In the workbook associated with this chapter, navigate to the **BigQuery** worksheet.

3. Press *Ctrl + D* to connect to a data source. In the resulting window, select **Google BigQuery** and, when prompted, provide your Gmail login information.

4. In the **Data Source** page, choose the **publicdata** project, the **samples** dataset, and the **natality** table.

5. The **natality** table provides birth demographics for the United States from 1969 to 2008:

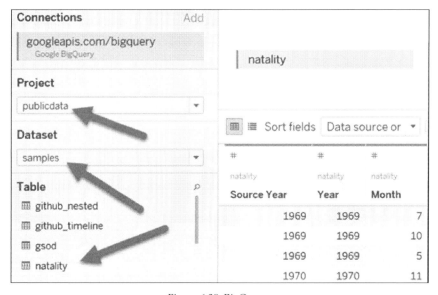

Figure 6.39: BigQuery

6. In the **Data** pane, double-click **Number of Records**.

7. From the **Data** pane, drag **Month** to the **Columns** shelf, and set it to **Discrete**.

8. Right-click on the *y* axis, **Number of Records**, and select **Edit Axis**. Deselect **Include Zero**.

9. Format as desired. This visualization displays the number of infants born in each month from 1969 to 2008:

Figure 6.40: BigQuery viz

 Knowing the fields on which the big data engine is partitioned will help a lot when facing performance issues. If, for example, your data is partitioned by **Year**, always try to make use of this field in filters and calculations. *Chapter 13, Improving Performance*, contains more information on this topic.

As you can see, BigQuery allows us to visualize datasets containing millions of records quickly and easily.

Summary

We began this chapter with a discussion of data densification and discovered that there are two types of data densification: domain completion and domain padding. When reviewing these two types of data densification, we learned how each can be deployed, when each is useful, and when each can be problematic. Next, we learned how to work with cubes. We discussed the Tableau Online Help articles as well as how to use data blending with cubes. Finally, we explored big data. We also surveyed MPP, and walked through an example of how to use Tableau to connect to Google BigQuery.

In the next chapter, we will explore another functionality: level of detail calculations. Although table calculations remain an important part of everyday Tableau usage, we will discover how level of detail calculations can easily accomplish tasks that were previously only possible through complex table calculations.

7
Level of Detail Calculations

When we talk about **Level of Detail (LOD)** calculations in Tableau, we mean three expressions: FIXED, INCLUDE, and EXCLUDE. These three expressions open a world of options by providing the ability to create calculations that target specific levels of granularity. In older versions of Tableau, data granularity for a worksheet was established by the dimensions in a view. If the view contained dimensions for, for example, Region, State, and Postal Code, but the author wanted to create a City-level calculation, the City dimension would need to be included on the view. Furthermore, there was no mechanism for excluding or ignoring a given **dimension** on a view. Admittedly, the desired results could normally be obtained through some complex and sometimes convoluted use of table calculations, data blends, and so on. Fortunately, LOD calculations greatly simplify these use case scenarios and, in some cases, enable what was previously impossible.

In this chapter, we will discuss the following topics:

- Introducing LOD calculations
- Playground I: FIXED and EXCLUDE
- Playground II: INCLUDE
- Building practical applications with LOD

Let's begin by introducing LOD calculations and how they are used.

Introducing LOD calculations

Tableau's default is to show measures in a view based on the dimensions also present in the view. If you have a dashboard with Sales data and dimensions like State and City, and you drag the State and Sales data onto the view, the Sales data will be divided by State, showing you Sales per State. If you want to divide the Sales data further into smaller chunks, you might add the City field, resulting in Sales data per City, per State. LOD calculations can manipulate this default behavior. After completing this chapter, you will be able to divide or partition measures by dimensions that are not in the view and show measures using fewer dimensions than are visible in the view.

To do this, we will build and use two **playgrounds**. Delivering reports as required by one's job duties may lead to a thorough knowledge of a limited set of capabilities; that is, a deep but narrow understanding. It can be difficult to set aside time (and also justify that time) to explore the capabilities of Tableau that on the surface may seem to have no direct correlation to job duties. Playground environments can help overcome any difficulties and objections, by providing efficient avenues of exploration. In this chapter, we'll build two playground environments specifically for LOD calculations, to help make the task of deep and broad understanding easier by providing an efficient avenue for exploration and understanding. You can always come back to the workbook accompanying this chapter and test functionality related to LODs.

Playground I: FIXED and EXCLUDE

The first playground we will build will be for the purpose of exploring two of the three LOD functions: FIXED and EXCLUDE. We will use a set of parameters and associated calculated fields to efficiently explore how these functions work.

Setting up the workbook

Much of the groundwork for this exercise has already been completed in the workbook associated with this chapter. The steps require more so to open different calculations and parameters and see how they have been set up and why this works. Explanations are given along the way. If you do not have ready access to the workbook, you should be able to construct a similar one by referencing the following information.

To complete the initial setup of a worksheet, take the following steps:

1. Navigate to `https://public.tableau.com/profile/marleen.meier` to locate and download the workbook associated with this chapter.

2. Open the workbook associated with this chapter and navigate to the **Fixed and Exclude** worksheet. The worksheet should look as follows:

Figure 7.1: The worksheet

3. Select the **Superstore** data source and inspect the parameter named **1st Dim** by right-clicking and selecting **Edit**:

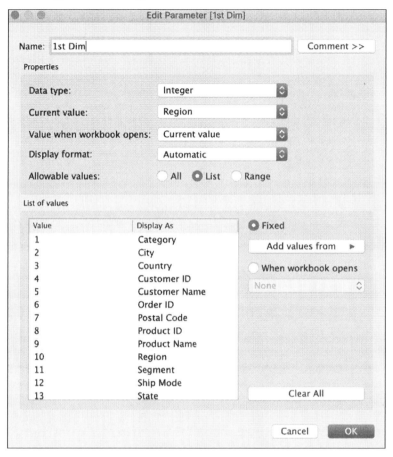

Figure 7.2: Parameter I

The parameters named **2nd Dim**, **3rd Dim**, and **4th Dim** are identical to **1st Dim**.

4. Note that except for **Order Date** and **Ship Date**, every dimension in the dataset is included in the list of values (see *Figure 7.2*). For the purposes of this exercise, **Category**, **Region**, **Segment**, **Ship Mode**, and **Sub-Category** are particularly important because those are dimensions with fewer members. Dimensions with many members are more difficult to use in this context.

5. Inspect the **Choose Fixed Dims, Choose Excluded Dims 1**, and **Choose Excluded Dims 2** parameters included in the workbook and note that we defined a number of integers under the **Value** column, each of which will later be visible as a string specified under the **Displays As** column in the parameter dropdown. The **Value** and **Display As** configurations for **Choose Fixed Dims** are as follows:

Figure 7.3: Parameter II

6. Inspect the calculated field named **1st Dim** (it is located under the **Practical: All** folder in the **Data** pane); this calculation makes use of the 1st Dim parameter and will cause a field to be displayed depending on the selection of the parameter. If the user selects **Category** in the **1st Dim** parameter, value 1 will be activated (according to the values specified in *Figure 7.2*). Value 1 then translates to the field **Category** in the calculated field **1st Dim** as shown in the following screenshot:

Figure 7.4: Calculated field 1st Dim

7. The calculated fields named **2nd Dim**, **3rd Dim**, and **4th Dim** are identical to **1st Dim** except that each references the parameter bearing its name; for example, the **2nd Dim** calculated field utilizes [Parameters].[2nd Dim].

    These Case statements, in conjunction with the associated parameters, will allow you to choose which dimensions to view from a dropdown in the view as described in *Step 5*.

8. Inspect the following calculated fields, which enable you to choose which LOD calculations to employ and thus to compare and contrast differences and similarities:

```
Case Fixed                    [icon] Superstore

CASE [Choose Fixed Dims]
WHEN 1 THEN SUM({FIXED [1st Dim]: SUM([Sales])})
WHEN 2 THEN SUM({FIXED [2nd Dim]: SUM([Sales])})
WHEN 3 THEN SUM({FIXED [3rd Dim]: SUM([Sales])})
WHEN 4 THEN SUM({FIXED [4th Dim]: SUM([Sales])})
WHEN 5 THEN SUM({FIXED : SUM([Sales])})
WHEN 6 THEN 0
END
```

Figure 7.5: Case Fixed

The **Case Fixed** calculation shows that if the user selects 1 in the **Choose Fixed Dims** parameter (which is being displayed as **1st**), the **1st Dim** will be fixed — no matter the dashboard setup. That means that **SUM(Sales)** will be partitioned over the **1st Dim**, no matter if it is part of the dashboard.

```
Case Exclude 1                    [icon] Superstore

CASE [Choose Excluded Dims 1]
WHEN 1 THEN SUM({EXCLUDE [1st Dim]: SUM([Sales])})
WHEN 2 THEN SUM({EXCLUDE [2nd Dim] : SUM([Sales])})
WHEN 3 THEN SUM({EXCLUDE [3rd Dim] : SUM([Sales])})
WHEN 4 THEN SUM({EXCLUDE [4th Dim]: SUM([Sales])})
WHEN 5 THEN 0
END
```

Figure 7.6: Case Exclude 1

The **Case Exclude 1** calculation shows that if the user selects 1 in the **Choose Excluded Dims 1** parameter (which will be displayed as **1st**), the **1st Dim** will be excluded from the calculation in the view. That means that **SUM(Sales)** won't be partitioned over the **1st Dim**, even if it is part of the view.

```
Case Exclude 2                    [icon] Superstore

CASE [Choose Excluded Dims 2]
WHEN 1 THEN SUM({EXCLUDE [1st Dim]: SUM([Sales])})
WHEN 2 THEN SUM({EXCLUDE [1st Dim],[2nd Dim] : SUM([Sales])})
WHEN 3 THEN SUM({EXCLUDE [1st Dim],[2nd Dim],[3rd Dim] : SUM([Sales])})
WHEN 4 THEN SUM({EXCLUDE [1st Dim],[2nd Dim],[3rd Dim], [4th Dim]: SUM([Sales])})
WHEN 5 THEN SUM({EXCLUDE : SUM([Sales])})
WHEN 6 THEN 0
END
```

Figure 7.7: Case Exclude 2

The **Case Exclude 2** calculation shows that if the user selects 1 in the **Choose Excluded Dims 2** parameter (which will be displayed as **1st**), the **1st Dim** will be excluded from the calculation in the view. That means that **SUM(Sales)** won't be partitioned over the **1st Dim**, even if it is part of the view.

9. Now, right-click and open the context filter on **Product Name** for inspection. In the resulting dialog box, click the **Wildcard** tab and note the settings as shown in the following screenshot. The filter has been set to show only product names that start with S (**Match value** is not case-sensitive.):

Figure 7.8: Wildcard filter

10. After clicking **OK**, right-click on the filter and note that context filters are denoted in gray:

Figure 7.9: Gray context filter

11. Place the following dimensions on the **Rows** shelf: **1st Dim, 2nd Dim, 3rd Dim**, and **4th Dim**.

12. Drag **Measure Names** onto the **Filters** shelf and select **Sales, Case Fixed, Case Exclude 1**, and **Case Exclude 2**.

13. Add **Measure Values** to **Text** and **Measure Names** to **Columns**:

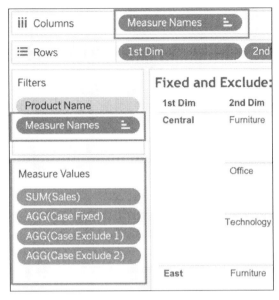

Figure 7.10: Measure Values

14. Display each parameter by right-clicking each one and selecting **Show Parameter Control**. Order the parameter controls as follows:

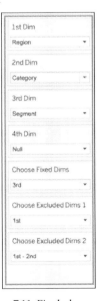

Figure 7.11: Final playground

By following those previous steps, we are now ready to build various tables in order to compare the different LOD calculations because the parameters will allow us to select different dimensions and the calculated fields that incorporated the FIXED and EXCLUDE functions from Tableau. We will now continue using the playground and explain how LODs change calculated fields.

Understanding FIXED

Now that the playground environment is complete, let's build scenarios to better understand FIXED and EXCLUDE functions. We'll begin with FIXED. The FIXED LOD considers only the dimensions to which it is directed. Thus, when fixed on a dimension, all other (if any) dimensions in the view are being ignored. When the FIXED LOD is used without defining any dimension, the result will be a calculation ignoring all (if any) dimensions in the view. Let's jump into the exercise and see this for ourselves:

1. Using the worksheet described previously, set the parameters as shown here:

Figure 7.12: First example

What we achieve with the different parameters is that we show the **SUM(Sales)** per **Region** and each **Region** per **Category**, but we also fixed the **SUM(Sales)** calculation for the dimension **Category** in the column **Case Fixed**.

2. The **Case Fixed** column now displays the totals for each **Category** and ignores **Region** because we told the calculation to fix the **2nd Dim** (**Region**) and ignore the dimensions in the view itself. The effect of this is visible by comparing the **Sales** column and the **Case Fixed** column:

Fixed and Exclude: 1st - **Region**; 2nd - **Category**; 3rd - **Null**; 4th - **Null**

1st Dim	2nd Dim	3rd Dim	4th Dim	Sales	Case Fixed
Central	Furniture			$10,072	47,379
	Office Supplies			$16,340	70,596
	Technology			$13,995	76,801
East	Furniture			$14,249	47,379
	Office Supplies			$21,560	70,596
	Technology			$20,646	76,801
South	Furniture			$4,494	47,379
	Office Supplies			$8,721	70,596
	Technology			$17,451	76,801
West	Furniture			$18,564	47,379
	Office Supplies			$23,975	70,596
	Technology			$24,710	76,801

Figure 7.13: Case Fixed I

3. Check for yourself and do the math for **Furniture**:

    10,072 + 14,249 + 4,494 + 18,564 = 47,379

    Even though the **Region** is visible in the view, the **SUM(Sales)** in column **Case Fixed** ignores the **Region** and shows the results as if the **Category** dimension is the only dimension in the view. We manipulated the granularity of the data. In the **Case Fixed** column, **Region** serves for informative purpose only but does not affect the calculation of **SUM(Sales)**.

4. Now change the **Choose Fixed Dims** parameter to **1st** and note that **Case Fixed** now displays the totals for each region:

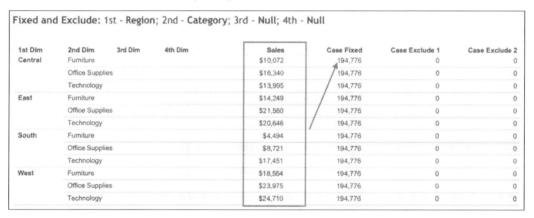

Fixed and Exclude: 1st - **Region**; 2nd - **Category**; 3rd - Null; 4th - Null

1st Dim	2nd Dim	3rd Dim	4th Dim	Sales	Case Fixed	Case Exclude 1	Case Exclude 2
Central	Furniture			$10,072	40,406	0	0
	Office Supplies			$16,340	40,406	0	0
	Technology			$13,995	40,406	0	0
East	Furniture			$14,249	56,455	0	0
	Office Supplies			$21,560	56,455	0	0
	Technology			$20,646	56,455	0	0
South	Furniture			$4,494	30,666	0	0
	Office Supplies			$8,721	30,666	0	0
	Technology			$17,451	30,666	0	0
West	Furniture			$18,564	67,249	0	0
	Office Supplies			$23,975	67,249	0	0
	Technology			$24,710	67,249	0	0

Figure 7.14: Case Fixed II

5. This time we fix the calculation in column **Case Fixed** to only take the **Region** into account but ignore the **Category**. Check for yourself and do the math for **Central**: 10,072 + 16,340 + 13,995 = 40,406

Change the **Choose Fixed Dims** parameter to **Fixed: Nothing** and note that the amount reflects the total **SUM(Sales)**:

Fixed and Exclude: 1st - **Region**; 2nd - **Category**; 3rd - Null; 4th - Null

1st Dim	2nd Dim	3rd Dim	4th Dim	Sales	Case Fixed	Case Exclude 1	Case Exclude 2
Central	Furniture			$10,072	194,776	0	0
	Office Supplies			$16,340	194,776	0	0
	Technology			$13,995	194,776	0	0
East	Furniture			$14,249	194,776	0	0
	Office Supplies			$21,560	194,776	0	0
	Technology			$20,646	194,776	0	0
South	Furniture			$4,494	194,776	0	0
	Office Supplies			$8,721	194,776	0	0
	Technology			$17,451	194,776	0	0
West	Furniture			$18,564	194,776	0	0
	Office Supplies			$23,975	194,776	0	0
	Technology			$24,710	194,776	0	0

Figure 7.15: Fixed: Nothing

This time we fixed the calculation to nothing, meaning that we ignore every dimension in the view. Check for yourself and do the math by summing the **Sales** values; the sum will be 194,776.

As is evident, the FIXED LOD considers only the dimensions to which it is directed. Thus, when fixed on **Category**, **Region** is ignored. And, as demonstrated, when fixed on **Region**, **Category** is ignored. Lastly, when **Choose Fixed Dims** is set to **Fixed: Nothing**, the entire dataset that is not restricted by the context filter on **Product Name** is displayed.

Next, let's look at a couple of new features introduced with Tableau 2021.1 that pertain to FIXED LODs.

Table-scoped expressions

A quick way to write a FIXED LOD expression when using a whole table as the scope is using code like the following:

```
{MAX([Order Date])}
```

If you use this calculation on the Superstore dataset, you will achieve the exact same as writing:

```
{FIXED: MAX([Order Date])}
```

No matter what you show in the view, this field will always retrieve the latest data from the whole table. Cool, right?

Quick LOD calculations

Tableau 2021.1 allows us to create FIXED LODs faster. Simply drag the desired measure on top of a dimension and press *Ctrl* (or *Cmd* on macOS). Now you will see the dimension highlighted in blue (see **Region** in *Figure 7.16*). Then drop the measure there and a new measure field (in this case, **Sales(Region)**) will be created.

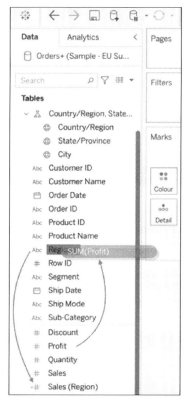

Figure 7.16: Quick LOD

Right click on **Sales(Region)** and note that a FIXED LOD has been created:

Figure 7.17: Quick LOD II

If you're working with Tableau 2021.1 or higher, you can use this shortcut for FIXED LODs.

The playground we built was not only meant for FIXED but also for EXCLUDE. Let us have a look at EXCLUDE next.

Understanding EXCLUDE

Let us start understanding the EXCLUDE LOD. The EXCLUDE LOD will exclude any dimension to which it is directed. If your view contains Region and Category and you write an EXCLUDE LOD on Category, only Region will be considered in the calculations. The following example will make this clearer—our goal in this exercise is to calculate SUM(Sales) by using fewer dimensions than in the view. We want to exclude visible dimensions only from the calculation but still show the dimension values in the dashboard:

1. Set the parameters as shown in the following screenshot:

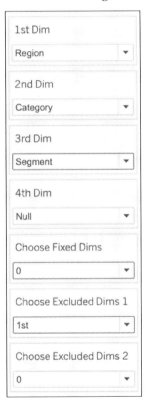

Figure 7.18: Fixed: Nothing

2. You can observe the following results:

Fixed and Exclude: 1st - Region; 2nd - Category; 3rd - Segment; 4th - Null							
1st Dim	**2nd Dim**	**3rd Dim**	**4th Dim**	**Sales**	**Case Fixed**	**Case Exclude 1**	**Case Exclude 2**
Central	Furniture	Consumer		$5,444	0	26,738	0
		Corporate		$2,779	0	13,050	0
		Home Office		$1,849	0	7,592	0
	Office Supplies	Consumer		$9,085	0	31,861	0
		Corporate		$3,462	0	24,179	0
		Home Office		$3,793	0	14,556	0
	Technology	Consumer		$5,144	0	39,955	0
		Corporate		$3,848	0	23,766	0
		Home Office		$5,003	0	13,081	0
East	Furniture	Consumer		$6,941	0	26,738	0
		Corporate		$4,415	0	13,050	0
		Home Office		$2,893	0	7,592	0
	Office Supplies	Consumer		$11,361	0	31,861	0
		Corporate		$7,217	0	24,179	0
		Home Office		$2,982	0	14,556	0
	Technology	Consumer		$12,459	0	39,955	0
		Corporate		$8,011	0	23,766	0
		Home Office		$176	0	13,081	0
South	Furniture	Consumer		$2,052	0	26,738	0
		Corporate		$2,193	0	13,050	0
		Home Office		$249	0	7,592	0
	Office Supplies	Consumer		$3,393	0	31,861	0
		Corporate		$2,349	0	24,179	0
		Home Office		$2,978	0	14,556	0
	Technology	Consumer		$10,024	0	39,955	0
		Corporate		$6,046	0	23,766	0
		Home Office		$1,381	0	13,081	0
West	Furniture	Consumer		$12,301	0	26,738	0
		Corporate		$3,663	0	13,050	0
		Home Office		$2,600	0	7,592	0
	Office Supplies	Consumer		$8,022	0	31,861	0

Figure 7.19: Exclude I

Case Exclude 1 displays the total of each **Category** and **Segment** and ignores **Region**. For example, the total of the **Segment Consumer** within the **Category Furniture** is $26,738. That total is repeated for each **Region**. The relevant code that is generating these results is

```
SUM({EXCLUDE [Region] : SUM([Sales])}).
```

3. Make the following changes to the parameters:

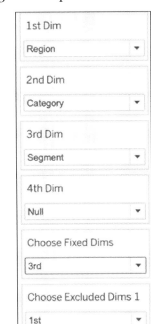

1st Dim

Region ▼

2nd Dim

Category ▼

3rd Dim

Segment ▼

4th Dim

Null ▼

Choose Fixed Dims

3rd ▼

Choose Excluded Dims 1

1st ▼

Choose Excluded Dims 2

1st - 2nd ▼

Figure 7.20: Exclude II

Any LOD calculation can be used with multiple dimensions in a view. In this case, **Case Exclude 2** ignores two dimensions: **1st Dim** and **2nd Dim**, which are associated with **Region** and **Category**. The associated code for **Case Exclude 2** is, therefore:

```
SUM({EXCLUDE [Region],[Category] : SUM([Sales])})
```

The associated code for **Case Fixed** is:

```
SUM({FIXED [Segment]: SUM([Sales])})
```

Case Exclude 2 and **Case Fixed** now have identical results. This is because excluding the first two dimensions is the same as fixing on the third dimension. Only the third dimension **Segment** is taken into account in both cases. You can observe the results in the following screenshot:

1st Dim	2nd Dim	3rd Dim	4th Dim	Sales	Case Fixed	Case Exclude 1	Case Exclude 2
Central	Furniture	Consumer		$5,444	98,554	26,738	98,554
		Corporate		$2,779	60,994	13,050	60,994
		Home Office		$1,849	35,228	7,592	35,228
	Office Supplies	Consumer		$9,085	98,554	31,861	98,554
		Corporate		$3,462	60,994	24,179	60,994
		Home Office		$3,793	35,228	14,556	35,228
	Technology	Consumer		$5,144	98,554	39,955	98,554
		Corporate		$3,848	60,994	23,766	60,994
		Home Office		$5,003	35,228	13,081	35,228
East	Furniture	Consumer		$6,941	98,554	26,738	98,554
		Corporate		$4,415	60,994	13,050	60,994
		Home Office		$2,893	35,228	7,592	35,228
	Office Supplies	Consumer		$11,361	98,554	31,861	98,554
		Corporate		$7,217	60,994	24,179	60,994
		Home Office		$2,982	35,228	14,556	35,228
	Technology	Consumer		$12,459	98,554	39,955	98,554
		Corporate		$8,011	60,994	23,766	60,994
		Home Office		$176	35,228	13,081	35,228
South	Furniture	Consumer		$2,052	98,554	26,738	98,554
		Corporate		$2,193	60,994	13,050	60,994
		Home Office		$249	35,228	7,592	35,228
	Office Supplies	Consumer		$3,393	98,554	31,861	98,554
		Corporate		$2,349	60,994	24,179	60,994
		Home Office		$2,978	35,228	14,556	35,228
	Technology	Consumer		$10,024	98,554	39,955	98,554
		Corporate		$6,046	60,994	23,766	60,994
		Home Office		$1,381	35,228	13,081	35,228
West	Furniture	Consumer		$12,301	98,554	26,738	98,554
		Corporate		$3,663	60,994	13,050	60,994
		Home Office		$2,600	35,228	7,592	35,228
	Office Supplies	Consumer		$8,022	98,554	31,861	98,554

Fixed and Exclude: 1st - **Region**; 2nd - **Category**; 3rd - Segment; 4th - Null

Figure 7.21: Exclude II table

4. Make the following changes to the parameters:

Figure 7.22: Change 4th dimension

5. You can observe the results as follows:

| Fixed and Exclude: 1st - **Region**; 2nd - **Category**; 3rd - **Segment**; 4th - **Ship Mode** | | | | | | | |
1st Dim	2nd Dim	3rd Dim	4th Dim	Sales	Case Fixed	Case Exclude 1	Case Exclude 2
Central	Furniture	Consumer	First Class	$740	98,554	2,961	8,843
			Second Class	$313	98,554	6,493	24,765
			Standard Class	$4,391	98,554	17,147	62,011
		Corporate	First Class	$164	60,994	779	10,622
			Second Class	$801	60,994	3,139	8,818
			Standard Class	$1,813	60,994	8,934	38,997
		Home Office	First Class	$746	35,228	1,202	3,121
			Same Day	$106	35,228	517	2,616
			Second Class	$24	35,228	2,286	6,953
			Standard Class	$973	35,228	3,586	22,537
	Office Supplies	Consumer	First Class	$251	98,554	1,854	8,843
			Same Day	$160	98,554	2,165	2,935
			Second Class	$1,046	98,554	7,930	24,765
			Standard Class	$7,627	98,554	19,913	62,011
		Corporate	First Class	$1,819	60,994	4,977	10,622
			Same Day	$41	60,994	274	2,558
			Second Class	$427	60,994	3,225	8,818
			Standard Class	$1,176	60,994	15,703	38,997
		Home Office	First Class	$834	35,228	1,551	3,121
			Same Day	$172	35,228	1,419	2,616
			Second Class	$400	35,228	1,866	6,953
			Standard Class	$2,586	35,228	9,720	22,537
	Technology	Consumer	First Class	$260	98,554	4,028	8,843

Figure 7.23: Exclude III

6. Note that **Case Exclude 2** and **Case Fixed** no longer have identical results. This is because **Ship Mode** was introduced and **Case Exclude 2** considers **Ship Mode** whereas **Case Fixed** does not.

7. Experiment with other settings to further enhance your understanding of the FIXED and EXCLUDE LODs.

EXCLUDE will cause any dimension addressed in the LOD calculation to be removed from the calculation. Multiple dimensions can be part of an EXCLUDE LOD and common use cases include the direct comparison of sales per category in a region versus total sales in a region. Without LODs it would not be possible to show those two sales figures and both dimensions in the same table.

I hope that by following the previous steps you were able to get a better feel for the EXCLUDE LOD. As a quick interlude after those exercises on FIXED and EXCLUDE, let's take a closer look at Tableau's order of operations, as getting the same result for FIXED and EXCLUDE as we have seen in this exercise is not always the case.

Understanding Tableau's order of operations

The previous exercise led us to believe that the same results for FIXED and EXCLUDE can be achieved by fixing the dimensions that are not excluded and vice versa. However, the order in which Tableau executes a FIXED and an EXCLUDE LOD differs and can hence cause unexpected results. In order to avoid this, I will show you what to consider when using either FIXED or EXCLUDE LODs.

Let's have a look at the order of filtering:

1. Set the parameters as follows:

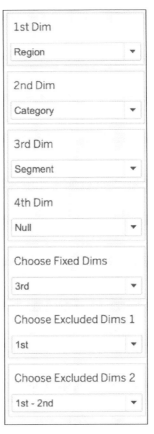

Figure 7.24: Set parameters

2. Observe the results:

Fixed and Exclude: 1st - **Region**; 2nd - **Category**; 3rd - **Segment**; 4th - **Null**

1st Dim	2nd Dim	3rd Dim	4th Dim	Sales	Case Fixed	Case Exclude 1	Case Exclude 2
Central	Furniture	Consumer		$5,444	98,554	26,738	98,554
		Corporate		$2,779	60,994	13,050	60,994
		Home Office		$1,849	35,228	7,592	35,228
	Office Supplies	Consumer		$9,085	98,554	31,861	98,554
		Corporate		$3,462	60,994	24,179	60,994
		Home Office		$3,793	35,228	14,556	35,228
	Technology	Consumer		$5,144	98,554	39,955	98,554
		Corporate		$3,848	60,994	23,766	60,994
		Home Office		$5,003	35,228	13,081	35,228
East	Furniture	Consumer		$6,941	98,554	26,738	98,554
		Corporate		$4,415	60,994	13,050	60,994
		Home Office		$2,893	35,228	7,592	35,228
	Office Supplies	Consumer		$11,361	98,554	31,861	98,554
		Corporate		$7,217	60,994	24,179	60,994
		Home Office		$2,982	35,228	14,556	35,228
	Technology	Consumer		$12,459	98,554	39,955	98,554
		Corporate		$8,011	60,994	23,766	60,994
		Home Office		$176	35,228	13,081	35,228
South	Furniture	Consumer		$2,052	98,554	26,738	98,554

Figure 7.25: Same results

Note that, as seen in the previous exercise, **Case Exclude 2** and **Case Fixed** are identical.

3. Right-click on the **Product Name** filter and select **Remove from context**:

Figure 7.26: Remove from context

4. Observe the results in the following screenshot:

4th - Null	≠	
Case Fixed	**Case Exclude 1**	**Case Exclude 2**
1,161,401	26,738	98,554
706,146	13,050	60,994
429,653	7,592	35,228
1,161,401	31,861	98,554
706,146	24,179	60,994
429,653	14,556	35,228
1,161,401	39,955	98,554
706,146	23,766	60,994
429,653	13,081	35,228
1,161,401	26,738	98,554
706,146	13,050	60,994
429,653	7,592	35,228
1,161,401	31,861	98,554
706,146	24,179	60,994
429,653	14,556	35,228
1,161,401	39,955	98,554
706,146	23,766	60,994
429,653	13,081	35,228
1,161,401	26,738	98,554
706,146	13,050	60,994

Figure 7.27: Without context filter

5. **Case Exclude 2** and **Case Fixed** are no longer identical. **Case Fixed** is no longer impacted by the **Product Name** filter because the context was removed.

The behavior difference observed between EXCLUDE and FIXED in the preceding exercise reflects the underlying filter order of operation. As shown in *Figure 7.26*, **Context Filters** will impact FIXED, EXCLUDE, and INCLUDE calculations because the **Context Filter** is being applied first to the dataset, then the LOD. **Dimension Filters**, however, will only impact EXCLUDE and INCLUDE LODs because the FIXED LOD will be applied to the dataset first and then the dimension filter, followed by EXCLUDE and INCLUDE LODs.

See the following diagram, a schematic representation of the order of operations in Tableau:

Figure 7.28: Order of operations

Figure 7.28 is sourced from Tableau's help pages, here: `https://help.tableau.com/current/pro/desktop/en-us/order_of_operations.htm`.

This page also contains more information on Tableau's order of operations.

We just saw that when using a context filter, EXCLUDE and FIXED LODs can result in the same numbers, whereas a dimension filter will cause the result to differ. This is happening because Tableau executes the different requests after one another. As can be seen in the preceding diagram, the order of operation goes:

1. Context filters
2. FIXED LOD
3. Dimension filters
4. INCLUDE and EXCLUDE LODs

This is important for you to know in order to choose the correct filter or LOD for your purpose.

Next, we will use a new playground, this time, to show how INCLUDE LODs work.

Playground II: INCLUDE

The second playground we will build will be for the purpose of exploring INCLUDE. Like in *Playground I: FIXED and EXCLUDE*, we'll start with setting up the workbook for effective exploration. If you do not have ready access to the workbook, you should be able to construct a similar one by referencing the following information.

Setting up the workbook

In the following, we will set up a worksheet with which we can practice the INCLUDE LOD calculations:

1. Open the workbook associated with this chapter and navigate to the **Exploring Include** worksheet

2. The parameters and calculated fields named **1st Dim**, **2nd Dim**, **3rd Dim**, and **4th Dim** created in the previous exercises are also utilized for this worksheet

3. Right-click on the **1st Dim** parameter and choose **Duplicate**

4. Rename the duplicate **Choose Included Dims**

5. Create a new calculated field named **Case Include** with the following code:

```
CASE [Choose Included Dims]
WHEN 1 THEN AVG({INCLUDE [Category]: SUM([Sales])})
WHEN 2 THEN AVG({INCLUDE [City]: SUM([Sales])})
WHEN 3 THEN AVG({INCLUDE [Country]: SUM([Sales])})
WHEN 4 THEN AVG({INCLUDE [Customer ID]: SUM([Sales])})
WHEN 5 THEN AVG({INCLUDE [Customer Name]: SUM([Sales])})
WHEN 6 THEN AVG({INCLUDE [Order ID]: SUM([Sales])})
WHEN 7 THEN AVG({INCLUDE [Postal Code]: SUM([Sales])})
WHEN 8 THEN AVG({INCLUDE [Product ID]: SUM([Sales])})
WHEN 9 THEN AVG({INCLUDE [Product Name]: SUM([Sales])})
WHEN 10 THEN AVG({INCLUDE [Region]: SUM([Sales])})
WHEN 11 THEN AVG({INCLUDE [Segment]: SUM([Sales])})
WHEN 12 THEN AVG({INCLUDE [Ship Mode]: SUM([Sales])})
WHEN 13 THEN AVG({INCLUDE [State]: SUM([Sales])})
WHEN 14 THEN AVG({INCLUDE [Sub-Category]: SUM([Sales])})
WHEN 15 THEN 0
END
```

6. Place the following measures and dimensions in their respective shelves:

Figure 7.29: Exploring INCLUDE

7. Display each of the following parameters by right-clicking each one and selecting **Show Parameter Control**:

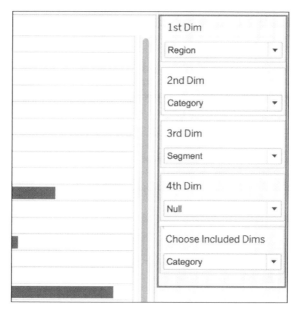

Figure 7.30: Parameters

After you have finished the initial setup, we can start to look into, last but not least, the INCLUDE LOD.

Understanding INCLUDE

Now that the playground environment is complete, let's build scenarios to better understand INCLUDE. By now you can probably imagine that if the FIXED and EXCLUDE LODs remove dimensions from a calculation, INCLUDE adds dimensions. Correct! It might happen that you want to include one or more dimensions in a calculation even though the view doesn't show them. The next example will make use of this functionality in order to show an average per sub-category without showing the sub-category. One would want to do so because the sub-category has so many additional values that the dashboard will be harder to read, and it will take longer to draw quick conclusions. Nevertheless, it is of interest to know the average per sub-category because the number of sub-categories might differ per region and other dimensions, and thus including it will give insights into the real average sales.

Let's see it in action:

1. Set the parameters on the right-hand side as shown here

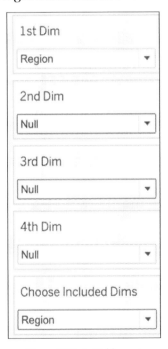

Figure 7.31: Initial layout

2. Add two reference lines by clicking on **Analytics** and edit them using the following settings:

Figure 7.32: Reference line settings

Figure 7.33: Reference line settings

3. Look at the following screenshot for the result. Note that both **Reference Lines** are equal:

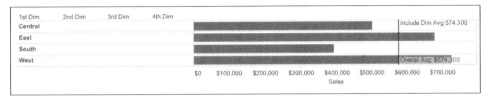

Figure 7.34: Sales per region and reference lines

4. If the **Reference Lines** are overlapping each other, edit the formatting and set **Alignment** to **Top**. To access the formatting, click on the **Reference Line** in the view:

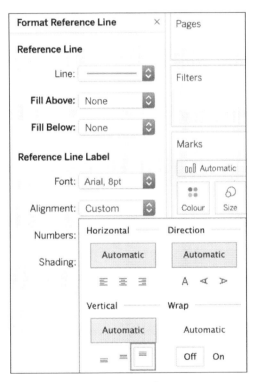

Figure 7.35: Format Reference Line

5. Now, set the parameters as shown here:

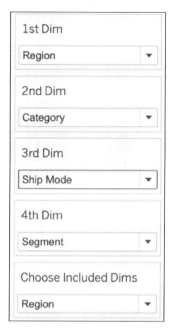

Figure 7.36: Format Reference Line

6. In Tableau Desktop, you should now see the following. As before, both **Reference Lines** are equal:

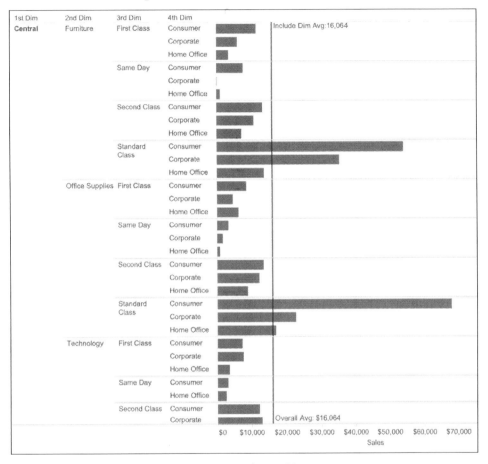

Figure 7.37: Reference Lines

7. Change the **Choose Included Dims** parameter to **Category**, **Ship Mode**, and **Segment**.

8. Note that the **Reference Lines** equal one another for each of these settings. This is because **Choose Included Dims** is only introducing dimensions already represented in the view.

9. Change the **Choose Included Dims** parameter to **Sub-Category**:

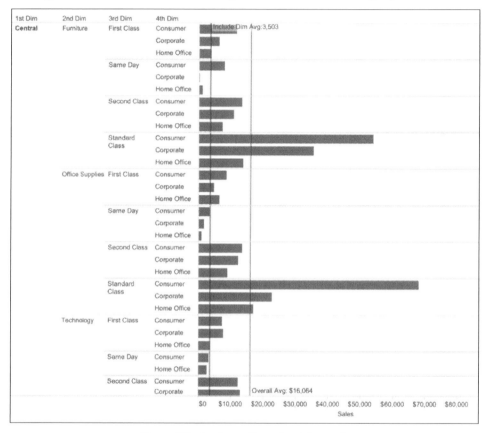

Figure 7.38: check caps throughout changed

The **Include Dim Avg** reference line now includes **Sub-Category** in the average and therefore differs from the **Overall Avg** reference line. The average is smaller because the total **Sales** amount is being divided over more points than are visible in the view. Adding **Sub-Category** to the LOD leads to more rows, which leads to a smaller average per row. Furthermore, note that the **Sub-Category** dimension is not used in the view. LOD calculations do not require a calculation to reside in the view.

To summarize, the INCLUDE LOD can manipulate a visualization in a way that partitions can be added that are not used in the view itself. Also, the naming convention for all three LODs will be your best mnemonic in understanding them: FIXED to fix the fields used, INCLUDE to add "missing" fields, and EXCLUDE to remove unwanted fields from the calculations that are already present.

To get more hands-on training, we will continue with a few practical applications.

Building practical applications with LODs

The first portion of this chapter was designed to demonstrate how LOD calculations work. The remainder will be dedicated to practical applications. Specifically, we will consider three typical challenges that previously were solved using other Tableau capabilities, such as table calculations and data blending.

This exercise will look at a problem that occurs when mixing a table calculation that calculates the percentage of the total with a dimension filter. We will consider the problem, a solution using a LOD calculation, and finish with a commentary section on the germane points of the solution.

Using the LOD calculation FIXED

First, we will start off with a common problem many Tableau users come across when working with the FIXED LOD. The following steps will guide you through the exercise:

1. Open the workbook associated with this chapter and navigate to the worksheet entitled **The Problem**.
2. Select the 2012_World_Pop dataset.
3. Create a calculated field named **Percent of Total** with the following code:

   ```
   SUM([Population]) / TOTAL(SUM([Population]))
   ```

4. Right-click on **Percent of Total** and select **Default Properties | Number Format | Percentage**.
5. Place **Country** on the **Columns** shelf, **Measure Names** on the **Rows** shelf, and **Measure Values** on the **Text** shelf.
6. Remove **Number of Records** from the **Measure Values** shelf.
7. Right-click on **Percent of Total** and set it to **Compute Using | Country**.

8. Create a filter on **Country** such that only **Afghanistan** displays:

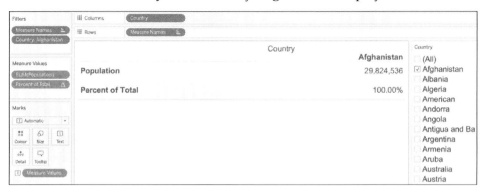

Figure 7.39: Population of Afghanistan

Afghanistan displays the percentage of the total as 100%. Obviously, this does not represent Afghanistan's percentage of the total population of the world. Let's look into a possible solution—to solve the issue with a LOD, follow along with the exercise steps:

1. Duplicate the worksheet entitled **The Problem** and rename it **Solution LOD**.

2. Create a calculated field named **Percent of Total LOD** with the following code:

   ```
   SUM([Population])/SUM({ FIXED : SUM([Population])})
   ```

3. Place **Percent of Total LOD** on the **Measure Values** shelf and note that the displayed percentage equals **0.43%**. If **0** displays, change the number formatting to percentage:

	Country
	Afghanistan
Population	29,824,536
Percent of Total	100.00%
Percent of Total LOD	0.43%

Figure 7.40: Percent of total

4. Remove the **Percent of Total** table calculation that was previously created from the **Measure Values** shelf:

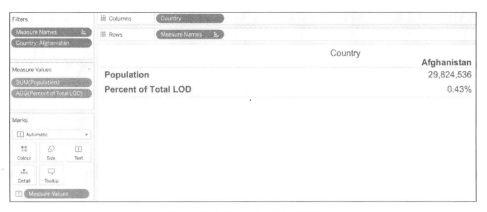

Figure 7.41: Percent of total LOD

As you can see, problem solved! To better understand what is happening in the background, let's look at a query that Tableau generates for the worksheet entitled **The Problem**. Generated queries can be viewed by clicking **Help | Settings and Performance | Start Performance Recording**. (See *Chapter 11, Visualization Best Practices and Dashboard Design*, for additional information regarding viewing Tableau's generated queries.)

The SQL statement is as follows:

```
SELECT
['2012_World_Pop$'].[Country] AS [Country],
SUM(['2012_World_Pop$'].[Population]) AS [sum:Population:ok]
FROM
[dbo].['2012_World_Pop$'] ['2012_World_Pop$']
WHERE
(['2012_World_Pop$'].[Country] = 'Afghanistan')
GROUP BY
['2012_World_Pop$'].[Country]]
```

Note that the WHERE clause in the query is limiting the returned dataset to only those rows that have Afghanistan as **Country**. This WHERE clause was generated as a result of placing **Country** on the **Filters** shelf. By limiting the returned data, the processing requirements are shifted from Tableau to the underlying data source engine. In other words, the data source engine does the work of executing the query, and Tableau thus works with a smaller dataset. The reasoning behind this design is that data source engines are specifically engineered to efficiently query large datasets and also typically have underlying hardware to support such activities. Furthermore, limiting the rows of data returned to Tableau can reduce inefficiencies due to latency.

Inefficiencies are further reduced because Tableau works from cache whenever possible. Often, a user can perform various operations without generating a call to the underlying data source. However, in the preceding case, if a user were to select a different **Country** from the filter, Tableau would generate a new query to the data source. For example, if a user interacts with the filter and deselects Afghanistan and selects Albania, a new query with a corresponding WHERE clause is generated. Although the logic of Tableau's reliance on the data source engine is demonstrable, the problem proposed in the preceding example still remains. What can a Tableau author do to calculate the percent of the whole regardless of filtering?

A solution is to create a table calculation that can also be used as a filter. The difference is that, unlike in the worksheet **The Problem**, the query generated by Tableau to the data source returns the entire dataset. When a table calculation is used in a filter, the filtering does not take place until the underlying data is returned. In other words, Tableau performs the filtering. This preserves a percent of the total percentages regardless of which country population totals the user chooses to view. But, a potential issue with table calculations is that the returned dataset may be quite large, which may cause performance challenges. Latency may be experienced due to increased time required to return a large dataset and Tableau may perform more slowly because of additional processing responsibilities to filter the dataset.

Our proposed solution, an LOD calculation, can address these challenges. Let's take a look at the SQL queries created by the Percent of Total LOD calculated field in the **Solution LOD** worksheet:

```
SELECT
[t0].[Country] AS [Country],
[t1].[ measure 0] AS
[TEMP(Calculation_418553293854285824)(2417030171)(0)],
[t0].[TEMP(Calculation_418553293854285824)(616435453)(0)] AS
[TEMP(Calculation_418553293854285824)(616435453)(0)]
FROM
( SELECT
['2012_World_Pop$'].[Country] AS [Country], SUM(['2012_World_Pop$'].
[Population])
AS [TEMP(Calculation_418553293854285824)(616435453)(0)]
FROM
```

```
[dbo].['2012_World_Pop$'] ['2012_World_Pop$']
WHERE
(['2012_World_Pop$'].[Country]= 'Afghanistan')
GROUP BY
['2012_World_Pop$'].[Country] ) [t0]
CROSS JOIN
( SELECT SUM(['2012_World_Pop$'].[Population]) AS [ measure 0] FROM
[dbo].['2012_World_Pop$'] ['2012_World_Pop$']
GROUP BY () ) [t1]
```

Note the term CROSS JOIN; the LOD calculation generates a query that instructs the underlying data source engine to return data in such a way as to allow Tableau to divide the population values of one or more countries by the world population total, thus returning the correct percentage of the total.

Using the LOD calculation INCLUDE

Next, we will practice the INCLUDE LOD. In this exercise, we will create a worksheet that displays the following:

- Total sales per region
- The average of total sales across all regions
- The average of total sales across all states in each region

Using a LOD calculation to display these values is pretty straightforward. Let's explore. Follow along with the exercise steps:

1. Select the **Practical Include** worksheet.
2. Select the **Superstore** dataset.
3. Create a calculated field named **Per State INCLUDE** with the following code:

    ```
    {INCLUDE [State]:SUM([Sales])}
    ```

4. Drag Region to the **Columns** shelf, SUM(Sales) to the **Rows** shelf, and AVG(Per State INCLUDE) to the **Details** shelf. Be sure to change **Per State INCLUDE** to an average aggregation.

5. Add two **Reference Lines** by right-clicking on the sales axis and selecting **Add Reference Line**. Use the following settings:

Figure 7.42: Reference lines

Figure 7.43: Reference lines

6. Complete the worksheet by formatting it as desired:

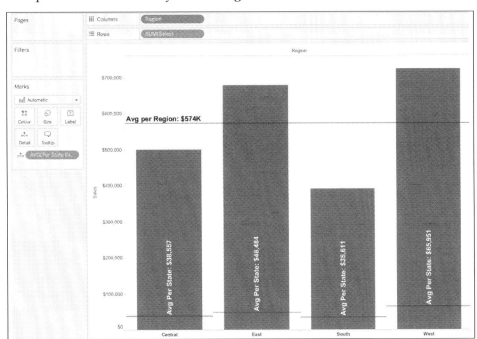

Figure 7.44: Average per region and state

As you can see, thanks to the LOD we can display a line chart per **Region**, as well as one for the whole dataset. This is possible because we included the **State** dimension in our **Per State INCLUDE** calculation. Using this calculated field to create a reference line allows Tableau to show not only the average per (visible) region but also the average per state (invisible) per region.

Using the LOD calculation EXCLUDE

In this exercise, we will create a worksheet using the **Superstore** dataset, which will calculate the percentage of sales generated by each city in a region.

Follow along with the exercise steps:

1. Select the **Practical Exclude** worksheet.
2. Select the **Superstore** dataset.

3. Create the following calculated fields:

Figure 7.45: Region Values and % Per Region LODs

4. Place **Region** and **City** on the **Rows** shelf.

5. Place **Measure Names** on the **Columns** shelf and **Measure Values** on the **Text** shelf.

6. Remove all instances of measures from the **Measure Values** shelf except **Sales**, **Region Values**, and **% Per Region LOD.**

7. In order for **% Per Region LOD** to display as a percentage, the number formatting must be adjusted. Simply right-click on the calculation in the **Data** pane and select **Default Properties | Number Format | Percentage**:

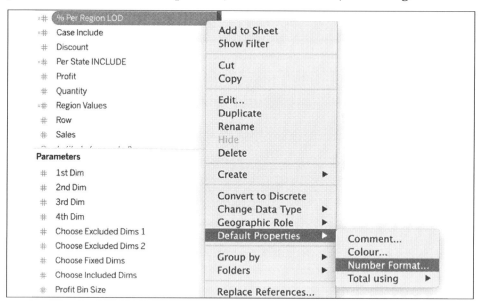

Figure 7.46: Change number format

8. Place an instance of **AGG(% Per Region LOD)** on the **Filter** shelf and adjust to display at least **0.1** (or, 10%):

Figure 7.47: % filter

9. Observe the current view, with **Region** and **City** on the **Rows** shelf:

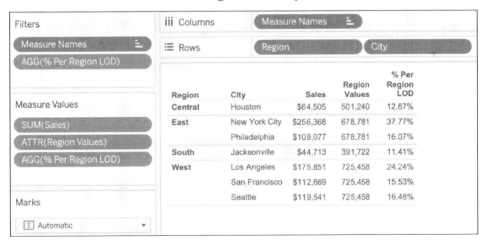

Figure 7.48: Jacksonville still visible

10. Now, place **State** on the **Rows** shelf between **Region** and **City**. Note that **Jacksonville** disappears:

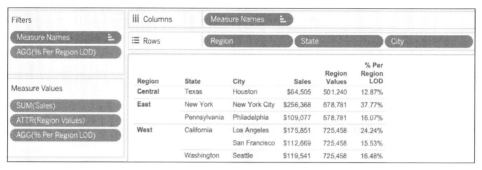

Figure 7.49: Jacksonville disappears when Region is added to Rows

This is happening because **Jacksonville** exists in two states of the **South** region, in **Florida** as well as in **North Carolina**:

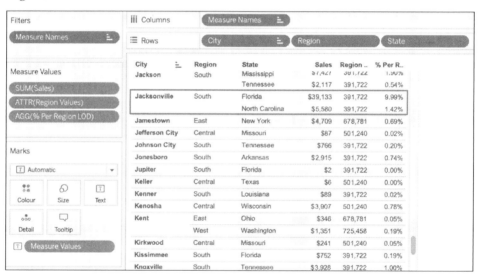

Figure 7.50: Jacksonville existing within two states

Our **Region Values** calculation excluded **City** and **State** and so the **% Per Region LOD** will take into account the **SUM(Sales)** for whatever is visible in the view, divided by the **Region Values**. With **Region** and **City** in the view only, the **SUM(Sales)** for Jacksonville is 44,713 (see *Figure 7.48*). That number divided by the **Region Values** of **391,722** (see *Figure 7.50*) is > 10%. But then we added **State** to the view, changing the **SUM(Sales)** to **39,133** for **Jacksonville** in **Florida** and 5,580 for **Jacksonville** in **North Carolina** (see *Figure 7.50*). Neither one of them when divided by **391,722** for the **Region Values** is above 10% and will therefore drop from the view due to our filter.

LOD calculations are one of the more advanced topics when using Tableau but they are very powerful and worth spending the time to understand. For more practical examples I would recommend you checking the following website: https://www.tableau.com/about/blog/LOD-expressions. I remember that, when I first started using Tableau, I didn't think that I would ever want to show data based on dimensions that are not in my view, or that I would want to exclude dimensions. But I needed them so many times. I went back to the documentation on LODs more often than you can imagine, and I can only encourage you to do the same; the more you read about LODs, the easier it will be to grasp the concept and use them naturally. The added flexibility LODs bring to your dashboard is incredible.

Summary

We began this chapter by exploring why LOD calculations are so impactful and why their inclusion in Tableau was so lauded. Next, we built two playgrounds to explore how the three LOD calculations—FIXED, EXCLUDE, and INCLUDE—work. Tableau's default is to base calculations on the dimensions visible in the view. For example, if you have states in your view, the sales amount will be presented by state. If you are adding cities, the sales amount will be adjusted by state, by city. But, if you want to manipulate this default logic, you can use LOD calculations. They allow you to calculate measures based on any dimension, no matter whether that dimension is represented in the view or not. We also saw that FIXED LODs are higher in the order of operations in Tableau than EXCLUDE and INCLUDE LODs. This is important to remember in order to use the correct LOD and/or filter in your dashboard.

In the next chapter, we'll turn our attention to the visual side of Tableau and explore different chart types and less common but very useful visualizations.

8

Beyond the Basic Chart Types

The assumption behind this chapter is that the reader is familiar with basic chart types such as bar, line graph, treemap, pie, and area. The focus will be on the middle ground, with the intent of relating how to improve visualization types you may already use on a regular basis, as well as introducing chart types with which you may be unfamiliar, but that are, nonetheless, widely useful. And, finally, I will introduce you to Tableau extensions, which offer some more exotic chart types.

Perhaps the most useful part of this chapter is actually not contained in the book at all, but rather in the workbook associated with the chapter. Be sure to download that workbook (the link is provided in the following section) to check out a wider range of visualization types.

This chapter will explore the following visualization types and topics:

- Improving popular visualizations
- Custom background images
- Tableau extensions

Keep in mind that the content of your dashboard is the most important thing, but if you can have the same content with a nicer design, go for the nicer design. Marketing sells and will make your users happy; I hope the next sections will help you find your path and eventually make you a better dashboard designer.

Improving popular visualizations

Most popular visualizations are popular for good reason. Basic bar charts and line graphs are familiar, intuitive, and flexible and are thus widely used in data visualization. Other, less basic visualizations such as bullet graphs and Pareto charts may not be something you use every day but are nonetheless useful additions to a data analyst's toolbox. In this section, we will explore ideas for how to tweak, extend, and even overhaul a few popular chart types.

Bullet graphs

The bullet graph was invented by Stephen Few and communicated publicly in 2006 through his book *Information Dashboard Design: The Effective Visual Communication of Data*. Stephen Few continues to be a strong voice in the data visualization space through his books and his blog, `www.perceptualedge.com`. Bullet graphs communicate efficiently and intuitively by packing a lot of information into a small space while remaining attractive and easy to read. Understandably, they have gained much popularity and are being utilized for many purposes, as can be seen through a web search. The following two exercises communicate the basics of bullet graphs and how to improve on those basics. That is not to say that I have improved on the bullet graph in this chapter! The intent is merely to relay how this important visualization type can be more effectively used in Tableau. Let's get started.

Using bullet graphs

The following steps are meant to teach you the basics of a bullet graph:

1. Navigate to `https://public.tableau.com/profile/marleen.meier` to locate and download the workbook associated with this chapter.

2. Navigate to the worksheet entitled **Bullet Graph** and select the **CoffeeChain** data source.

3. Place these fields on their respective shelves: **Profit** on **Columns**, **Market** on **Rows**, and **BudgetProfit** on **Detail** in the **Marks** card.

4. Right-click on the *x* axis and select **Add Reference Line**.

5. From the upper left-hand corner of the **Edit Reference Line, Band or Box** dialog box, select **Line**. Also, set **Scope** to **Per Cell**, **Value** to **SUM(Budget Profit) as Average**, and **Label** to **None**. Click **OK**:

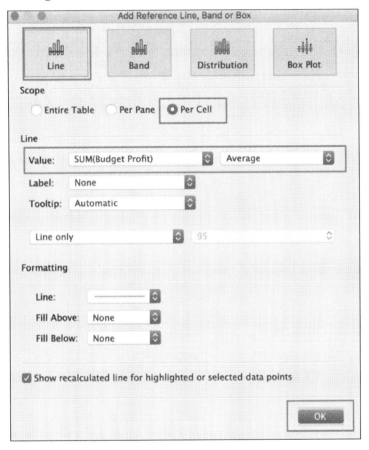

Figure 8.1: Reference line

6. Let's add another reference line. This time, as an alternative method, click on the **Analytics** pane and drag **Reference Line** onto your dashboard. (You could obviously repeat the method in *Step 4* instead.)

7. Within the dialog box, select **Distribution** and set **Scope** to **Per Cell**. Under **Computation**, set **Value** to **Percentages** with **90,95,100** and **Percent of** to **SUM(Budget Profit)**. Set **Label** to **None**. Click **OK**:

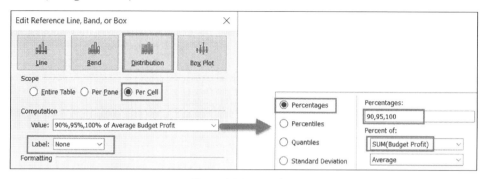

Figure 8.2: Percentiles

8. Create a calculated field called Profit to Budget Profit Ratio with the following code:

```
SUM([Profit])/SUM([Budget Profit])
```

9. Create another calculated field called Quota Met? with the following code:

```
SUM([Profit])>=SUM([Budget Profit])
```

10. Right-click on **Profit to Budget Profit Ratio** and select **Default Properties | Number Format | Percentage**.

11. Place **Profit to Budget Profit Ratio** on the **Label** shelf in the **Marks** card and **Quota Met?** on the **Color** shelf in the **Marks** card:

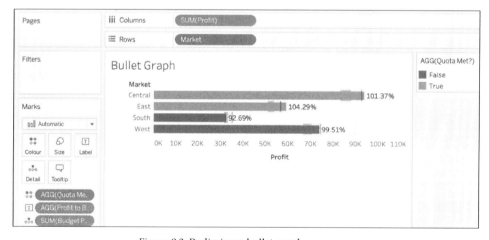

Figure 8.3: Preliminary bullet graph

As you survey our results thus far, you will notice that there are some important aspects to this visualization. For example, the reference lines and the colored bars clearly delineate when a quota was met and missed. Furthermore, the percentages communicate how close the actual profit was to the budgeted profit for each market. However, there are also some problems to address:

- The percentage associated with the **South** market is partially obscured.

- The background colors represented by the reference distribution are obscured.

- The colors of the bars are not intuitive. Orange is set to **True**, which signifies, in this case, the markets that made the quota. However, psychologically speaking, orange is a warning color used to communicate problems and therefore would be more intuitively associated with those markets that failed to make the quota. Furthermore, these colors are not easily distinguishable when presented in grayscale.

- The words **False** and **True** in the legend are not immediately intuitive.

In the upcoming steps, we will address those issues and show you possible solutions.

Bullet graphs – beyond the basics

To address the problems with the graph in the previous section, take the following steps:

1. Continuing from the previous exercise, access the **Data** pane on the left-hand portion of the screen, right-click on **Quota Met?**, and adjust the calculation as follows:

   ```
   IF SUM([Profit])>=SUM([Budget Profit])
   THEN 'Quota Met'
   ELSE 'Quota Missed'
   END
   ```

2. This calculation will create the string Quota Met if the profit is higher than the budgeted profit or the string Quota Missed if the profit isn't higher than the budgeted profit. These two strings can be used as a legend and are more intuitive than the previous **True** and **False**.

3. Create a calculated field named Greater of Profit or Budget Profit with the following code:

   ```
   IF SUM(Profit)>SUM([Budget Profit])
   THEN SUM(Profit)
   ELSE SUM([Budget Profit])
   END
   ```

This calculation will show the profit amount if it is more than the budgeted amount, or the budgeted amount if the profit is smaller. This will help us to always show the bigger amount of the two.

4. Place **Greater of Profit or Budget Profit** on the **Columns** shelf after **Profit**. Also, right-click on the pill and select **Dual Axis**.

5. Right-click on the axis for **Greater of Profit or Budget Profit** and select **Synchronize Axis**.

6. Within the **Marks** card, select the pane labeled **All**:

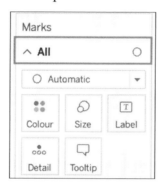

Figure 8.4: Marks card

7. Set the mark type to **Bar**.

8. Remove **Measure Names** from the **Color** shelf.

9. Within the **Marks** card, select the pane labeled **AGG(Greater of Profit or Budget Profit)**.

10. Click on the **Color** shelf and set **Opacity** to **0%**.

11. Within the **Marks** card, select the pane labeled **SUM(Profit)**.

12. Remove **AGG(Profit to Budget Profit Ratio)** from the **Marks** card and note that the percentage labels are no longer obscured.

13. Click on the **Color** shelf and select **Edit Colors**. Within the resulting dialog box, complete the following steps:

    1. Double-click on **Quota Met** and set the color to white

    2. Double-click on **Quota Missed** and set the color to black

14. After you have clicked **OK** for each dialog box and returned to the main screen, once again click on the **Color** shelf and select black for **Border**.

15. Click on the **Size** shelf to narrow the width of the bars by dragging the slider to the left.

16. Right-click on the **Profit** axis and select **Edit Reference Line**. Then set **Value** to **90%,95%,100% of Average Budget Profit**:

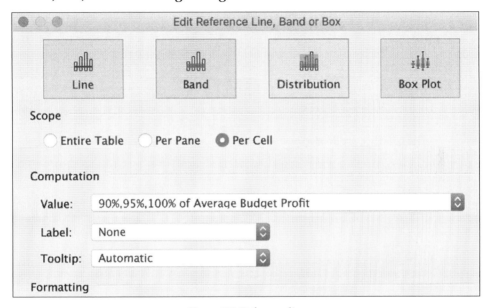

Figure 8.5: Reference line

17. Moving down to the **Formatting** section, set the fill color to **Grey**. Click the **Fill Below** checkbox and the **Reverse** checkbox. Note that the background colors are now more easily distinguishable:

Figure 8.6: Background colors

18. Right-click on the axis labeled **Greater of Profit or Budget Profit** and deselect **Show Header**. You may wish to make some additional tweaks, but our result looks as follows:

Figure 8.7: Improved bullet graph

Note that each of the aforementioned problems has now been addressed:

- The percentage numbers are no longer obscured.

- The background colors are easier to distinguish due to having narrowed the bars.

- The color of the bars is more intuitive. Furthermore, using black, white, and gray has circumvented any readability problems arising from color blindness or grayscale print.

- The words **False** and **True** in the legend have been replaced with the more descriptive terms **Quota Met** and **Quota Missed**.

By completing this section, you will have learned how small or bigger tweaks can improve your visualization and the type of graph you chose. You can do this whenever the current choices you have made do not tell the full story yet. In addition to that, it is also a selling point. Your users like a nice design and clear dashboards. By improving your visualization with more advanced techniques, you will be able to improve your storytelling and marketing.

In the next section, we will continue to add complexity to known **visualizations**. This time we will create pie and donut charts and eventually combine the two.

Pies and donuts

Pie charts are normally frowned upon in data visualization circles. They simply have too many drawbacks. For instance, pie charts don't utilize space well on a rectangular screen. Treemaps fit much better. Also, the number of slices that are reasonable on a pie chart is fairly limited, perhaps six to eight at best. Once again, treemaps are superior because they can be sliced at a finer level of granularity while remaining useful. Lastly, when using pie charts it can be difficult to discern which of two similarly sized slices is largest. Treemaps are no better in this regard; however, if the viewer understands that treemap sorting is from top left to bottom right, that knowledge can be used to distinguish size differences. Of course, bar charts circumvent that particular problem entirely, since the eye can easily distinguish widths and heights but struggles with angles (pie charts) and volume (treemaps).

Despite these drawbacks, because of their popularity, pie charts will likely continue to be widely used in data visualization for years to come. For the pessimistic Tableau author, the best course of action is to grin and bear it. But for one willing to explore and push frontier boundaries, good uses for pie charts can be discovered. The following exercise is one contribution to that exploration.

Pies and donuts on maps

Occasionally, there is a need (or perceived need) to construct pie charts atop a map. The process is not difficult (as you will see in the following exercise), but there are some shortcomings that cannot be easily overcome. We will discuss those shortcomings after the exercise.

The following are the steps:

1. Within the workbook associated with this chapter, navigate to the worksheet entitled **Pie Map** and select the **Superstore** data source.

2. In the **Data** pane, double-click on **State** to create a map of the United States.

3. Place **Sales** on the **Color** shelf. Click on the **Color** shelf and change the palette to **Grey**:

Figure 8.8: Edit Colours

4. Drag an additional copy of **Latitude (generated)** on the **Rows** shelf by holding *Ctrl* for Windows and *Command* for Mac and simultaneously dragging the pile to create two rows, each of which displays a map:

Figure 8.9: Latitude

5. In the **Marks** card, you will notice that there are now three panes: **All**, **Latitude (generated)**, and **Latitude (generated) (2)**. Click on **Latitude (generated) (2)** and set the mark type to **Pie**:

Figure 8.10: Marks card panes

6. Place **Category** on the **Color** shelf and **Sales** on the **Size** shelf.

7. Right-click on the second instance of **Latitude (generated)** in the **Rows** shelf and select **Dual Axis**:

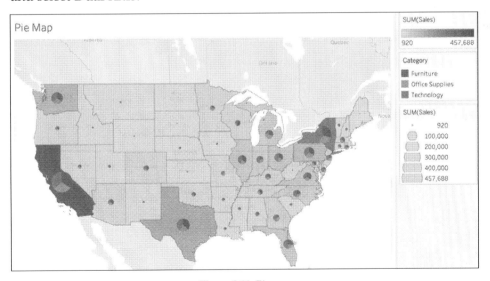

Figure 8.11: Pie map

Can you see issues in the visualization? Two should be immediately apparent:

- First, the smaller pies are difficult to see. Clicking on the drop-down menu for the **Size** legend and selecting **Edit Sizes** could partially address this problem, but pies on smaller states such as **Rhode Island** will continue to be problematic.

- Second, many states have the same light-gray background despite widely varying sales amounts.

The following approach will address these issues while adding additional functionality.

Pies and donuts – beyond the basics

The following are the steps required to create a pie and donut chart on top of a map. By combining the different methods, we will be able to show more information at once without overloading the view:

1. Within the workbook associated with this chapter, navigate to the worksheet entitled **Altered Pie Map** and select the **Superstore** data source.

2. Create the following calculated fields:

Name	Code
Category State Sales	`{FIXED State, Category: SUM(Sales)}`
State Max	`{FIXED State : MAX([Category State Sales])}`
Top Selling Category per State	`MAX(If [State Max] = [Category State Sales] then Category END)`

3. We need those first two **Level of Detail (LOD)** calculations and the last calculation in order to show the sales per category, while also showing the best-selling category per state.

4. Within the **Marks** card, set the mark type to **Pie**.

5. Within the **Data** pane, select the **States** data source.

6. Click the chain link next to **State** in the **Data** pane in order to use **State** as a blended field:

Figure 8.12: Linking dimensions

7. Drag **Column** to the **Columns** shelf and **Row** to the **Rows** shelf.

8. From the **Superstore** data source, place **Category** on the **Color** shelf and **Sales** on the **Angle** shelf.

9. Click on the **Size** shelf and adjust the size as desired.

10. At this point, you should see a rough map of the United States made up of pie charts. Next, we will further enhance the graphic by changing the pies into donuts:

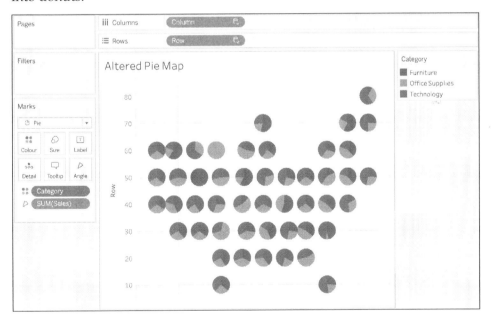

Figure 8.13: Map

11. Return to the **States** data source and place another instance of **Row** on the **Rows** shelf.

12. In the **Marks** card, select **Row (2)** and change the view type to **Circle**.

13. From the **Superstore** dataset, place **Top Selling Category per State** on the **Color** shelf:

Figure 8.14: Map II

14. Place **Sales** on the **Label** shelf. Right-click on the instance of **Sales** you just placed on the **Label** shelf and select **Format**. Make the following adjustments in the **Format** window:

1. Set the **Numbers** formatting to **Currency (Custom)** with **0** decimal places and **Display Units** set to **Thousands (K)**:

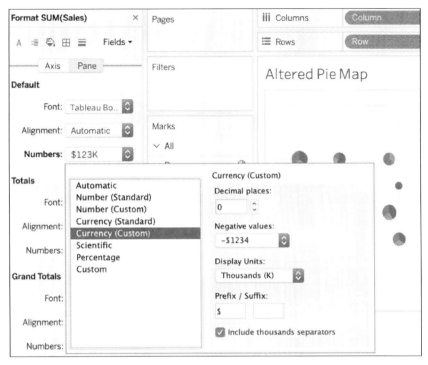

Figure 8.15: Formatting

2. Set **Alignment** to **Middle Center** as shown in the following
    screenshot, so that the numbers are centered over the circles:

Figure 8.16: Alignment

15. In the **Rows** shelf, right-click on the second instance of **Row** and select **Dual Axis**.

16. Right-click on an instance of the **Row** axis and select **Synchronize Axis**.

17. Within the **Row (2)** instance on the **Marks** card, make sure that **Size** exceeds the **Size** of the **Row** instance in the **Marks** card in order to show the pie chart as an outer ring.

18. Within the **Row (2)** and **Row** instances of the **Marks** card, click on the **Color** shelf and select **Edit Colors**. Adjust the color settings as desired so that the color of the overlaying circle (the hole of the donut) can be distinguished from the underlying colors and yet continues to recognize which **Category** sold best. I selected the following:

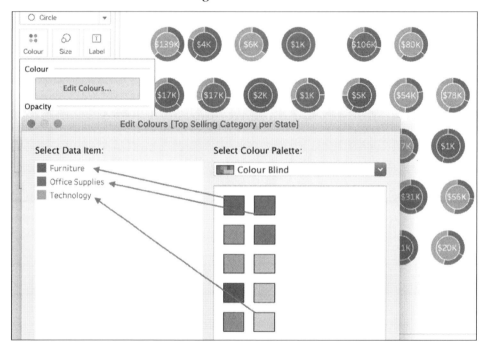

Figure 8.17: Color selection

19. Also within the **Color** shelf, set **Border** to the desired color. I used white. I also used white as the color for **Label**.

20. Right-click on each axis and deselect **Show Header**. Select **Format | Lines** and set **Grid Lines** to **None**. Make other formatting changes as desired:

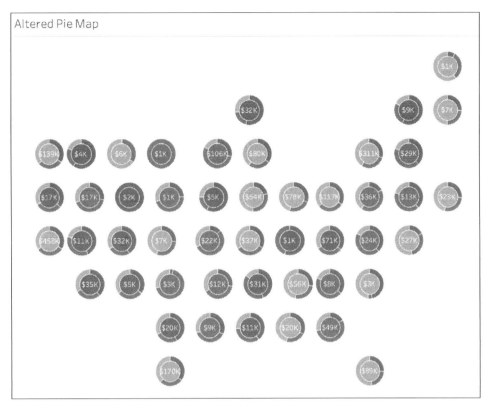

Figure 8.18: Tile grid map

At first glance, the visualization may look peculiar. It's called a **tile grid map** and although it's fairly new to the data visualization scene, it has begun to see usage at media outlets such as NPR. In the right setting, a tile grid map can be advantageous. Let's consider a couple of advantages the preceding exercise gives us.

First, the grid layout in combination with the **Log Sales** calculated field creates a map immediately evident as of the United States, while ensuring that the sizing of the various pie charts changes only moderately from greatest to least. Thus, each slice of each pie is reasonably visible; for example, the district of Columbia sales are as easily visible as California sales.

Second, the end user can clearly see the top-selling category for each state via the color of the inner circle (that is, the hole of the donut). This was accomplished with the LOD calculations. Thanks to the LOD, we were able to differentiate the best-selling category from the other two. Since all three categories live in the same column, you need to use an LOD calculation. You can refer to *Chapter 7, Level of Detail Calculations*, for more details on LOD calculations. The end result is an information-dense visualization that uses pie charts in a practical, intuitive manner.

This section demonstrated some more creative approaches to show data from different angles in the same visualization. Next, we will continue to discuss another advanced visualization, Pareto charts.

Pareto charts

In the late-19th century, an Italian economist named Vilfredo Pareto observed that 80% of the land in Italy was owned by 20% of the people. As he looked around, he observed this mathematical phenomenon in many unexpected places. For example, he noted that 80% of the peas in his garden were produced from 20% of the peapods. As a result, although Vilfredo Pareto is not a household name, the 80/20 rule has found its way into the popular vernacular. In the following exercise, we'll discuss how to build a basic Pareto chart and then how to expand that chart to make it even more useful.

Using Pareto charts

Of course, not every dataset is going to adhere to the 80/20 rule. Accordingly, the following exercise considers loan data from a community bank where 80% of the loan balance is not held by 20% of the bank's customers. Nonetheless, a Pareto chart can still be a very helpful analytical tool.

Take the following steps:

1. Within the workbook associated with this chapter, navigate to the worksheet entitled **Pareto - Basic** and select the **Bank data source**.

2. In the **Data** pane, change **Account #** to **Dimension**. Place **Account #** on the **Columns** shelf and **Current Loan Balance** on the **Rows** shelf.

3. Click on the **Fit** drop-down menu and choose **Entire View**.

4. Right-click on the **Account #** pill and select **Sort**. Set **Sort By** to **Field**, **Sort Order** to **Descending**, **Field Name** to **Current Loan Balance**, and **Aggregation** to **Sum**:

Figure 8.19: Sorting

5. Right-click on **SUM(Current Loan Balance)** located on the **Rows** shelf and select **Add Table Calculation**. Choose the settings as shown in the following screenshot:

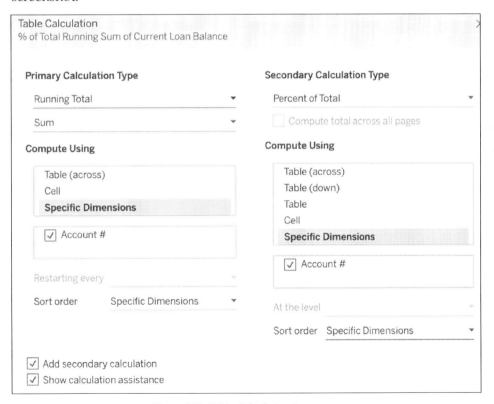

Figure 8.20: Table Calculation I

6. Drag an instance of **Account #** to the **Detail** shelf.

7. Click on the **Color** shelf and set **Border** to **None**.

8. Right-click on the instance of **Account #** that is on the **Columns** shelf and select **Measure | Count (Distinct)**. Note that a single vertical line displays:

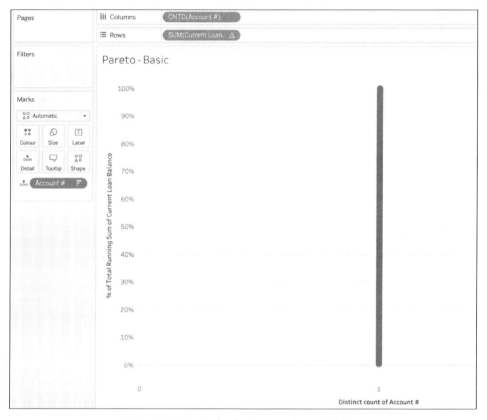

Figure 8.21: Pareto displaying a single vertical line

9. Once again, right-click on the instance of **CNTD(Account #)** on the **Columns** shelf and select **Add Table Calculation**. Configure the settings as shown in the following screenshot:

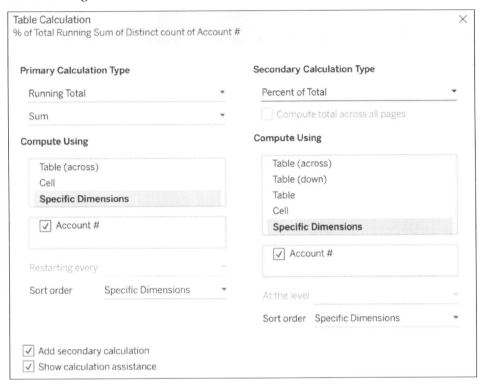

Figure 8.22: Table Calculation II

10. Click the **Analytics** tab in the upper left-hand corner of the screen and perform the following two steps:

    1. Drag **Constant Line** to **Table | SUM(Current Loan Balance)**

2. In the resulting dialog box, select **Constant** and set **Value** to **0.8** as shown in the following screenshot:

Figure 8.23: Constant Line

11. Repeat the previous step with the following differences:

1. Drag **Constant Line** to **Table | CNTD(Account #)**

2. In the resulting dialog box, select **Constant** and set **Value** to **0.2**

12. Drag **Current Loan Balance** to the **Rows** shelf. Place it to the right of the **SUM(Current Loan Balance)** Δ that is currently on the **Rows** shelf. Note that the axis is affected by a single loan with a much larger balance than the other loans:

Figure 8.24: Pareto Basic

13. Right-click on the **Current Loan Balance** axis and select **Edit Axis**. In the resulting dialog box, set **Scale** to **Logarithmic** and close the window. This addresses the problem of the single large loan affecting the axis and thus obscuring the view of the other loans.

14. Within the **Marks** card, select the second instance of **SUM(Current Loan Balance)** and set the mark type to **Bar**:

Figure 8.25: Select Bar

15. Right-click on **SUM(Current Loan Balance)** on the **Rows** shelf and select **Dual Axis**.

16. Right-click on the % **of Total Running Sum of Current Loan Balance** axis and select **Move Marks Card to Front**. Change the colors, tooltips, and formatting as desired:

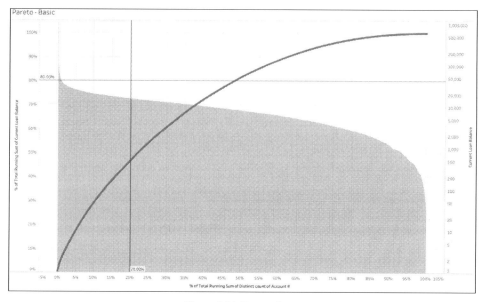

Figure 8.26: Pareto chart

There are positive aspects of this visualization to consider. First, the end user can quickly gain an initial understanding simply by observing both portions of the graph in conjunction with the values on the axes. The y axis on the left, for example, shows the percentage of each current loan in regard to the total amount of current loans, presented in a running sum such that we end up at 100%. The y axis on the right side shows the amount of those same loans. The x axis simply presents us with the unique account IDs or numbers. We can see that in this example, 20% of the accounts hold almost 60% of the loans and around 50% of the accounts hold 80% of the loans. Those are the two cross points of the red line and the two reference lines. Furthermore, the end user can hover the cursor over any part of the curve and see the resulting tooltip.

However, there are a number of ways this visualization could be improved. For example, adding parameters to the two reference lines and rewording the axis labels to be less verbose would be quick ways to add additional value. Therefore, in the next exercise, we'll see if we can go a little beyond the current visualization.

Pareto charts – beyond the basics

In the previous exercise, we had to take a closer look in order to figure out what percentage of accounts account for how many of the loans. The following steps will show us how to create a parameter in order to make it easier for us to spot the intersection:

1. Duplicate the sheet from the previous exercise and name the duplicate **Pareto - Improved**.

2. Remove both reference lines by selecting them and dragging them out of the dashboard.

3. Drag **SUM(Current Loan Balance)** Δ (the table calculation) from the **Rows** shelf to the **Data** pane. When prompted, name the field **Running % of Balance**.

4. Create and display a parameter with the following settings. This parameter will allow us to set any given value between 0 and 100% and we will be able to see that area on the Pareto viz in color:

Figure 8.27: Edit Parameter

5. Right-click on the newly created parameter and select **Show Parameter**.

6. Create the following calculated fields:

Name	Code
Running % of Loans	`RUNNING_SUM(COUNTD([Account #]) /` `TOTAL(COUNTD([Account #])))`

Pareto Split	`IF [Running % of Balance] < [% of Balance] THEN`
	`"Makes up X% of Balance" ELSE "Makes up rest of`
	`Balance" END`

Pareto Split (label)	`IF LOOKUP([Pareto Split], -1) != LOOKUP([Pareto`
	`Split], 0) THEN`
	`MID(STR([Running % of Loans] * 100), 1, 5) + "% of`
	`loans make up " +`
	`MID(STR([% of Balance] * 100), 1, 5) +`
	`"% of balance" END`

7. The configuration that will result in the coloring of a selected area on the Pareto chart needs some extra attention, therefore we created three calculations. With the help of those, we can change the color of parts of the viz and add some explanatory text as well as labels.

8. Select the **All** portion of the **Marks** card.

9. Drag **Pareto Split** to the **Detail** shelf. Click on the drop-down menu to the left of the **Pareto Split** pill on the **Marks** card and select **Color**:

Figure 8.28: Pareto Split to Color

10. Select the **Running % of Balance Δ** portion of the **Marks** card. Set the mark type to **Line**.

11. Drag **Pareto Split (label)** to the **Label** shelf. Note that the expected label does not display:

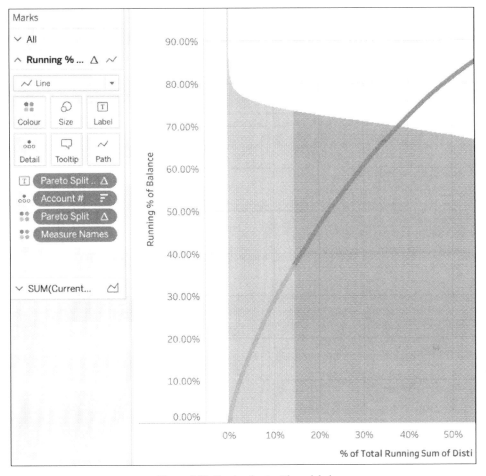

Figure 8.29: Pareto chart with no label

12. To address this, first click on the **Label** shelf and select **Allow labels to overlap other marks**.

13. Then, right-click **Pareto Split (label)** on the **Marks** card and select **Compute Using | Account #**. Now you will see the label:

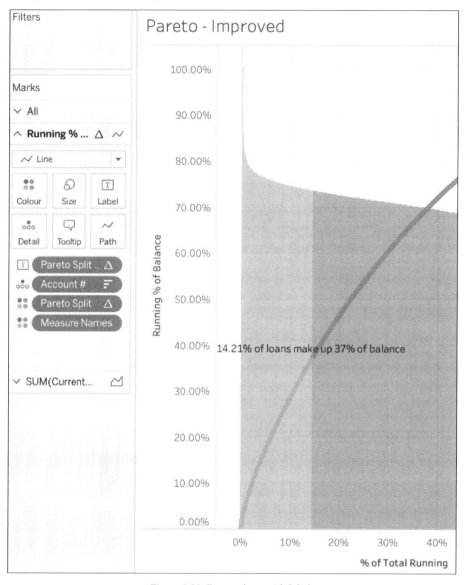

Figure 8.30: Pareto chart with label

14. Click the **Analytics** tab in the upper left-hand corner of the screen and perform the following two steps:

    1. Drag **Reference Line** to **Table | Δ Running % of Balance**:

Figure 8.31: Reference line

    2. In the resulting dialog box, select **% of Balance** from the **Value** drop-down menu and set **Label** to **None**:

Figure 8.32: Reference line II

15. Change the colors, tooltips, and formatting as desired:

Figure 8.33: Pareto improved

As you will see in the screenshot, the end user now has a single parameter to slide (top-right corner) that moves the horizontal reference line on the chart. As the end user moves the reference line, the text updates to display the loan and balance percentages. The colors also update as the end user adjusts the parameter to vertically communicate the percentage of loans under consideration. We were able to achieve this by creating the calculated fields Pareto Split and Pareto Split (Label), which perform calculations on the data in the view in combination with the parameter.

The next section discusses a very powerful and still rarely used feature that will bring your dashboards to the next level! Imagine a street view with houses in Tableau, where by hovering over each house you will be able to see the rent/buy price, the size, and maybe other characteristics. You can't imagine how to achieve this in Tableau? Well, continue reading! We will discuss diverse examples of maps, images, and even games like chess and darts in the next section.

Custom background images

Custom background images in Tableau open a world of potential. Imagine the ability to visualize any space. Possibilities encompass sports, health care, engineering, architecture, interior design, and much, much more. Despite this wealth of potential, background images in Tableau seem to me to be underutilized. Why? Part of the reason is because of the difficulty of generating datasets that can be used with background images.

Like the tile grid map discussed before, background images require a grid layout to pinpoint *x* and *y* coordinates. In the following section, we will address how to use Tableau to create a grid that can be superimposed on an image to instantly identify locations associated with *x* and *y* coordinates and relatively quickly produce datasets that can be accessed by Tableau for visualization purposes.

Creating custom polygons

Geographic areas for which Tableau natively provides polygons include country, state/province, county, and postcode/ZIP code. This means, for example, that a filled map can easily be created for the countries of the world. Simply copy a list of countries and paste that list into Tableau. Next, set the view type in Tableau to **Filled Map** and place the country list on the **Detail** shelf. Tableau will automatically draw polygons for each of those countries.

Furthermore, special mapping needs may arise that require polygons to be drawn for areas that are not typically included on maps. For example, an organization may define sales regions that don't follow usual map boundaries. Lastly, mapping needs may arise for custom images. A Tableau author may import an image of a basketball court or football pitch into Tableau and draw polygons to represent particular parts of the playing area. To create a filled map for each of these examples for which Tableau does not natively provide polygons, custom polygons must be created.

In this section, we will start with the basics by drawing a simple square around the mythical Null Island, which is located at the intersection of the prime meridian and the equator.

Drawing a square around Null Island

We will progress to a more robust example that requires drawing polygons for every city in Texas. There is an option in Tableau that allows an author to **Show Data at Default Position** for unknown locations. Selecting this option will cause Tableau to set latitude and longitude coordinates of 0 (zero) for all unknown locations, thus creating a symbol on the world map 1,600 kilometers off the western coast of Africa. Tableau developers affectionately refer to this area as Null Island.

 Null Island even has its own YouTube video: https://youtu.be/bjvIpI-1w84.

In this exercise, we will draw a square around Null Island:

1. Recreate the following dataset in Excel:

	A	B	C
1	Point	Latitude	Longitude
2	0	-1	-1
3	1	-1	1
4	2	1	1
5	3	1	-1
6	4	-1	-1

2. Copy and paste the dataset into Tableau. By doing so, a new data source called **Clipboard_...** will appear:

Figure 8.34: Null Island coordinates

3. Remove all fields from the worksheet.

4. Convert **Point** to a dimension. This can be accomplished by either right-clicking on **Point** and selecting **Convert to Dimension**, or by dragging it to the dimensions portion of the **Data** pane.

5. Double-click on **Latitude** and **Longitude**. It doesn't matter in which order, Tableau will automatically place longitude on the **Columns** shelf and latitude on the **Rows** shelf.

6. Select **Map | Background Maps | Streets**. You might have to zoom out a bit to see the land line:

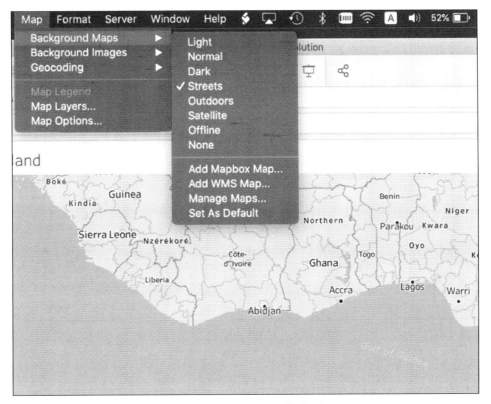

Figure 8.35: Locating Null Island

7. Change the view type to **Line**, and drop **Point** on the **Path** shelf. You should see the following results:

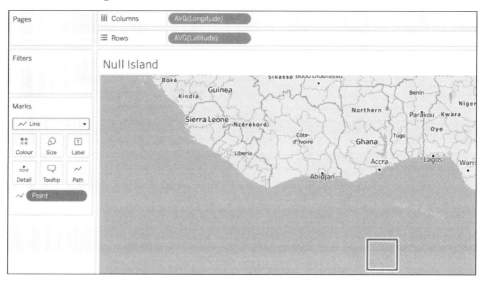

Figure 8.36: Locating Null Island II

8. Go back to your Excel file, switch the rows containing data for points 1 and 2, and copy the data again into Tableau.

9. Follow *Steps 2–7* and observe the resulting image:

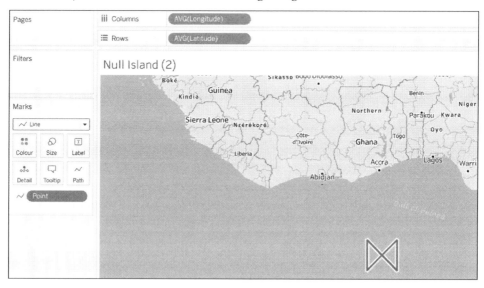

Figure 8.37: Incorrectly delineating Null Island

This interesting but incorrect image occurred because of incorrect point ordering. As a rule of thumb, when determining point order, select an order that would make sense if you were physically drawing the polygon. If you cannot draw the desired polygon on a sheet of paper using a given point order, neither can Tableau.

It is likely that you found completing this exercise in Tableau relatively easy. The challenge is in getting the data right, particularly the polygon points. A useful (and free) tool for generating polygon data can be found at http://powertoolsfortableau.com/tools/drawing-tool. This is one of many tools created by InterWorks that are helpful for addressing common Tableau challenges.

We will use it next to show which books in our library are available and which aren't.

Creating an interactive bookshelf using polygons

I am not very good at drawing myself, but I always loved the fancy polygon backgrounds I saw on Tableau Public, having shapes of all kinds and being able to have Tableau interact with them, color them depending on a measure, or link an action to a specific area. Did you know, for example, that the continents can be reshaped to build the shape of a chicken? Well, Niccolo Cirone made a Tableau dashboard out of it, using polygons: https://www.theinformationlab. co.uk/2016/06/01/polygons-people-polygon-ize-image-tableau/.

Do you want to build fancy dashboards too but your drawing skills are mediocre just like mine? Don't worry! This section will give you the tools to achieve it anyway. InterWorks has developed a tool similar to paint by numbers, the perfect application to build polygons without drawing too much yourself. You can find it here: http://powertoolsfortableau.com/tools/drawing-tool. All you need to do is find an image, upload it to the tool, and start drawing along the lines.

For this exercise, I searched for an image of a bookshelf on the internet. You can do the same and find an image for this exercise or download the image I used, which can be downloaded here: https://github.com/PacktPublishing/Mastering-Tableau-2021.

1. Open the free drawing tool from InterWorks and upload your image.

2. Now start at the edge of one book and click. A red dot will appear. Now go to the next edge of the same book and click again. A line will be drawn along that edge of the book and the coordinates automatically appear in the list at the bottom left:

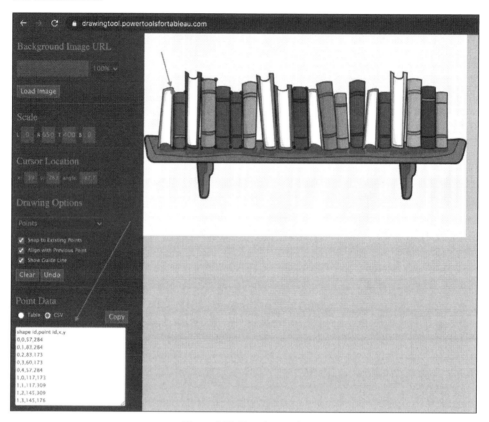

Figure 8.38: Drawing tool

3. The last dot of a book should be on top of the first dot, which will finish the first polygon. The next dot you set somewhere else will get a different shape number and hence can be distinguished as a different shape by Tableau later on. And remember, move along the outside of a book to avoid crossing lines.

4. When you are done outlining the books, copy the **Point Data** values (shown in the bottom left of the preceding screenshot) to Tableau, just like we did with Null Island, by clicking *Ctrl + C* and *Ctrl + V* (use *Command* for Mac).

5. If you have lots of data points, you can also copy the data to Excel first and save the file to be used as a data source in Tableau. I did so and in addition, I added the **Name** and **Available** columns. You can also see that each book has a unique shape ID, the point ID is the order in which you clicked on the screen, and *x* and *y* represent the location on the screen:

	A	B	C	D	E	F
1	shape id	point id	x	y	Name	Available
2	0	0	57	284	The brown book	No
3	0	1	83	284	The brown book	No
4	0	2	83	173	The brown book	No
5	0	3	60	173	The brown book	No
6	0	4	57	284	The brown book	Yes
7	1	0	117	173	The green book	Yes
8	1	1	117	309	The green book	Yes
9	1	2	145	309	The green book	Yes
10	1	3	145	176	The green book	Yes
11	1	4	117	173	The green book	Yes
12	2	0	175	176	The blue book	Yes
13	2	1	175	283	The blue book	Yes
14	2	2	196	283	The blue book	Yes
15	2	3	196	176	The blue book	Yes
16	2	4	175	176	The blue book	Yes
17	3	0	303	176	The purple book	No
18	3	1	303	292	The purple book	No
19	3	2	327	292	The purple book	No
20	3	3	327	173	The purple book	No
21	3	4	303	176	The purple book	No

Figure 8.39: Excel

6. Next, load the data in Tableau and place **X** on **Columns** and **Y** on **Rows**. Can you recognize the bookshelf yet? I only used four books for this exercise:

Figure 8.40: Bookstore

7. Before we can add the image to Tableau, we need the coordinates of the outermost points for the Tableau settings. Simply go back to the drawing tool and hover over the edges. Note down the x and y coordinates for the four edges. Either **x** or **y** should be 0 in each of the corners:

Figure 8.41: Drawing tool

8. Back in Tableau, click on **Map | Background Image** and select a random one. In the following popup, define a name and upload the image you used in the drawing tool. Also fill in the coordinates for the **X** and **Y** fields to represent the edges of the image:

Figure 8.42: Edit Background Image

9. Click on **Options** and select **Always Show Entire Image**. Then close this window:

Figure 8.43: Edit Background Image options

10. Your image should appear on your worksheet now, with matching dots surrounding the books:

Figure 8.44: Bookshelf with dots

11. To create a surrounding line instead of dots, change the mark type to **Line** and place **Shape Id** on **Detail** and **Point Id** on **Path**:

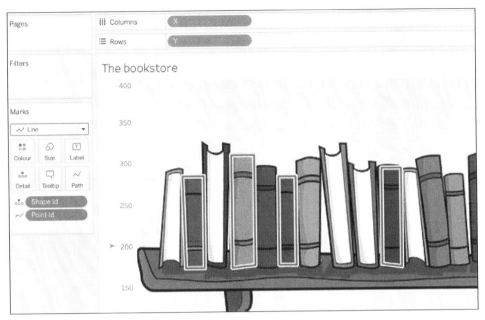

Figure 8.45: Bookshelf with lines

12. To create a polygon, change the mark type to **Polygon** and set **Opacity** in the **Color** shelf to **0%**.

13. In addition, you can add a tooltip with the book name and availability after placing both fields on the **Detail** shelf:

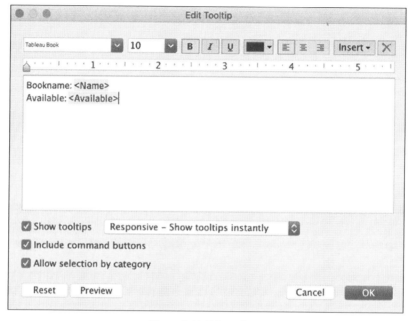

Figure 8.46: Edit tooltip

14. If you now hover over the books, you can see the name as well as the availability:

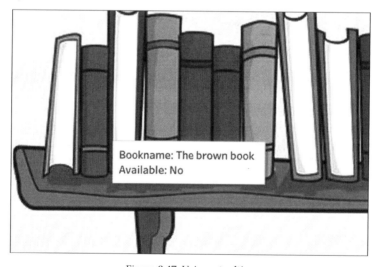

Figure 8.47: Using a tooltip

The best part about polygons is that they fill the whole area. In this example, no matter where you hover or click, the complete back of the book is covered because we drew an area rather than a point or a certain default shape. And this comes with endless options; imagine a big library where every book is a polygon, and you can connect live data to the polygon dataset with the up-to-date availability of any book. Aside from books, you can draw anything. What I have seen most in Tableau are floor plans, supermarket shelves, office layouts, shapes split into parts... polygons really allow you to get creative with your visualizations.

But, if you don't have an image at hand and you want to draw something very specific to your dashboard, you can use paid or free software like Adobe Illustrator Draw, Sketch, Sketsa SVG Editor, Boxy SVG, Gravit Designer, Vecteezy Editor, Vectr, Method Draw, Inkpad, iDesign, Affinity Designer, macSVG, Chartist.js, Plain Pattern, Inkscape, and many others.

Analyzing a game of chess in Tableau

In this exercise, we will use Inkscape. But instead of drawing something in one of the tools, transforming it into polygons, and loading it in Tableau, we will create the code for an SVG file in Tableau, load it in Inkscape to see if it worked, and then transform it into polygons and load the converted version with x and y coordinates back into Tableau to analyze a game of chess. By creating an SVG file yourself, you will be able to recognize which are the x and y coordinates Tableau needs and thus you will always be able to transform SVGs.

Creating an SVG file in Tableau

In this section, we will use Tableau to generate the XML required to construct an SVG file that can be opened with the vector graphic tool Inkscape, which is open source and is thus available free of charge. Visit `inkscape.org` to download the latest version. We will also need the `Chessboard.png` image available on the Packt GitHub page: `https://github.com/PacktPublishing/Mastering-Tableau-2021`. Please download that one as well.

Usually, polygons show their power even more when used in non-linear drawings. Our chessboard, however, is a good example in this case, because we will create the locations used by Tableau ourselves—creating a square is easier than a more complex shape because we can work with increments. Note that a grid with 10 rows and 10 columns is used in the following examples, which of course generates a grid of 100 cells. This will perform satisfactorily in Inkscape. However, if a large cell count is required, a professional graphics tool such as Adobe Illustrator may be required. I tested grids with up to 10,000 cells and found the performance in Inkscape unacceptable—however, the same grids performed adequately in Illustrator.

Creating a grid

The following exercise serves multiple purposes. The first purpose is to demonstrate how to use Tableau to create a grid. This chapter provides another opportunity to use data scaffolding, which was discussed in *Chapter 4*, *All About Data – Joins, Blends, and Data Structures*. The difference is that in that chapter, dates were used for scaffolding purposes whereas in the following section, bins are utilized. Additionally, this exercise requires many table calculations that will help reinforce the lessons learned in *Chapter 5*, *Table Calculations*. Lastly, this exercise makes use of data densification, which was discussed in *Chapter 6*, *All About Data – Data Densification, Cubes, and Big Data*.

To get started, take the following steps:

1. Open a new Tableau workbook and name the first sheet **Header**.

2. Using Excel or a text editor, create a **Records** dataset. The following two-row table represents the **Records** dataset in its entirety:

	A	B	C
1	Records		
2	1		
3	2		
4			
5			
6			
7			

Figure 8.48: Excel

3. Connect Tableau to the Records dataset:

   * For convenience, consider copying the dataset using *Ctrl + C* and pasting it directly in Tableau using *Ctrl + V*.

   * Tableau will likely consider **Records** a measure. Drag **Records** to the **Dimensions** portion of the **Data** pane.

4. Create two parameters. Entitle one Overall Pixel Count and the other Rows Down/Columns Across. The settings for both are as follows:

   * Data type: **Integer**

   * Allowable values: **All**

5. Show both parameters. Set **RowsDown/Columns Across** to `10` and **Overall Pixel Count** to `1,000`:

Figure 8.49: Show parameter

6. Create a calculated field named `Concatenate Header` with the following code:

```
<?xml version="1.0" encoding="utf-8"?><svg version="1.1"
id="Squares"
xmlns="http://www.w3.org/2000/svg"
xmlns:xlink="http://www.w3.org/1999/xlink" x="0px" y="0px"
viewBox="0 0 ' +
STR( [Overall Pixel Count] ) + " " + STR([Overall Pixel Count])+
'"
style="enable-background:new 0 0 '+ STR([Overall Pixel Count]) +
' ' +
STR([Overall Pixel Count]) + ';" xml:space="preserve">
<style type="text/css"> .st0{fill:none;stroke:#000000;stroke-
miterlimit:10;}
</style>
```

 Note that entering line breaks in the Calculated Field dialog box may make the results difficult to extract from Tableau. In other words, remove all line breaks.

7. Now we have created a skeleton or template that will help us create multiple locations in order to draw a grid in Tableau.

8. Place the newly created calculated field on the **Text** shelf.

9. In the toolbar, choose to fit to **Entire View** to view the results; you can see that the parameters fill in **STR([Overall Pixel Count])** from **Concatenate Header**:

Figure 8.50: Concatenate Header

10. Create a new worksheet named **Location Codes**.

11. Create the following calculated fields:

Name	Code
Rows Down/ Columns Across	`[Parameters].[Rows Down/Columns Across]`
Which Column?	`LAST()+1`
Which Row?	`INDEX()`
Grid Size	`[Overall Pixel Count]/LOOKUP([Which Column?],FIRST())`
X	`[Overall Pixel Count] - ([Grid Size] * ([Which Row?]))`
Y	`[Overall Pixel Count] - ([Grid Size] * ([Which Column?]-1))`
Count	`If [Records] = 1 THEN 1 ELSE [Rows Down/Columns Across] END`
Decicount	`If [Records] = 1 THEN 1 ELSE [Rows Down/Columns Across] END`
Location Codes	`Index()`

Concatenate Locations	`'<text transform="matrix(1 0 0 1 ' + STR([X]) + " " + STR([Y])`
	
	`+')">' + STR( [Location Codes] ) + '</text>'`

12. The created calculated fields will be used in the next steps to create a table of values, similar to the table of values that we generated in the drawing tool. Only now, we will do it ourselves and use SVG code instead of longitude and latitude values.

13. Right-click on **Count** and select **Create | Bins**. In the resulting dialog box, set **Size of bins** to **1**:

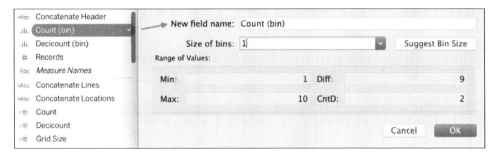

Figure 8.51: Count bin

14. Right-click on **Decicount** and select **Create | Bins**. In the resulting dialog box, set **Size of bins** to **1**:

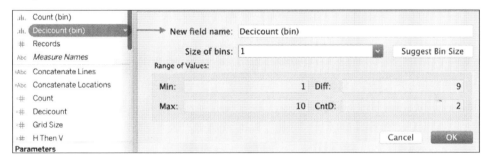

Figure 8.52: Count bin II

15. Place **Count (bin)**, **Decicount (bin)**, **Location Codes**, **X**, and **Y** on the **Rows** shelf. Be sure to place those fields in the order listed:

Figure 8.53: Location Codes worksheet

16. If your fields are green (meaning continuous), right-click on each field on the **Rows** shelf and set it to **Discrete**. Then:

    1. Right-click on **Count (bin)** and **Decicount (bin)** and ensure that **Show Missing Values** is selected

    2. Right-click on **Location Codes** and select **Compute Using | Table (Down)**

    3. Set the **Compute Using** value for **X** to **Count (bin)**

    4. Set the **Compute Using** value for **Y** to **Decicount (bin)**

17. Place **Concatenate Locations** on the **Text** shelf.

18. Right-click on the instance of **Concatenate Locations** you just placed on the **Text** shelf and select **Edit Table Calculations**.

19. At the top of the resulting dialog box, note that there are four options under **Nested Calculations**: **Grid Size**, **Which Column?**, **Which Row?**, and **Location Codes**. Set the **Compute Using** definition for each as follows:

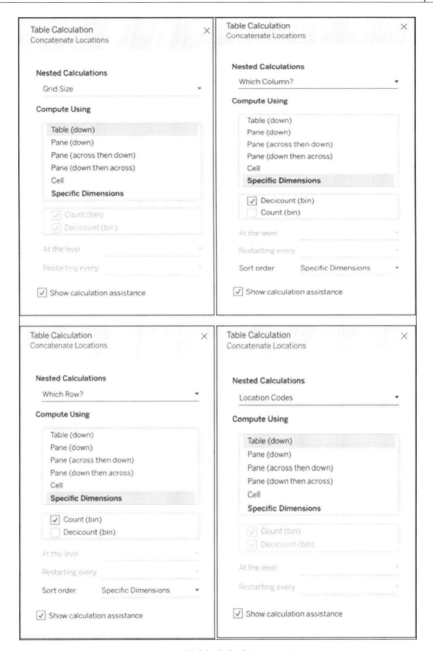

Figure 8.54: Table Calculation settings

20. In the toolbar, choose to fit to **Fit Width** to view the results; you can already see that multiple rows have been created. Those rows will later be used to draw a grid:

Figure 8.55: Fit width

21. Now, create a new worksheet named **Lines**.

22. Create the following calculated fields:

Name	Compute Using Setting
H Then V	Index()
HLine	Last()
VLine	Index()-1
X1	IF [H Then V] = 1 THEN 0 ELSE [Overall Pixel Count] - ([Grid Size] * ([VLine])) END
Y1	IF [H Then V] = 2 THEN 0 ELSE [Overall Pixel Count] - ([Grid Size] * ([VLine])) END
X2	IF [H Then V] = 1 THEN [Overall Pixel Count] ELSE [Overall Pixel Count] - ([Grid Size] * ([VLine])) END
Y2	IF [H Then V] = 2 THEN [Overall Pixel Count] ELSE [Overall Pixel Count] - ([Grid Size] * ([VLine])) END

23. Next, place the following fields on the **Rows** shelf in the following order: **Count (bin)**, **Decicount (bin)**, **H Then V**, **HLine**, **VLine**, **Grid Size**, **X1**, **Y1**, **X2**, and **Y2**. Note that each should be cast as discrete.

24. Right-click on **Count(bin)** and **Decicount(bin)** and set each to **Show Missing Values**.

25. Right-click on each of the remaining fields on the **Rows** shelf and select **Edit Table Calculations**. Set the **Compute Using** definition of each field as shown in the following table:

Name	Nested Calculations	Compute Using Setting
H Then V	N/A	Count (bin)
HLine	N/A	Count (bin)
VLine	N/A	Decicount (bin)
Grid Size	Grid Size	Table (Down)
Grid Size	Which Column?	Decicount (bin)
X1, Y1, X2, Y2	H Then V	Count (bin)
X1, Y1, X2, Y2	Grid Size	Count (bin)
X1, Y1, X2, Y2	Which Column?	Count (bin)
X1, Y1, X2, Y2	VLine	Decicount (bin)

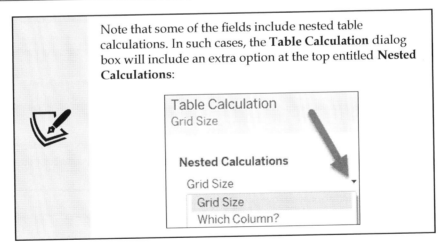

Note that some of the fields include nested table calculations. In such cases, the **Table Calculation** dialog box will include an extra option at the top entitled **Nested Calculations**:

X1, X2, Y1, and Y2 need to be configured for 4 nested calculations. Start by opening the X1 table calculation and then selecting **H Then V** from the **Nested Calculations** dropdown, and set **Compute Using** to **Count (bin)**. Then, in the same window, select **Grid Size** from the dropdown and enter the corresponding **Compute Using** setting. After all 4 dropdowns have been set, continue with X2 and do the same.

26. Filter **H Then V** to display only **1** and **2**:

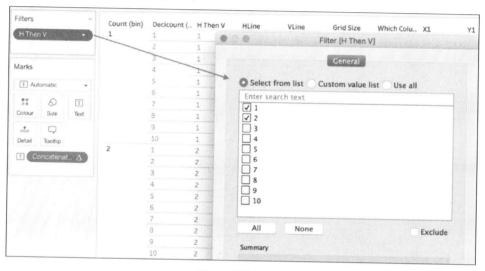

Figure 8.56: Filter

27. Create a calculated field called `Concatenate Lines` with the following code:

```
<line class="st0" x1="' + STR([X1]) + '" y1="' + STR([Y1]) +
'" x2="' + STR( [X2] ) + '" y2="'
+ STR([Y2]) + '"/>
```

28. This calculation will create a new string by including the fields **X1**, **X2** and **Y1**, **Y2**. By doing so we multiply one row of code by as many rows as we want, each with a specific combination of **X1**, **X2**, **Y1**, and **Y2**.

29. Place **Concatenate Lines** on the **Text** shelf. Your worksheet should look as follows:

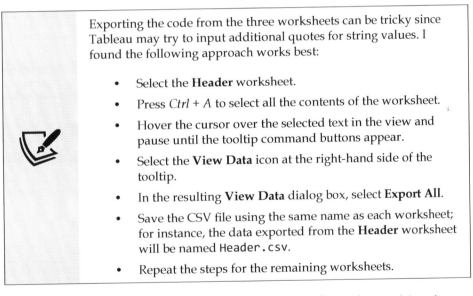

Count (bin)	Decicount (..	H Then V	HLine	VLine	Grid Size	Which Colu..	X1	Y1	X2	Y2		Rows Down/Columns A..
1	1	1	9	0	100	10	0	1,000	1,000	1,000	<.	10
	2	1	9	1	100	10	0	900	1,000	900	<.	
	3	1	9	2	100	10	0	800	1,000	800	<.	Overall Pixel Count
	4	1	9	3	100	10	0	700	1,000	700	<.	1,000
	5	1	9	4	100	10	0	600	1,000	600	<.	
	6	1	9	5	100	10	0	500	1,000	500	<.	
	7	1	9	6	100	10	0	400	1,000	400	<.	
	8	1	9	7	100	10	0	300	1,000	300	<.	
	9	1	9	8	100	10	0	200	1,000	200	<.	
	10	1	9	9	100	10	0	100	1,000	100	<.	
2	1	2	8	0	100	9	1,000	0	1,000	1,000	<.	
	2	2	8	1	100	9	900	0	900	1,000	<.	
	3	2	8	2	100	9	800	0	800	1,000	<.	
	4	2	8	3	100	9	700	0	700	1,000	<.	
	5	2	8	4	100	9	600	0	600	1,000	<.	
	6	2	8	5	100	9	500	0	500	1,000	<.	
	7	2	8	6	100	9	400	0	400	1,000	<.	
	8	2	8	7	100	9	300	0	300	1,000	<.	
	9	2	8	8	100	9	200	0	200	1,000	<.	
	10	2	8	9	100	9	100	0	100	1,000	<.	

Figure 8.57: Concatenate Lines

30. Export the code from the three worksheets just created.

> Exporting the code from the three worksheets can be tricky since Tableau may try to input additional quotes for string values. I found the following approach works best:
>
> - Select the **Header** worksheet.
> - Press *Ctrl + A* to select all the contents of the worksheet.
> - Hover the cursor over the selected text in the view and pause until the tooltip command buttons appear.
> - Select the **View Data** icon at the right-hand side of the tooltip.
> - In the resulting **View Data** dialog box, select **Export All**.
> - Save the CSV file using the same name as each worksheet; for instance, the data exported from the **Header** worksheet will be named Header.csv.
> - Repeat the steps for the remaining worksheets.

31. Open an instance of your favorite text editor and save it as Grid and LocationCodes.svg.

32. Using Excel, copy the data from `Header.csv` and paste it into `Grid and LocationCodes.svg`. Be sure not to include the header information; include only the XML code. For example, in the next screenshot, don't copy row 1, only copy row 2:

Figure 8.58: Excel

33. Using Excel, copy the required data from `Location.csv` and paste it into `Grid and LocationCodes.svg`. The required data only includes the column labeled `Concatenate Locations`. Do not include the other columns or the header. Include only the XML code. For example, in the following screenshot, we only copy column **F**:

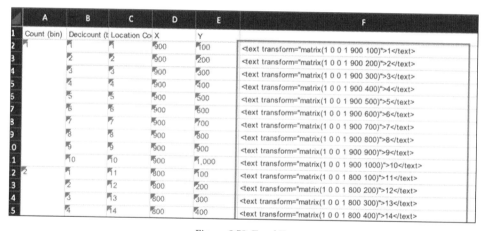

Figure 8.59: Excel II

34. Using Excel, copy the required data from `Lines.csv` and paste it into `Grid and LocationCodes.svg`. Again, the required data only includes the column labeled `Concatenate Lines`. Do not include the other columns or the header, only the XML code.

35. Lastly, complete the SVG file by entering the `</svg>` closing tag. The full code has been added for your convenience on the **Generated SVG Code** tab:

```
<text transform="matrix(1 0 0 1 200 300)">73</text>
<text transform="matrix(1 0 0 1 200 200)">72</text>
<text transform="matrix(1 0 0 1 200 100)">71</text>
<text transform="matrix(1 0 0 1 300 1000)">70</text>
<text transform="matrix(1 0 0 1 300 900)">69</text>
<text transform="matrix(1 0 0 1 300 800)">68</text>
<text transform="matrix(1 0 0 1 300 700)">67</text>
<text transform="matrix(1 0 0 1 300 600)">66</text>
<text transform="matrix(1 0 0 1 300 500)">65</text>
<text transform="matrix(1 0 0 1 300 400)">64</text>
<text transform="matrix(1 0 0 1 300 300)">63</text>
<text transform="matrix(1 0 0 1 300 200)">62</text>
<text transform="matrix(1 0 0 1 300 100)">61</text>
<text transform="matrix(1 0 0 1 400 1000)">60</text>
<text transform="matrix(1 0 0 1 400 900)">59</text>
```

| Null Island (2) | The Bookstore | Lines | Location Codes | Header | ⊞ Generated SVG Code | Chessboard |

Figure 8.60: Full code

36. Now, open the SVG file in Inkscape (https://inkscape.org/) and observe the grid:

Figure 8.61: Inkscape II

If for some reason your code does not create a grid or you rather want to use the version that I created, you can find the SVG file together with all the other datasets on the following GitHub page: https://github.com/PacktPublishing/Mastering-Tableau-2021.

We will cover an example of how to use the grid for a polygon data source in Tableau in the next exercise.

Using a grid to generate a dataset

Skilled chess players will complete a game in about 40 moves. In chess tournaments, data is routinely captured for each game, which provides opportunities for data visualization. In this exercise, we will use data from a chess game to visualize how often each square of a chessboard is occupied:

1. Within the workbook associated with this chapter, navigate to the worksheet entitled **Chessboard**.

2. Download the Chessboard.png pictures from this book's GitHub repository if you haven't done so yet. Open the SVG file created in the previous exercise in Inkscape.

> If you did not complete the previous exercise, you can copy the XML code located on the dashboard entitled **Generated SVG Code** in the solution workbook associated with this chapter. Paste that code in a text editor and save it with an SVG extension, then open the file with Inkscape.

3. Within **Inkscape**, press *Ctrl + A* to select all. Group the selection using *Ctrl + G*.

4. From the **Inkscape** menu, select **Layer | Layers**. The keyboard shortcut is *Shift + Ctrl + L*.

5. Within the **Layers** palette that displays on the right-hand side of the screen, press the + icon to create a layer. Name the layer **Chessboard**. Then, create another layer named **Grid**:

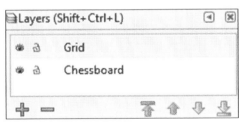

Figure 8.62: Layers

6. Click on any line or number in the view. Right-click on that same line or number and select **Move to layer**. Choose the **Grid** layer.

7. Select **File | Import** and choose the Chessboard.png image.

8. Make sure that the image is placed on the **Chessboard** layer so that the location code numbers are not obscured. Position the chessboard image such that location code 81 is centered over the top left-hand square of the chessboard. Since the chessboard is only composed of 64 squares, it will not encompass all 100 squares the grid provides.

At this point, you can generate a dataset based on how often each location is occupied. For example, you might note that for one game, position 81 was occupied for 40 moves, in which case the player may simply have never moved that rook. However, in another game the position may be occupied for only 10 moves, perhaps indicating the player performed a castle early in the game.

Visualizing a chess game

In this exercise, we will take a look at a dataset generated from a chess game and discover how to visualize the results based on the work done in the previous exercises. The following are the steps:

1. Within the workbook associated with this chapter, navigate to the worksheet entitled **Chessboard** and select the **Chessboard** data source.

> Note: In order to follow the next step, you will need to download the assets associated with this chapter. To do so, simply follow the link to the GitHub repository for this book: https://github.com/PacktPublishing/ Mastering-Tableau-2021.

2. Right-click on the **Chessboard** data source and select **Edit Data Source** in order to examine the dataset.

3. In the dialog box asking **Where is the data file?** steer to the Chessboard.xlsx file provided with the assets associated with this chapter.

4. The table named **Board Grid** contains each location code and the **X** and **Y** coordinates associated with each location code. This dataset was taken from the **Location Codes** worksheet created earlier in this chapter. The table named **Squares Occupied** contains the fields **Location Code** and **Moves Occupied**. **Board Grid** and **Squares Occupied** are connected using a left join on **Location Code**:

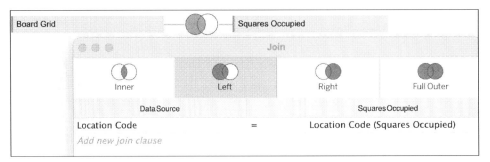

Figure 8.63: Join

5. On the **Chessboard** worksheet, select **Map | Background Images | Chessboard**.

6. In the resulting dialog box, click **Add Image** to add a background image.

7. Fill out the **Add Background Image** dialog box as shown:

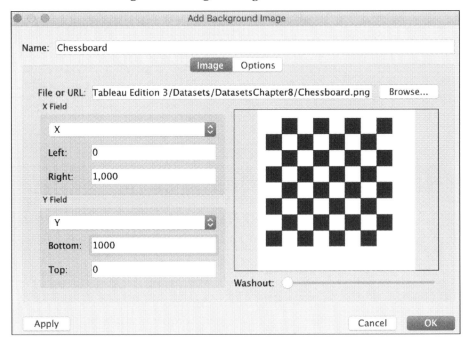

Figure 8.64: Chessboard background image

8. Place the fields **X**, **Y**, and **Location Code** on the **Columns**, **Rows**, and **Detail** shelves respectively, and the **Moves Occupied** field on **Color** and **Size**:

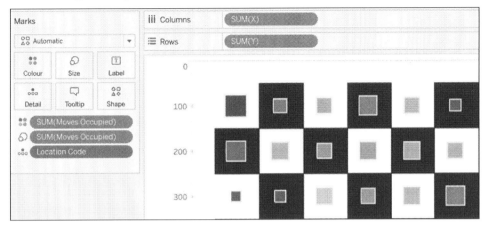

Figure 8.65: Chessboard background image II

9. Right-click on the **X** and **Y** axes and set both to **Fixed** with a **Fixed start** value of 0 and a **Fixed end** value of 875:

Figure 8.66: Fixed end

10. Edit the **Y** axis and set it to **Reversed**. Do not reverse the *x* axis.

 This last step was performed because the data has been structured to mirror the **X** and **Y** coordinate setup that is the default in most graphic tools. In these, the upper left-hand corner is where **X** and **Y** both equal **0**.

11. Adjust **Color**, **Size**, **Shape**, and so on as desired:

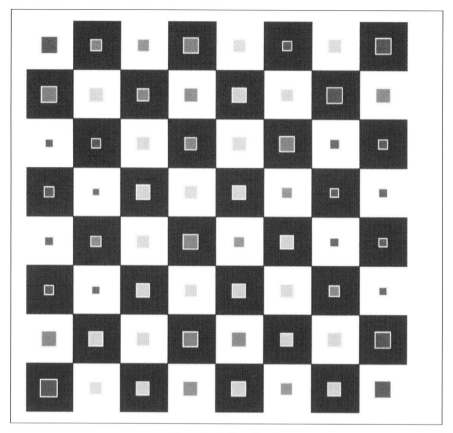

Figure 8.67: Chessboard

In the screenshot, the larger and bluer the square, the more frequently this space was occupied for a move. The smaller and the redder a square, the less frequently it was occupied. By hovering over a field, the amount of occupation will show as well.

To recap, we started off by creating an SVG file. We did so by creating three different code types, Header, Location Codes, and Lines, according to the standards of an SVG file. We then copied those three code pieces into a text editor program and saved it as an SVG file. Then we downloaded the Inkscape application and opened the SVG file to check and see the result of our work, a 10-by-10 square field.

We added an image of a chessboard to Inkscape and aligned the two. Now we could see which square number will be associated with which chessboard field. Just like in the bookshelf example, it is necessary to identify the shape ID, that is, the chessboard field ID. Based on the chessboard field IDs, we were able to generate a second dataset containing the number of moves for which a field was occupied. By joining the Board Grid dataset with the Occupied Moves dataset, we got ourselves a use case. We added a background image of a chessboard to Tableau and on top of it, we drew squares and colored as well as sized them depending on the number of moves those fields were occupied for during the chess games. The numbers are very specific to each game, of course, but by collecting the data for multiple games, we would be able to visually analyze chess strategies and maybe even tell who the better player was. If you like chess, feel free to try it out and compare the different visual results per game, or see whether you usually end up with the same pattern, and is this also true for your opponent?

Talking about games, in the next exercise, we will visualize a dartboard. This exercise will be shorter than the chess one but also advanced. Follow along with the steps and learn more about polygons.

Creating polygons on a background image

Utilizing shapes on specific points of a visualization was sufficient for the previous exercise, but sometimes it may be advantageous to use polygons to outline shapes. In this section, we will utilize polygons on a background image and unlike with the books, we will fill out the areas such that the background image is not needed (as much) anymore.

The following are the steps:

1. Within the workbook associated with this chapter, navigate to the worksheet entitled **Dashboard - Polygon** and select the **DartBoard_W_Polygons** data source.

 If you have not already done so when completing the previous exercise, download the images provided on GitHub. Unzip the contents to a directory of your choosing.

2. Select **Map | Background Images | Dartboard_W_Polygons**. In the **Background Images** dialog box, select **Add Image**. Fill out the dialog box as shown:

Figure 8.68: Dartboard background image

3. Create a parameter with the following configuration:

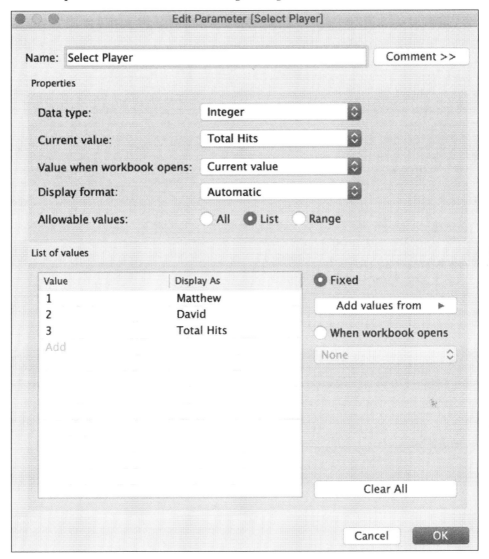

Figure 8.69: Parameter

4. This parameter will be used to either switch between player 1: **Matthew** and player 2: **David** or will show the dart hits of both.

5. Display the parameter created in the previous step by right-clicking on it at the bottom of the **Data** pane and selecting **Show Parameter Control**.

6. Create a calculated field called Total Hits with the following code:

   ```
   [David]+[Matthew]
   ```

7. Then, create a calculated field called Case with the following code:

   ```
   CASE [Select Player]
   WHEN 1 THEN SUM([Matthew])
   WHEN 2 THEN SUM([David])
   WHEN 3 THEN SUM([Total Hits])
   END
   ```

8. Set the **Marks** card to **Polygon**.

9. Survey the **Data** pane to ensure that **Point** and **Shape** are both dimensions (blue color). The other fields are measures:

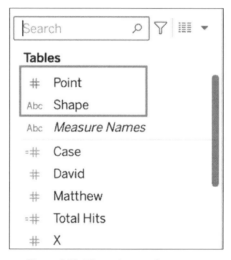

Figure 8.70: Dimensions and measures

10. Place the fields **X**, **Y**, **Point**, **Shape**, and **Case** on their respective shelves:

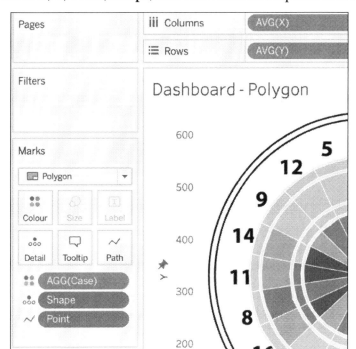

Figure 8.71: Dartboard polygon

11. Right-click on each axis and set the **Range** from **0** to **650**:

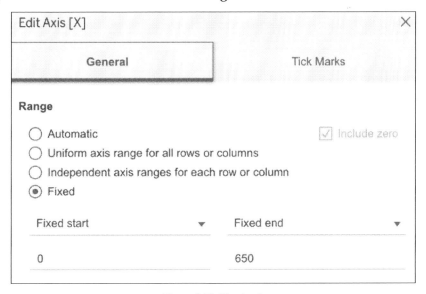

Figure 8.72: Fixed axis

12. Click on the **Color** shelf and select **Edit Colors**. Adjust the color as desired. One possibility is represented in the following screenshot:

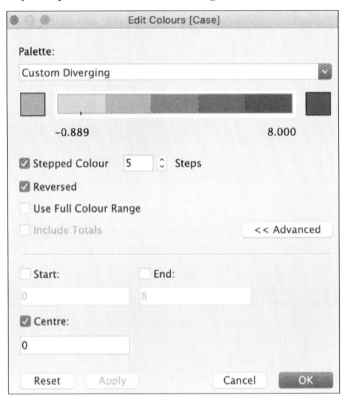

Figure 8.73: Custom Diverging

Your final worksheet should look like the following:

Figure 8.74: Final dartboard polygon

The final dashboard shows a dartboard with different colors. Gray color means that this area has not been hit during the game whereas the redder the color, the more often this field has been hit. By using the parameter, you can compare Matthew's score with David's, or you can show the total hits, like in the preceding screenshot.

It is likely that you found completing this exercise in Tableau relatively easy. The challenge is in getting the data right, particularly the polygon points. A useful (and free) tool for generating polygon data can be found at `http://powertoolsfortableau.com/tools/drawing-tool`. This is one of many tools created by InterWorks that are helpful for addressing common Tableau challenges. We used it in the bookshelf exercise.

You may have noticed that the curved sections of the polygons in this exercise aren't quite perfect. Look, for example, at the triple ring and double ring areas surrounding the bullseye; you can see that the area is not 100% even. That's simply the nature of working with points on a Cartesian grid in Tableau. This means that Tableau is based on a grid structure, so every curve we draw will still be many small lines connecting dots on a grid layout. The more dots you have and the shorter the lines between the dots, the more likely you will draw curves evenly. But if you followed along with the bookshelf exercise, you can imagine that a lot of effort has to go into such a background image. Nevertheless, I believe that polygons are absolutely worth it.

The next topic is a little bit different from the rest of this chapter. Have you heard about Tableau extensions yet? Extensions can help you get functionality into your dashboard that Tableau does not offer by default. Interested? Continue with the next section!

Tableau extensions

Another very helpful tool when it comes to going "beyond the basic chart types" is the Tableau Extensions API, which was released to the public in 2018. What does the Extensions API do? Basically, it allows you to use third-party tools directly in Tableau. Some selected extensions are available here: `https://extensiongallery.tableau.com`, and the list is always growing.

Please be aware that Tableau does not provide support or guarantees/security measures for extensions. Those APIs are built by external parties and should be treated as such. Check with your IT security team first if you want to use them at work.

Let's have a look at one example from Infotopics—a Sankey chart extension.

Using Show me More

In the associated workbook, create a new sheet called **Show me More** and select the **Coffee Chain** dataset. Now please reproduce the following worksheet layout by adding **Type** to **Columns**, **Product Type** to **Rows**, and **Profit** to the **Text** shelf:

Figure 8.75: Show me More

We want to utilize a Sankey chart for this worksheet, which is a kind of flow chart that shows based on the size of flow-lines how much of a given measure and a given dimension flows into a second given dimension. In this case, we want to know how much **Profit** of **Regular** type products comes from **Coffee**, **Espresso**, **Herbal Tea**, or **Tea**, and how much **Profit** can be associated with the **Decaf** types?

Say you know how to build a Sankey chart using calculated fields, but it is time-consuming. Instead, there is an **extension** to do so. The following are the steps required to use the extension and ultimately save us time when building a Sankey chart:

1. In the associated workbook, open a **Dashboard** tab.

2. Drag the **Show me More** sheet onto the dashboard. Now also drag the **Extension** object onto the dashboard:

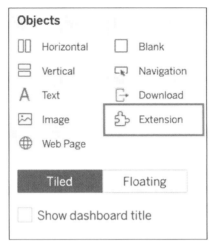

Figure 8.76: Extension

3. From Tableau 2021.1, you will see the following pop-up window:

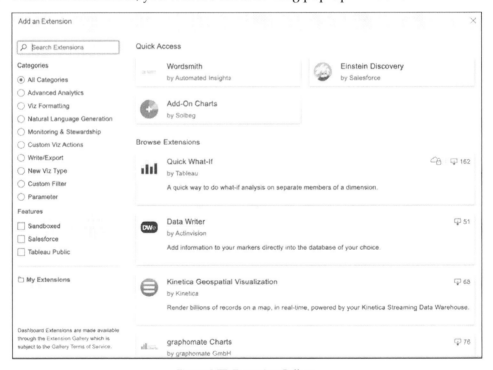

Figure 8.77: Extension Gallery

4. In the **Extension Gallery** search for the **Show Me More** extension. Click on it and select **Add to Dashboard** in the next screen:

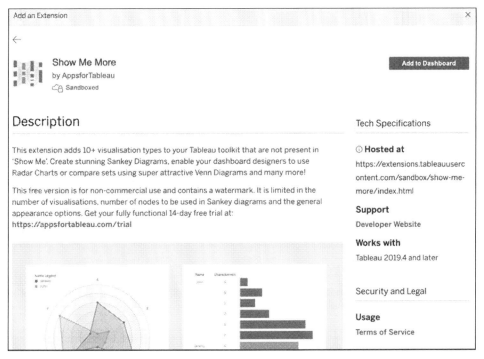

Figure 8.78: Show Me More

5. Then, select the **Show me More** sheet and the **Sankey Diagram** visualization:

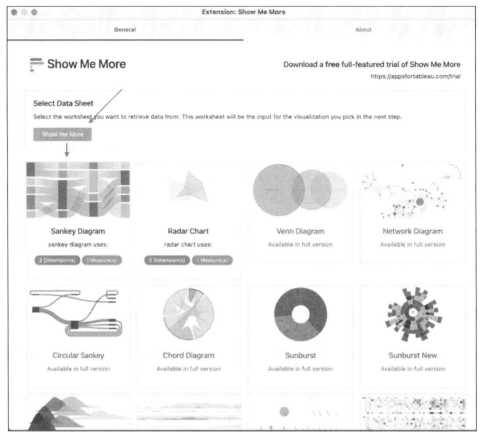

Figure 8.79: Show Me More II

6. After selecting the Sankey diagram, configure the variables as follows:

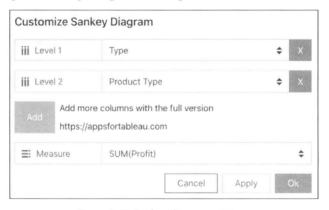

Figure 8.80: Sankey diagram settings

7. Hit the **Ok** button and voilà, you have your Sankey diagram:

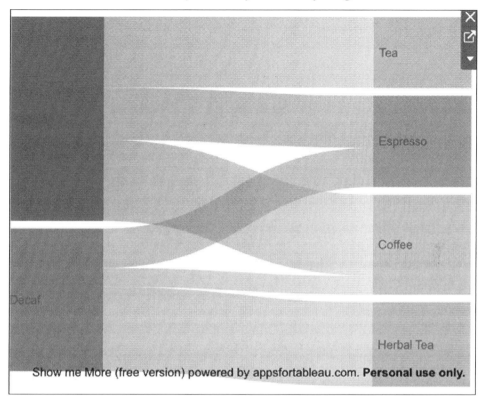

Figure 8.81: Sankey diagram

Besides this Sankey chart, I would highly recommend you have a look at the extensions library. There are many extensions for multiple different use cases; some are free, some have to be paid for, but you can also build your own. It is worth taking a look! The next section will be dedicated to a special extension, which is the most advertised new feature in Tableau 2021.1, **Einstein Discovery**.

Einstein Discovery

We have discussed extensions in the previous section, however, one deserves a little extra attention. But before we continue, a bit of a backstory. In August 2019 Tableau was acquired by Salesforce. Probably most of you know Salesforce and even work with it, but for all other readers, Salesforce is a cloud-native **Customer Relationship Management (CRM)** tool. Next to that, the company also developed an analytics portion, which allows Salesforce users to analyze data from the CRM system and other data sources.

Connecting Salesforce to Tableau was possible long before the acquisition, but what's new in Tableau 2021.1 is that the analytics piece of Salesforce is available to be called into Tableau, as an extension and in calculated fields. The Tableau community is very excited about this feature because of the built-in machine learning capability and real-time prediction power. This piece of software is called Einstein Discovery.

 In order to make use of Einstein Discovery you need a Salesforce license and more specifically, the analytics license for Salesforce. The licensing details can be found here: `https://www.salesforce.com/editions-pricing/crm-analytics/`.

Now, to give you an idea what Einstein Discovery can do for you, I will walk you through an imaginary use-case. On a supply chain data dashboard you discover that shipment time can be improved, but you don't know which factors cause the delays. In this instance, you might decide to use Einstein Discovery for its analysis capabilities.

First, you would drag the **Extensions** object on to the dashboard, just like we did with the **Show me More** extension. You would then select the **Einstein Discovery** item, at which point a browser window will open to ask you to log in to Salesforce. After you have done so, you can select which model you want to use on your Tableau dashboard. The model (for example, a machine learning model) has to be prepared in Salesforce beforehand. Then, Einstein Discovery will be a part of your dashboard, and your worksheet will show the output from the model running in the background on Salesforce. In our example, the model will more easily be able to find the relevant variables used on your dashboard that are best suited for predicting the time of delivery and will recommend actions you can take to improve the shipment time.

 A video of the described use-case and another use-case can be viewed under: `https://youtu.be/dMWuy6mVE_o`.

Alternatively, you can call a Salesforce model directly in a calculated field. How this works is described here: `https://help.tableau.com/current/pro/desktop/en-us/einstein_discovery_predictions.htm`.

If you want to try out these new features, there is a way to test out the new Einstein capabilities if you do not have a Salesforce license yet. It is a longer process to set up but for those of you who do want to try, please check this video for assistance: `https://youtu.be/ZReSwXK0reo`.

Those are the cornerstones of the bespoke new Einstein features in Tableau 2021.1. Going into detail on the functionality of the Salesforce platform is unfortunately out of the scope of this book, but if you have Salesforce in place, I would most certainly set up the connection and test out running some models. If you do not use Salesforce, the licensing might change over time, so hopefully we can all run those models soon. For the time being, don't worry, as we will discuss machine learning model integration in *Chapter 15, Programming Tool Integration*.

Summary

We began this chapter by considering how to tweak popular visualization types. Specifically, we fine-tuned a bullet graph, considered a very different approach for using pie charts in mapping, and ended by tweaking a Pareto chart. Next, we turned our attention to custom background images, where we considered how to build a grid using XML to generate an SVG file to expedite generating data to use with background images. Then, we completed the chapter by building polygons on a background image and had a quick excursion into the world of Tableau extensions and Einstein Discovery.

There are too many options to put them all in this book but since you are an expert in replicating by now, I added more sheets with other visualizations to the solutions workbook for you to play with. You will find sheets with bar charts, stacked bar charts, diverging stacked bar charts, crosstabs, highlight tables, discrete highlight tables, trend lines, area charts, spark lines, combo charts, dual axis, histograms, box and whisker plots, scatterplots, filled maps, symbol maps, treemaps, tree bar charts, Gantt charts, KPI charts, funnel charts, jittered distribution, calendar, bump charts, slopegraphs, waterfall, target, and bar in bar charts. Always make sure to use the chart that is most suitable for your data and will add value to the story you are trying to tell. If you still need a little bit of help with deciding on the appropriate visualization technique, I advise you to look at the following dashboard published on Tableau Public: `https://public.tableau.com/en-us/gallery/visual-vocabulary`. This dashboard was made to show you which visualization type to use depending on the data you have.

In the next chapter, we will turn our attention to mapping, where we will consider how to extend Tableau's native mapping capabilities without ever leaving the interface, as well as how to extend Tableau's mapping capabilities with other technology.

9
Mapping

When I conduct Tableau classes and workshops for people who are using Tableau for the first time, I find that demonstrating **mapping** is always a big hit, sometimes resulting in murmurs of appreciation and surprise. People have told me on multiple occasions that Tableau's mapping capability was the key feature that caused them to take notice of and consider Tableau's offerings more seriously. Tableau's out-of-the-box mapping capabilities are powerful and flexible. You may be surprised at how much you can accomplish without ever leaving the user interface. But these out-of-the-box capabilities are just the tip of the iceberg. With proper guidance (which I will attempt to provide in this chapter), you can expand beyond the native mapping functionality and explore techniques that will greatly enhance your workbooks' functionality and aesthetics.

In this chapter, we will discuss the following topics:

- Extending Tableau's mapping capabilities without leaving Tableau
- Creating custom polygons
- Heatmaps
- Dual axes and map layering
- Extending Tableau mapping with other technology
- Swapping maps

The default mapping capability of Tableau already is a big selling point. Take any city, region, country, or other geographical location, place it on a Tableau worksheet, and you get a nice map; add a measure like **Sales** to the **Colour** shelf and your map colors change according to sales figures. In the following first section, we will go a step further and enhance this capability with the less obvious features Tableau has to offer, like measuring distances on a map and plotting additional data (for example, weather data) in the background.

Extending Tableau's mapping capabilities without leaving Tableau

In our everyday lives, a map can be helpful for better understanding the world around us. For instance, maps are often used on websites, television, or in printed media to present demographic information. In such instances, the mapping requirement is **static** since the immediate goal does not require movement. Some businesses only have static mapping requirements—for example, a retail chain might create a visualization that includes a map to better understand sales performance in a given region. In such cases, movement between locations is not a direct need.

Often, however, a map is needed to navigate from point A to point B. This kind of mapping requirement is more complicated, because it encompasses static needs (what restaurant is nearby?), but must also deliver additional information, such as routes and distances (how can I get to that restaurant?). These **dynamic** mapping needs assume that movement is *required* to fulfill a demand. Many businesses need to understand routes and mileages, that is, how to get from point A to point B and the distances involved. These dynamic mapping requirements can vary greatly but most of these needs share at least two things in common: routes and distances.

In the following exercise, we will consider flight routes and associated distances in Australia. Specifically, we will cover how to extract longitude and latitude numbers from Tableau and use that information in conjunction with trigonometry to calculate the mileage between various points. Along the way, we will utilize data blending, table calculations, mapping, and **Level of Detail** (LOD) calculations for a robust exercise that touches on many advanced features.

Please take the following steps:

1. Navigate to `https://public.tableau.com/profile/marleen.meier` to locate and download the workbook associated with this chapter.

2. Open the workbook and navigate to the **Map** worksheet.

3. Select **Transit Data** in the **Data** pane and double-click on **City**, then change **City** from **Detail** to **Text** in the **Marks** card.

4. In the following screenshot, note that the cities Mackay and Brisbane are the only cities that display. This issue depends on your country setting, but the following is an example of an issue that may be encountered. If you see it, click on **14 unknown**:

Figure 9.1: Australia

 Caveat: If you are in the **United States**, Melbourne in Florida will display. If you are in another country, you may get different results.

5. Select **Edit Locations...**:

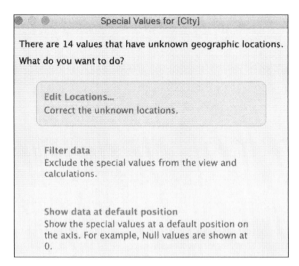

Figure 9.2: Edit Locations…

6. Change **Country/Region** to **Fixed | Australia**:

Figure 9.3: Select Australia

Australia is now displayed on the map:

Figure 9.4: Australia

7. Navigate to the **Miles** worksheet and place the **Trip ID** and **City** fields on the **Rows** shelf, and **Latitude (generated)** and **Longitude (generated)** on the **Text** shelf, as seen in the following screenshot:

Trip ID	City	
1	CANBERRA	-35.28 149.13
	MELBOURNE	-37.81 144.96
2	ADELAIDE	-34.93 138.60
	SYDNEY	-33.87 151.21
3	MELBOURNE	-37.81 144.96
	PERTH	-31.95 115.86
4	MELBOURNE	-37.81 144.96
	PERTH	-31.95 115.86

Figure 9.5: Distances

Your screen should look like the preceding screenshot. Note that the crosstab is pretty cluttered. Ideally, **Latitude** and **Longitude** should display in separate columns. Unfortunately, we can't do this with the generated latitude and longitude because, although they are listed under the **Measures** portion of the **Data** pane, Tableau doesn't treat them as measures. In order to complete the exercise, we will need to be able to access the latitude and longitude coordinates from a separate data source.

8. To do this, begin by clicking on the **Map** worksheet tab.

9. Right-click on the visualization and select **View Data**. Copy all the data in the **Summary** tab of the resulting dialog box, by selecting every cell and clicking **Copy**.

10. Close the dialog box and press *Ctrl + V* (*Command + V* for Mac) to create a new dataset in Tableau. Rename the resulting dataset (now called **Clipboard_[timestamp]**) to **Lat Long**. Also name the worksheet **Lat Long**.

11. In the **Lat Long** worksheet, rename **Latitude (generated)** and **Longitude (generated)** to **Lat** and **Long**.

12. Return to the **Miles** worksheet and, within the **Transit Data** data source, create two calculated fields: one called **LAT**, containing the code AVG([Lat Long].[Lat]), and one called **LONG**, containing the code AVG([Lat Long].[Long]).

13. Remove **Latitude (generated)** and **Longitude (generated)** from **Text** on the **Marks** card.

14. Place **Measure Names** on the **Columns** shelf and the **Filter** shelf and select **Lat** and **Long**. Also, place **Measure Values** on the **Text** shelf. Now, we have the ability to treat latitude and longitude as true measures.

15. Create two more calculated fields: one called **Lookup Lat**, containing the code Lookup(Lat,-1), and one called **Lookup Long**, containing the code Lookup(Long, -1). Place the two newly created calculated fields on the **Measure Values** shelf.

16. Create a calculated field named **Great Circle Distance Formula** with the following code:

```
3959 * ACOS (
SIN(RADIANS([Lat])) * SIN(RADIANS([Lookup Lat]))+
COS(RADIANS([Lat])) * COS(RADIANS([Lookup Lat])) *
COS(RADIANS([Lookup Long]) - RADIANS([Long]))
)
```

For kilometers, change 3959 to 6378. This number represents the radius of the Earth and it needs to be updated from miles to kilometers.

17. Place the newly created calculated field **Great Circle Distance Formula** on the **Measure Values** shelf.

18. Change the calculation for **Great Circle Distance Formula** so that it computes using **City** by clicking on the field itself and selecting **Compute Using: City**.

19. Adjust the following calculations accordingly:

Name	Code
Lookup Lat	IFNULL(LOOKUP(Lat,-1), LOOKUP(Lat,1))
Lookup Long	IFNULL(LOOKUP(Long,-1), LOOKUP(Long,1))

20. Select the **Map** worksheet and set the **Marks** type to **Line**.

21. Place **Trip ID** on the **Detail** shelf.

22. Drag **City** to the bottom of the **Marks** card view.

23. Place the **Great Circle Distance Formula** field on the **Tooltip** shelf. Double-check that it is still set to **Compute Using: City**:

Figure 9.6: Australia distances

24. Create two more calculated fields, one called **Source City**, containing the following code:

```
{ FIXED [Trip ID]:MIN(IF [Dest/Orig]='Source' THEN City END)}
```

The second calculated field should be called **Destination City** and contain the following code:

```
{ FIXED [Trip ID]:MIN(IF [Dest/Orig]='Destination' THEN City END)}
```

25. Use the newly created calculated fields to format as desired. In particular, notice that in the following screenshot, **Source City** is on the **Colour** shelf and **Destination City** is used on the **Tooltip** shelf:

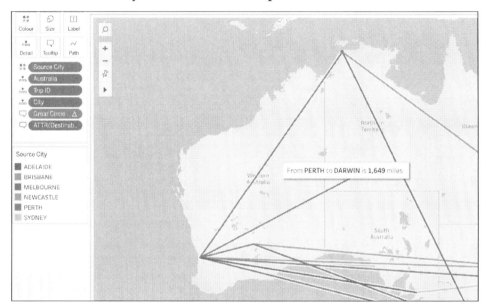

Figure 9.7: Flights

To sum up what we have done here, initially we added a dataset to Tableau. We then needed to copy the latitudes and longitudes per city out of the workbook in order to create a second data source, which we then used as a blend to look up latitude and longitude values. With the help of LOD calculations, we could identify the source and destination cities and lastly, we were able to measure the distance between cities by using the so-called great circle formula. Each color in the viz represents a starting city; for example, all green lines measure distances from Perth to other cities. By hovering over a line, the source and destination city, as well as the distance measured in miles (or kilometers), will show.

If you wanted to analyze shipment routes or any other distances between two points, you now know exactly how to visualize this kind of data in Tableau. Another, similar viz can be seen at the following address, which is definitely worth checking out (try to replicate it!): `https://www.tableau.com/solutions/workbook/big-data-more-common-now-ever`.

In the next section, we will discuss Tableau's map and polygon functionalities.

Creating custom polygons

Geographic areas for which Tableau natively provides polygons include worldwide airport codes, cities, countries, regions, territories, states, provinces, and some postcodes and second-level administrative districts (county-equivalents): U.S. area codes, **Core-Based Statistical Areas** (**CBSA**), **Metropolitan Statistical Areas** (**MSA**), congressional districts, and ZIP codes. This means, for example, that a filled map can easily be created for the countries of the world. Simply copy a list of the world's countries (*Ctrl + C*) and paste that list into Tableau by pressing *Ctrl + V* while your mouse is located on an empty worksheet in Tableau Desktop. A new data source will be added at the top right under **Data**. Next, set the **View** type in Tableau to **Filled Map** and place the country list on the **Detail** shelf. Tableau will automatically draw polygons for each of those data points:

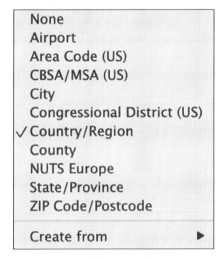

Figure 9.8: Native polygons

There are some geographic types for which Tableau will not automatically provide polygons. These include telephone area codes. For these geographic types, Tableau will draw a symbol map but not a filled map, like so:

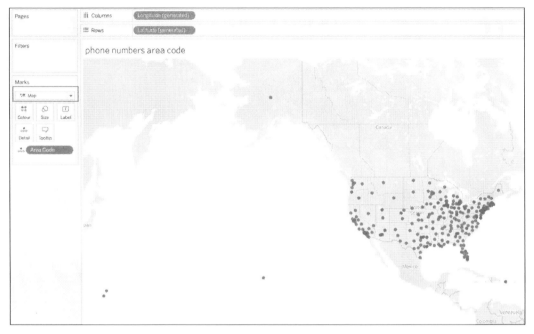

Figure 9.9: Filled map failed

Even though the filled map **Marks** type is chosen, Tableau is not able to fill the map because the outlines of those areas are unknown to Tableau. Furthermore, special mapping needs may arise that require polygons to be drawn for areas that are not typically included on maps. For example, an organization may define sales regions that don't follow usual map boundaries. Or, a Tableau author may import an image of a basketball court or football pitch into Tableau and draw polygons to represent particular parts of the playing area. An alternative, which we discussed in more detail in *Chapter 8, Beyond the Basic Chart Types*, could be mapping bookshelves in a store.

But other than drawing polygons yourself, there are also file types that support drawing polygons. One of those file types is .shp. In the next exercise, we will make use of such a file and create polygons for Texas.

Polygons for Texas

We got to know polygons in *Chapter 8*, *Beyond the Basic Chart Types*, already. We even drew them ourselves. But other than drawing polygons, in some cases, Tableau can create them. For example, Tableau natively provides polygons for several shape files. In the next exercise, we will use a `.shp` file to show the population of Texas as polygons on a map of Texas:

1. Open the **Texas Department of Transportation** page: `https://gis-txdot. opendata.arcgis.com/datasets/txdot-city-boundaries`.

2. Use the **Download** dropdown and download **Shapefile**:

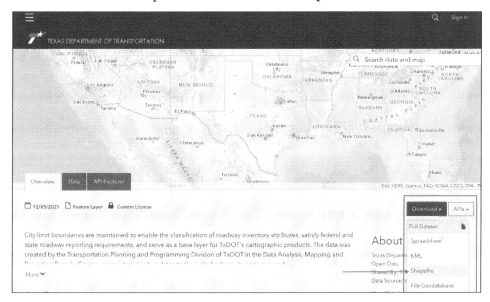

Figure 9.10: Texas data

In your download directory, you should find multiple files:

Figure 9.11: Texas city boundaries

If you were to open a `.shp` file in a text editor, you would see the following:

Figure 9.12: .shp in a text editor

3. Luckily, Tableau has native capabilities to read `.shp` files. In the workbook associated with this chapter, navigate to the **Texas_Cities** worksheet and select **Data** | **New Data Source** | **Text File**.

4. Navigate to your download directory or the path where you saved the Texas shape files and select the `.shp` file:

Figure 9.13: Loading spatial file

5. In the next screenshot, you can see how Tableau was able to read the `.shp` file and how it created an additional field called **Geometry** that indicates that we are looking at polygons and multipolygons in this file:

Figure 9.14: Geometry

6. Open a new worksheet and drag **Geometry** onto the empty canvas:

Figure 9.15: Adding geometry

7. And look at that! Tableau created polygons around areas in Texas right away:

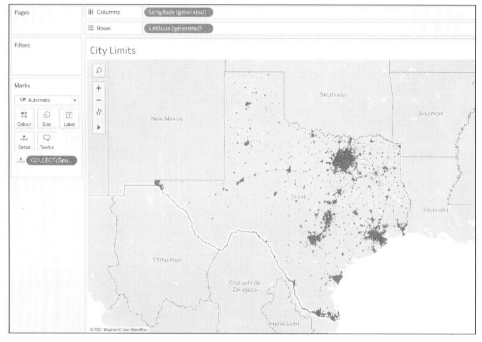

Figure 9.16: Texas polygons

8. Feel free to adjust the formatting via **Map | Background Maps | Dark**.

9. Put the **City Nm** field on **Detail** and **Pop2010** on **Colour** in the **Marks** card. (The color used in *Figure 9.17* is **Temperature Diverging**.)

10. Your dashboard should look as follows:

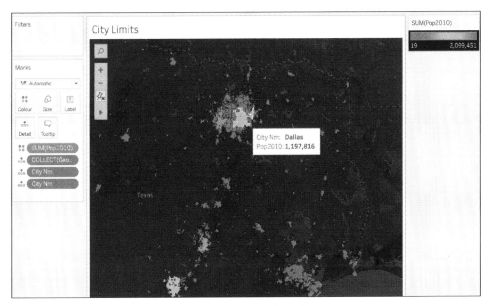

Figure 9.17: Texas city boundaries

You can see that we have a nice dark map now with polygons on top. The polygons define the area per city name (using the field **City Nm**) as published by the government of Texas. By placing the measure of the population in 2010 (using the field **Pop2010**) on the **Colour** shelf, we can also see that the areas with red polygons had the highest number of inhabitants in 2010 and dark green the least.

You might not like the polygons or maybe you are wondering if a spatial file like a .shp will only allow you to use polygons. Luckily, the answer is we can change the map, no matter whether it's a spatial file or not. I really like heatmaps to display geographical density, so let's use them in the next section.

Heatmaps

I want to share a feature with you that was part of an earlier Tableau release and has proven to be very useful when working with geographical data. It is the mark type **Density** with which you can create heatmaps. This new feature is not limited to maps; you can also use it for any other type of chart. However, it is most efficient for dense data where patterns cannot be spotted easily.

The following steps will illustrate an example of creating a **heatmap**:

1. Open the **Citylimits** tab in the workbook related to this chapter. If you did not complete the previous exercise, please open the **Citylimits** tab from the solutions workbook of this chapter.

2. Duplicate the worksheet, and call it **City Limits (2)**.

3. Set the **Marks** card type to **Density**:

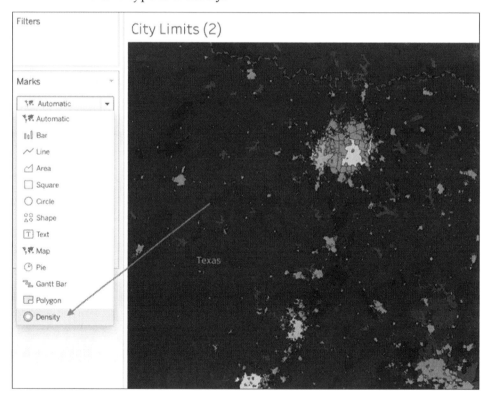

Figure 9.18: Texas city density

4. Click on **Colour** in the **Marks** card and select any color you like. I chose Density Gold Dark.

5. Decrease **Size** in the **Marks** card by dragging the slider to the left. Drag until you like the size of the circles on your map:

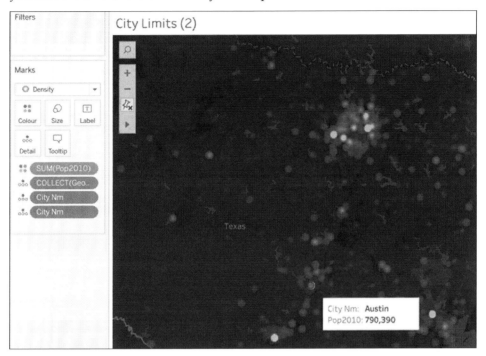

Figure 9.19: Heatmap

Heatmaps can show you a spatial concentration and are perfect for very dense datasets. In the preceding figure, you can see that we lost the surroundings of the city, the polygon structure; however, we can still see the densely populated areas and now every city has the same size, making it easier to compare smaller with bigger geographic locations. And we were able to prove that a spatial file does not need to be used with polygons.

In the Tableau 2020.4 release, another feature was added: map layers. What it is and what it is used for will be described in the next section.

Dual axes and layering maps

You might recall that on many different occasions throughout the previous chapters, we used dual axes. A dual axes visualization can also be achieved with maps, and, even better, since the Tableau 2020.4 release, maps can be layered. We simply put another layer with the same structure (which in this case is a map), and per layer, we can display different data.

We will look at two exercises, the first one being about the use of dual axes and the second one will include map layers.

Using dual axes

Let's get started:

1. First, we need a dataset. I simply created one in Excel myself; feel free to create your own, copy what you see in the following screenshot, or download the file from this book's GitHub repository (`https://github.com/PacktPublishing/Mastering-Tableau-2021`). Name the file `freight`:

Transportation	Goods	Ordered	Delivered	Origin	Origin Country	Destination	Destination Country	Weight
Plane	Furniture	01/01/2021	02/01/2021	Lisbon	Portugal	London	United Kingdom	85
Train	Furniture	01/01/2021	10/01/2021	London	United Kingdom	Paris	France	58
Ship	Furniture	01/01/2021	04/01/2021	Venice	Italy	Palma	Italy	66
Ship	Furniture	01/01/2021	11/01/2021	Rotterdam	Netherlands	Hamburg	Germany	82
Plane	Office	01/01/2021	03/01/2021	Rotterdam	Netherlands	Rome	Italy	80
Plane	Office	01/01/2021	08/01/2021	Rome	Italy	Kiev	Ukraine	53
Transporter	Office	01/01/2021	12/01/2021	Rome	Italy	Vienna	Austria	74
Plane	Office	02/01/2021	15/01/2021	Amsterdam	Netherlands	Warsaw	Poland	68
Plane	Office	02/01/2021	30/01/2021	London	United Kingdom	Reykjavík	Iceland	76
Transporter	Books	02/01/2021	17/01/2021	Hamburg	Germany	Berlin	Germany	55
Plane	Books	02/01/2021	25/01/2021	Athens	Greece	Tallinn	Estonia	76
Train	Books	02/01/2021	10/01/2021	Paris	France	Madrid	Spain	69
Train	Books	02/01/2021	28/01/2021	Warsaw	Poland	Budapest	Hungary	63
Ship	Books	02/01/2021	17/01/2021	Helsinki	Finland	Glasgow	United Kingdom	96
Ship	Clothes	03/01/2021	10/01/2021	Glasgow	United Kingdom	Reykjavík	Iceland	92
Plane	Clothes	04/01/2021	19/01/2021	Reykjavík	Iceland	Istanbul	Turkey	72
Plane	Clothes	05/01/2021	11/01/2021	Istanbul	Turkey	Naples	Italy	97
Plane	Clothes	06/01/2021	17/01/2021	Palermo	Italy	Tunis	Tunisia	85

Figure 9.20: Excel

2. Connect the new dataset to Tableau and open a new worksheet called **Dual-axis map**.

3. Double-click on **Origin Country** and the following map will appear:

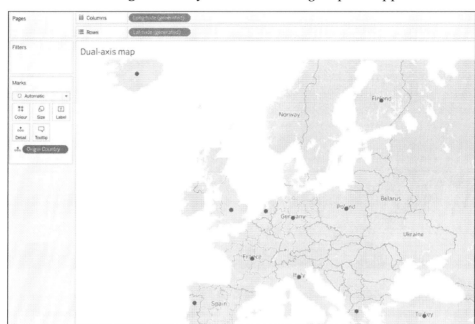

Figure 9.21: Dual-axis map

4. Change the **Mark** card type to a filled map and drag **Goods** onto the **Colour** shelf:

Figure 9.22: Dual-axis map II

5. Click on **Longitude** in the **Columns** shelf, press *Ctrl* (or *Command* on Mac), and simultaneously move the field to its right. You should have copied a second copy of the **Longitude** field to the **Columns** shelf:

Figure 9.23: Copying Longitude

6. You can also see that the **Marks** card maintains two layers now, plus an additional **All** layer, just like dual axes on a bar chart would:

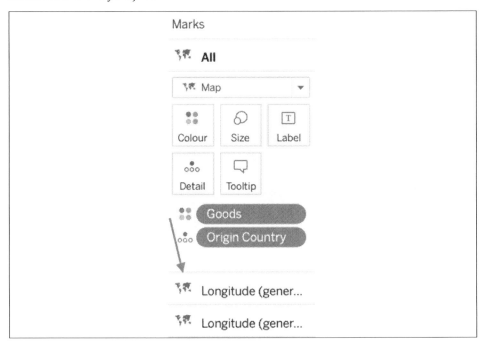

Figure 9.24: Marks card

7. On the bottom layer, replace **Goods** with **Origin** on the **Colour** shelf and see how the second map now shows colored dots representing cities:

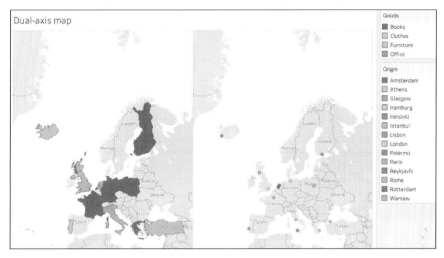

Figure 9.25: Dual-axis map

8. Click on the right **Longitude** field in the **Columns** shelf and select **Dual Axis**.

You created your first layered map! Each country's color represents the types of goods they ship. The dots indicate the cities for train, ship, plane, or truck transport:

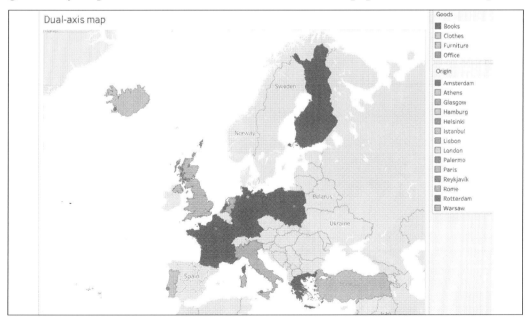

Figure 9.26: Dual-axis map

After completing the first basic exercise, we will move on to a more complex one, using the newer map layering functionality.

Adding map layers

We want to visualize the transport routes with a line from the start to the destination city. We also want to show the time to delivery as well as the weight of the shipment. We will continue using the freight dataset from before; we just need to do some adjustments:

1. The freight dataset does not have longitudes or latitudes, which are crucial for some of Tableau's spatial calculated fields, like **MAKEPOINT**, which we will need later on. Open Google Maps and type in a city from the dataset, for example, **Lisbon**. In the URL, you will be able to find the longitude and latitude:

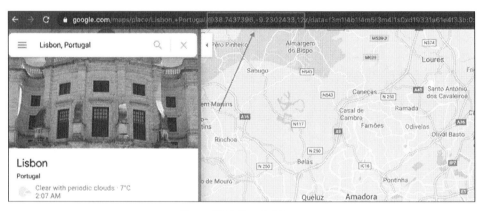

Figure 9.27: Google Maps

2. Copy them and add them to a separate Excel sheet, as shown in the following screenshot, and call it **latlong**:

City	Lat	Long
Lisbon	38.722252	-9.139337
London	51.507351	-0.127758
Venice	45.440845	12.315515
Rotterdam	51.924419	4.477733
Rome	41.902782	12.496365
Amsterdam	52.3547925	4.7638775
Hamburg	53.5586526	9.6476426
Athens	37.9908997	23.7033199
Paris	48.8589507	2.2770201
Warsaw	52.2330653	20.9211112
Helsinki	60.11021	24.7385058
Glasgow	55.8555734	-4.3725409
Reykjavík	64.1335484	-21.922482
Istanbul	41.0055005	28.7319933
Palermo	38.1406578	13.2872484
Palma de Mallorca	39.5812177	2.6355079
Kyiv	50.4021368	30.2525097
Vienna	48.2208286	16.2399765
Berlin	52.5069312	13.1445522
Tallinn	59.4717925	24.5981597
Madrid	40.4381311	-3.8196211
Budapest	47.4813602	18.9902194
Naples	40.8540421	14.1765623
Tunis	36.7949999	10.0732375

Figure 9.28: Excel

3. We needed to use a new Excel sheet because we have to create a spatial field for destinations as well as the origin. Since some cities are an origin as well as a destination, we will create two inner joins; both times the initial **freight** Excel sheet will connect to the recently created **latlong** Excel sheet:

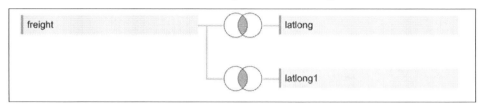

Figure 9.29: Join

4. The only difference will be that the first join is made on **Origin** and **City** and the second on **Destination** and **City**. Rename the **latlong** data sources by double-clicking on the name, to avoid confusion:

Figure 9.30: Join II

5. Open a new workbook and name it 4-layer map. Create a calculated field called **Line**, with the following code:

```
MAKELINE(MAKEPOINT([Lat (Origin)], [Long (Origin)]),
MAKEPOINT([Lat (Destination)], [Long (Destination)]))
```

6. The Tableau description shows that to make a point based on a spatial location, Tableau needs the longitude and latitude, or coordinates.

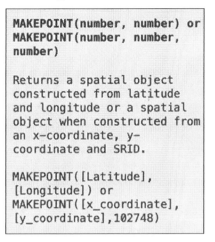

```
MAKEPOINT(number, number) or
MAKEPOINT(number, number,
number)

Returns a spatial object
constructed from latitude
and longitude or a spatial
object when constructed from
an x-coordinate, y-
coordinate and SRID.

MAKEPOINT([Latitude],
[Longitude]) or
MAKEPOINT([x_coordinate],
[y_coordinate],102748)
```

Figure 9.31: MAKEPOINT

7. Create another calculated field called **Days to delivery**, with the following code:

```
[Delivered]-[Ordered]
```

8. Double-click on **City** from the **Origin** file and a map will appear, but you will encounter **12 unknown**. Click on the error and then **Edit Locations...**:

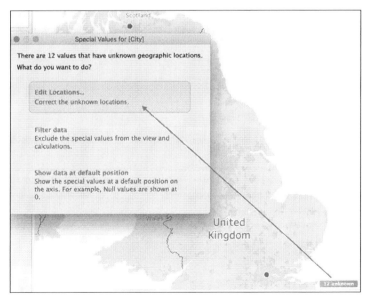

Figure 9.32: Unknown cities

9. You will see that Tableau uses **United Kingdom** (might be different for you) as a default country to find every city, but Tableau is unsuccessful because we have cities all over Europe in our dataset. Instead of a **Fixed** location, use the **From field** option and select **Origin Country**. Now this field will be used as a country per city in our dataset:

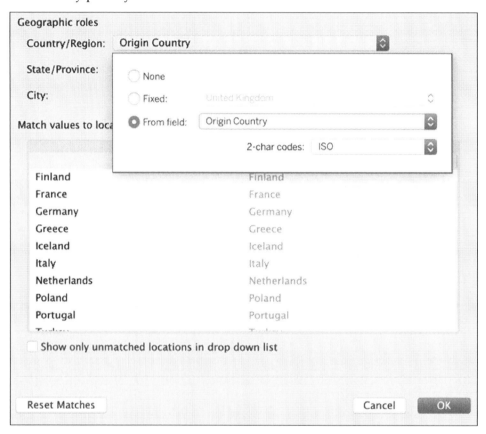

Figure 9.33: Origin Country

10. Tableau automatically adds **Origin Country** to the view on the **Detail** shelf and displays the cities correctly now. You can also achieve the previous step by placing **Origin Country** on the **Detail** shelf directly:

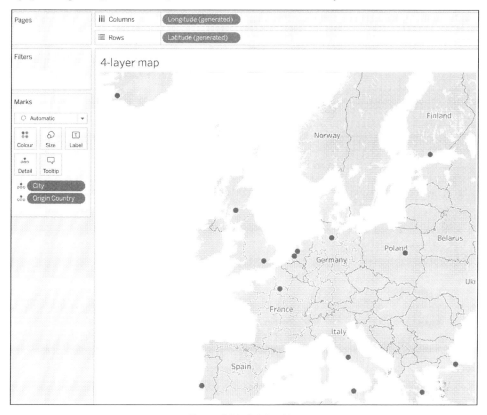

Figure 9.34: Origin cities

11. Since one of our goals is to draw lines between the **Origin** and **Destination** cities, it only makes sense to also add **Destination**, correct? Double-click on **Destination** to add it to the visualization.

12. We now have all **Origin** and **Destination** cities in our view, but we won't be able to distinguish between them because they are all on the same layer. Therefore, drag the just-added **Destination** field from the **Detail** shelf to the upper-left corner of your view, until the **Add a Marks Layer** sign appears:

Figure 9.35: Freight II

13. You will now see that the **Marks** card shows two layers:

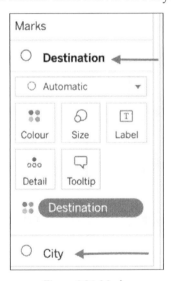

Figure 9.36: Marks

14. Rename the **Destination** layer to **Destination Country** by double-clicking on the name.

15. Add another layer and add **Days to Delivery** to **Colour** and **Line** to **Detail**. Name this layer **Line** and select the **Automatic** type from the **Marks** card dropdown:

Figure 9.37: Marks layer

16. Add another layer called **City (2)**, and add **City (Destination)** to **Detail** and **Destination Country** to **Detail**. Select the **Automatic** type from the **Marks** card dropdown:

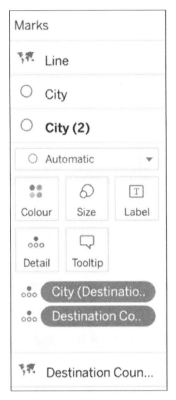

Figure 9.38: Marks layer

17. Lastly, go back to the **Destination Country** layer, change **Destination Country** to **Detail**, and put **Weight** on **Colour**. Select **Map** from the **Marks** card dropdown:

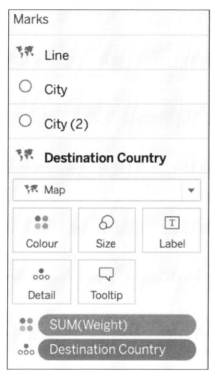

Figure 9.39: Marks layer

18. Sort the layers in the following order: **Line**, **City**, **City (2)**, **Destination Country**. Your worksheet should now look as follows:

Figure 9.40: Map

19. In order to make the viz a bit easier to interpret, put **Origin** on the **Filters** shelf and select only a few origins of your choosing.

20. And to distinguish the **Origin** from the **Destination**, open the **City** and **City (2)** map layers and change **City** and **City (Destination)** respectively from **Detail** to **Shape**. Select one shape for the **Origin** and another for the **Destination**, for example, filled circles for **Origin** and crosses for **Destination**. You can also give the shapes color by clicking on the **Colour** shelf:

Figure 9.41: Final layered map

Now, let's look at what we have created. We can see that goods are being transported from every circle to a cross city. Both cities are connected by a yellow-to-red range colored line. More yellow-toned means that the delivery was fast, more red-toned means that the delivery took longer. The destination country is colored in a turquoise-to-dark blue color range. The darker the color, the more weight has been transported there. We can easily spot that Italy received the heaviest transport, coming from Istanbul and being delivered within 6 days. The slowest delivery was from Budapest to Warsaw, which took 26 days.

I hope that this exercise showed you the benefits of layered maps. Each layer allows you to use **Colour**, **Shape**, **Size**, **Label**, and other **Marks** in its unique way, opening new paths for your analysis. But if this is not enough, in the next section we will go even further and use external technology for maps in Tableau.

Extending Tableau mapping with other technology

Next, we will consider how to extend Tableau's mapping capabilities with other tools. Tableau developers were careful to create a mapping interface that is readily extensible. Some areas of this extensibility, such as connecting to a **Web Map Service (WMS)** server, are available directly from the interface.

Using custom maps with a Web Map Service

The easiest way to bring a custom map into Tableau is directly from Desktop. We need a properly formatted URL that points to a WMS server. Tableau Desktop can connect to any WMS server that supports the WMS 1.0.0, 1.1.0, or 1.1.1 standards.

 A good place to find a list of such URLs is http://directory.
spatineo.com, which provides information for a ton of different
mapping services.

The following exercise was inspired by Jeffrey A. Shaffer's article *Building weather radar in Tableau in under 1 minute*, which can be accessed here: https://www.dataplusscience.com/TableauWeatherRadar.html. However, we will include a different map and our source is the NASA earth observation data (https://neo.sci.gsfc.nasa.gov/). In this exercise, we will see that by plotting additional data—in the form of background images—underneath your dataset, you will be able to make better decisions for your business. For example, if your sales figures are dependent on good (or bad) weather or your production is at risk of close-by wildfires, you will be able to see this all in one Tableau dashboard:

1. Open the workbook associated with this chapter and navigate to the **WMS Server** worksheet via the desktop.

2. Select the **Superstore** data source.

3. Place **State** on the **Detail** shelf.

4. Copy the `http://neowms.sci.gsfc.nasa.gov/wms/wms?` URL, then in Tableau, navigate to **Map | Background Maps | Add WMS Map**. Paste the URL and click **OK**:

Figure 9.42: Add WMS Map

5. In the **Marks** card, set the view type to **Map**.

6. Click on the **Colour** shelf to turn on **Border**, set the color to white, and set **Opacity** to 0%:

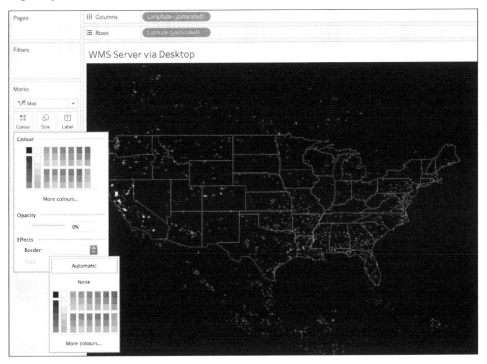

Figure 9.43: Active fires map

7. You can now see the active fires from the last month. But, by clicking on **Map | Map Layers**, more options will appear. Take a look at the left-hand side on your screen and select any other info domain you are interested in; how about **Average Land Surface Temperature**?

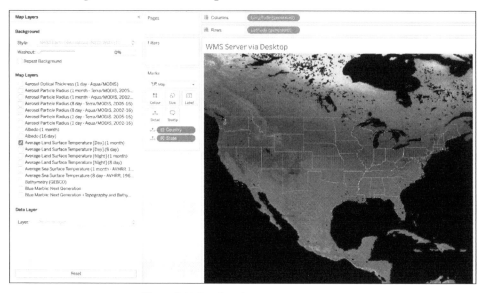

Figure 9.44: Land surface temperature map

Or **Cloud Fraction** (don't forget to first deselect a map before you select a new one):

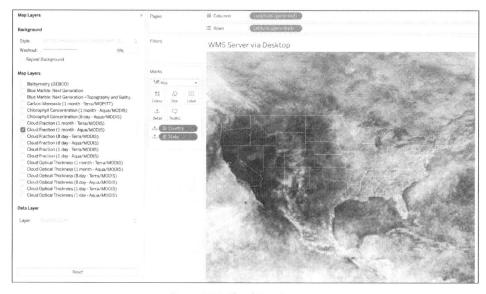

Figure 9.45: Cloud Fraction map

This feature will give you endless ways to analyze data related to geographic locations. Let's say you own an online store. You could check if the sale of specific products is higher in specific areas, for example, umbrellas in rainy areas and sun protection in hotter regions. You can then continue to analyze if the market is already satisfied or if it makes sense to invest in marketing for those regions. Or maybe you want to move stock to regions where more sales are expected due to a weather change. Feel free to share your findings on Tableau Public and make sure to use the tag #MasteringTableau.

Before we proceed, here's a note on tiling and zooming. Since high-resolution maps may be many gigabytes, it's impractical to require you to download an entire map in order to zoom in on one small area. Tiles solve this problem by enabling multiple zoom levels. A zoom level of 0 results in a single tile (often a 256 x 256-pixel PNG image) that displays the entire map. As the zoom levels increase, the number of map tiles increases exponentially. Also, a proportionally smaller section of the map displays; that is, as the zoom level increases, the area of the entire map that displays decreases and the total number of tiles required to fill the display remains constant. This helps control the amount of data downloaded at any given time.

Exploring Mapbox

Mapbox provides custom maps and integrates natively with Tableau. To learn how to build your own custom maps, you can check out their website here: https://www.mapbox.com/. Starting with Tableau 2019.3, multiple Mapbox styles are even available by default:

Figure 9.46: Background maps

Next to that, Mapbox itself provides an extended mapping service with an accompanying web application that enables users to customize maps. This customizability encompasses fonts, colors, background images, and more. Mapbox provides basic services free of charge but, of course, more maps and greater bandwidth needs will require an upgrade with an accompanying fee.

This exercise will show you how to connect to **Mapbox**:

1. Navigate to `https://www.mapbox.com` and create an account.

2. After completing the signup and logging into **Mapbox**, click on the **Studio** link:

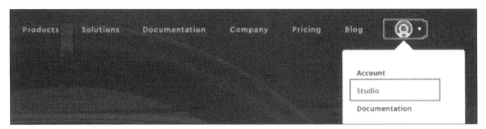

Figure 9.47: Mapbox

3. Click **New Style** and start creating a map. I chose **Monochrome | Dark | Customize Monochrome**.

4. The Mapbox editor should open. Adjust the map based on your needs:

Figure 9.48: Mapbox integration

5. Click **Share** (top-right corner) once you are done. Select **Third Party |
   Tableau** and copy the URL:

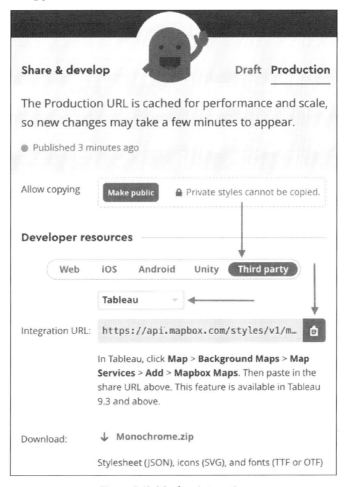

Figure 9.49: Mapbox integration

6. In the workbook associated with this chapter, navigate to the **Mapbox
   Classic** worksheet and select **Map | Background Maps | Add Mapbox Map**.

7. Add a **Style Name** (I used MasteringTableau) and copy the URL. Click **OK**.

8. Select the **Superstore** data source, double-click on **State**, and select the **MasteringTableau** map style via the **Map | Background Maps | MasteringTableau** path:

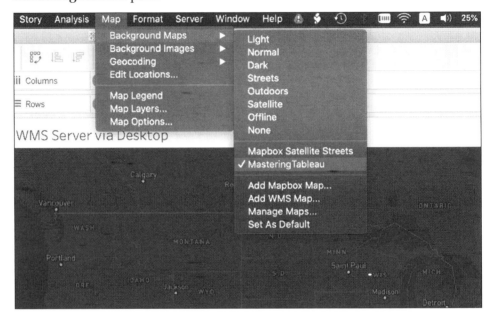

Figure 9.50: Background Maps

As you can see, Tableau makes use of the map we previously created in Mapbox. Great! So, this means you can customize your map just the way you like it.

A manual on how to create custom maps and everything else you need to know about Mapbox can be found here: https://docs.mapbox.com/studio-manual/guides/.

Swapping maps

We will now create a dashboard that allows the end user to choose between the various maps we just discussed. The technique used for this exercise is known as **sheet swapping**. However, a deeper dive into this technique is presented in *Chapter 11, Visualization Best Practices and Dashboard Design*.

Let's look at the necessary steps:

1. Navigate to the sheet **MapSwap** in the workbook associated with this chapter. Double-click on **State** Set the **Marks** card view to **Map**, click on **Colour**, set **Opacity** to **0%**, and lastly set **Border** to **Automatic**:

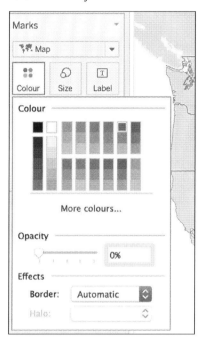

Figure 9.51: Colour

2. Duplicate the **MapSwap** sheet twice:

Figure 9.52: Duplicate MapSwap sheet

3. Select the **MapSwap** sheet and navigate to **Map | Background Maps | Normal**

4. Select the **MapSwap (2)** sheet and navigate to **Map | Background Maps | Dark**

5. Select the **MapSwap (3)** sheet and navigate to **Map | Background Maps | Satellite**.

6. Create a parameter called **Show Sheet** like so:

Figure 9.53: Parameter

7. Right-click on the parameter in the **Data** pane and select **Show Parameter Control**.

8. Create a calculated field called Show Sheet Filter like the following:

    ```
    [Show Sheet]
    ```

9. Select the **MapSwap** worksheet and place **Show Sheet Filter** on the **Filters** shelf. Select **Select from list** and **Normal**:

Figure 9.54: Sheet filter

10. Select the **MapSwap (2)** worksheet and place **Show Sheet Filter** on the **Filters** shelf. This time select **Custom value list** and type Dark:

Figure 9.55: Custom value list

11. Repeat the previous step on the **MapSwap (3)** sheet and type Satellite.

12. Create a dashboard and call it **db_MapSwap**. Place a vertical container on the dashboard.

13. Place all three **MapSwap** sheets in the vertical container, and hide their titles.

14. Select a different map style and see how your map changes:

Figure 9.56: Swap map

You might have seen a feature like dark/light or day/night background on your own computer or maybe on websites like YouTube or IDEs like PyCharm. With the MapSwap function, you can now offer the same comfort to your users on your Tableau dashboards.

Summary

In this chapter, we explored how to extend Tableau's mapping capabilities without leaving the interface by capturing Tableau-generated latitude and longitude data and how to look this up on Google. We created polygons and a heatmap for Texas based on a .shp file as well as a dashboard with a dual map axis and another dashboard with 4 map layers. Next, we explored various ways to extend Tableau's mapping using other technology. We connected to a WMS server and then explored the Mapbox offering, followed by an excursion to the world of polygons.

In the next chapter, we will explore using Tableau for presentations. Specifically, we will look at how to get the best images out of Tableau, how to effectively and efficiently use Tableau with PowerPoint, and how to use Tableau directly for presentations without relying on third-party tools.

10
Tableau for Presentations

All Tableau authors are essentially storytellers. Analyzing data is more than just puzzle- solving; it is a search for a story that will make a difference. Topics can range from Airbnb to the Zika virus, and may be pleasantly diverting or life-changing, but they all serve a common need: to tell a story. This chapter is dedicated to helping you stock your toolkit of knowledge with ideas and methods for using Tableau to make presentations that engage, delight, and make a difference.

This chapter will explore the following presentation-centric topics:

- Getting the best images out of Tableau
- From Tableau to PowerPoint
- Embedding Tableau in PowerPoint
- Animating Tableau
- Story points and dashboards for presentations
- Presentation resources

For the content of this chapter, I'm particularly indebted to Robert Mundigl and Cathy Bridges.

Getting the best images out of Tableau

In this section, we will review options for exporting an image from Tableau into other applications and discuss the pros and cons of each method. We'll begin by surveying various screenshot applications and then we will consider methods that are available directly in Tableau.

Perhaps the easiest way to capture an image in Tableau is to use a screen capture tool. The following are some screen capture tools that won't impact your pocketbook:

- **Snipping Tool** is installed by default with Windows and, although a very simple tool with few bells and whistles, is easy to use and effective.

- **Greenshot** is an open-source screen capture tool with many features similar to SnagIt. Visit `http://getgreenshot.org/` to download the application and learn more.

- **Microsoft Office OneNote** includes a screen capture feature. If you have OneNote installed with Windows 7 or earlier, simply press *Windows + S* to activate the screen capture. If you are on Windows 8 or 10, press *Windows + N* and then the *S* key for activation.

- **Grab** is a screen capture utility natively available on macOS. Grab is located in the **Utilities** folder under **Applications**. You can also access it via the following shortcuts: *Shift + Command + 3* for a screenshot, *Shift + Command + 4* for a partial screenshot, and *Shift + Command + 5* for a timer screenshot.

Now that we have covered the tools and methods for image capturing, let us have a look into the native capabilities that ship with Tableau.

Tableau's native export capabilities

One of the shortcomings of screen capture tools is that they are limited to **raster images**. Raster images are often sufficient for documentation or a PowerPoint presentation, but are subject to pixilation if enlarged. Vector images, on the other hand, do not pixelate when enlarged and may therefore provide sharper image quality. Natively, Tableau includes both raster and vector export options. These options are discussed in the following section.

Tableau can export images in three formats, accessible via **Worksheet** | **Export** | **Image**:

- **JPEG** is a raster image format that is good for high resolution images such as photographs, but does not work very well for low color images, such as those typically deployed in Tableau. Export an image from Tableau in JPEG format and then zoom in close. Note that the white space (especially white space surrounding text) includes stray pixels of various colors. These are known as **artifacts** or **noise**. Although these pixels are not visible unless zoomed in, the overall impact on an exported image is that it can look blurry. Thus, there is rarely, if ever, a reason to export to JPEG from Tableau.

- Like JPEG images, **PNG** images are raster. The advantage of the PNG format is that it works well with both high color images such as photographs and low color images like those typically used in Tableau. Export an image from Tableau in PNG format and zoom in to observe that, although pixilation occurs, the white space comprises only white. Unlike JPEG images, no artifacts or noise appear. PNG should be considered the format of choice when using a raster image.

- **BMP** is a raster image format that looks quite nice but is uncompressed and can thus result in large image files. Today, the BMP format is considered antiquated and should typically be avoided.

I suggest you try all three of them. Luckily, Tableau also provides us with a native feature to export to a PDF as a vector image, as well as exporting to PowerPoint directly. In the next section, we will take a look at the PowerPoint export feature and some variations to it.

From Tableau to PowerPoint

PowerPoint is ubiquitous. Some may argue that other presentation tools such as Prezi are superior, but for many organizations (probably the vast majority) PowerPoint remains the software of choice.

 Prezi is a tool that can be accessed via the web. Typically, you won't see classical slides but an interactive, moving presentation. Templates are available online and they offer free as well as paid tiers. You can check it out here: www.prezi.com.

As such, it's important to integrate Tableau and PowerPoint efficiently and effectively. Starting from Tableau Desktop version 2019.1, it is possible to export your dashboard directly to PowerPoint. You will find the option under **File | Export As PowerPoint:**

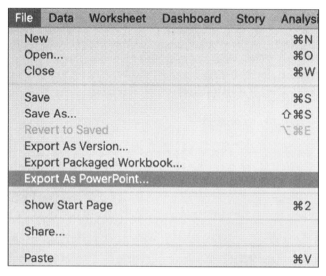

Figure 10.1: Export as PowerPoint

After making this selection, you will be asked whether you want to export the current view or a selection of sheets from the workbook:

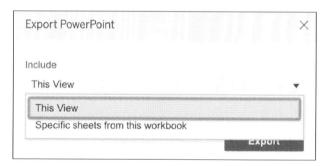

Figure 10.2: Export PowerPoint

Try both options to see how the native Tableau export functionality appears in PowerPoint. If you want to put in a little extra effort, there are options to create a PowerPoint implementation of Tableau via a different route. These alternatives might present added value for you. The following exercises explore the various techniques for doing so.

Creating a template

For this first PowerPoint-centric exercise, you will create a template that will be utilized in future exercises. It will include common PowerPoint elements such as a header and a footer. The size of the template will be 1200 x 900, which adheres to the 4:3 aspect ratio typically used for PowerPoint presentations. Of course, other sizes may be targeted, but the aspect ratio should always be kept in mind. Let us look at the following steps:

1. Navigate to `https://public.tableau.com/profile/marleen.meier` to locate and download the workbook associated with this chapter.

2. Create a new worksheet and select the **Superstore** dataset.

3. Name the worksheet **Header**.

4. Place **Sales** on the **Color** shelf in the **Marks** card.

5. Click on **Color** in the **Marks** card, click **Edit Colors...**, and then select the gray color palette and set **Opacity** to 50%:

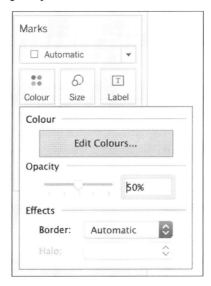

Figure 10.3: Opacity

6. Duplicate the **Header** worksheet and name the duplicate **Footer1**.

7. Click on **Color** in the **Marks** card, click **Edit Colors...**, and then select the blue color palette:

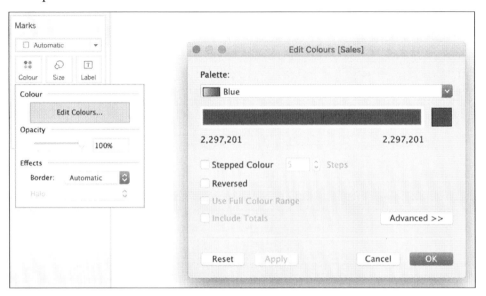

Figure 10.4: Color palette

8. Duplicate the **Footer1** worksheet and name the duplicate **Footer2**.

9. Click on **Color** in the **Marks** card, click **Edit Colors...**, and then select the gray color palette and set **Opacity** to **50%**.

10. Create a new dashboard called **Template**.

11. Within the **Dashboard** pane, set the size to 1200 x 900:

Figure 10.5: Custom size the dashboard

12. Display the dashboard title via **Dashboard | Show Title**.

13. Double-click on the **title**. In the resulting dialog box, left-justify the text if needed.

14. In the **Dashboard** pane, make sure that **Tiled** is selected. This way, you make sure that the single worksheets stay in place and don't overlap one another:

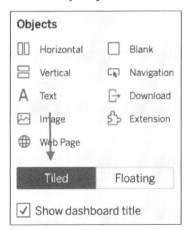

Figure 10.6: Tiled

15. From the **Dashboard** pane, drag **Blank** from the **Objects** panel and place it on the left-hand side of the dashboard. Be careful to place it so that it stretches from the top to the bottom of the dashboard, as shown in the following screenshot:

Figure 10.7: Adding a blank space

16. Repeat the previous step for the right-hand side, the middle, and the bottom of the dashboard. When creating the bottom margin, be sure to position the object so that it stretches from the far right to the far left of the dashboard. Your final layout should contain four containers and a left-aligned title at the top, like so:

Figure 10.8: Layout

17. Size the blank objects to create appropriate margins. This can be accomplished by dragging the inner edge of each **Blank** object (that is, the edges facing the center) as far to the right or left or bottom as possible:

Figure 10.9: Increasing size

18. Change the bottom margin one more time by approximately doubling the height by selecting the container and dragging the bottom line downward, as indicated by the arrows in *Figure 10.9*.

19. In the **Objects** portion of the **Dashboard** pane, click **Floating**.

20. Drag the **Header**, **Footer1**, and **Footer2** assets onto the dashboard. It does not matter where you place them; we will align the worksheets shortly. If a **Sales** legend appears, delete it.

21. Right-click on the title of each asset and select **Hide title**.

22. In the **Layout** pane, enter the following values for each worksheet:

Figure 10.10: Changing position

23. Set each worksheet to **Entire View** by clicking in the toolbar on the **Fit** drop-down menu next to the word **Standard** and selecting **Entire view**:

Figure 10.11: Changing view

24. The results should be a line for the header just under the title stretching across 80% of the dashboard and two bars at the bottom stretching across the entire dashboard:

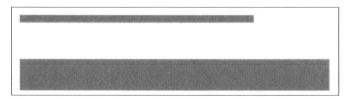

Figure 10.12: Layout

25. Click on the container located underneath the **Template** title.

26. If you have not already done so, download the assets associated with this chapter. A link is provided in the workbook.

27. Drag an **Image** object from the **Objects** portion of the **Dashboard** pane onto the dashboard. When prompted, select the tableau-logo.png image supplied with this chapter:

Figure 10.13: Adding an image

28. Select the option **Centre Image** and then click **OK**.

29. Position the image via the **Layout** pane as follows:

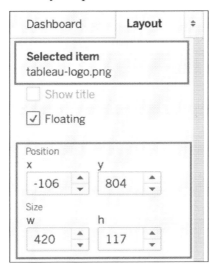

Figure 10.14: Position logo

Your PowerPoint template is now ready to use:

Figure 10.15: Template

For every screenshot you will take now, you will always have the same design surrounding it. By doing so, your presentations will look more professional and your audience will soon recognize your work by its design. A template such as this can also help you follow company design guidelines. As an extra tip, make sure that you use matching colors for headers, footers, and your graphs!

Next, we will go through some examples in order for you to see the template in use.

Creating a dashboard for print

This exercise will utilize the template created previously to make a dashboard. Basic instructions are provided, but specifics are left to individual preference:

1. Right-click on the tab entitled **Template** created in the previous exercise, *Creating a template*, and select **Duplicate**.

2. Rename the duplicate dashboard to **Superstore Loss Leaders**.

3. Populate the **Superstore Loss Leaders** dashboard with the worksheets **HexMap** and **Loss Leaders States**. Arrange as desired. An example layout is given as follows:

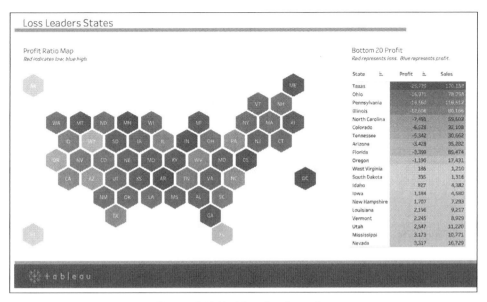

Figure 10.16: Dashboard and template

The dashboard on top of the template looks really great, doesn't it? It immediately looks more professional and presentation-worthy. But are you asking yourself why did I choose to work with that specific layout? Well, let me elaborate: If you want to show a Tableau dashboard in a printed version or you have to export the dashboard to PowerPoint, it is important to remember that all interactivity will be lost. One of the highlights and biggest selling points of Tableau — interactivity — doesn't work on a 2D print. But obviously you don't want to recreate graphs that already exist in some form on your Tableau Server, and you don't have to. Just make sure that your audience understands the viz without being able to click on a field or hover over to show more info:

- **Tip 1**: The dashboard in *Figure 10.17* has been adjusted to the colors of the template to make it appear as if the two belong together.

- **Tip 2**: A hexagon map (**hexmap**) has been used instead of the default map that comes with Tableau. The reason is that smaller states on the east coast disappear when printed in the actual ratio and Alaska and Hawaii are so far away that they usually don't fit on the map either. A hexmap gives the same space to each state and hence, even if printed, the user can see what's going on in Alaska, as well as in Rhode Island.

- **Tip 3**: The colors indicate that the profit ratio is especially bad in Ohio and Colorado, but your audience might want to know more. That's when the table comes into play. The profit ratio is profit divided by sales and the table shows both numbers so that the audience can get a better picture of the current situation and you can avoid them asking.

- **Tip 4**: In order to avoid a printed scroll down bar, I selected the bottom 20 states only. If the topic is loss leaders, it is not very likely that you will need to show all the states that do really well.

I hope this example gave you some ideas on how to prepare your dashboard for a print! If a print happens more frequently, I would advise you to add a page to your interactive dashboard on Tableau Server such that you always have it ready to go if asked for. If you are interested in replicating the hexmap, go ahead and check the following article: `https://www.tableau.com/about/blog/2017/1/viz-whiz-hex-tile-maps-64713`.

Next, we will look at another example, this time an automation for a weekly PowerPoint presentation.

Semi-automating a PowerPoint presentation

The previous exercises (*Creating a template* and *Creating a dashboard for print*) demonstrated two methods for generating a template for PowerPoint presentation and gave you some tips on how to adjust your dashboard for printing and/or PowerPoint presentations. Usually, however, your Tableau dashboard isn't static, and the data will change for the next time when you need it. You can, of course, export a new PowerPoint file with the updated data, but you might have other slides as well that you don't want to lose. The following steps will help you a bit with a semi-automated way of updating your PowerPoint presentation:

1. Open the dashboard created previously entitled **Superstore Loss Leaders**.
2. Click on **Dashboard | Export Image...**:

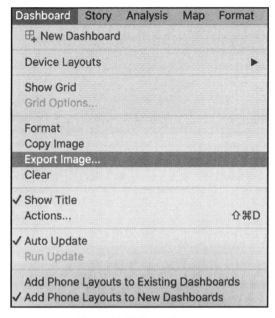

Figure 10.17: Export Image

3. Click **OK** and, in the resulting dialog box, choose to save the image as `SuperstoreLossLeaders.png`.

4. Open the PowerPoint presentation. Open a slide.

5. Select the **Insert** ribbon and choose **Pictures | Picture from File**:

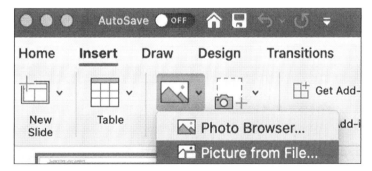

Figure 10.18: Inserting a picture into PowerPoint

6. Navigate to the PNG image you just exported.

7. In the **Insert** dialog box, choose the drop-down selector next to **Insert** and select **Insert and Link** for Windows, or select **Options | Link to File | Insert** for Mac. Note that this step is important because it will allow pictures to be swapped out easily, as will be demonstrated:

Figure 10.19: Link to File

8. Save the PowerPoint presentation as AutoUpdate.pptx.

9. Close PowerPoint. In Tableau, modify the dashboard; for example, remove a state from the table.

10. Overwrite the previously exported SuperstoreLossLeaders.png image via **Dashboard | Export Image ....**

11. Open AutoUpdate.pptx and note that the new image of the dashboard displays.

Something I come across frequently when I teach in Tableau classes is that I encounter people who are responsible for providing PowerPoint presentations on a weekly or monthly basis. These presentations include charts and graphs that are updated, but the overall layout remains unchanged. The technique covered in the preceding exercise can make that process much quicker. Although Tableau Desktop only allows the author to update one image at a time, Tableau Server can be configured to export multiple images simultaneously, thereby making the process even more efficient. Exporting images from Tableau Server is discussed in *Chapter 14, Interacting with Tableau Server/Online*.

Wouldn't it be even nicer if we could present our web browser, Tableau Server, directly on a slide, including all the interactivity? The next section will cover this while sharing some thoughts on doing so.

Embedding Tableau in PowerPoint

It is possible to embed Tableau directly in a PowerPoint presentation or, to be more accurate, it's possible to embed a web browser through which an instance of Tableau Server may be accessed. There are various methods for accomplishing this, including the Web Viewer app, a third-party add-in called LiveWeb, and VBA code.

The Web Viewer app is available at https://appsource.microsoft.com/en-us/ product/office/WA104295828?tab=Overview. Although it works well for Tableau Public, the default Tableau Server settings disallow access via Web View. LiveWeb (available at http://skp.mvps.org/liveweb.htm) works well, but requires an additional installation. You have to download the installation from the URL provided and start PowerPoint. You will then be able to add another add-in to your PowerPoint ribbon, which, in return, allows you to add a Tableau Server URL that will be displayed directly in Tableau. Detailed instructions can be found on the website too.

The third method mentioned previously, using VBA, is perhaps the most workable method and will be discussed next. The following steps utilize PowerPoint 2016. Other versions of PowerPoint may require a slightly different approach, but any differences should be relatively easy to figure out. Also, the exercise assumes that the **Developer** toolbar is activated. If the **Developer** toolbar is not activated for your instance of PowerPoint, instructions to enable it can be found here: https://support. microsoft.com/en-us/office/show-the-developer-tab-e1192344-5e56-4d45-931b-e5fd9bea2d45.

> The following exercise currently only works on Windows due to the fact that PowerPoint for Mac does not provide a developer add-in.

Perform the following steps:

1. Open PowerPoint. If it's not already enabled, enable the **Developer** tab in the Excel ribbon by selecting **File | Options | Customize Ribbon** and then, under **Main Tabs**, add **Developer**.

2. Create a new single blank slide.

3. Select the **Developer** tab in the ribbon and click on the **Command Button** icon located in the **Controls** group:

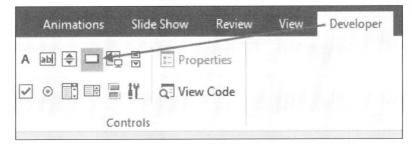

Figure 10.20: Command button

4. In the lower-left hand portion of the slide, create a command button by clicking and dragging:

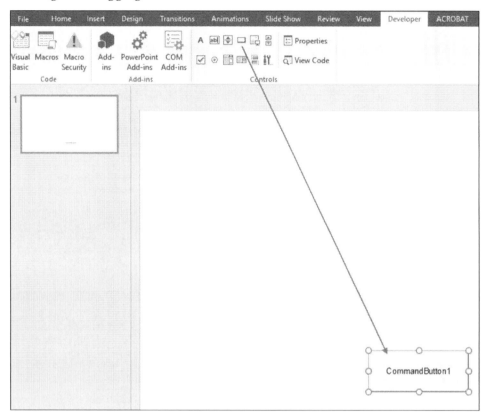

Figure 10.21: Creating a command button

5. Right-click on the command button just created and select **Property Sheet**.

6. Within **Property Sheet**, locate **Caption** and set the text to **Launch Workbook**:

Figure 10.22: Properties

The command button should now be labeled **Launch Workbook**.

7. Within the **Controls** group in the **Developer** ribbon, select **More Controls**.

8. Within the resulting dialog box, choose **Microsoft Web Browser** and then click **OK**:

Figure 10.23: More Controls

9. If this process works and you do *not* get an error message at this point, skip to *Step 16*. However, if a warning dialog box displays stating that **The ActiveX control cannot be inserted**, continue reading the next few steps.

 Note that the following steps provide instructions regarding the adjustment of registry settings. Adjusting registry settings can be a tricky business and can cause problems on your machine if done incorrectly. Proceed at your own risk!

10. Save the file and close PowerPoint.

11. Press the *Windows* button + *R* to open the **Run** dialog box. Within the **Run** dialog box, type Regedit.

12. In the Registry Editor, locate the following class ID: 8856F961-340A-11D0-A96B-00C04FD705A2. This class ID will be located differently based on the different installation methods for Office. The following three locations are likely candidates:

    • HKEY_LOCAL_MACHINE\SOFTWARE\Microsoft\Office\15.0\Common\COM Compatibility\

    • HKEY_LOCAL_MACHINE\SOFTWARE\Microsoft\Office\15.0\Click ToRun\ REGISTRY\MACHINE\Software\Wow6432Node\Microsoft\Office\15.0\ Common\COM Compatibility\

    • HKEY_LOCAL_MACHINE\SOFTWARE\Wow6432Node\Microsoft\Office\15.0\ Common\COM Compatibility

13. Click on the class ID and note the type REG_DWORD in the right-hand panel. Right-click on **REG_DWORD** and then select **Modify**.

14. Change the textbox labeled **Value data** to **0** and then click **OK**:

Figure 10.24: Registry editor

15. Start PowerPoint and open the file saved previously. Now you should be able to add the Microsoft Web Browser control as instructed in *Step 8*.

16. Draw a marquee over most of the slide, allowing only enough room for the **Launch Workbook** command button created previously:

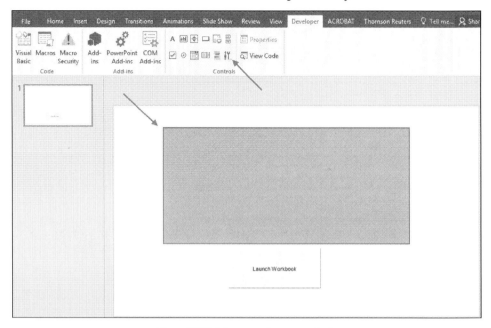

Figure 10.25: Marquee of more controls

17. Right-click on the **Launch Workbook command** button and then select **View Code**.

18. Within the **Visual Basic for Applications (VBA)** console that appears, delete any existing code and enter the following code:

```
Private Sub CommandButton1_Click()
'Begin Comment: The above line of code gives instructions
regarding what action to take when clicking on the command
button. End Comment.
WebBrowser1.Navigate ("https://public.tableau.com/
profile/vizpainter#!/vizhome/TheChangingShapeofHistory/
FromColoniestoUS")
'Begin Comment: WebBrowser1 is the name of the Microsoft
WebBrowser control that the command button controls. End
Comment. 'Begin Comment: The URL can be replaced with a URL of
your choosing. End Comment.
'Begin Comment: '"Navigate" is the Property/Method that accepts
the URL. End Comment.
End Sub
```

19. Close the VBA console.

20. Press *F5* and click the **Launch Workbook command** button. An instance of a Tableau workbook should now display in PowerPoint:

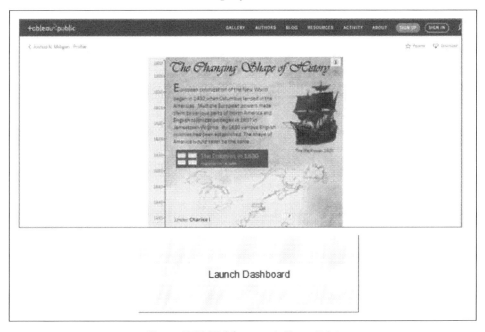

Figure 10.26: Web browser in PowerPoint

 Note that the preceding VBA code includes comments. The statements **Begin Comment** and **End Comment** are included for clarity, but are not required. For this example, I used a link to a very well-designed Tableau Public dashboard by Joshua N. Milligan, a Tableau Zen Master.

Robert Mundigl explores various techniques for embedding Tableau in PowerPoint similar to the preceding example on his blog, clearlyandsimply.com. Perform a search on the blog for PowerPoint to explore these methods. Robert's creative ideas include a technique for accessing multiple workbooks on a single PowerPoint slide and a technique for embedding the Tableau Desktop authoring environment in PowerPoint for on-the-fly authoring without leaving the presentation interface.

In this section, you have learned how you can embed a web browser in a PowerPoint presentation. Next, we will discuss ways to bring animation to Tableau that can support your data storytelling.

Animating Tableau

Including animation in a presentation can be very effective for engaging an audience. Hans Rosling accomplishes this admirably with his popular YouTube video *200 Countries, 200 Years, 4 Minutes* (https://youtu.be/jbkSRLYSojo). In this video, Rosling uses data visualization to track wealth and life expectancy over time. His combination of data visualization with insightful commentary and a passion for his message makes Rosling's video a must-see for anyone interested in making appealing presentations using data.

Animations are easy to implement and are available via Tableau Reader as well as Tableau Server (since the 2020.1 release). At the time of writing, I have only encountered one drawback; worksheets with animation that are uploaded to Tableau Server will provide a single-speed level, whereas Tableau Desktop will show three. But as you can see, nothing too pressing.

The following exercise tracks ACT testing scores from 1991 to 2015. Complete the exercise to learn how to create an animation in Tableau and also discover whether standardized testing results in the United States have improved over time.

Perform the following steps:

1. Open the workbook associated with this chapter and navigate to the worksheet entitled ACT 1991–2015.
2. Select the **ACT** data source.
3. Rename the sheet ACT scores.
4. Place **Year** on the **Columns** shelf, **Score Value** on the **Rows** shelf, and **Score Type** on **Color** in the **Marks** card.
5. Right-click on **Score Value** axis and select **Edit Axis...** In the resulting dialog box, deselect **Include zero**.

6. Place **Year** on the **Pages** shelf. Your view should look like the following:

Figure 10.27: ACT scores – 1991

7. In the **Current Page** panel that appears on the worksheet, check **Show history**. Click on the arrow to open the dropdown and align all parameters as shown in the following screenshot:

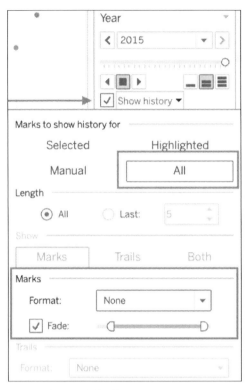

Figure 10.28: Aligning parameters

8. In the **Marks** card, click on the drop-down menu to change the view type from **Automatic** to **Circle**.

9. Click on the **Show history** drop-down menu again and note that both the **Show** options and the **Trails** options are now available. Under **Show**, select **Both**.

10. Click on the **Format** drop-down menu under **Trails** and then select the dashed line option:

Figure 10.29: Dashed line

Sometimes, the question "How can I create a dashed line in Tableau?" arises. One method is demonstrated in the preceding steps. By setting the view type to **Circle** and adjusting the **Show history** options, a dashed line was created. If a dashed line without animation is required, simply hide the page panel.

To briefly extend the theme of creating dashed lines in Tableau, to discover how to create multiple lines with varying dash types, check out `https://boraberan.wordpress.com/2015/11/22/quick-tip-creating-your-own-dashed-line-styles-in-tableau/`, where Bora Beran has pioneered a method using calculated fields to insert null values to achieve differing line effects.

11. Now, click on the play button and see how Tableau walks through each year, one at a time:

Figure 10.30: Animation

Even though this functionality is not a good use case for thorough analytics, it does help when visualizing change over time, for example, while giving a presentation or for any other kind of storytelling. I most recently used it to show how product clusters changed over time, with the conclusion that clusters should not remain static. I then continued to search for early identification of such change in clusters in order to adjust pricing and marketing accordingly.

To conclude, animations are possible in Tableau using a functionality called **pages**. I hope you will find many use cases for this feature. Next, we will use the animation features in a different way, by showing you how to export multiple images with it.

Using an animation to export many images

There are at least two reasons why it may be necessary to export many images from a timeline. First, it may be analytically advantageous to see separate images for each time snapshot; for example, a separate image for each day in a month. Second, it may be necessary to create an animation outside of Tableau, perhaps in PowerPoint.

The next two exercises (*Using an animation to export many images* and *Using an animation in Tableau to create an animation in PowerPoint*), cover both scenarios:

> Note that the following steps assume that the previous exercise was completed.

1. Open the workbook associated with this chapter and navigate to the worksheet entitled **ACT scores**:

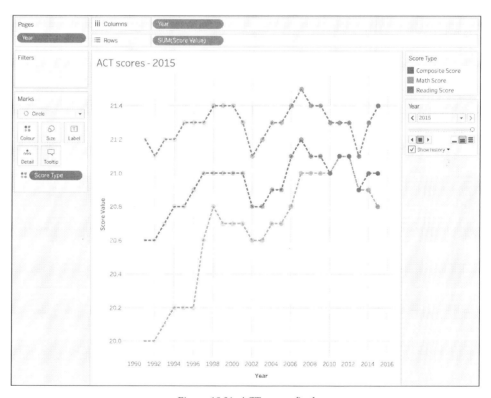

Figure 10.31: ACT scores final

2. Select **File | Page Setup...**. At the bottom of the resulting dialog box, under **Pages Shelf**, select **Show all pages**:

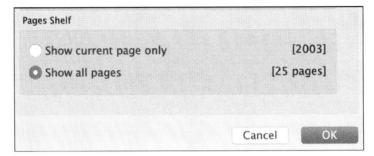

Figure 10.32: Show all pages

3. Select **File | Print to PDF**. Mac users should select **File | Print.**

4. In the resulting dialog box, set **Range** to **Active Sheet**. Also set the orientation to **Landscape**.

5. Click **OK** and save the PDF as Animation.pdf to a location of your choice.

6. Navigate to https://www.pdftoppt.com/. Upload Animation.pdf and convert it to PowerPoint. An email will be sent a few minutes after conversion.

7. Download the file via the link provided in the email and open it in PowerPoint.

8. Within PowerPoint, select **File | Save As**. Within the **Save As** type drop-down menu, select ***.png**:

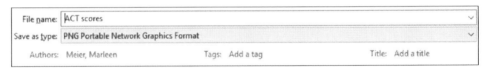

Figure 10.33: Animation.png

9. When prompted, choose to export **All Slides**:

Figure 10.34: All Slides

10. Save the PowerPoint presentation. Note that when PowerPoint finishes saving, a dialog box will display stating that each slide in the presentation has been saved as a separate file:

Name	Date modified	Type	Size
Slide1	1/11/2021 8:58 PM	PNG image	41 KB
Slide2	1/11/2021 8:58 PM	PNG image	42 KB
Slide3	1/11/2021 8:58 PM	PNG image	44 KB
Slide4	1/11/2021 8:58 PM	PNG image	45 KB
Slide5	1/11/2021 8:58 PM	PNG image	46 KB
Slide6	1/11/2021 8:58 PM	PNG image	46 KB
Slide7	1/11/2021 8:58 PM	PNG image	49 KB
Slide8	1/11/2021 8:58 PM	PNG image	50 KB

Figure 10.35: All slides saved

11. Open and inspect the saved PNG files as desired:

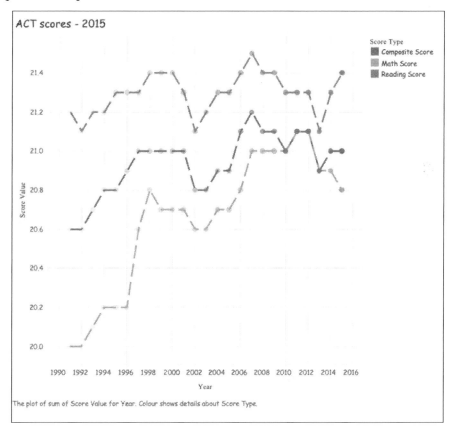

Figure 10.36: Last slide as .png

By following all the preceding steps, you should have been able to save multiple images at once. This is hopefully a time saver for you, and even though it might not happen too often, it will benefit you knowing about this option.

Using an animation in Tableau to create an animation in PowerPoint

This exercise will show you how to create an animation from the mass of images we saved in the preceding exercise. Hence, we will use the files created previously to animate in PowerPoint:

1. Access the PowerPoint presentation downloaded from `https://www.pdftoppt.com/` in the previous exercise.

2. In the **View** ribbon, select **Slide Sorter** under the **Presentation Views** group.

3. Select **All slides** in the PowerPoint presentation except for the last one.

4. On the **Transition** ribbon under **Timing** group, set to advance the slide after 0.1 seconds:

Figure 10.37: Advancing the slide

5. Press *F5* to see the animation.

Isn't this cool? You can see a similar simulation to what you would see in Tableau using Pages! To further improve the animation in PowerPoint, consider the following additional steps:

*   Upload the initial PDF to `https://pdfresizer.com/crop` and crop the size as desired.

*   If the animation is too slow in PowerPoint, it is likely that all the text and drawing elements are maintained. For example, the background grid is made up of individual lines. Rendering all text and drawing elements is resource-intensive. Consider creating a separate PowerPoint presentation using the PNG images created in the *Using an animation to export many images exercise*. This will lead to a quicker, smoother running animation.

I hope that this section has given you some ideas on how you can improve and impress with PowerPoint. Using these newly acquired techniques, you might not even need Prezi after all. However, this chapter wouldn't be complete without mentioning story points, a feature that will bring you a long way if you don't want PowerPoint at all.

Story points and dashboards for presentations

Story points are Tableau's answer to PowerPoint. As such, both share fundamental similarities. A PowerPoint presentation provides a linear approach to communication. So do story points in Tableau. A PowerPoint presentation provides slides, each of which is a blank canvas that provides a user with infinite possibilities to communicate ideas. A story in Tableau provides story points for the same purpose.

Although there are fundamental similarities, it is important to understand that Tableau story points and PowerPoint presentations often do not fulfill the same role. Each has advantages over the other, and so a list of pros and cons should be considered.

We can view the pros and cons of PowerPoint and Tableau story points in the following table:

PowerPoint		Tableau story points	
Pros	**Cons**	**Pros**	**Cons**
Can be quick and easy to create	Difficult to automate based on changes to underlying data	Automatically updates as underlying data changes	Can be more difficult to create
Easily fits different resolutions	Difficult to create a presentation that allows for departure from linear thought	Easily allows nonlinear exploration in the middle of a presentation	Requires forethought regarding resolution size

So how do you decide between using PowerPoint and Tableau when making presentations? Perhaps the following list will help:

When to Use PowerPoint	When to Use Tableau story points
A presentation where the audience has little opportunity for immediate feedback	A presentation where immediate feedback is likely and exploratory questions may be asked
A one-time presentation comprising clearly delineated points	A reusable presentation with updates mostly based on changes to underlying data
A presentation where the monitor resolution size may not be known in advance	A presentation where the monitor resolution size is known or assumed

The basics of creating and using story points are straightforward, nor, at the time of writing, is there much beyond the basics. Since the focus of this book is on more advanced Tableau ideas and concepts, those basics will not be considered here. If you need to quickly understand story point basics, I recommend reading through the following pages: `https://help.tableau.com/current/pro/desktop/en-us/stories.html`.

I like story points and I like to use them especially when my audience has its own version of Tableau open in front of them and can follow along with their own actions. It is a great way to give people a deeper understanding because it allows you to show more complexity than a static screenshot. If you are looking to improve your presentation skills in general, continue reading the next section.

Presentation resources

Using story points effectively in Tableau is perhaps more of an artistic consideration than a technical one. Although this book attempts to consistently consider best practices for data visualization and to encourage attractive and user-friendly worksheets and dashboards, a discussion of effective presentation techniques is beyond its scope.

If you would like to improve your ability to create effective presentations, consider the following resources:

- **Presentation Zen**: Garr Reynolds is a bestselling author and a repeat speaker at Tableau conferences. His books and website (`https://www.presentationzen.com/`) provide provocative ideas for effective presentations.

- **Tableau Public**: Learning by example is invaluable. Fine examples of story points can be found on Tableau. To learn from one of the most engaging, navigate to `https://help.tableau.com/current/pro/desktop/en-us/story_example.htm`.

- **Blogs**: One of the more interesting posts discussing Tableau story points in combination with good presentation methodology can be found on Matt Frances' blog, `wannabedatarockstar.blogspot.com`. The post is entitled *Five Tips for Better Tableau Story Points*.

Even though these presentation skills are beyond the scope of this chapter, I hope that the preceding resources have given you food for thought.

Summary

We began this chapter by exploring various screen capture tools as well as Tableau's native export capabilities. Next, we turned our consideration to PowerPoint, where we explored various methods for creating PowerPoint presentations from Tableau workbooks, and even explored how to embed a live instance of Tableau in PowerPoint. Next, we considered Tableau animation. Lastly, we explored how to use story points and dashboards for presentations. In *Chapter 11*, *Visualization Best Practices and Dashboard Design*, we will turn our attention to dashboarding, where we will push beyond the normal boundaries of the typical dashboard, but not lose focus of the practical applications.

11

Visualization Best Practices and Dashboard Design

This chapter was particularly influenced by some giants in data visualization and dashboard design—Edward Tufte and Stephen Few. I would also like to draw attention to Alberto Cairo, who has been providing new insights in more recent years. Each of these authors should be considered a must-read for anyone working in data visualization.

This chapter has been written with the intent of empowering you with design knowledge and Tableau-centric techniques for creating effective dashboards.

In this chapter, we will cover the following topics:

- Visualization design theory
- Formatting rules
- Color rules
- Visualization type rules
- Compromises
- Keeping visualizations simple
- Dashboard design
- Dashboard best practices for user experience

Now that we have discussed the topics of this chapter, let's dive into design theory, which will provide you with rules that can be applied to every single dashboard you are going to build.

Visualization design theory

Any discussion about designing dashboards should begin with information about constructing well-designed content. The quality of the dashboard's layout, and the utilization of technical tips and tricks, do not matter if the content is subpar. In other words, we should first consider the worksheets displayed on dashboards and ensure that those worksheets are well-designed. Therefore, our discussion will begin with a consideration of visualization design principles. Regarding these principles, it's tempting to declare a set of rules, such as the following:

- To plot change over time, use a line graph.
- To show breakdowns of the whole, use a treemap.
- To compare discrete elements, use a bar chart.
- To visualize correlations, use a scatter plot.

But of course, even a cursory review of this list brings to mind many variations and alternatives! Thus, in the next section, *Formatting rules*, we will consider various rules, while keeping in mind that once you're comfortable with the basics, rules can be broken to serve a purpose.

Formatting rules

The following formatting rules encompass **fonts**, **lines**, and **bands**. Fonts are, of course, an obvious formatting consideration. Lines and bands, however, may not be something you typically think of when formatting—especially when considering formatting from the perspective of Microsoft Word. But if we broaden formatting considerations to think of Adobe Illustrator, InDesign, and other graphic design tools, lines and bands should certainly be considered. This illustrates that data visualization is closely related to graphic design and that formatting considers much more than just textual layout.

Keep the font choice simple

Typically, using one or two fonts on a dashboard is advisable. More fonts can create a confusing environment and interfere with readability.

Fonts chosen for titles should be thick and solid, while body fonts should be easy to read. In Tableau, choosing appropriate fonts is simple because of the new Tableau font family. Select **Format | Font** to display the **Format Font** window to see and choose these new fonts.

Assuming your dashboard is primarily intended for the screen, sans-serif fonts are best. On the rare occasion that a dashboard is primarily intended for print, you may consider serif fonts, particularly if the print resolution is high.

Use lines in order of visibility

We tend to order line visibility in the following order: trend line, chart line, reference line, drop line, and grid line. For example, trend-line visibility should be greater than fever-line visibility. Visibility is usually enhanced by increasing line thickness, but may be enhanced via color saturation or by choosing a dotted or dashed line over a solid line. Let's look at each of the line types, in order of decreasing visibility:

- **Trend lines**: The trend line, if present, is usually the most visible line on the graph. Trend lines are displayed via the **Analytics** pane and can be adjusted via **Format | Lines**.

- **Chart lines**: The chart line (for example, the line used on a time-series chart) should not be so heavy as to obscure twists and turns in the data. Although a chart line may be displayed as dotted or dashed by utilizing the **Pages** shelf, this is usually not advisable because it may obscure visibility. The thickness of a chart line can be adjusted by clicking on the **Size** shelf in the **Marks remove bold** area.

- **Reference lines**: Usually less prevalent than fever or trend lines and can be formatted via **Format | Reference lines**.

- **Drop lines**: Not frequently used. To deploy drop lines, right-click in a blank portion of your **view** and select **Drop lines | Show drop lines**. Next, click a point in the view to display a drop line. To format drop lines, select **Format | Drop Lines**. Drop lines are relevant only if at least one axis is utilized in the visualization.

- **Zero lines**: These are sometimes referred to as base lines, and only display if zero or negative values are included in the view, or positive numerical values are relatively close to zero. Format zero lines via **Format | Lines**.

- **Grid lines**: These should be the most muted lines on the view and may be dispensed with altogether. Format grid lines via **Format | Lines**.

Use bands in groups of three to five

Visualizations composed of a tall table of text or horizontal bars should segment dimension members in groups of three to five.

Please follow along with the steps to experience an efficient use of bands in Tableau:

1. Navigate to `https://public.tableau.com/profile/marleen.meier` to locate and download the workbook associated with this chapter.

2. Navigate to the **Banding** worksheet.

3. Select the **Superstore** data source and place **Product Name** on the **Rows** shelf.

4. Double-click on **Discount**, **Profit**, **Quantity**, and **Sales**. Note that after completing this step, Tableau defaulted to banding every other row. This default formatting is fine for a short table but is quite busy for a tall table.

5. Navigate to **Format | Shading** and set **Band Size** under **Row Banding** so that three to five lines of text are encompassed by each band. Be sure to set an appropriate color for both **Pane** and **Header**:

Figure 11.1: Format Shading

The Band in Groups of Three to Five rule is influenced by Dona W. Wong, who, in her book *The Wall Street Journal Guide to Information Graphics*, recommends separating long tables or bar charts with thin rules to separate the bars in groups of three to five to help readers read across.

Color rules

It seems slightly ironic to discuss color rules in a book that will be printed in black and white (of course, that may not be true if you are reading this book on an electronic device). Nevertheless, even in a monochromatic setting, a discussion of color is relevant. For example, exclusive use of black text communicates something different than using variations of gray. The following survey of color rules should be helpful for ensuring that you use colors effectively in a variety of settings.

Keep colors simple and limited

Stick to the basic hues and provide only a few (perhaps three to five) hue variations. In his book, *The Functional Art: An Introduction to Information Graphics and Visualization*, Alberto Cairo provides insight as to why this is important:

> *"The limited capacity of our visual working memory helps explain why it's not advisable to use more than four or five colors or pictograms to identify different phenomena on maps and charts."*

Respect the psychological implications of colors

There is a color vocabulary in every region of the world so pervasive that it's second nature. Red is often used for love or danger; in some Asian countries, it can also mean fortune and is common for wedding dresses. Green can mean luck, whereas in Mexico, green represents independence. Green traffic signals tell us to go, red to stop. Similarly, colors on dashboards are often used with purpose. Reds and oranges are usually associated with negative performance, while blues and greens are associated with positive performance. Using colors counterintuitively can cause confusion, so be aware of color usage and of your audience and their interpretation.

Be colorblind-friendly

Colorblindness is usually manifested as an inability to distinguish red and green, or blue and yellow. Red/green and blue/yellow are on opposite sides of the color wheel.

Consequently, the challenges these color combinations present for colorblind individuals can be easily recreated with image editing software such as Photoshop. If you are not colorblind, convert an image with these color combinations into grayscale and observe. The challenge presented to the 8.0% of men and 0.5% of women who are colorblind becomes immediately obvious! Or, use the following website to upload an image of your dashboard and experience how your user might see the colors used: `https://www.color-blindness.com/coblis-color-blindness-simulator/`.

Use pure colors sparingly

The resulting colors from the following exercise should be a very vibrant red, green, and blue. Depending on the monitor, you may even find it difficult to stare directly at the colors. These are known as **pure colors** and should be used sparingly, perhaps only to highlight particularly important items.

Please follow these steps:

1. Open the workbook associated with this chapter and navigate to the **Pure Colors** worksheet.

2. Select the **Superstore** data source and place **Category** on both the **Rows** shelf and the **Color** shelf.

3. Set **Fit** to **Entire View**.

4. Click on the **Color** shelf and choose **Edit Colors...**.

5. In the **Edit Colors** dialog box, select one after the other member; that is, **Furniture**, **Office Supplies**, and **Technology**, and select blue, green, and red, respectively:

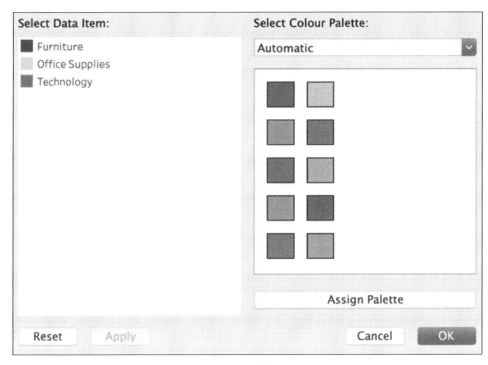

Figure 11.2: Colors

See for yourself how you experience looking at those pure colors and select three other, less vibrant, colors to compare. Too vibrant colors can be very heavy on your eye and make it hard to focus. Colors that are too similar, however, make it hard to distinguish. Finding a good balance is key.

Choose color variations over symbol variation

Deciphering different symbols takes more mental energy for the end user than distinguishing color. Therefore, color variation should be used over symbol variation. This rule can actually be observed in Tableau defaults. Create a scatter plot and place a dimension with many members on the **Color** shelf and the **Shape** shelf, respectively. Note that, by default, the view will display 20 unique colors but only 10 unique shapes. Older versions of Tableau (such as Tableau 9.0) display warnings that include text such as "the recommended maximum for this shelf is 10."

See the following diagram for an example of symbol variation:

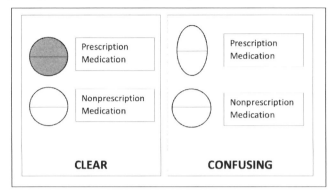

Figure 11.3: Color versus shape

To sum up, keep your color palette simple and be aware of your regional, cultural meanings of color. Also, take into account that people in your audience might be color-blind or have a color deficiency; tools can help you choose colors wisely and Tableau also offers a colorblind palette. Lastly, use pure colors sparingly, since too many highlight colors will make it hard for the audience to focus on the most important items. Also don't use too many shapes; instead, use color to distinguish between values.

Visualization type rules

Since there's a chapter dedicated to visualization types, *Chapter 8*, *Beyond the Basic Chart Types*, and since much of this book explores various visualizations, we won't take the time here to delve into a lengthy list of visualization type rules.

 If you want to get additional information on this topic, I highly recommend checking out the Visual Vocabulary that Andy Kriebel created, and which was inspired by the Financial Times (`https://ft-interactive.github.io/visual-vocabulary/`), available on Tableau Public: `https://public.tableau.com/profile/andy.kriebel#!/vizhome/VisualVocabulary/VisualVocabulary`.

However, it does seem appropriate to review at least a couple of rules. Here, we will consider keeping shapes simple and effectively using pie charts.

Keep shapes simple

Too many shape details impede comprehension. This is because shape details draw the user's focus away from the data. Consider the following exercise using two different shopping cart images.

Let's look at the following exercise steps:

1. Open the workbook associated with this chapter and navigate to the **Simple Shopping Cart** worksheet. Note that the visualization is a scatter plot that shows the top-10-selling sub-categories in terms of total sales and profits.

2. Navigate to the **Shapes** directory located in the **My Tableau** repository. On my computer, the path is C:\Users\Marleen Meier\Documents\My Tableau Repository\Shapes.

3. Within the **Shapes** directory, create a folder named **My Shapes**.

4. Reference the link included in the comment section of the worksheet to download assets associated with this chapter. In the downloaded material, find the images entitled **Shopping_Cart** and **Shopping_Cart_3D**, and then copy those images into the **My Shapes** directory.

5. In Tableau, access the **Simple Shopping Cart** worksheet.

6. Click on the **Shape** shelf and then select **More Shapes**.

7. Within the **Edit Shape** dialog box, click the **Reload Shapes** button:

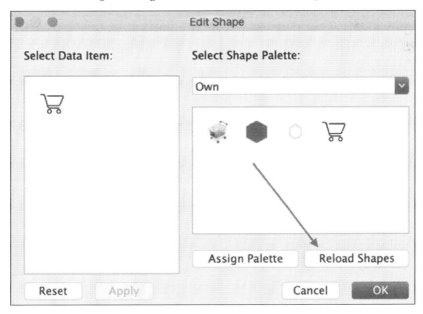

Figure 11.4: Reload Shapes

8. Select the **My Shapes** palette and set the shape to **Simple Shopping Cart**.

9. After closing the dialog box, click on the **Size** shelf and adjust as desired. Also, adjust other aspects of the visualization as desired.

10. Navigate to the **3D Shopping Cart** worksheet and then repeat *Steps 8-11* above. Instead of using **Simple Shopping Cart**, use **3D Shopping Cart**. See the following screenshot for a comparison of the simple and 3D shopping carts:

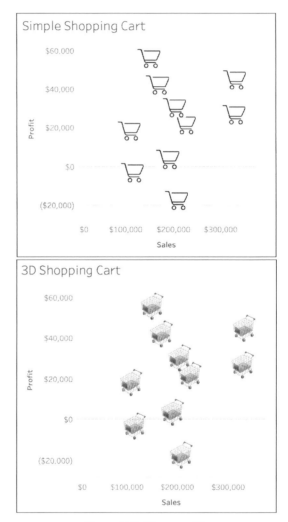

Figure 11.5: 2D versus 3D

Compare the two visualizations. Which version of the shopping cart is more attractive? It's likely that the cart with the 3D look was your choice. So, why not choose the more attractive image? Making visualizations attractive is only a secondary concern. The primary goal is to display the data as clearly and efficiently as possible. A simple shape is grasped more quickly and intuitively than a complex shape. Besides, the cuteness of the 3D image will quickly wear off.

Use pie charts sparingly

Edward Tufte makes an acrid comment against the use of pie charts in his book *The Visual Display of Quantitative Information*, saying that a table is always better than a pie chart, because we humans fail to interpret the visual dimension of pie charts.

The present sentiment in data visualization circles is largely sympathetic to Tufte's criticism. There may, however, be some exceptions; that is, some circumstances where a pie chart is optimal. Consider the following visualization:

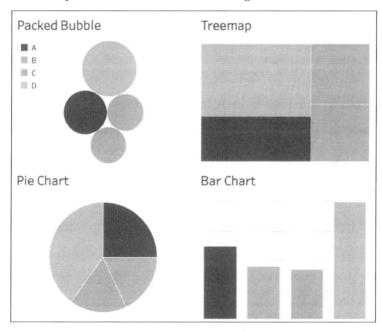

Figure 11.6: Comparing visualizations

Which of the four visualizations best demonstrates that A accounts for 25% of the whole? Clearly, it's the pie chart! Therefore, perhaps it is fairer to refer to pie charts as limited and to use them sparingly, as opposed to considering them inherently undesirable.

Compromises

In this section, we will transition from more or less strict rules to compromises. Often, building visualizations is a balancing act. It's not uncommon to encounter contradictory direction from books, blogs, consultants, and within organizations. One person may insist on utilizing every pixel of space while another advocates simplicity and whitespace. One counsels a guided approach, while another recommends building wide-open dashboards that allow end users to discover their own path. Avant-garde types may crave esoteric visualizations, while those of a more conservative bent prefer to stay with convention. Let's explore a few of the more common competing requests and then suggest compromises.

Making the dashboard simple and robust

Recently, a colleague showed me a complex dashboard he had just completed. Although he was pleased that he had managed to get it working well, he felt the need to apologize by saying, I know it's dense and complex, but it's what the client wanted. Occam's Razor encourages the simplest possible solution for any problem. For my colleague's dashboard, the simplest solution was rather complex. This is OK! Complexity in Tableau dashboarding need not be shunned. But a clear understanding of some basic guidelines can help the author intelligently determine how to compromise between demands for simplicity and demands for robustness:

- *More frequent data updates necessitate simpler design*: Some Tableau dashboards may be near real-time. Third-party technology may be utilized to force a browser that displays a dashboard via Tableau Server to refresh every few minutes, to ensure the latest data is displayed. In such cases, the design should be quite simple. The end user must be able to see, at a glance, all pertinent data and should not use that dashboard for extensive analysis. Conversely, a dashboard that is refreshed monthly can support high complexity and thus may be used for deep exploration.

- *Greater end user expertise supports greater dashboard complexity*: Know thy users. If they want easy, at-a-glance visualizations, keep the dashboards simple. If they like deep dives, design accordingly.

- *Smaller audiences require more precise design*: If only a few people monitor a given dashboard, it may require a highly customized approach. In such cases, specifications may be detailed, which are complex and difficult to execute and maintain. This is because the small user base has expectations that may not be natively easy to produce in Tableau.

- *Screen resolution and visualization complexity are proportional*: Users with low-resolution devices will need to interact fairly simply with a dashboard. Thus, the design of such a dashboard will likely be correspondingly uncomplicated. Conversely, high-resolution devices support greater complexity.

- *Greater distance from the screen requires larger dashboard elements*: If the dashboard is designed for conference room viewing, the elements on the dashboard may need to be fairly large to meet the viewing needs of those far from the screen. Thus, the dashboard will likely be relatively simple. Conversely, a dashboard to be viewed primarily on end users' desktops can be more complex.

Although these points are all about simple versus complex, do not equate simple with easy. A simple and elegantly designed dashboard can be more difficult to create than a complex dashboard.

As Steve Jobs said, simplicity can be harder than complexity; however, simplicity can move mountains.

Presenting dense information

Normally, a line graph should have a max of four or five lines. However, there are times when you may wish to display many lines. A compromise can be achieved by presenting many lines and empowering the end user to highlight as desired. The following line graph displays the percentage of internet usage by country from 2000-2012. The user can select a country and compare it to the rest.

We can see this example in the following screenshot:

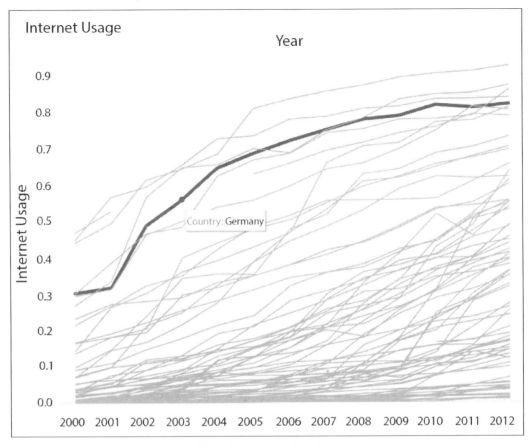

Figure 11.7: A many-line chart

When using line charts versus many line-charts, it should not be important how a line performs compared to a specific other line, but rather how one line behaves in a lake of other lines.

Telling a story

In his excellent book, *The Functional Art: An Introduction to Information Graphics and Visualization*, Alberto Cairo includes a section where he interviews prominent data visualization and information graphics professionals. Two of these interviews are remarkable for their opposing views. Jim Grimwade mentions that visualization designers should not try to make editors out of users; expecting them to make up a story on their own is not the approach he likes. On the contrary, Moritz Stefaner is fascinated by being able to explore key insights on big datasets on his own.

Fortunately, the compromise position can be found in the Jim Grimwade interview, where he states that the New York Times lets you explore complex datasets, but that beforehand, they give the reader some context.

Although the scenarios considered here are likely quite different from the Tableau work you are involved in, the underlying principles remain the same. You can choose to tell a story or build a platform that allows the discovery of numerous stories. Your choice will differ, depending on the given dataset and audience. If you choose to create a platform for story discovery, be sure to take the New York Times approach suggested by Grimwade. Provide hints, pointers, and good documentation to lead your end user to successfully interact with the story you wish to tell or to successfully discover their own story.

Maximizing documentation on a dashboard

In the *Telling a story* section, we considered the suggestion of providing hints, pointers, and good documentation, but there's an issue. These things take up space. Dashboard space is precious. Often, Tableau authors are asked to squeeze more and more stuff on a dashboard and are hence looking for ways to conserve space. Here are some suggestions for maximizing documentation on a dashboard while minimally impacting screen real estate:

- **Craft titles for clear communication**: Titles are expected. Not just a title for a dashboard and worksheets on the dashboard, but also titles for legends, filters, and other objects. These titles can be used for effective and efficient documentation. For instance, a filter should not just read Market. Instead, it should say something such as Select a Market. Notice the imperative statement. The user is being told to do something and this is a helpful hint. Adding a couple of words to a title will usually not impact dashboard space.

- **Use subtitles to relay instructions**: A subtitle will take up some extra space, but it does not have to be much. A small, italicized font immediately underneath a title is an obvious place a user will look for guidance. Consider an example: Red represents loss. This short sentence could be used as a subtitle that may eliminate the need for a legend and thus actually save space.

- **Use intuitive icons**: Consider a use case of navigating from one dashboard to another. Of course, you could associate an action with some hyperlinked text that states Screentext style to navigate to another dashboard. But this seems unnecessary when an action can be associated with a small, innocuous arrow, such as is natively used in PowerPoint, to communicate the same thing.

- **Store more extensive documentation in a tooltip associated with a help icon**: A small question mark in the upper-right corner of an application is common. Currently, I'm composing this chapter in Word 2013, which has such a question mark. This clearly communicates where to go if additional help is required. As shown in the following exercise, it's easy to create a similar feature on a Tableau dashboard.

Follow these steps to create an informative tooltip to help users:

1. Open the workbook associated with this chapter and navigate to the **Help** worksheet.

2. Hover over the light bulb on the worksheet and note the text that appears:

Figure 11.8: Lorem ipsum

 Note that the *Lorem ipsum...* text shown in the preceding screenshot is commonly used by web designers, who borrowed it from typesetters, who have been using this Latin text as a placeholder for centuries. Visit www.loremipsum.io to learn more.

The text in this worksheet was deployed via **Worksheet | Tooltip**. This worksheet could be thoughtfully placed on a dashboard (for example, in the upper-right corner) to give very detailed documentation that minimally impacts space.

Keeping visualizations simple

Some people tire of seeing the same chart types over and over. This leads to requests such as, can we spice up the dashboard a bit? Normally, such sentiments should be resisted. As stated at the beginning of this chapter, introducing variety for its own sake is counterproductive. Nevertheless, there are times when a less common visualization type may be a better choice than a more popular type. When are those times?

Use less common chart types in the following scenarios:

- The chart is used to catch the end user's attention.
- The chart type presents the data more effectively.

Sometimes, a less common chart type can be effectively used to catch the end user's attention for some particular goal, such as humor, making a salient point, or making the visualization more memorable. One such example can be found on the Tableau 404 error page. Navigate to `http://www.tableau.com/asdf` and observe Sasquatch in a packed bubble chart. Note that this page changes from time to time, so you may see Elvis, aliens, or some other visualization.

An example of the second point is using a treemap over a pie chart. Both are non-Cartesian chart types (visualizations with no fields on the **Rows** or **Columns** shelves) used to show parts of a whole. Pie charts are the more common of the two, but treemaps usually present the data better. There are at least three reasons for this:

- A treemap can represent more data points.
- The rectangular nature of a treemap fits monitor space more efficiently.
- Pie slice sizes are more difficult to distinguish than sizes of treemap segments.

Sometimes, using a less common visualization type may elicit complaints: *I like pie charts. Give me a pie chart!* In such cases, a compromise may be possible. Later in this chapter, we will consider sheet swapping. As you will learn, sheet swapping can allow the end user to determine which visualization type to view. In the end, if a compromise is not possible and the person responsible for your paycheck desires a less-than-ideal chart type... well, I recommend you doing so!

Dashboard design

Now that we have completed our discussion of visualization theory, let's turn our attention to dashboard design. We'll begin by asking the question, what is a dashboard? This is rather difficult to answer; however, its usage in everyday conversation in many organizations would suggest that people have a definite idea as to what a dashboard is. Furthermore, search engine results provide no shortage of definitions. But those definitions can differ significantly and even be contradictory.

Why is it so difficult to define dashboard? In part, it is because data visualization as a whole, and dashboarding specifically, is an emerging field that combines many other disciplines. These disciplines include statistical analysis, graphic and web design, computer science, and even journalism. An emerging field with so many components is a moving target, and as such is difficult to define.

For our purposes, we will begin with Stephen Few's definition as it first appeared in an issue of *Intelligent Enterprise* in 2004. He states that a dashboard is a visual display of vital statistics we need to reach, and how all these details are present on a sole screen, so that this information can be observed at first sight. Then, we'll extend and adapt that definition for Tableau dashboards.

Although this definition is good, Tableau takes a broader approach. For instance, a Tableau dashboard may be contained on a single screen but can be designed (and quite effectively so) to require scrolling. More importantly, Tableau dashboards are typically interactive, which opens up a world of exploration, analysis, and design options. Therefore, let's attempt a Tableau-centric dashboard definition:

A Tableau dashboard is a display that contains one or more data visualizations designed to enable a user to quickly view metrics. This display may provide interactive elements, such as filtering, highlighting, and drill-down capabilities that enable further exploration and analysis.

Dashboard layout

The layout of a dashboard is important for the same reason that the layout of a magazine foldout or a web page is important. Placing the right information in the right place helps the viewer quickly and efficiently gather information and draw conclusions. In order to appreciate this fact, consider the last time you had to hunt through a poorly constructed web page to find important information. Your time could have been better used actually applying that important information!

The golden ratio layout

You have probably heard of the Fibonacci sequence or the golden ratio. Since it may have been a few years since you attended a math class, a brief reminder may prove helpful.

The Fibonacci sequence is a series of numbers where every number is the sum of the previous two numbers; for example, 1, 1, 2, 3, 5, 8, 13, 21.

A Golden Rectangle is achieved when the ratio of the longest side to the shortest side of a rectangle is approximately 1.618. This ratio is known as the Golden Ratio. Mathematically, the Golden Ratio is represented as follows:

$$\varphi = \frac{1 + \sqrt{5}}{2} \approx 1.61803398874989$$

You can see the connection between the Fibonacci sequence and the Golden Ratio when dividing each number of the Fibonacci sequence by the previous number; for example, take the following sequence:

0, 1, 1, 2, 3, 5, 8, 13, 21, 34

This leads to the following:

$$\frac{1}{1} = 1, \frac{2}{1} = 2, \frac{3}{2} = 1.5, \frac{5}{3} = 1.67, \frac{8}{5} = 1.6, \frac{13}{8} = 1.625, \frac{21}{13} = 1.615, \frac{34}{21} = 1.619$$

Now, let's consider a dashboard layout using the Golden Ratio. The layout shown here is constructed of rectangles so that each is 1.618 times longer or taller than the next. The spiral (known as the golden spiral) is displayed to demonstrate the order of the rectangles:

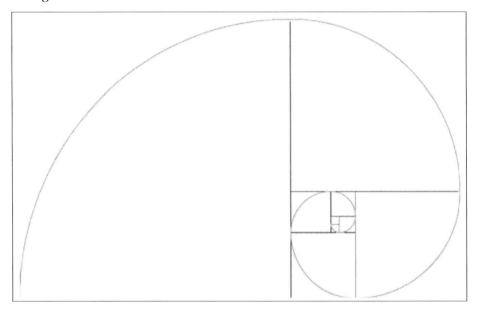

Figure 11.9: Golden ratio

The Fibonacci sequence/Golden Rectangle/Golden Ratio appears endlessly in nature and throughout history. Many seashells and flowers adhere to the Fibonacci sequence. The Great Pyramid of Giza appears to have been constructed with the Golden Ratio in mind. Phidias likely used the Golden Ratio to design his statues for the Athenian Parthenon. Indeed, the Parthenon itself was designed with Golden Rectangle proportions.

So, does the golden ratio, as pictured in the preceding diagram, represent the ideal dashboard layout? Perhaps it's truer to say that this image represents one acceptable dashboard layout. The ideal is not so much found in the abstract as it's found in the application. Dashboard layouts may sometimes approximate the golden ratio but, as we will see, other dashboard layouts may be better for different scenarios.

The dashboard pictured here (which is also available in the Tableau workbook that accompanies this chapter) utilizes the Golden Rectangle:

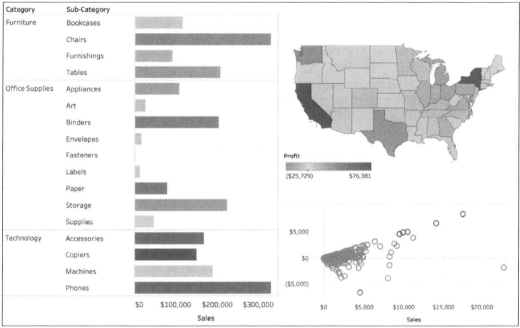

Figure 11.10: Golden Rectangle

Notice that this example does not attempt to follow the Golden Ratio through to smaller and smaller rectangles. There are practical limits.

The Golden Rectangle layout is particularly good for guiding the viewer from coarser to finer granularity. In this example, the left portion of the dashboard displays the coarsest granularity, 17 subcategories. The map is next. Finally, the scatter plot displays the finest granularity. Creating actions that follow this path would make a natural interaction for the end user. For example, an end user might first click on **Tables** and then click on the state of **Pennsylvania** in order to observe outliers in the scatter plot.

The quad layout

The quad layout divides a dashboard into four more or less equal quadrants. It's easy to implement. On a blank dashboard, simply double-click on four worksheets in the **Dashboard** pane. The result is a quad layout, though some small adjustments may need to be made to account for legends, filters, and parameters. To observe a quad layout, refer to the diagram in *Figure 11.6*.

The small multiple layout

A small multiple layout displays many views on a single dashboard. Like the quad layout, a small multiple layout can be implemented simply by double-clicking on each desired worksheet in the **Dashboard** pane. Small multiples are useful when viewing information that utilizes the same visualization type repeatedly. Also, a consistent theme is helpful; for example, the following screenshot demonstrates a theme of profit performance per state in the USA. Attempting to create a small multiple with multiple visualization types and multiple themes will likely be messy and difficult to interact with:

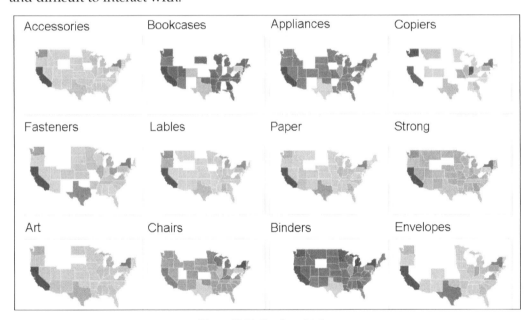

Figure 11.11: Small multiples

Some layouts are essentially variations of a theme. For instance, a layout that displays three views where one view on the dashboard covers double the real estate of each of the other views may essentially be a variation of the quad layout. Other layouts defy easy categorization and are unique to a given dashboard. Regardless, this will hopefully provide some food for thought as you design dashboards in the future.

The next section was already announced when we discussed compromises; sheet swapping is a great feature for that. If your stakeholder asks you to build something you know might not be as good or not following visualization best practice, you can always add a sheet swap, making your stakeholders happy and deliver an alternative for other users. We will walk through a sheet swapping exercise in the next section.

Utilizing sheet swapping

Sheet selection, often referred to as sheet swapping, allows the Tableau author to hide and display visualizations, as well as to move worksheets on and off the dashboard. These techniques have been used in creative ways with some very impressive results. For example, Tableau Zen Master Joshua Milligan has built various games, including Tic-Tac-Toe and Blackjack, using sheet selection. For our purposes, we will stick to using sheet selection to assist with creating dashboards that adhere to the design principles we've discussed.

In the *Use pie charts sparingly* section, we discussed pie charts and treemaps, and we noted that a treemap is a better visualization. However, people are often more comfortable with pie charts. As a compromise, in the first exercise, we will review an example that allows the end user to choose whether to see a pie chart or a treemap.

Please follow these steps:

1. Open the workbook associated with this chapter and navigate to the **Population Pie** worksheet.

2. Select the **World Indicators** data source and note the calculated field, called **Blank**. The code is composed of single quotes with a space in-between.

3. Place **Blank** on the **Columns** shelf.

4. In the view, select all pie slices via *Ctrl + A* or by dragging a marquee around the entire pie. Non-Cartesian visualization types (for example, visualizations with no fields on the **Rows or Columns** shelves) require this step for sheet swapping to work. Otherwise, when placing the worksheet in a vertical container on a dashboard, the worksheet will not properly stretch to fill the width of the container.

5. Right-click on any pie slice and choose **Annotate | Mark**.

6. In the resulting dialog box, delete all the text except `<Country>`:

Figure 11.12: Annotation

7. Position and format the annotations as desired. Note that additional adjustments may be required once the pie chart has been deployed on a dashboard.

8. Create a parameter named **Select Chart Type** with the following settings:

Figure 11.13: Parameter

9. Create a calculated field entitled **Sheet Swap** containing the following code:

    ```
    [Select Chart Type]
    ```

10. Place **Sheet Swap** on the **Filters** shelf and select **Pie Chart** in the resulting dialog box.

11. Display the parameter by right-clicking on **Select Chart Type** and choosing **Show Parameter Control**.

12. Navigate to the **Population Tree** worksheet.

13. Place **Blank** on the **Columns** shelf.

14. Place **Sheet Swap** on the **Filters** shelf and select **Treemap** in the resulting dialog box.

15. If **Treemap** does not display as a choice, make sure that the **Select Chart Type** parameter is toggled to **Treemap** and click **OK**:

Figure 11.14: Filter

16. Create a new dashboard entitled **Latin American Population**.

17. In the **Dashboard** pane, double-click on **Vertical** to place a vertical container on the dashboard.

18. In the **Dashboard** pane, double-click on **Population Tree** and **Population Pie** in order to add them to the view.

19. Right-click on the titles **Population Tree** and **Population Pie**, then select **Hide Title** for both.

20. Place **Population Map** and **Population Line** on our dashboard, then position them as desired:

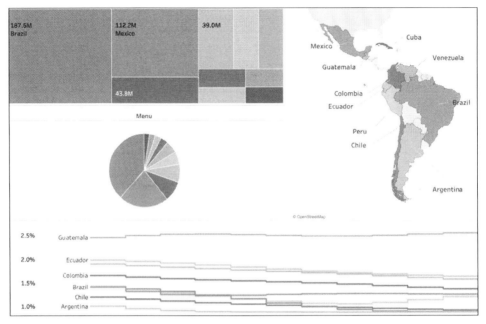

Figure 11.15: Dashboard

21. Shift-drag the **Select Chart Type** parameter over our **Treemap** in order to float the control; position it as desired.

22. Delete all legends and quick filters. Format, document, and position all dashboard elements as desired. The user can now determine whether to view a **Treemap** or a **Pie Chart**.

The following is an example of the dashboard with a treemap:

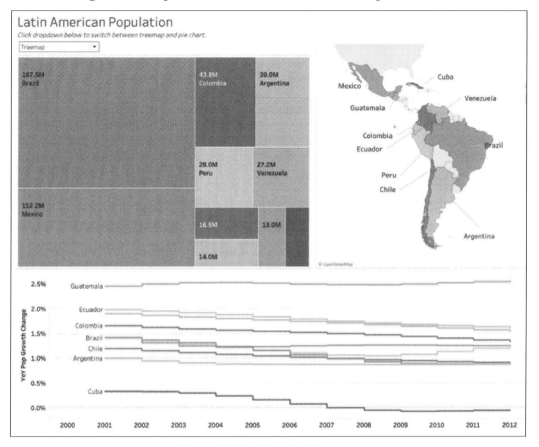

Figure 11.16: Dashboard with treemap

The following is with a pie chart:

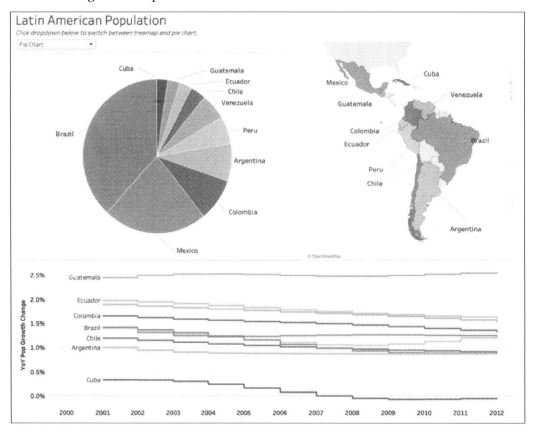

Figure 11.17: Pie chart

You can use the sheet swap feature in case some of your users prefer one visualization over the other. Next, we will create a filter menu that can be hidden on the dashboard. In the *Maximizing documentation on a dashboard* section, the point was made that dashboard space is precious. Therefore, in the second exercise, *Creating a collapsible menu*, we will review an example that will use sheet selection to allow the end user to show or hide filters, and thus make more efficient use of screen real estate.

Creating a collapsible menu

Please follow these steps to learn how to add a collapsible filter menu to your dashboards:

1. Duplicate the dashboard we created in the preceding exercise and rename it **Collapsible Menu**. If you did not complete the preceding exercise, utilize the dashboard included with the solution workbook provided with this chapter.

2. In the bottom portion of the **Dashboard** pane, select **Floating**:

Figure 11.18: Floating

3. Drag the **Menu Icon** worksheet from the dashboard pane onto the dashboard.

4. Right-click on the title and select **Hide Title**.

5. Set the fit of the **Menu Icon** worksheet to **Entire View**:

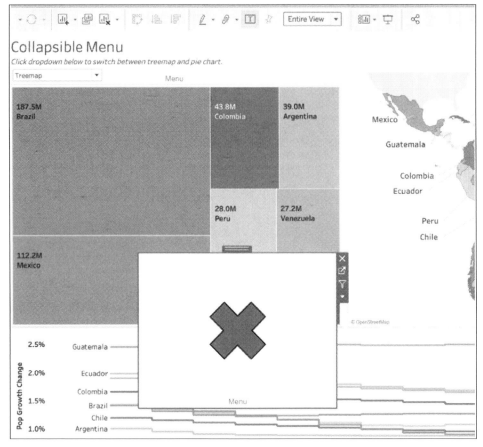

Figure 11.19: Menu

6. Size and position the **Menu Icon** worksheet so that it fits in the upper-right corner of the dashboard:

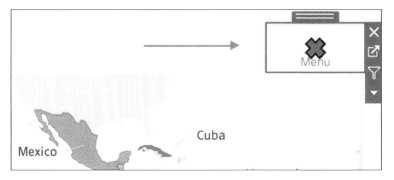

Figure 11.20: Menu II

7. In the bottom portion of the **Dashboard** pane, select **Tiled**.

8. Place the **Menu** worksheet anywhere on the dashboard. The filters for **Years** and **Country** should display on the right-hand side of the dashboard:

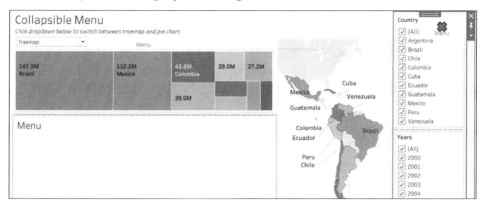

Figure 11.21: Collapsible Menu

9. Navigate to the **Menu** worksheet and take a moment to explore the settings of each dimension on the **Filters** shelf. Note that the region filter (**Latin American Countries**) is set to **Context** and that **Country Copy** is displayed as a quick filter. Also, note that the **Country (copy)** quick filter is set to **Show All Values in Context.** It is necessary to display the **Country (copy)** filter as opposed to the **Country** filter because **Country** displays the condition (that is, AVG([Population Total]) | 1000000) in the quick filter:

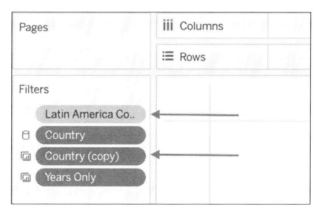

Figure 11.22: Filters

10. Return to the **Collapsible Menu** dashboard. Right-click on the **Menu** title and select **Hide Title**.

11. Make the **Menu** worksheet floating by clicking on the arrow next to the worksheet and selecting **Floating**:

Figure 11.23: Floating

12. Then, size and position with the following dimensions:

Figure 11.24: Menu position

Note that the goal of this step is to make the **Menu** worksheet as small as possible. It is necessary for the **Menu** worksheet to remain on the dashboard so that the accompanying **Year** and **Country** filters can be used.

13. On the **Dashboard** pane, select **Floating** and drag a **Horizontal** container onto the view in approximately the middle of the dashboard.

14. Within the **Layout** pane, set the width of the **Horizontal** container to **400**:

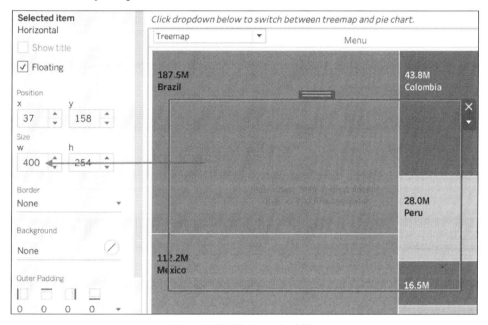

Figure 11.25: Horizontal widths

15. In the lower-right section of the dashboard, right-click the container that houses the **Country** and **Years** filters. In the resulting pop-up menu, choose **Edit Width** and set the value to 200:

Figure 11.26: Edit Width...

16. Drag the filter container selected in the previous step and place it in the container that is floating in the center of the dashboard:

Figure 11.27: Floating filter

17. From the **Dashboard** pane, press *Shift* to drag a vertical container and place it inside the left portion of the floating horizontal container:

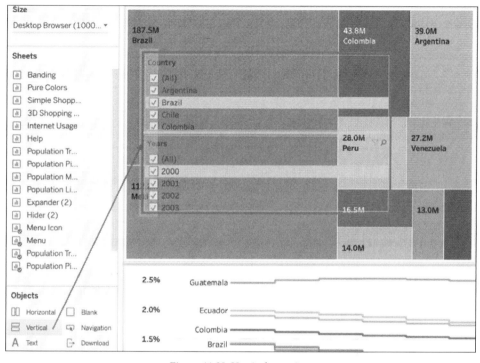

Figure 11.28: Vertical container

18. Right-click on the newly created vertical container and select **Fix Width**. The width of the vertical container should now be 200 pixels:

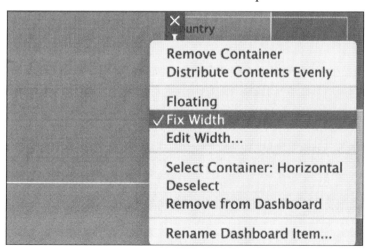

Figure 11.29: Fix width

19. Place the **Expander** worksheet in the newly created vertical container by pressing *Shift* and dragging.

20. The **Expander** worksheet contains a small, transparent image that will be used to expand and collapse the menu we are creating. However, an image does not have to be used; for example, text could be used instead. A transparent image is sometimes used in web design to stretch tables; we will make use of this method from web design here.

21. Set the fit for the **Expander** worksheet to **Entire View**.

22. Right-click on the **Expander** worksheet title and select **Hide Title**. The results should look similar to the following screenshot:

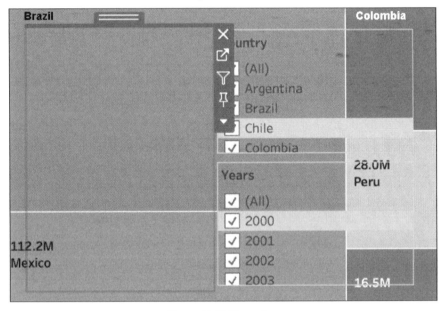

Figure 11.30: Expander

23. Within the **Layout** pane, select the horizontal container that contains the **Country** and **Years** filters and the **Expander** worksheet by right-clicking it and selecting **Select Container: Horizontal**, or by selecting the horizontal container from **Item hierarchy** under **Layout**:

Figure 11.31: Item hierarchy

 You can change the naming convention in the Item hierarchy to create different Dashboard Zone Names and find container and/or worksheets faster.

24. Enter the following dimensions:

Figure 11.32: Horizontal position

25. Select **Dashboard | Actions** and create the following filter action, called **Collapse/Expand**:

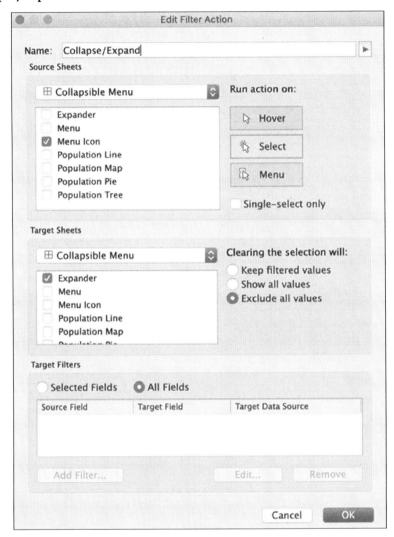

Figure 11.33 Filter action

26. In **Item hierarchy**, right-click on the vertical container that is housing the **Expander** worksheet and deselect **Fix Width**.

> This step is necessary so that the **Collapse/Expand** action will work properly. It was necessary to fix the container's width previously to properly align the contents of the container.

27. On the dashboard, click on **Menu Icon**. The **Expander** worksheet should appear and disappear, causing the filters to move on and off the dashboard. When you're finished with this step, make sure that the **Expander** worksheet is visible/the filters are located off the dashboard.

28. From the **Dashboard** pane, press *Shift* and drag two blank containers onto the dashboard. Position one directly above the **Expander** worksheet and one directly below. Size the blank containers so that the **Expander** worksheet is as small as possible, as indicated by the red arrow:

Figure 11.34: Add blanks

29. Be sure to continually test the **Menu** action as you adjust the size so as to not inadvertently break the collapsing functionality of the container.

30. Click the drop-down menus associated with both the **Country** and **Years** filters, then choose **Apply to Worksheets | Selected Worksheets**. In the resulting dialog boxes, choose **Population Line**, **Population Map**, **Population Pie,** and **Population Tree.**

31. Adjust the formatting and positioning as desired. The **Country** and **Years** filters can be hidden or shown by selecting the **Menu** button:

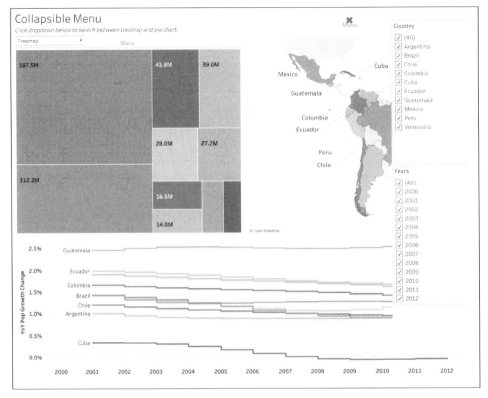

Figure 11.35: Collapsed Menu, which can be hidden by selecting the Menu button

In this section, we learned that by using containers and a filter, Tableau is able to automatically resize the selected worksheet within the container. This feature can be used to make it seem as if a worksheet can be swapped. However, Tableau basically just minimizes one and maximizes the other, even though this is not visible to the user's eye. Brilliant, isn't it?

After completing this exercise, you may think, OK: the filters do not technically display on the dashboard, but they are still visible to the side. While this is true in Tableau Desktop, if you are able to upload the workbook to an instance of Tableau Server, you will note that when clicking on the menu icon, the filters appear and disappear and do not display to the side. In the solution workbook provided with this chapter, the **Hider** worksheet has been floated off the right-hand side of the dashboard to completely hide the filters from view. Review the **Hider** approach if your design needs require completely hiding material that is beyond the confines of the dashboard.

The collapsible menu is a very nice add-on and contributes to the simplicity of your dashboard. The users can focus on the data and use the filter only if needed.

Dashboard best practices for user experience

Visualization best practices are not limited to visual features; actions, filters, and organizing data can be as important. A few of those features that Tableau has to offer shall be mentioned in this section. Each of them will help you to either improve the user experience or keep track of what you have built—since sometimes, you can get lost when working with many different worksheets.

In total, we will be discussing four features, two of each category mentioned previously. Actions (six in total) and export buttons contribute to a better user experience, and "Used In" as well as item hierarchy are part of a better dashboard building experience. Let's start!

Actions

Implicitly, we have discussed this a few times before, but let's have an explicit look at what we can achieve with regards to visualization and dashboard design by using **Actions**. Actions come into play if you want your user to be redirected by clicking or hovering on data in a viz. This can be helpful if you have a lot of data to show and don't want to put it all on the same dashboard. Neither should you, because it is distracting and if it is hierarchical data, actions are the perfect way to implement a drill-down technique.

The following sections will explain all the different actions you can use in Tableau for the purpose of adding interactivity to support a clean and effective dashboard design.

Filter actions

In this example, we will use a filter action to show data initially hidden. By doing so, we will make sure to present smaller chunks of data at a time and the user can drill down to any point of interest. Follow these steps:

1. Please open the worksheet **Quantity by State**:

Figure 11.36: Map

You can see in the preceding screenshot that each state represents the quantity of a given product sold. But wouldn't it be nice to see more details by clicking on a given state? In order to do so, we must set up actions.

2. First, we need a second worksheet we want to use in our action. Please open the worksheet **Profit by State by Category**:

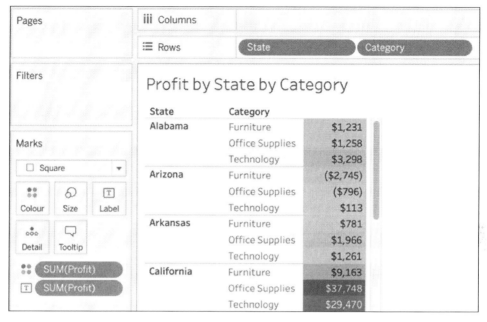

Figure 11.37: Table

You can see in the preceding screenshot that every state, every category, and the corresponding profit are shown.

3. Now, go back to the worksheet **Quantity by State** to enable an action that will prompt the user to go to the **Profit by State by Category** worksheet, and then filter it on the state they clicked on.

4. On the **Quantity by State** worksheet, select **Worksheet | Actions**; the following window will appear. Click on the **Add Action** button and select **Filter...**:

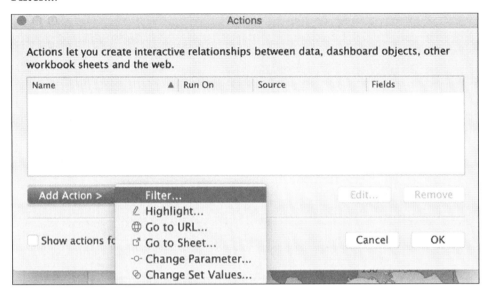

Figure 11.38: Filter action

5. In the next window, add a filter action called **Map to table (quantity to profit)** and copy the settings, as shown in the screenshot. Then, click **OK**:

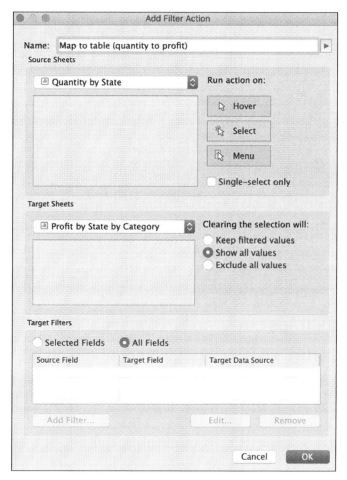

Figure 11.39: Filter action parameter

6. If you now click on a state on the worksheet **Quantity by State** (**Source Sheet**), Tableau will look for that same **State** on **Target Sheet** and filter accordingly. The following is an example after clicking on Texas:

Figure 11.40: Filtered table

The filter action discussed in this section can be used to declutter your dashboard. Following design principles often means less is more, and if you have lots of datapoints to share, a drill down or filter action can help you achieve this goal. Present high-level data first, then present a more detailed data layer behind a filter action. You can also add a sentence for your users below the title, like "Click on a state to see more details."

Highlight actions

Other options are, for example, a highlight action. This is more useful for worksheets on the same page because it will simply highlight applicable fields. You can show all data on the same dashboard, but the highlight action makes it easier for your users to find related data points. Follow these steps:

1. Therefore, please open the dashboard **Qty & Profit**, which combines the two worksheets we used previously:

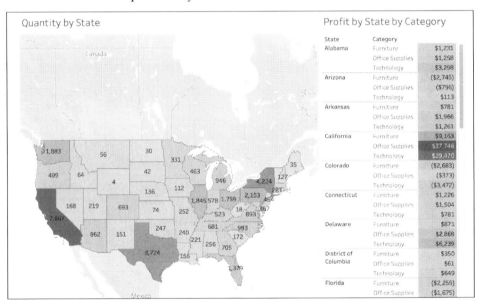

Figure 11.41: Dashboard

2. Click on **Dashboard | Actions** and this time, copy the following **Highlight Action** parameters:

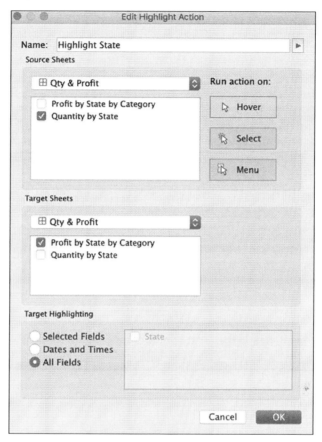

Figure 11.42: Highlight action

3. The preceding parameters mean that, on the **Qty & Profit** dashboard, our source worksheet will be **Quantity by State** and by hovering over it, the corresponding data on the target sheet will be highlighted. In this case, the only common data is **State**, so the highlighter will only take **State** into account. The result looks like this:

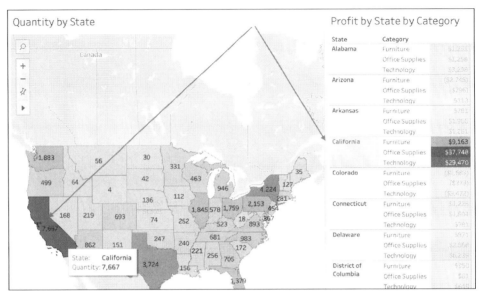

Figure 11.43: Highlight action dashboard

By hovering over California on the map, the same state will be highlighted in the right-hand table. As you can see, implementing a highlight filter can help your users find related data points faster. In contrast to the navigation action, this filter should be used for worksheets on the same page and as visual help to find a value.

URL actions

The next action is the URL action. This one allows you to open a URL when clicking on a data point in the dashboard. Follow these steps:

1. Go to the **Quantity by State** worksheet and open **Worksheet | Actions**.
2. Delete every action that is visible.

3. Now, select **Add Action** and select **Go to URL**. Copy all the parameters, as shown, and click on the arrow next to the Wikipedia URL. Fields from your data source will appear, which enables you to add a field to the URL that will automatically return a value based on the dashboard. Select **State**:

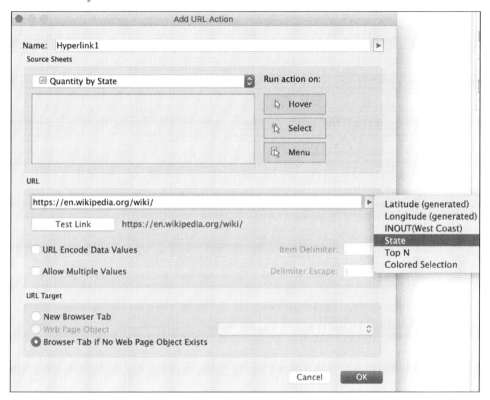

Figure 11.44: URL action

4. Click on a state on your map on the **Quantity by State** worksheet and see how Wikipedia will open the respective web page.

URL actions are very useful when you want to show your users additional information available on websites. You can also use latitude and longitude values to open Google Maps, link the URL action to company internal websites with regulations, or maybe a ticketing system.

Navigation actions

The next action used to be commonly used in combination with a button to give the user a more interactive experience. Instead of clicking on tabs to go from one to another page, you will add buttons with an action to go to a specific sheet:

1. Go to the **Qty & Profit** dashboard and create a calculated field called **String** with the code "Go back to [...]". This will serve as our button shortly.

2. Open a new worksheet and call it **Button**.

3. Place the calculated field **String** by dragging and dropping **Details** as well as **Label** on it.

4. Select **Shape** from the **Marks** card dropdown and select any shape (and color) of your choice.

5. Hide the title and disable **Tooltip**.

6. Click on **Label** and select **Bottom-Centre Alignment**. The result will look as follows:

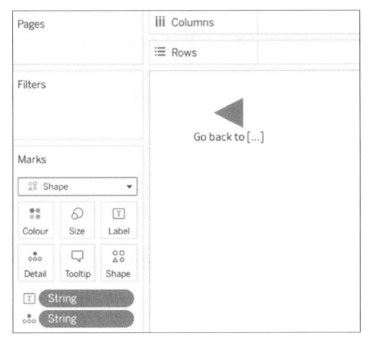

Figure 11.45: Button

7. Go back to the **Qty & Profit** dashboard, select **Floating**, and drag the **Button** worksheet onto the dashboard; for example, into the bottom-left corner:

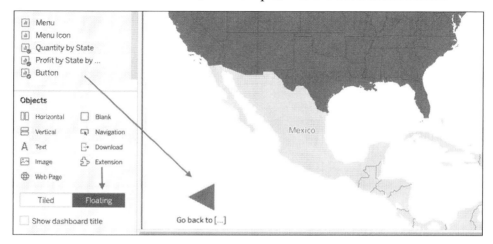

Figure 11.46: Button on the dashboard

8. Click on **Dashboard | Actions** and copy the following parameter:

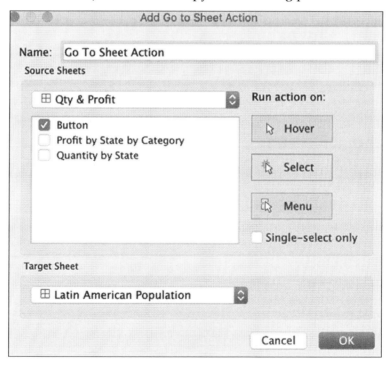

Figure 11.47: Go to Sheet action

9. Click **OK** and click on the **Button** worksheet on the **Qty & Profit** dashboard.

It will now take you back to the **Latin American Population** dashboard! Nowadays, this action is less used since the release of a specific navigation object, but it is useful to know about it for the sake of completeness.

Parameter actions

The next one in line is **Parameter Action**. This one is used to change a parameter by clicking on a data point in the dashboard rather than using the parameter control. Follow these steps:

1. Place the **Categories** worksheet on the **Qty & Profit** dashboard; for example, in the top-right corner:

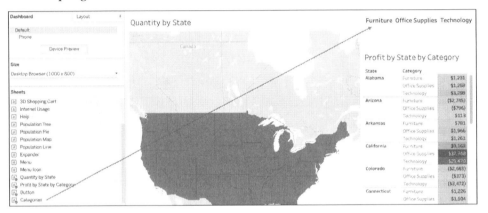

Figure 11.48: Parameter action

2. Click on **Dashboard | Actions** and copy the following parameters:

Figure 11.49: Parameter action setup

3. Create a calculated field called `Cat Param` with the following code:

```
If [Parameter Action] = [Category]
Then [Category]
Else ""
END
```

4. Place **Cat Param** on the **Filter** shelf on the worksheet **Profit by State by Category** and select the empty value and enable **Exclude**, as shown here, before selecting **OK**:

Figure 11.50: Category filter

5. If you now hover over any **Category** at the top, the following table will adjust accordingly:

Figure 11.51: Category filtered dashboard

Set actions

The last action that we will discuss is the set action. A set splits your data in two, **In** or **Out**. If you were to create a set called animals based on the following list: [cat, tree, dog, leopard, house, car], you would mark cat, dog, and leopard as **In** and tree, house, and car as **Out**. You can then use the set as a new field for your dashboard. Follow these steps:

1. Go to the **Qty & Profit** dashboard and select the western states California, Oregon, and Washington. Note that the pop-up window shows two rings in the top-right part. Using this icon is one way to create a set; go ahead and click on it:

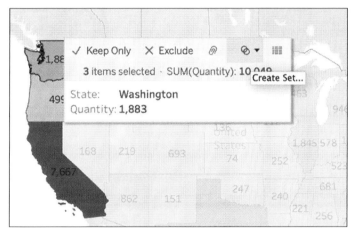

Figure 11.52: Set action

2. The following window will open; click **OK**:

Figure 11.53: Set

In the data pane, a new field has been created—a set called **West Coast**.

3. See how it works by changing the **Profit by State by Category** worksheet as follows, removing **State** from **Rows**, and adding **West Coast** instead (you can remove **Cat Param** from the filter shelf or leave it; both will work):

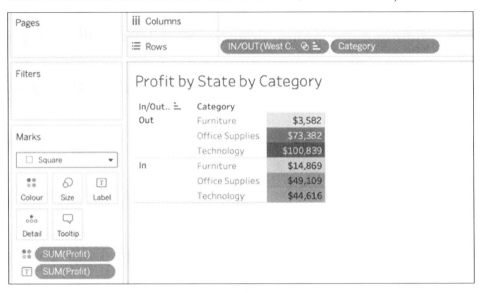

Figure 11.54: Setting field states

The profit in the **Out** band takes into account all states except for California, Oregon, and Washington, whereas the **In** band shows numbers relative to those three mentioned states.

4. Go back to the **Qty & Profit** dashboard and select **Dashboard | Actions** to copy the following parameter into a **Set Action**:

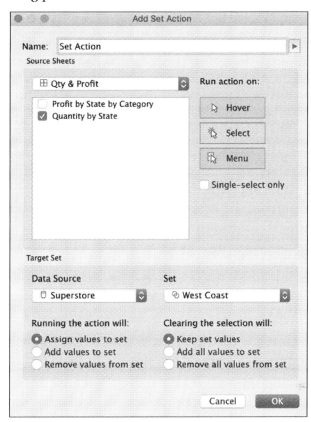

Figure 11.55: Set action parameter

5. If you now click on any one or multiple states, all selected states will be the **In** group of your set. Therefore, the profit numbers will show the profit of your selection against the rest, like so:

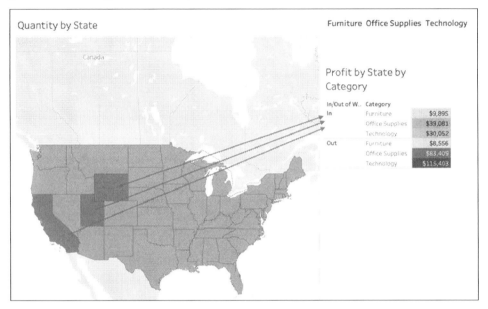

Figure 11.56: Set action dashboard

6. You can also rename the **In** and **Out** values by clicking and selecting **Edit Alias…** :

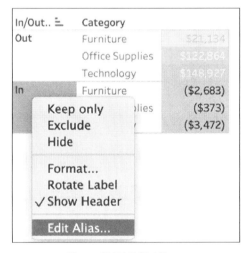

Figure 11.57: Edit Alias…

Those were the six Tableau actions; with the Filter and Highlight actions, you can make it easier for your users to find more detailed information by drilling down. The Go to Sheet and Go to URL actions can be seen as interactive buttons that will redirect your user to additional information, either on the web or on another sheet. And lastly, the Change Parameter and Change Set actions can be used to adjust a predefined value or multiple values, which will allow your users to interact with and analyze the data from different angles.

Export Dashboard Button

Next to actions, another item that's part of the user experience is a built-in download button. Adding such a button to your dashboard will allow your users to share an image or a screenshot, if they like, with others, use it for documentation, or for presentation purposes. Adding a button is super easy, just follow the steps:

1. Open the dashboard **Golden Rectangle**, select **Floating** in the bottom-left corner, and drag **Download** to the top-right corner:

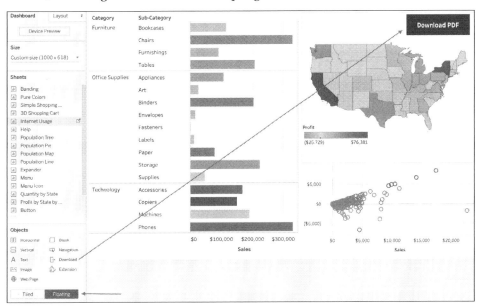

Figure 11.58: Download button

2.   Click on the newly added button; a **Print to PDF** popup will appear:

Figure 11.59: Print to PDF

3.   Click **OK**, after which you can open the dashboard as a PDF from your desktop.

That's it! In only one simple step, you can make many users that like to have a printout very happy. A Tableau workbook as well as Tableau dashboards can become very overwhelming, depending on how many worksheets are being used to create them. Luckily, Tableau helps us with organizational features like **Item hierarchy** and **Used In**.

Item hierarchy

As we briefly mentioned in the *Creating a collapsible menu* section, if you open the **Latin American Population** dashboard, you will notice **Item hierarchy** at the bottom-left of the **Layout** pane. By clicking on the arrow next to the word **Tiled**, you will be able to see all the different part of the dashboards and the worksheets used in each container. You can also spot containers in containers and the structure of your layout:

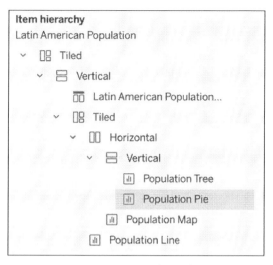

Figure 11.60: Item hierarchy extended

Try to keep a logical order within your item hierarchy. This will make it easier for you to make changes to your dashboard later on. Which logic you choose is up to you; one I use often is high-level to more detailed, or most important to least important, or from spacious worksheets to smaller ones. A nice article on keeping your dashboard clean can be found here: `https://www.thedataschool.co.uk/joe-beaven/layout-containers-how-to-get-your-item-hierarchy-under-control`.

Used In

The **Used In** feature shows you on which dashboards a certain worksheet is used. Just right-click on a worksheet and select **Used In**:

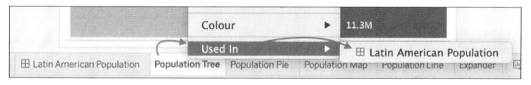

Figure 11.61: Used In

This feature is especially useful if you want to make changes to a worksheet. Before execution, you can check which dashboards will be affected, and the risk of breaking an existing dashboard will decrease tremendously.

Summary

We began this chapter by considering visualization design theory. We looked at formatting rules, color rules, and rules about which visualization types to use and which we need to avoid. We also explored how to compromise when contradictory design goals are expressed by end users. Then, we discussed dashboard design principles. We covered three popular layouts: the Golden Rectangle, quad, and small multiple.

Afterward, we looked at how to use sheet selection techniques as an ally in good design. Specifically, we explored how to allow the end user to choose which visualization type to view, and how to hide and display filters so as to make the best use of screen real estate. Finally, we discussed actions and download buttons for a better user experience, as well as item hierarchies and the **Used In** feature, which is very handy for organizing your dashboard. This, in turn, will help to improve the layout design.

In the next chapter, we will focus on use cases. Going from a dataset to a product will be the theme, and we will practice doing this with a World Index dataset and a couple of geospatial ones. The knowledge you gained from the previous chapters will be very useful!

12
Advanced Analytics

This chapter focuses on advanced self-service analytics. Self-service analytics can be seen as a form of business intelligence, where people in a business are encouraged to execute queries on datasets themselves, instead of placing requests for queries in a backlog with an IT team. Then, query analysis can be done, which should lead to more insights and data-driven decision-making. But how do you start creating useful self-service dashboards if it's your first time doing so? How do you go from a dataset to a product? Have you ever asked yourself how other people start working on a dashboard, how they clean data, and how they come up with a dashboard design? If so, this is the right chapter for you! I want to share three use cases with you, written as a train of thought in order to give you an idea about how I work. Please note that this is just my personal experience; there are many different ways that can lead you to your goal.

We will cover the following topics:

- Visualizing world indices correlations
- Geo-spatial analytics with Chicago traffic violations
- Extending geo-spatial analytics with distance measures

Now that we have had this introduction, we are good to go and can start with the first use case.

Visualizing world indices correlations

Imagine you are working on the world indices dataset and your line manager gives you the following task:

Create a dashboard for me in which I can easily spot all correlated world indices and their distribution. I need it by tomorrow morning.

Now, take a few minutes before you continue reading and think about how you would tackle this task. The dataset contains 67 columns with various indices, like birth registrations or emission values, exports and imports, and forest areas, divided into 188 rows, where each row represents one country.

Write down your planned steps, open the workbook related to this chapter from https://public.tableau.com/profile/marleen.meier, and follow your steps; time it in order to get a better feel for time estimates when working with Tableau. This way, you can make sure that you can deliver on time and manage expectations if you are ever asked how long it will take to build a certain dashboard.

Plotting a scattergraph

And now, I will illustrate one way I could imagine solving this task:

1. First, I open the world-indices file in Tableau Prep Builder in order to get more details on the dataset itself; this will help us to describe the data but also to spot obvious data flaws like null values, duplicate entries, and so on:

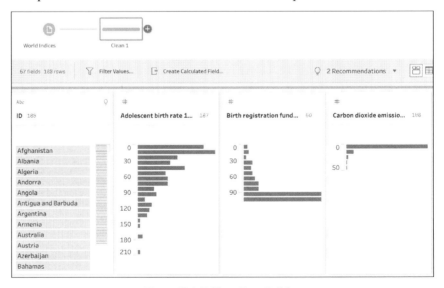

Figure 12.1: Tableau Prep Builder

With this dataset, I actually didn't spot any obvious data quality issues in Prep Builder, nor a need to further prepare the data. It's 1 row per country — which you can see in the evenly distributed bars in the **Id** column — and 65 columns for the different indices per country. Since no data preparation is needed, I decide to continue directly with Tableau Desktop. I close Tableau Prep Builder and open Tableau Desktop.

2. My next thought is, how can I visualize all correlations at once, yet not have it be too much information? I do have 65 different columns, which makes for 4,225 possible combinations. No, I decide that displaying everything won't work. The task is very generic; therefore, I decide to go for a two-parameter approach, which will enable my end user to select each of the index combinations themselves. I start sketching what the dashboard might look like and come up with the following:

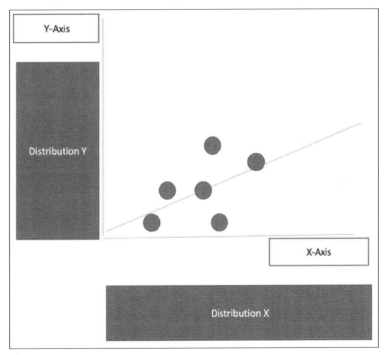

Figure 12.2: Sketch

3. In order to execute my plan, I first create two parameters, which I name **X-Axis** and **Y-Axis**, which will be used to define the respective axes *x* and *y*.

4. I define both parameters as **String** and paste all field names from the clipboard into both of the parameters. To do this, I open the input file in Excel, transpose the header row to a column, and press *Ctrl + C*. The data can now be pasted into the parameter via the **Paste from Clipboard** option. This saves time and is less error-prone:

Figure 12.3: Paste to parameter

5. I also want the parameters to be visible on the dashboard, so I select **Show Parameter**:

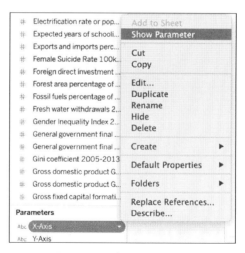

Figure 12.4: Show Parameter

6. If you were to test the parameter now, nothing would happen. We need a calculated field that defines that if a selection from the parameter has been made, Tableau will select the appropriate field. I create the following calculated field to achieve this (this field has been made part of the `Starter` and `Solution` workbook to make your life easier):

Figure 12.5: Calculated field

7. Now we will do the same thing for the **Y-Axis** parameter.

 In order to create the calculated field for **Y-Axis** quicker, copy and paste the **X-Axis** calculated field into Excel and find and replace [Parameters].[X-Axis] with [Parameters].[Y-Axis].

8. Drag the **X-Axis** calculated field to **Columns** and **Y-Axis** to **Rows**. Also, put the **ID** field on the **Detail** shelf.

9. In order to see the correlation analytics from Tableau, drag **Trend Line** onto the sheet:

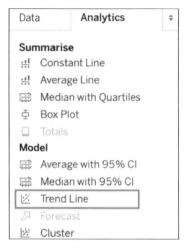

Figure 12.6: Trend Line

The sheet with the trend line looks as follows. When hovering over the trend line, you will see the equation of the line, the **R-Squared** value, and the value for **P-value**:

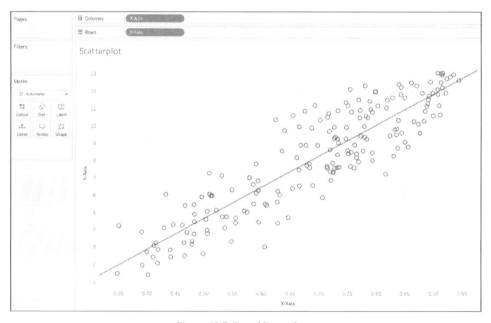

Figure 12.7: Trend line values

The **Y-Axis** equation means that, for each point on the *x*-axis, the *y*-axis value will increase by 17.9717, starting at point 0 on the *x*-axis and point -4.33685 on the *y*-axis. Thus, overall the *y*-term increases faster than the (also increasing) *x*-term. The **R-Squared** value explains how much variance is explained by the trend line (80.81%), and lastly **P-value** explains the significance of the model. A **P-value** value smaller than 0.05 is considered significant and means there is a 5% chance that the data is following the trend line randomly. The trend line in the preceding figure has a **P-value** of less than 0.01%. We can safely assume, therefore, that there is a real relationship between the two variables.

10. In order to see more coefficients, right-click on the line and select **Describe Trend Line...**:

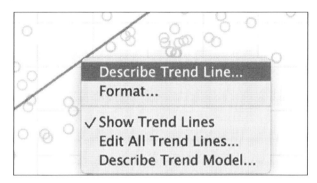

Figure 12.8: Describe Trend Line...

The following window will appear:

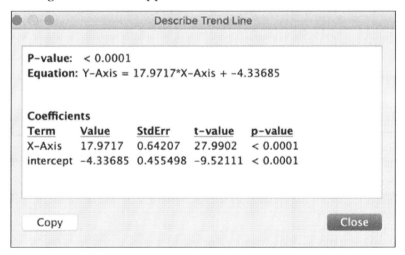

Figure 12.9: Trend line information

Alternatively, you can select the **Describe Trend Model...** option and you will see this:

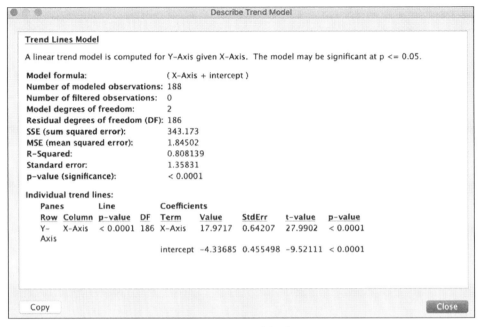

Figure 12.10: Trend model information

 If you want to learn more about interpreting trend lines, you can read the following article: https://onlinehelp. tableau.com/current/pro/desktop/en-us/ trendlines_add.htm.

11. I get a bit distracted by the grid lines, so I decide to remove them by right-clicking on the screen and selecting **Format...**:

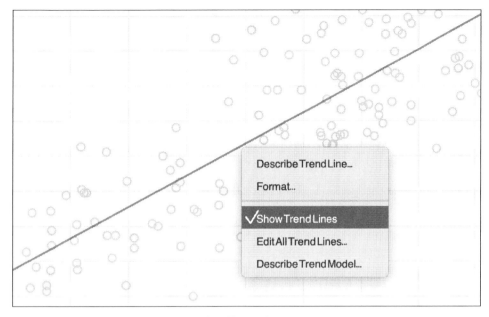

Figure 12.11: Formatting

12. I select the fifth option in the **Format** window, the lines, and remove the **Grid Lines** value:

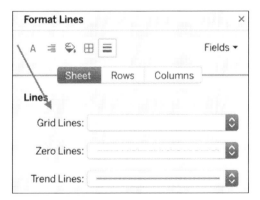

Figure 12.12: Removing grid lines

13. I also change **Marks** from **Automatic** to **Circle** and change the color to black.

14. Now, I think it would be helpful to show on the scatterplot which country each point represents, so I change the **ID** field from **Detail** to **Label** in the **Marks** card; however, this looks a bit too chaotic:

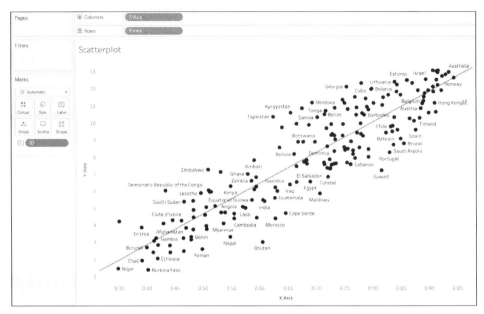

Figure 12.13: ID to text

15. I click on the undo arrow and I add a highlighter function by right-clicking on **ID** and selecting **Show Highlighter**. Now, the end user will be able to search a country and that point will be highlighted in the scatterplot:

Figure 12.14: Show Highlighter

16. I also want the country name to show clearly and in red when hovering over any points, and I achieve this by changing the **ID** color in **Edit Tooltip** to red and increase the size:

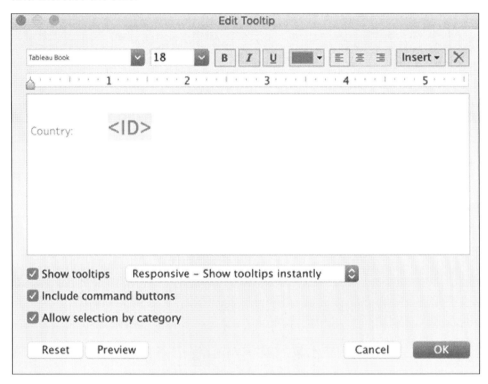

Figure 12.15: Tooltip

The result looks as follows:

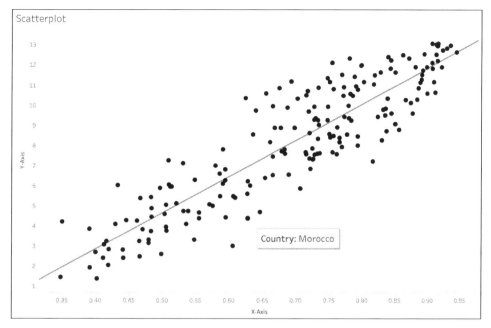

Figure 12.16: Hovering over a point

17. I have already added the trend line, and I now want to show the **Pearson R**, also called **R-Squared**, value in the view such that the user knows if two indices are correlated; however, it is not possible to set the **Describe Trend Line** or **Describe Trend Model** option to always be shown. Hence, I will calculate the value myself in a new field; I use the CORR() function to do this:

Figure 12.17: Pearson R

18. But I want to show some text that indicates if two variables are correlated or not instead of the value itself, because I want to make my dashboard clear. Therefore, I create another calculated field called `Correlation yes or no` with the following code:

```
IF [Pearson R] > 0.7 then 'The two indices <' + [Parameters].
[X-Axis]+ '> and <'+ [Parameters].[Y-Axis]+ '> have a very
strong positive correlation of: ' + STR([Pearson R])
ELSEIF [Pearson R] < 0.7 and [Pearson R] > 0.4 then 'The two
indices <' + [Parameters].[X-Axis] + '> and <'+ [Parameters].
[Y-Axis]+ '> have a strong positive correlation of: '  +
STR([Pearson R])
ELSEIF [Pearson R] < 0.4 and [Pearson R] > 0.2 then 'The two
indices <' + [Parameters].[X-Axis] + '> and <'+ [Parameters].
[Y-Axis]+ '> have a moderate positive correlation of: ' +
STR([Pearson R])
ELSEIF  [Pearson R] <0.2 and [Pearson R] > -0.2 then 'The two
indices <' + [Parameters].[X-Axis] + '> and <'+ [Parameters].
[Y-Axis]+ '> have no or a weak correlation of:' + STR([Pearson
R])
ELSEIF [Pearson R] < -0.2 and [Pearson R] >-0.4 then 'The two
indices <' + [Parameters].[X-Axis] + '> and <'+ [Parameters].
[Y-Axis]+ '> have a moderate negative correlation of: '+
STR([Pearson R])
ELSEIF [Pearson R] < -0.4 and [Pearson R] > -0.7 then 'The two
indices <' + [Parameters].[X-Axis] + '> and <'+ [Parameters].
[Y-Axis]+ '> have a strong negative correlation of: ' +
STR([Pearson R])
ELSEIF [Pearson R] < -0.7 THEN 'The two indices <'  +
[Parameters].[X-Axis] + '> and <'+ [Parameters].[Y-Axis]+ '>
have a very strong negative correlation of: ' + STR([Pearson R])
END
```

19. This being done, I create a new sheet and place **Correlation yes or no** on the **Text** shelf. The sheet looks very simple, as you can see:

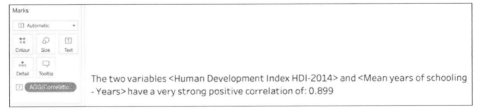

Figure 12.18: Correlation on text

20. I right-click on the title and choose **Hide Title**.

Finally, almost everything is ready to build the dashboard from the sketch at the beginning of this section. Only the distributions for each of the two axes are still missing.

Adding axis distributions

We have made a start, but now I want to add the distribution plots for the *x*- and *y*-axes next to the scatterplot. I take the following steps:

1. I start with the *x*-axis, open another worksheet, and drag **ID** to **Columns** and **X-Axis** to **Rows** and change the color to gray in the **Marks** card. I also select **Entire View** at the top of the page.

2. The *x*-axis distribution should be aligned to the scatterplot; therefore, I want the bars to form from top to bottom. I achieve this by clicking on the *x*-axis and selecting **Reversed** for **Scale**:

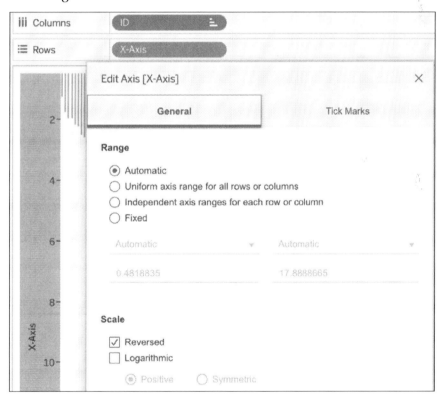

Figure 12.19: Edit Axis [X-Axis]

3. After I close the **Edit Axis [X-Axis]** window, I right-click on **X-Axis** and deselect **Show Header** to not show the header anymore.

4. The values should also be sorted from smallest to biggest, just like in the scatterplot. I click on **ID** in **Columns** and select **Field** for **Sort By**, as shown in the dialog box below:

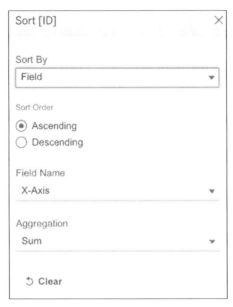

Figure 12.20: Sort by field

5. I continue with **Y-Axis** on another new worksheet and drag **Y-Axis** to **Columns** and **ID** to **Rows** and change the color to gray in the **Marks** card. I also select **Entire View** at the top of the page.

6. Just like in *step 2*, the *y*-axis distribution should be aligned to the scatterplot; therefore, I want the bars to form from right to left. I achieve this by clicking on the *y*-axis and selecting **Reversed** for **Scale**.

7. After I close the **Edit Axis [Y-Axis]** window, I right-click on **Y-Axis** and deselect **Show Header** to not show the header anymore.

8. The values should also be sorted from biggest to smallest, just like in the scatterplot. I click on **ID** in **Columns** and select **Field** for **Sort By**, as shown in the next figure:

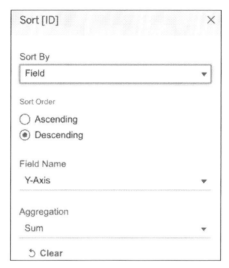

Figure 12.21: Sorting by field

9. In order to put everything together, I open a dashboard page and call it **Distribution 1**, then I put the scatterplot worksheet at the bottom of the page and the correlation text worksheet at the top of the dashboard canvas:

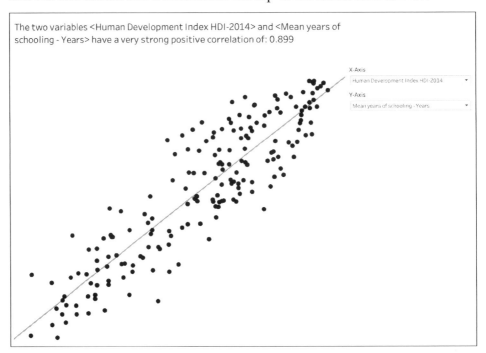

Figure 12.22: Dashboard

10. I add the distribution worksheet to the related site of the scatterplot (Y to the *y*-axis and X to the *x*-axis).

11. Then I add a blank in the lower left-hand corner to align the distribution with the scatterplot edges:

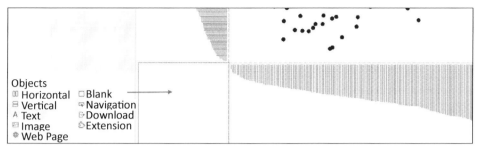

Figure 12.23: Adding a blank

The final layout looks like this:

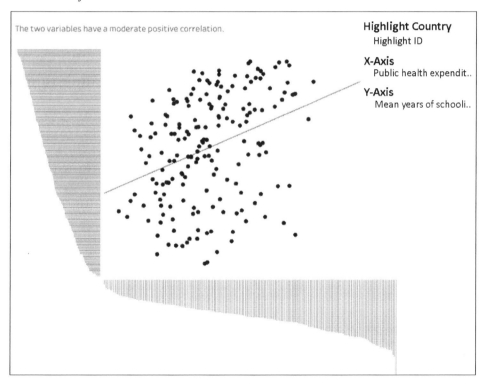

Figure 12.24: Final layout

12. I want to give the distribution more meaning and add an action that will highlight the country in both distribution plots. I do this so the user can see where a country is located in the range of all countries within one index because it can be hard to see in the scatterplot sometimes. The scatterplot, on the other hand, can be used to get more insights into the relationship between the two indices. For the **Highlight** action, I need to set the parameters as follows:

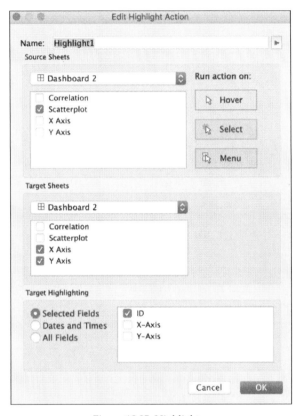

Figure 12.25: Highlighter

Look at the following screenshot: I hovered over the dot that represents the Netherlands. I can see that the Netherlands is quite high in both selected indices and that it is close to the trend line, but I can also see in the distribution bar chart that in the *y*-index **Mean years of schooling**, quite a few countries score higher than the Netherlands, whereas in the *x*-index **Public health expenditure percentage of GDP 2013**, there is only one more country that scores higher:

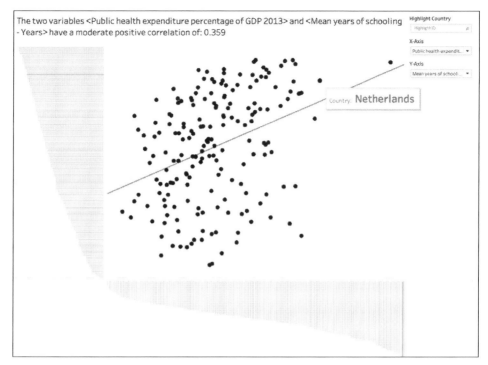

The two variables <Public health expenditure percentage of GDP 2013> and <Mean years of schooling - Years> have a moderate positive correlation of: 0.359

Highlight Country

X-Axis
Public health expendit...

Y-Axis
Mean years of school...

Country: Netherlands

Figure 12.26: Final layout II

13. Another idea is to change the distribution plots to a count of values per bin. A bin is a range of values, which is more likely what you will see when people talk about distribution plots. This would basically show which bin contains the most countries, and if the plot is normally distributed or maybe another distribution such as Poisson, Log-Normal, or Student's t-distribution. I think that in this context either factor would add value; therefore, I will add them both and present both to my boss, so there are two options to choose from.

14. I duplicate the two worksheets that contain the distribution plot by clicking on the tabs and selecting **Duplicate**.

15. I click on **X-Axis | Create | Bins…**, leave the settings as they are, and click **OK**. A new **X-Axis (bin)** field will be created:

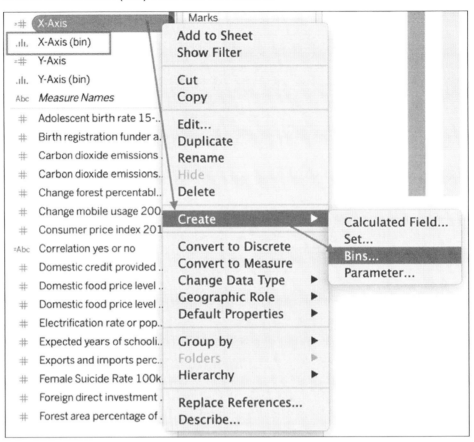

Figure 12.27: Create bins

16. I repeat the previous step for **Y-Axis**.

17. Next, for the **Y-Axis**, I add **Count of Y-Axis** to **Columns**, **Y-Axis (bin)** to **Rows**, and **ID** to **Detail** in the **Marks** card. Sort **Y-Axis (bin)** in descending order:

Figure 12.28: Layout

18. For **X-Axis**, I add **Count of X-Axis** to **Rows**, **X-Axis (bin)** to **Columns**, and the **ID** field to **Detail** in the **Marks** card. Sort **X-Axis (bin)** in ascending order.

19. I duplicate the previously created dashboard **Distribution 1** by clicking on the tab and clicking **Duplicate**. In this new version, I replace the former distributions with the new ones with the bins. The result looks as follows:

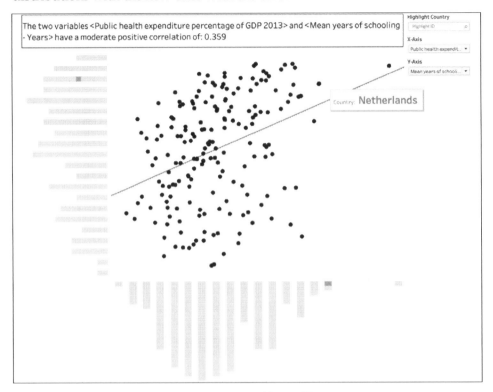

Figure 12.29: Final layout III

Adding a correlation matrix

After clicking through the dashboard and testing the functionality, I realize that it's hard to remember which combinations I have already tried, and also I wish I could filter on highly correlated combinations. To address this, I want to add one more dashboard to this workbook: a correlation matrix with all combinations, color-coded and with an option to filter:

1. First, I go back to my data source tab and add the same dataset again, but with a new name: **World Indices Correlation Matrix**. And I even add it twice because I need every index correlated against every other index:

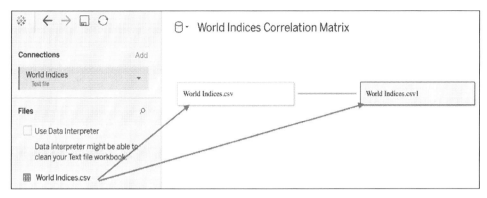

Figure 12.30: World Indices Correlation Matrix

2. The key used is **ID**:

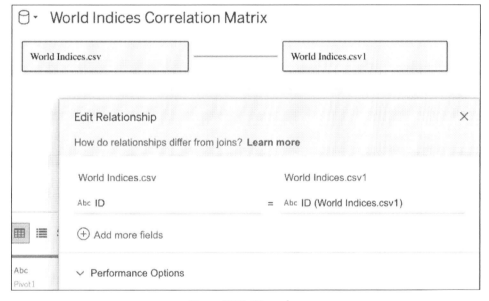

Figure 12.31: ID as a key

3. Then, I need to pivot both tables because instead of having one column per index, I need one column with all index names and a second column with all values in order to create a table with each of them. I select all fields except **ID** and use **Pivot**:

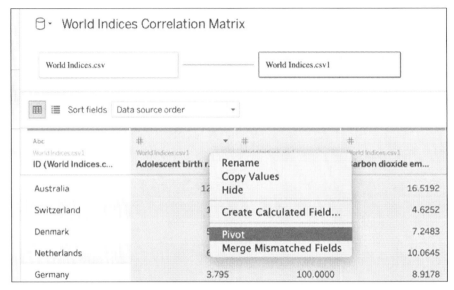

Figure 12.32: Pivoting

4. This results in three columns, I rename **Pivot Field Values** as **Value Index A** and **Pivot Field Names** as **Index A**:

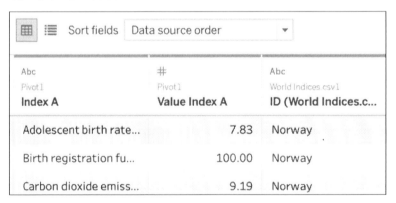

Figure 12.33: Renaming columns

5. Now I do this again with the second table and rename the columns **Index B** and **Value Index B**.

6. I open a new worksheet and place **Index B** on **Columns**, and **Index A** on **Rows**. I create a calculated field named **Pearson R** with the code `CORR([Value Index B], [Value Index A])` and place it on **Filters**, **Colour**, and **Text**. After right-clicking on **Pearson R** in the **Filters** shelf, I select **Show Filter**:

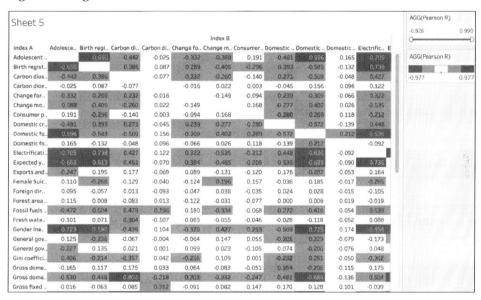

Figure 12.34: Correlation matrix

The colors can be adjusted as you like; I chose a 5-stepped color scheme from red to black, indicating that red fields are negatively correlated and black ones positively.

7. I open a new dashboard tab and place the worksheet on it. Try adjusting the filter such that you only see the highly correlated range 0.89–0.99, just to have a smaller dataset to work with for now:

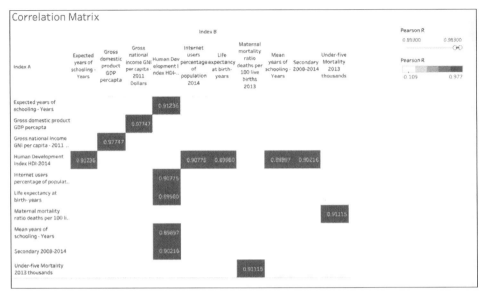

Figure 12.35: Filter correlation matrix

This section helped us to create a heatmap of all possible combinations, and we color-coded the correlation value and added a filter to it in order to focus on points of interest. In the preceding screenshot, you can see the highly correlated indices.

Finalizing the dashboard

To avoid any confusion, I want to explain the **Pearson R** filter for the user and finalize the dashboard:

1. I start by adding a text field to the dashboard. With more time, I could make it a drop-down parameter just like the **X-Axis** and **Y-Axis** fields:

Figure 12.36: Adding text about Pearson R

2. To finalize everything, three actions are needed. First, two **Parameter** actions are needed to enable a click in the correlation matrix to change the values for the **X-Axis** and **Y-Axis** parameters, the first of which should be customized as follows:

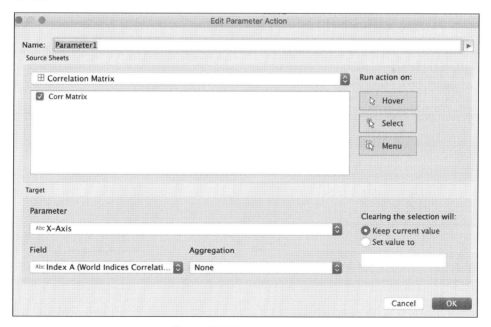

Figure 12.37: Parameter action 1

The action in the preceding screenshot will change the **X-Axis** parameter to the value from **Index A**.

3. Now, I edit the second parameter action as follows:

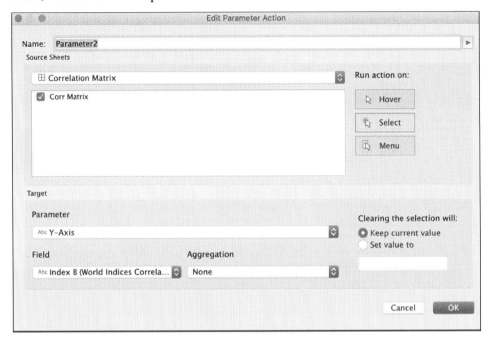

Figure 12.38: Parameter action 2

The action in the preceding figure will change the **Y-Axis** parameter to the value from **Index B**.

4. Lastly, I add a **Sheet Navigation** action called **GoToScatterplot** that allows the user to change the dashboard after selecting an index combination:

Figure 12.39: Sheet navigation action

5. The preceding action will show a menu to go to the trend line dashboard.

6. The user can now select a value and click on it. In the background, the parameters **X-Axis** and **Y-Axis** will be adjusted to the two indices that relate to that same field. For example, for **Mean years of schooling** and **Human Development Index**, a hyperlink appears:

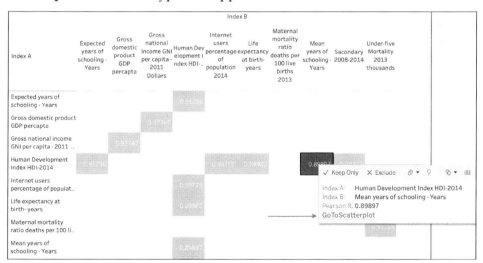

Figure 12.40: Menu

7. The user will be redirected to the dashboard with a trend line that is now prefiltered and shows the same two indices: **Mean years of schooling** and **Human Development Index**:

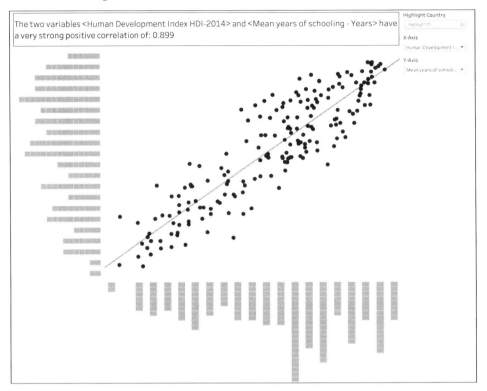

Figure 12.41: Filtered visualization

From this, we can see that the two selected indices are positively correlated by 89.9%. We can also see the distribution per index on the *x*- and *y*-axes.

This was a lengthy exercise, but I wanted to present you with my full thought process and look at dashboard creation. With more time, I would definitely add some more insights; for instance:

- Add an explanation for each index
- Add a more thorough explanation for the correlation
- Add the p-value or other coefficients to the analysis and change the text accordingly

And don't forget to get feedback and check with your stakeholders if you are on the right track. Some people use sketches, then work on a draft, and then ask for feedback again, until the product is finalized. I tend to ask my stakeholders questions to better understand what they need and let them walk me through the process they want to replace or change with the Tableau dashboard. Then I present a full version or intermediate version, depending on complexity and timelines. It should be avoided that you spend hours or days on something that is not what the stakeholder wants.

But now, let us have a look at a second short use case that incorporates geo-spatial data.

Geo-spatial analytics with Chicago traffic violations

It's Wednesday morning; your manager comes into your office wanting to check the red-light violations of the last year in Chicago. They ask if you can build a dashboard for that purpose. In particular, you're asked to highlight where the most violations happen and whether there is an overall trend in Chicago traffic light violations over the last few years. You are given two datasets, one with the camera locations and one with the violations, and told that the dashboard is needed within the next hour. What do you do?

Before you continue reading, think about how you would approach this problem. Take five minutes, think about the steps you would take, and sketch a dashboard design.

The following is an overview of how I would do it:

1. Open the datasets in Tableau Prep Builder
2. Join the two datasets
3. Clean the data if needed
4. Open the output in Tableau
5. Use a map to visualize the locations of cameras, if possible
6. Add the number of violations per camera
7. Establish whether there is a monthly trend

What follows is a rough sketch of how I would design the dashboard:

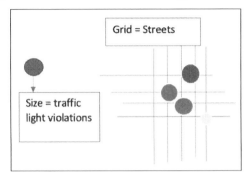

Figure 12.42: Sketch

Up next is a step-by-step description of what I would do. The corresponding Tableau dashboard can be downloaded from Tableau Public, the Tableau Prep Builder file is available on GitHub (`https://github.com/PacktPublishing/Mastering-Tableau-2021`), and the dataset itself is publicly available here: `https://data.cityofchicago.org/Transportation/Red-Light-Camera-Violations/spqx-js37`.

Preparing the data

After loading both files into Tableau Prep Builder, I see that a join on **Longitude** and **Latitude** doesn't get me anywhere, because almost all records are mismatches:

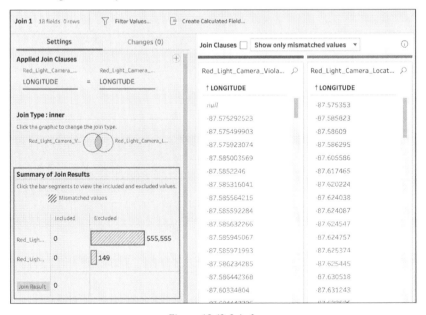

Figure 12.43: Join I

I try a different approach: a join on the intersections. This results, again, in **0** joined rows, but this time I see why. In one dataset, the **Intersection** values are separated with a dash (-) and in the other dataset it's **AND**; also, one uses capital letters, and the other one doesn't:

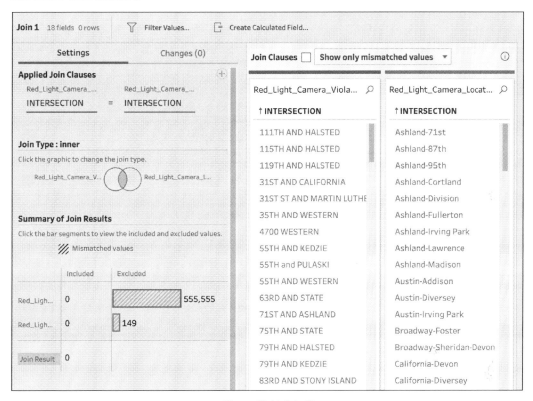

Figure 12.44: Join II

I could add a cleaning step to make all the letters uppercase and split the intersections into two parts. I can execute **Custom Split...** on - as well as on **AND**:

Figure 12.45: Data prepping

Then, I notice that the intersection order is different; for example, **Ashland-71st** and **71ST AND ASHLAND**. I might consider restructuring the datasets and creating a loop that would put the two streets in alphabetical order in the two splits, but I don't have time for this now.

Another solution is to first join split 1 and split 1 as well as split 2 and split 2. In a second join, I could join split 1 and split 2 as well as split 2 and split 1. Afterward, I could union the two joins and create an output file (or directly load the Prep Builder dataset into Tableau Desktop). With this approach, I would still not include all the data, but I would have 380,000 rows out of 444,000. This could be enough to get a rough idea of patterns. If I have any time left, I can continue mapping the remaining mismatches.

However, I instead decide to drop the locations dataset altogether and just use the violations dataset, because it has the location of every violation and therefore the location dataset is not even needed.

Building a map of intersections

I continue by opening the violations dataset in Tableau:

1. Longitude and latitude values are not automatically recognized, so I have to change both to **Number (decimal)** by clicking on the data type icon:

Figure 12.46: Change data type

2. Then, I change the **Longitude** and **Latitude** fields to **Measure** by clicking on the drop-down arrow on the field as shown in the preceding figure and select **Convert to Measure**.

3. Now I can click on the data type icon again and change the two fields to **Latitude** and **Longitude**:

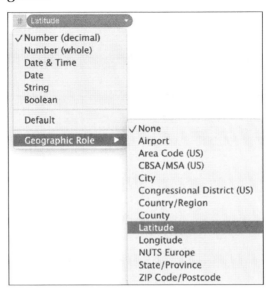

Figure 12.47: Changing the geographic role

4. By dragging **Longitude** to **Columns**, **Latitude** to **Rows**, and **Intersection** to the **Text** shelf, I visualize the red-light locations—at least the ones that have ever had a violation:

Figure 12.48: Intersections Chicago

5. The name of the worksheet will be **Intersection**, and since I am looking at violations, I change the color in the **Marks** card to red. Lastly, I don't need to see the intersection name, so I change **Intersection** from **Text** to **Detail**.

6. Next, I like the map better when it shows a few more details, so I use **Map Layers...** to select some more options:

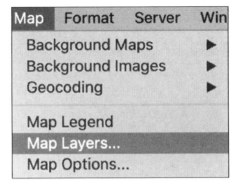

Figure 12.49: Map Layers...

Select all the layers you want to see on the map:

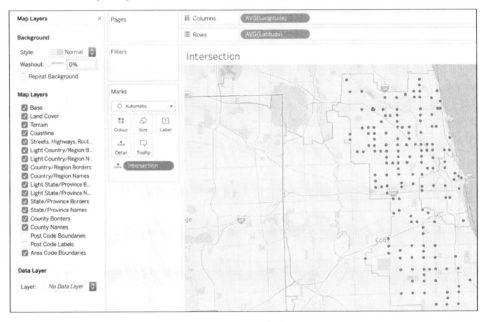

Figure 12.50: Map of Chicago

Another nice functionality of Tableau is that you can add **Data Layer** to your view. You can see the option in the bottom-left corner of the preceding screenshot.

7. I use the **Population** layer by **Census Tract**, as I hope it will give me some details on whether more or fewer violations happen in densely populated areas:

Figure 12.51: Data layers

In the following screenshot, you can see how it looks — note that the darker the red, the denser the area is populated:

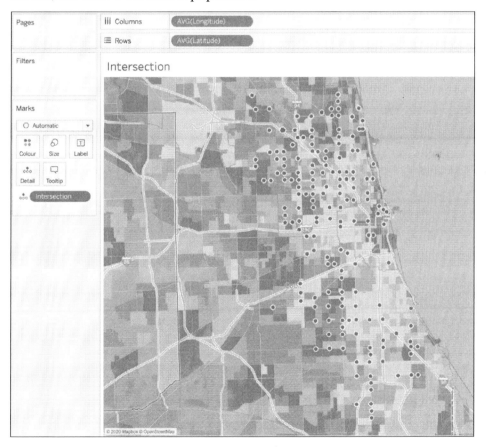

Figure 12.52: Intersection vizualization

8. I add **MONTH(Violation Date)** to **Pages**; this way, my boss can play through the months and see where and when the amount of violations changes:

Figure 12.53: Pages

9. Of course, I need to add the **Violations** field to make **Pages** work properly. I decide to use the density feature of Tableau, using red as the color:

Figure 12.54: Density visualization

Adding a corresponding heatmap worksheet

After clicking on the **Pages** play button, I notice a pattern in some months. I want to take a closer look, so I open a new worksheet:

1. I call the new worksheet **Heatmap** and place **MONTH(Violation Date)** on **Columns** and **YEAR(Violation Date)** on **Rows**. Then, I drag **Violations** to the **Colour** shelf and select red-gold to get the following:

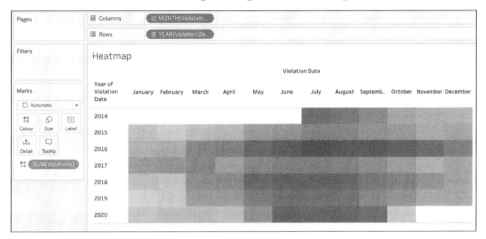

Figure 12.55: Heatmap

There are definitely more red-light violations in the summertime, and 2016 and 2020 show the most violations.

2. Last but not least, I add a new worksheet called **Trend?**. I drag
   MONTH(Violation Date) and drop it on the **Columns** shelf. The **Violations**
   field should be placed on **Rows**. I make sure that both measures are
   continuous (green). From the **Analytics** pane, I drag the linear **Trend Line**
   onto the worksheet. Next, I drag **Forecast**:

Figure 12.56: Line chart

In the preceding figure, you can see that the overall trend of red-light
violations increases slightly over the years. The forecast shows us that the
seasonality of there being more red-light violations in the summertime will
probably continue in 2021.

 Feel free to check by the end of 2021 how good Tableau's forecast
model was! The City of Chicago datasets are continuously
refreshed.

Finalizing the dashboard

The hour is almost over and I am just placing the three worksheets onto a dashboard, calling it **Red-Light Violations**, and formatting it a bit; it looks as follows:

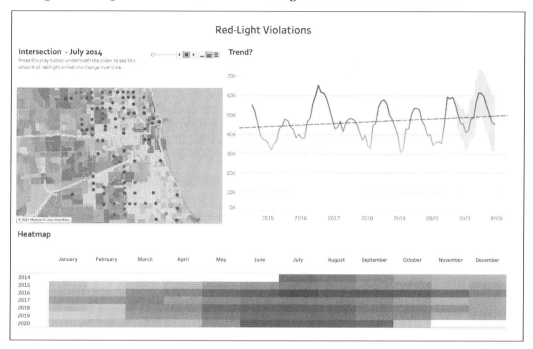

Figure 12.57: Final dashboard

You can find the final dashboard in the Tableau workbook associated with this chapter on Tableau Public, here: `https://public.tableau.com/profile/marleen.meier/`.

Can the dashboard be improved? Yes, it always can. But after this first iteration, my boss can let me know if anything needs to be adjusted and I can do so. I am sure that I could spend many more hours improving it, but most of the time dashboarding is more about delivering promptly. And a full production model is a different story than an ad hoc question or a one-off exercise, especially if you work in an agile manner, split your work into deliverables, get feedback, and continue working on it.

Extending geo-spatial analytics with distance measures

Our last use case is also geo-spatial analysis on the same Chicago traffic dataset, but this time, we will be adding another component. We will be looking to rent a new place but with the requirement that there are no more than n intersections in a radius of x and Navy Pier should be at most y miles away. The variables n, x, and y should be interactive in order for us to make changes and have a very flexible dashboard experience. The questions to ask about this task are:

- How can we add any given location in Chicago to our dataset? It is currently only showing intersections and violations.
- How can we make the n, x, and y variables?
- How can we add a radius indicator to any given point on the map?
- How can we measure the distance between two variable points?

All those questions will be answered in the following steps:

1. Go back to the workbook related to this chapter.
2. Right-click on the worksheet called **Intersection** and click on **Duplicate**.
3. Rename the new worksheet **Rental**.

4. Remove **MONTH(Violation Date)** from **Pages** and **SUM(Violations)** from the **Colour** shelf and the red text (sub-heading) from the title, to make the worksheet look like this:

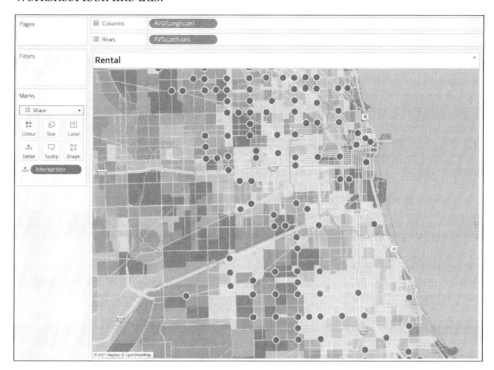

Figure 12.58: Intersections

5. Change the **Marks** type to **Map**.

6. Click on **Map** | **Map Layer** and change **Data Layer** to **No Data Layer**:

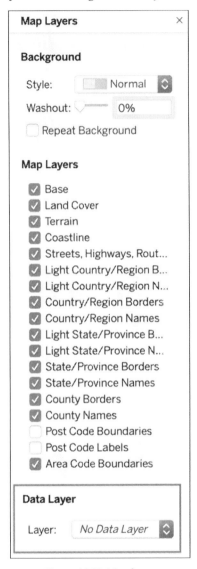

Figure 12.59: Map layer

7. Place **Violation Date** on the **Filters** shelf and select the year **2020**.

8. Drag **Violations** on the **Colour** shelf and select the **Red** color palette:

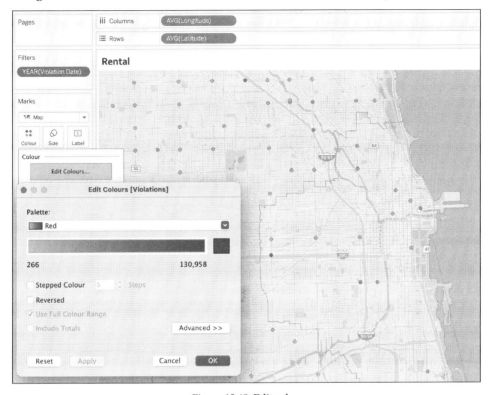

Figure 12.60: Edit colors

We now have a map of Chicago in front of us, on which each point represents an intersection at which violations have happened in 2020. The darker the dot, the more violations there are that were registered at that intersection.

Adding measure points to the map

Next, we have to add functionality that will allow us to set a mark on the map and start measuring from there. This can be achieved by creating longitude and latitude parameters and using them in a calculated field:

1. Create the following parameters, **Lat** and **Long**:

Figure 12.61: Parameters

2. Right-click each of the parameters and select **Show Parameter**.

3. Create a calculated field called **Address manual**:

    ```
    MAKEPOINT([Lat], [Long])
    ```

4. Drag **Address manual** onto the map, on top of the **Add a Marks Layer** pop-up:

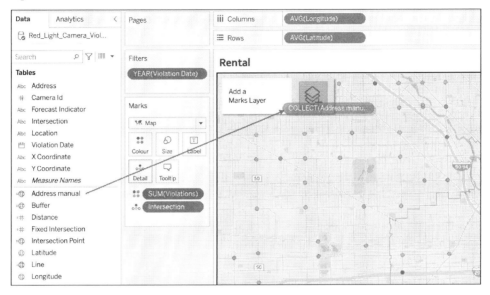

Figure 12.62: Add a layer

5. Change the **Marks** type of the new layer to **Map**.

6. After these steps, we have a map with intersections and color-coded amounts of violations and a point that we can change by using the Lat and Long parameters. The user can use, for example, Google Maps to find the latitude and longitude; simply select a point on Google Maps that represents a rental home location:

Figure 12.63: Google Maps

7. The latitude and longitude will show in the URL and at the bottom of the page. Type them into the Lat and Long parameters and the same points will appear on our Tableau map:

Figure 12.64: Latitude and longitude

Adding the distance line

In the next steps, we will add a radius and a distance line starting at Navy Pier:

1. Create another parameter called **Radius in miles** as follows:

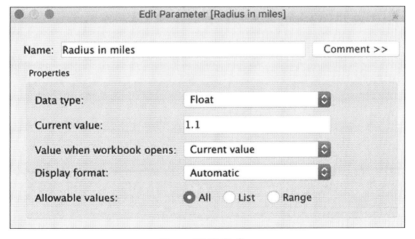

Figure 12.65: Radius

2. Right-click on the **Radius in miles** parameter and select **Show Parameter**

3. Create a calculated field called **Buffer** that will be used as our radius around the **Address manual** point:

```
BUFFER([Address manual],[Radius in miles], 'miles')
```

4. Drag the **Buffer** field onto the map just like we did with the **Address manual** field, on top of the **Add a Marks Layer** popup.

5. Change the **Marks** type of this new layer to **Map**.

6. Click on **Colour**, change the opacity to **50%**, and choose a gray color:

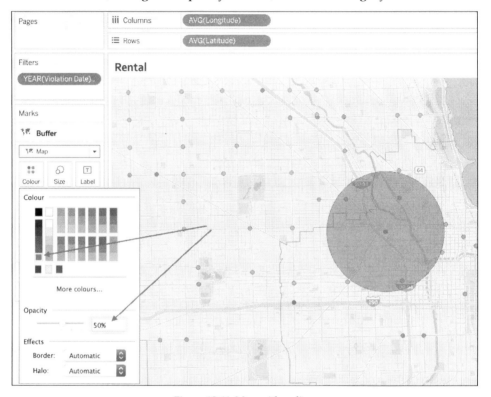

Figure 12.66: Map with radius

The Navy Pier coordinates are shown in the URL in the following figure:

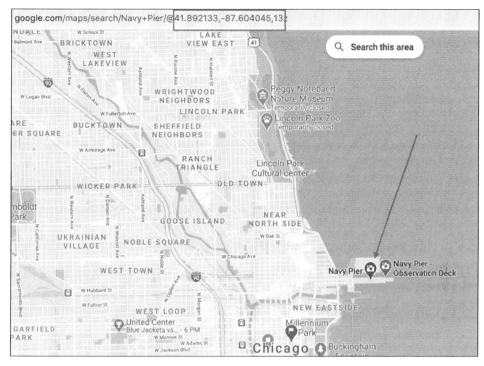

Figure 12.67: Navy Pier

7. Create a calculated field as follows:

```
MAKEPOINT(41.892133, -87.604045)
```

8. Drag the **Navy Pier** field on the map on top of the **Add a Marks Layer** popup.

9. Change the **Marks** type to **Map**.

10. In order to connect **Navy Pier** to our **Address manual** point and measure the distance, create another calculated field called **Line**:

```
MAKELINE([Address manual], [Navy Pier])
```

11. To measure the distance between the two, create a **Distance** field with the following code:

```
DISTANCE([Address manual], [Navy Pier], 'miles')
```

12. Place the **Line** field on the map on top of the **Add a Marks Layer** popup.

13. Change the **Marks** type in the new layer to **Map**.

14. Place **Distance** on the **Label** shelf, change the measure to **Average**, and click on **Label** to add the text miles:

Figure 12.68: Edit label

Our dashboard now looks as follows:

Figure 12.69: Final dashboard

And this makes it complete. The radius clearly shows how many intersections are within a certain distance; you can see the amount of intersection violations by hovering over the points. The line from Navy Pier to our current location **Address Manual** tells us how far away those two points are from each other.

To answer our questions from the beginning:

- *How can we add any given location in Chicago to our dataset? It is currently only showing intersections and violations.* By using the `Makepoint()` function in a calculated field.

- *How can we make the n, x, and y variables?* By using parameters.

- *How can we add a radius to any given point on the map?* By using the `Buffer()` function.

- *How can we measure the distance between two variable points?* By using the `Distance()` function; by adding the `MakeLine()` function, a line will be drawn.

This use case can be recreated for the number of supermarkets in an area, schools, public transport points, and so on. Be creative and feel free to upload your dashboards to Tableau Public, and don't forget to add the `#MasteringTableau` tag!

> If you work a lot with spatial data, I would also recommend that you check out these links:
>
> - https://www.tableau.com/about/blog/2019/6/
>   geospatial-analysis-made-easy-two-new-spatial-
>   functions-makepoint-and-makeline
> - https://www.tableau.com/about/blog/2020/3/
>   seeing-and-understanding-proximity-made-easy-
>   buffer-calculations

Summary

In this chapter, we looked at three use cases of self-service analytics. One was about world indices, one was about traffic-light violations, and the last one used distance measures to find the radius within which a house could be located given some key variables. Our main takeaway was that you should always start by planning your work, then get to know the data, use descriptive statistics, and adjust your plan according to your intermediate results.

A dashboard is never really finished: you can always change things; your audience might change; stakeholder wishes might differ. Deliver a working visualization with basic functionality and continue to develop after you get feedback. Depending on your backlog or other circumstances, the basics might be enough.

The next chapter will be all about improving performance. With more and more data, performance is key and could mean the difference between success and failure.

13
Improving Performance

Recently, while teaching a Tableau Desktop class, a gentleman approached me regarding a dashboard he had built that was performing inadequately. He stated that his dashboard probably flouted several best practices regarding performance. He was correct! The dashboard had close to a dozen filters, most of which were set to show only relevant values. Also, the dashboard was full of worksheets, some of which included thousands of marks. Although we did not look at the underlying data sources, based on our conversation, some of those data sources likely included complex joins. I was amazed that the dashboard performed as well as it did! This underscores a truth that many Tableau authors have experienced: Tableau can perform abysmally if best practices are not followed.

This chapter will address various aspects of performance with the intent of empowering you with techniques to create workbooks that load quickly and respond snappily to end user interaction.

In this chapter, we will discuss the following topics:

- Understanding the performance-recording dashboard
- Hardware and on-the-fly techniques
- Connecting to data sources
- Working with extracts

- Using filters wisely
- Efficient calculations
- Other ways to improve performance

As you can see, there are many topics we have to cover with regard to performance improvement. Therefore, let's not lose any time and dive right in. Our first topic will be performance recording, which is the first thing you should look at when experiencing a drop in performance because it helps you identify the source of all the slowness.

Understanding the performance-recording dashboard

Tableau includes a performance-recording feature as part of the installation package and ships as a dashboard named `PerformanceRecording.twb`. The dashboard gives the Tableau author an easy way to understand and troubleshoot performance problems. The following exercises and associated discussion points will review various aspects of the performance-recording dashboard, including how to generate it, how to use it to improve performance, and how it's constructed.

Perform the following steps:

1. Navigate to `https://public.tableau.com/profile/marleen.meier` to locate and download the workbook associated with this chapter.
2. Navigate to the **Types of Events** worksheet.
3. Select **Help | Settings and Performance | Start Performance Recording**.
4. Press *F5* on Windows or *Command* + *R* on macOS to refresh the view.
5. Select **Help | Settings and Performance | Stop Performance Recording**. A new dashboard will open:

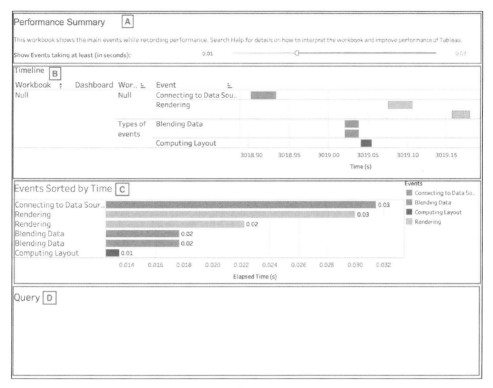

Figure 13.1: Performance summary

There are four main parts to be looked at:

a. **Performance Summary** shows the amount of time the dashboard needed to execute all the steps that happened between *step 3* (start performance recording) and *step 5* (stop performance recording). The slider can be used to filter.

b. **Timeline** shows which step happened when and how long it took.

c. The steps are also color-coded and can be found in the **Event** bar chart as well.

d. **Query** will only show details when clicking on any event in (**B**) or (**C**).

1. Drag the **Events** timeline slider in (**A**) to the far left to show all events.

2. Within **Events Sorted by Time** (C), click on any green bar entitled **Executing Query**. Note that the **Query** section is now populated by the VizQL belonging to the highlighted bar:

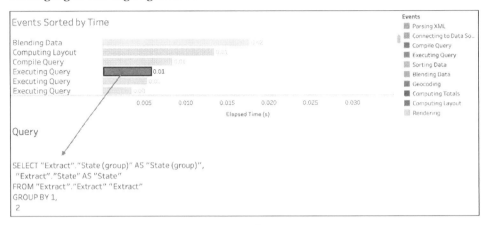

Figure 13.2: Events

3. To see the query in its entirety, navigate to the **Query** worksheet and set the fit to **Entire View** (by **Query**, Tableau is referring to a VizQL query). Note that an especially long query may not be recorded in its entirety. In order to see every line of such a query, reference the log files located in **My Tableau Repository**.

The preceding steps were intended to provide you with an initial look at what the performance-recording dashboard can be used for. I usually use it to check whether a particular query took significantly longer than others. I then look at the query on the **Query** tab and check which part is affected by reading the fields used, try to change it, and then run the performance dashboard again. Now, let's look at some more details.

If you access the **Events** worksheet from the performance-recording dashboard, you will see the different events. We will now discuss those events and their impact on performance in more detail:

Event type	Performance considerations
Connecting to Data Source	Poor performance when connecting to the data source could indicate network latency or database issues, or even outdated drivers.

Generating Extract	Aggregating data before you extract can increase performance because it will decrease the total row count.
Compile Query	Compile Query performance problems could indicate database issues.
Executing Query	If a query takes too long, you can improve performance by filtering data you don't need or hiding fields you don't use. Refer to the *Using filters wisely* section in this chapter for more information.
Sorting Data	Performance issues related to sorting issues may indicate too many marks in the view. This sorting issue can also be caused by table calculations that depend on sorting data in the view.
Geocoding	Geocoding performance issues may indicate too many marks in the view, internet latency issues, poor hardware, or a poor graphics card.
Blending Data	Blending Data performance may be improved by reducing the amount of underlying data or by filtering.
Computing Table Calculations	Since table calculations are typically performed locally, complex calculations may tax the end user's computer.
Computing Totals	The Computing Totals performance may be improved by reducing the amount of underlying data or by filtering.
Computing Layout	Computing Layout performance issues may be indicative of a dashboard with too many worksheets or elements such as images.

After this overview, which you can always come back to, we will dive a little deeper and research what happens when performance recording is activated. Note that the following assumes that the author is working on Tableau Desktop, and not Tableau Server. In *Chapter 14, Interacting with Tableau Server/Online*, we will cover the performance recording on Tableau Server.

When recording performance, Tableau initially creates a file in My Tableau Repository\Logs, named performance_[timestamp].tab. Additionally, there is a file named PerformanceRecording_new.twb located in the Tableau program directory, for example, C:\Program Files\Tableau\Tableau.[version]\Performance. That file is automatically opened once the recording stops, thereby allowing the author to peruse the results.

Hardware and on-the-fly techniques

The number-one performance inhibitor for Tableau Desktop that I have observed while training in many different companies is underpowered machines. Developers almost invariably have excellent computers. Analysts and other business users, regrettably, often do not. In many cases, a few modest upgrades can make a significant improvement. Unfortunately, upgrading a computer may be impossible at many organizations due to a variety of factors, and procuring a new machine may also be quite difficult. Therefore, in this section, we will consider both: optimal computer specifications and techniques for working with Tableau on underpowered machines.

The currently published minimum requirements for Tableau Desktop are as follows:

Windows	Mac
Microsoft Windows 7 or newer (64-bit)	iMac/MacBook computers 2009 or newer
Microsoft Server 2008 R2 or newer	macOS High Sierra 10.13, macOS Mojave 10.14, and macOS Catalina 10.15
Intel or AMD 64-bit processor or newer	1.5 GB minimum free disk space
2 GB memory	
1.5 GB minimum free disk space	

The specifications listed for macOS are adequate assuming sufficient RAM (a minimum of 8 GB). Those for Windows, however, are insufficient for many use cases. Instead, consider the following recommendations:

Recommended Specifications for Windows Computers	Notes
Microsoft Windows 7 or newer	Note that most Windows performance reviews report, at best, modest gains when upgrading. Therefore, don't expect Tableau to run noticeably faster if upgrading beyond Windows 7. *Performance improvement expected by upgrading: Moderate.*
Intel i7 processor	The i5 processor works fine with Tableau, but the larger cache and faster processing of the i7 processor enables better multitasking and improves performance overall. *Performance improvement expected by upgrading: Moderate.*

8 GB memory or more	RAM is a major performance factor. In short, the more the better. 8 GB will suffice for most purposes, but 4 GB is often unsatisfactory, especially if running multiple instances of Tableau. More RAM is particularly important when using a TDE file as a data source, since a TDE file is typically loaded in RAM. *Performance improvement expected by upgrading: High.*
SSD (solid-state drive)	An SSD outperforms an HDD by a wide margin. Part of the reason is simply better I/O (input/output) performance. Also, over time, an HDD will fragment, that is, data is scattered throughout the drive and performance consequently suffers. Fragmentation is irrelevant for an SSD due to its technical specifications. *Performance improvement expected by upgrading: High.*
NVIDIA graphics card	Rendering performance can be improved via OpenGL. OpenGL enables the Accelerated Graphics option within Tableau. This, in turn, allows Tableau to utilize a GPU (graphic processing unit) instead of a CPU (central processing unit) for some rendering operations. Accelerated Graphics requires a graphics card. NVIDIA is recommended here because, according to Dan Cory, a technical advisor to the Tableau Development leadership team, Tableau Software (the company) predominately uses NVIDIA graphics cards. Other graphics cards include ATI and Intel HD Graphics 2000, 4000, and 5000. Note that the Intel HD Graphics 4000 card might require updated video drivers. You can update video drivers via the device manager located in the Windows Control Panel. Accelerated Graphics is activated in Tableau via **Help | Settings and Performance | Enable Accelerated Graphics**. *Performance improvement expected by upgrading: Moderate.*

You may have noticed that the preceding table mostly does not address specific brands, nor are there considerations of different brands of RAM or hard drives. Despite the proliferation of computer and component types (or perhaps as a result of this proliferation), computers and components have become commodities. In short, any brand name equipment should work fine. In fact, off-brand equipment will often perform just as well, although the relatively small price savings may not justify additional risks. A little research combined with common sense should lead to satisfactory results when considering which brand of computer or component to purchase.

Perhaps, as a result of the preceding section, you have ordered a new, more optimal computer. Or, more likely, you may keep it in mind should you have the opportunity to obtain a new machine in the near future, but for now, you have to make do with what you have. This section discusses tips that will help the Tableau author work more efficiently irrespective of the equipment used.

Configuring auto updates

Auto updates can be accessed either via the icon located on the toolbar, via **Worksheet | Auto Updates**, or by using the shortcut key *F10* on Windows or *Option + Command + 0* on Mac. Auto updates give the author the option of pausing/ resuming auto updates for the worksheet and/or for filters, and can come in very handy if you want to make multiple changes to your layout but want to avoid Tableau loading after every change. You can simply pause the update, make your changes, and then run the update once.

The following exercise demonstrates how this works:

1. Open the workbook associated with this chapter and navigate to the **Auto Updates** worksheet.

2. In the **Data** pane, select the **Superstore** dataset.

3. Place **State** on the **Rows** shelf.

4. Deselect **Auto Update Worksheet** via the toolbar:

Figure 13.3: Auto Update Worksheet

5. Place **City** on the **Rows** shelf to the right of **State**. Note that the view does not update.

6. Enable **Auto Update Worksheet** via the toolbar. The view now updates.

7. Right-click on **State** on the **Rows** shelf and select **Show Filter**.

8. Right-click on **City** on the **Rows** shelf and select **Show Filter**.

9. On the **City** filter, click the drop-down menu and select **Multiple Values (list)** and **Only Relevant Values**:

Figure 13.4: Only Relevant Values

10. Deselect **Auto Update Filters** as shown in *Figure 13.3*.

11. In the **State** filter, select only **Alabama**. Note that the **City** filter does not update.

12. Enable the **Auto Update Filters** via the toolbar. The **City** filter now updates.

Auto updates can be very helpful. The author may pause auto updates, make multiple changes, and then resume auto updates, thereby saving time and increasing performance indirectly.

As a sidenote, cascading filters such as **Only Relevant Values** or **All Values in Context** may not populate when using the pause button or auto updates as they are reliant on a query being passed first.

The Run Update feature

The **Run Update** icon to the right of the pause/resume auto updates is meant to refresh once, while the user can keep the disabled **Auto Update** feature in place. The following brief example should help clarify this option:

1. Duplicate the **previous** worksheet called **Auto Updates** and name the duplicate **Run Updates**.

2. Pause all updates by clicking on the **Pause Auto Updates** icon.

3. Select several states at random in the **State** filter.

4. Click on the **Run Update** icon as shown in *Figure 13.5* and select either **Update Dashboard** or **Update Worksheet**. The shortcut key for running an update is *F9* on Windows. The shortcut on macOS is *Shift + Command + 0*:

Figure 13.5: Running an update

5. Select several more states at random in the **State** filter. Note that auto updating is still paused.

To repeat, **Run Update** allows the Tableau author to intermittently refresh the view while still keeping auto updates paused. The two update features that we just discussed will make your life as a dashboard developer easier, but if you want to tackle performance issues at their core, you need some more tools at hand. The following section will introduce extracts, a really good feature for speeding up calculations and rendering in general.

Small extracts

Although extracts will be discussed in more detail in the *Working with extracts* section, it seems fitting to mention extracts in the context of performance considerations while authoring. Even under optimal conditions, working with large data sources can be slow. If constant access to the entire dataset while authoring is not necessary, consider creating a small, local extract. Author as much of the workbook as possible and then when all the underlying data is truly needed, point to the original data source.

The following steps show a brief example of this technique in action:

1. In the workbook associated with this chapter, navigate to the **Small Local Extract** worksheet.

2. Select **Data | New Data Source** to choose a desired data source. This exercise assumes Sample - Superstore.xls, which installs with Tableau, but you can take any dataset you like.

3. Drag any field to the **Text** shelf. In my example, I used **Number of Records**.

4. Right-click on the data source (for me: **Superstore**) and select **Extract Data...**:

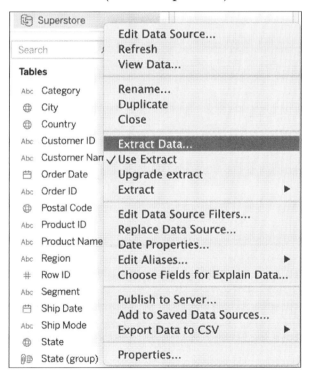

Figure 13.6: Extracting data

5. At the bottom of the **Extract Data…** dialog box, select **Top**, your data source, and choose **1000**. In the following figure, **Orders** has been chosen, which is one of the two parts of the superstore join:

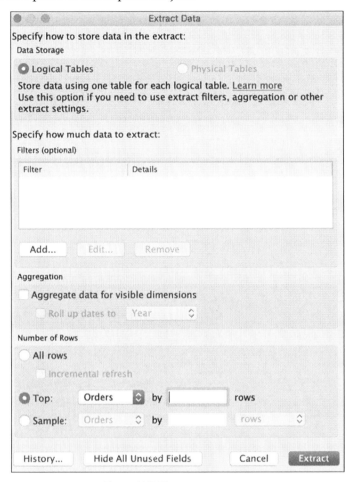

Figure 13.7: Top rows

6. Click the **Extract** button and note that **Number of Records** now displays **1000** rows.

7. In the **Data** pane, right-click on **Superstore** and deselect **Use Extract**. Note that **Number of Records** has reverted to its original value.

 By creating a small, local extract, the Tableau author alleviates two performance inhibitors: network latency and dataset size.

This section gave you the knowledge of how to reduce your dataset temporarily and the option to get back to the original size, both without leaving the Tableau interface. This is a great way to speed up your dashboard building process and avoid long waits. In the next section, we will talk about how to connect to data sources to achieve the best possible performance.

Connecting to data sources

One of the beauties of Tableau is the ease with which you can connect to many different data sources in various ways. As mentioned earlier in this book, there are many connectors defined in Tableau for interfacing with a variety of data sources. Furthermore, this flexibility extends beyond simply connecting to single tables or files.

 Although Tableau makes it easy to connect to various data sources, it should be stressed that Tableau is not an **Extract, Transform, and Load** (**ETL**) tool. If complex joins and complex data blending are required to generate useful results, it may be advisable to perform ETL work outside of Tableau, for example, in Tableau Prep Builder (see *Chapter 3, Tableau Prep Builder*, for more information on this service). ETL work will ideally lead to better data modeling and thus easier authoring and quicker performance in Tableau.

The four ways in which Tableau connects to data are as follows:

- Tableau may connect to a single table. This is ideal as it allows the most functionality and easiest troubleshooting, while enabling Tableau to send the simplest queries and thus perform optimally. However, it is not always possible to connect to a single table and, although ideal, it is not reasonable to have such a strict limitation. The relationship between data sources and reporting tools is constantly changing. A reporting tool that is inflexible in the way it can connect to data will likely not be successful, no matter how elegant and beautiful the end results.

- The second option is relationships, a newer, more flexible way to combine two or more datasets. The level of detail will be defined per worksheet rather than in the data source tab, which makes this feature very powerful.

- The third way in which Tableau may connect to data is via joining. One table may not supply all the necessary data, but by joining two or more tables, all the needed data may be accessible. As the joins become more and more complex, performance may be impacted, and troubleshooting may become difficult. Fortunately, Tableau can assume referential integrity and thus work quite efficiently with even complex joins.

- Finally, Tableau may utilize data blending. Data blending often performs admirably, provided no more than one of the blended data sources is large and dimensions that are used for blending have relatively few members.

Relationships should be chosen over joining and joining should be chosen instead of blending whenever possible. When blending multiple, large data sources, performance can be seriously impacted. The problem is further compounded when blending on high-cardinality dimensions. Also, data blending limits some functionality, such as the ability to use dimensions, row-level calculations, or LOD expressions, from a secondary data source.

However, there are exceptions, two of which are discussed here:

- First, data blending is advantageous (and usually necessary) when there is no common key shared between two tables.
- Secondly, in some instances, cross-joining will not work, and a data blend is required. For example, use data blending when you work with two datasets that have different granularities and relationships are not possible, or when a cross-database join is not possible (for example, to cubes or extract only connections), or when you have big datasets for which a blend will improve performance.

 More info can be found here: `https://help.tableau.com/current/pro/desktop/en-us/multiple_connections.htm`.

For these reasons, consider as a guideline that data blending should normally be avoided if a joining option exists.

Chapter 4, All About Data – Joins, Blends, and Data Structures, provides detailed information about joining and blending. For the purposes of this chapter, joining and blending discussions will be limited to performance considerations.

Working efficiently with large data sources

This section will cover some basics of database tuning and ways to work efficiently with large data sources. Since the topic is more focused on data sources than on Tableau, no exercises are included.

If you are connecting to large data sources and are experiencing performance problems, a conversation with a **database administrator (DBA)** may be beneficial.

Clear communication coupled with a small amount of database work could dramatically improve performance. The conversation should include database-tuning points, such as explicitly defining primary and foreign keys, defining columns as *not null*, and indexing. Each point will be discussed here.

Defining primary and foreign keys

Primary and foreign keys are essential for joining tables. A primary key is composed of one or more columns in a table. The primary key should be unique for every row. Joining on a non-unique, row-level key may lead to erroneous results, as explored in *Chapter 4, All About Data – Joins, Blends, and Data Structures*. Explicitly defining primary keys in the database helps to ensure that each key value is unique:

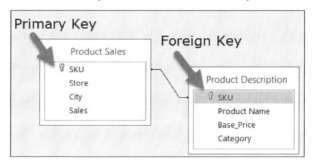

Figure 13.8: Database keys

A foreign key is composed of one or more columns in a table that uniquely identify rows in another table. This unique identification occurs as a result of the foreign key in one table referencing the primary key in another table. Explicitly defining foreign keys in the database enables Tableau to bypass many integrity checks, thereby improving performance.

Defining columns as NOT NULL

Tableau has published multiple white papers on performance improvement tips and tricks (`https://help.tableau.com/current/pro/desktop/en-us/performance_tips.htm`) that state that programmers and Tableau Desktop do not like NULL data. Define each column in your tables with an explicit NOT NULL if possible.

In practice, database admins debate when it is and isn't appropriate to define columns as NOT NULL; however, two things are clear:

- A primary or foreign key should be defined as NOT NULL. This is self-evident since primary and foreign keys must be unique by definition.

- Also, any column that is to be indexed should be defined as NOT NULL since otherwise an index may be unusable.

Indexing is discussed more fully in the next section.

Indexing

Let's consider the following two questions regarding indexing:

- What is an index?
- What should be indexed?

The first of our two questions may be easily answered by a DBA, but is likely uncharted waters for the Tableau author. So, to clarify, an index is a copy of selected columns in a database table that has been optimized for efficient searching. Since these copied columns include pointers to the original columns, they can be accessed to quickly find given rows and return the required data.

A small example may prove helpful. According to The Boeing Company, the 787 Dreamliner has about 2.3 million parts. Imagine a table that lists all of these parts in the **Part_Name** column. Your task is to search this column for every part starting with the "fuse" string. On a non-indexed column, this would require the examination of every row of data in the database. Such a search could be quite slow. Fortunately, indexes can be used to reduce the number of rows searched, thus making the process much faster. One type of structured data used for indexing is B-tree. A B-tree data structure is sorted. Thus, when accessing an index using a B-tree data structure to search for all parts starting with *fuse*, not every row has to be considered. Instead, the database can skip straight to *fs* and quickly return the desired rows.

Now let's move on to the second question on indexing. What should be indexed? This question can be answered fairly succinctly: ideally, all columns used for joining or filtering should be indexed in the data source.

Although there are some basic performance considerations for creating more efficient joins in Tableau (for example, avoid an outer join when a left join will suffice), join performance is largely determined outside of Tableau. Therefore, it is typically more important to index columns used in joins than those used for filtering.

To continue with our discussion of manipulating data sources, the next section will cover how Tableau can be used to create summarized datasets through extracting.

Working with extracts

This section will discuss what a Tableau data extract is as well as how to efficiently construct an extract. A colleague of mine recently consulted with a relatively small mobile phone service provider. Even though the company was small, the volume could be in excess of 1,000,000 calls per day. Management at the company insisted on the ability to interface with detailed visualizations of individual calls in Tableau workbooks. The performance of the workbooks was, understandably, a problem. Was such low-level detail necessary? Might less detail and snappier workbooks have led to better business decisions?

In order to balance business needs with practical performance requirements, businesses often need to ascertain what level of detail is genuinely helpful for reporting. Often, detailed granularity is not necessary. When such is the case, a summary table may provide sufficient business insight while enabling quick performance. In the case of the mobile phone service provider, a daily snapshot of call volumes may have sufficed. Even an hourly snapshot would have greatly reduced the table size and improved Tableau's performance.

To address this common business need, an extract is a proprietary compressed data source created by Tableau Desktop. Since its release, the file extension for an extract changed from .tde to the .hyper format. Thus, the new format makes use of the Hyper engine, which was discussed in *Chapter 1, Getting Up to Speed – A Review of the Basics*. An extract can be stored locally and accessed by Tableau to render visualizations.

Consider the following points that make an extract file an excellent choice for improved performance:

- Extracts can be quickly generated at an aggregate level
- Extracts are a columnar store, which records as sequences of columns
- Relational databases typically store data using a Row Store methodology

In the following example, note that **Row Store** is excellent for returning individual rows, whereas **Column Store** is much better for returning aggregated data.

Here is an example table:

	Table		
	Instrument	Store	Price
Row 1	Selmer Trumpet	North	$3,500
Row 2	Conn French Horn	East	$4,500
Row 3	Getzen Trombone	South	$2,500
Row 4	Miraphone Tuba	West	$9,000

Here is a **Row Store** table in a database:

Row 1	Selmer Trumpet
	North
	$3,500
Row 2	Conn French Horn
	East
	$4,500
Row 3	Getzen Trombone
	South
	$2,500
Row 4	Miraphone Tuba
	West
	$9,000

Here is a **Column Store** table in a database:

Instrument	Selmer Trumpet
	Conn French Horn
	Getzen Trombone
	Miraphone Tuba
Store	North
	East
	South
	West
Price	$3,500
	$4,500
	$2,500
	$9,000

I hope you could see that in a column store table, each *n* row of a certain attribute makes up for the first row. For example, the first row of `Instrument`, the first row of `Store`, and the first row of `Price` all relate to one entry, whereas in a row store table, all rows that belong to the same entry are in consecutive order.

To sum up what we have learned so far in this section, extracts use compression techniques to reduce file size while maintaining performance, and utilize RAM and hard drive space for optimal performance. Neither of those two points are given when using a live connection to a database—therefore, extracts can improve the performance of your dashboard whenever the database can't.

Constructing an extract

This section will discuss extracts from a performance aspect. Other aspects of extracts, such as scheduling and incremental refreshes, will not be considered here:

As we discussed in the *Small extracts* section earlier, an extract is created via **Data | [Data Source] | Extract Data**. From the resulting dialog box, we can take the following actions:

- **Filter the extract as needed**: Sometimes, an extract that precisely reflects a data source is warranted, but often filtering various fields will still populate the extract with the required data while shrinking the size and improving performance. To add a filter, simply click **Add...** to access a dialog box identical to the filter dialog box used within a worksheet:

Figure 13.9: Filter extract

- **Aggregate to the level of granularity represented in the view**: Aggregation not only reduces the file size, but can also be helpful from a security standpoint. Without aggregation, an extract is constructed using row-level data. Therefore, the Tableau author should note that if the extract is built without choosing to aggregate, any sensitive row-level data is accessible:

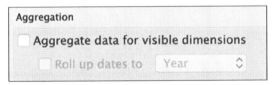

Figure 13.10: Aggregation

- **Reduce the number of rows**: As shown in the *Small extracts* section, reducing the number of rows can allow the author to create a small, local extract for quick workbook building, after which the original data source can be accessed for complete analysis:

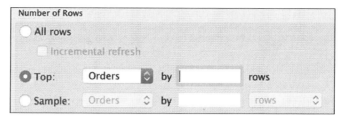

Figure 13.11: Reducing rows

- **Hide all unused fields**: This option excludes all columns that are not used in the workbook from the extract. This can significantly reduce the extract size and increase performance:

Figure 13.12: Hiding fields

By taking these four measures, your performance should improve immediately. Feel free to test it yourself by using the performance-recording tool and creating different extracts of the same data source. Using aggregation and performance-recording actions will be discussed next.

Aggregation

The following exercise will use two aggregates from a single data source, one at the **State** level and the other at the **City** level. These aggregated data sources will be used to create two worksheets. Each of these worksheets will be placed on a dashboard along with a third worksheet with row-level information. Finally, filter actions will be created to tie the three worksheets together. The purpose of the exercise is to demonstrate how small extracts might be used in conjunction with a larger dataset to create a more performant dashboard:

1. Open the workbook associated with this chapter and navigate to the **State Agg** worksheet.
2. In the **Data** pane, select the **SS - State Agg** data source.
3. Create a filled map using state by placing **State** on the **Detail** shelf and selecting **Filled Map** from the **Marks** card.
4. Right-click on the **SS - State Agg** data source and select **Extract Data**.
5. Note that Tableau displays an error stating that it cannot find the referenced file. You can either point to the instance of **Sample - Superstore** that ships with Tableau or you can use the instance provided via the GitHub link: https://github.com/PacktPublishing/Mastering-Tableau-2021.

6. After connecting to the data source, Tableau will display the **Extract Data** dialog box. Within the dialog box, select **Aggregate data for visible dimensions** and **All rows**. Click the **Hide All Unused Fields** button and then click on **Extract**:

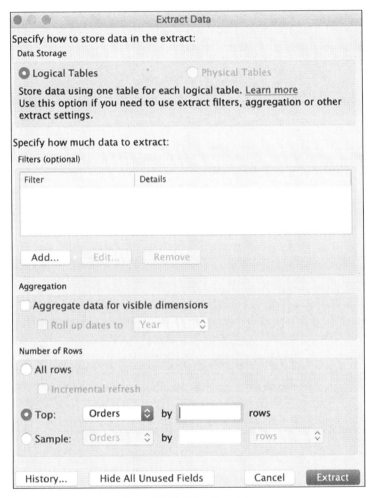

Figure 13.13: Extracting data

Note that the resulting extract only contains **State**. Also note that the data has been aggregated so that no underlying data is available.

7. Navigate to the **City Agg** worksheet.

8. In the **Data** pane, select the **SS - City Agg** data source. Note that this data source has already been extracted and so only contains **State**, **City**, and **Sales**. Also note that the data has been aggregated so that no underlying data is available.

9. Place **City** on the **Rows** shelf, **Sales** on the **Text** shelf, and **State** on the **Detail** shelf. Don't forget to include **State** even though it does not display on the view. It must be used so that the dashboard created at the end of the exercise works correctly.

10. Navigate to the **Row Detail** worksheet and select the **Superstore** dataset.

11. Create a crosstab view that displays **Customer Name**, **Order ID**, **Row ID**, **Profit**, and **Sales**. One quick way to create this view is to double-click on each field.

12. Navigate to the **Agg Dash** dashboard and place each of the three worksheets on the dashboard.

13. Create the following actions via **Dashboard | Actions | Add Action | Filter**:

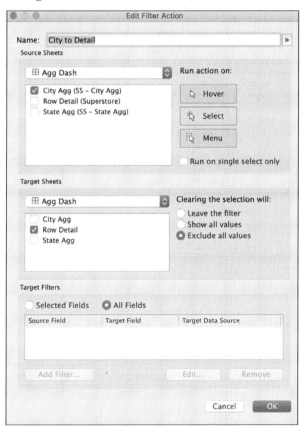

Figure 13.14: Adding City to Detail action

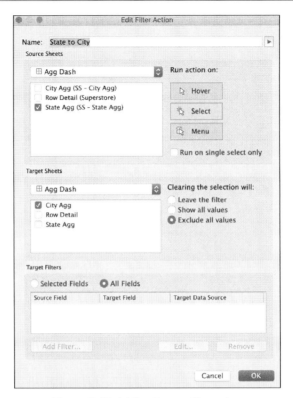

Figure 13.15: Adding State to City action

14. After creating these two actions, in the dashboard, click on the **State** field.

15. Then, click on the **City** field.

16. Click on a blank portion of the **City Agg** worksheet to exclude all values on **Row Detail**.

17. Click on a blank portion of the **State Agg** worksheet to exclude all values on **City Agg**.

18. Format the dashboard as desired:

Figure 13.16: Action on dashboard

Having completed this exercise, note that the resulting dashboard is quite performant:

- When the user first opens the dashboard, only **State Agg** displays. This is performant for two reasons. First, displaying a single worksheet as opposed to every worksheet when opening the dashboard causes fewer initial queries and less rendering. Second, accessing a small extract is quicker than accessing a larger data source.

- Since the **City Agg** worksheet is also accessing a small extract, when the user clicks on a state, the **City Agg** worksheet will appear quickly.

- When the user clicks on **City**, a call is made to the data source that only includes the information for that particular city. A relatively small amount of data is pulled, and performance should be good for even larger datasets.

Another aspect of good performance practice, apart from using aggregate extracts, should be considered for this exercise. The dashboard contains no quick filters. Often, using quick filters on a dashboard is unnecessary. If the worksheets on the dashboard can be used to filter, those worksheets can essentially do double duty. That is to say, worksheets can provide valuable analysis while simultaneously acting as filters for other worksheets on the dashboard. This represents a performance improvement over using quick filters, since adding quick filters would cause additional queries to be sent to the underlying data source.

In the preceding dashboard, each worksheet references a different data source. Therefore, you may ask, how are the action filters able to function across the different data sources? The answer can be found in the filter action dialog box. As shown in *Figure 13.14* and *Figure 13.15*, **All Fields** are considered **Target Filters**. Tableau simply matches any fields of the same name across each data source. Extracts can be optimized for even better performance results. We'll cover this in the next section.

Optimizing extracts

Optimization accelerates performance by materializing calculated fields when possible. This means that Tableau actually generates values for calculated fields in the extract so that those values can be looked up instead of calculated. If you were to use table calculations, Tableau would have to calculate the values each time you change the view.

 Note that not all calculated fields are materialized. Fields that are not materialized include table calculations, changeable or unstable functions, such as NOW( ) and TODAY( ), and calculated fields using parameters.

When an extract is first created, it is automatically optimized. In other words, calculated fields are automatically materialized when possible. However, over the course of time, calculated fields may be altered that will cause the extract to drop materialized fields. At such times, open **Data | [Data Source] | Extract** and click on **Compute Calculations Now** in order to regenerate the materialized fields:

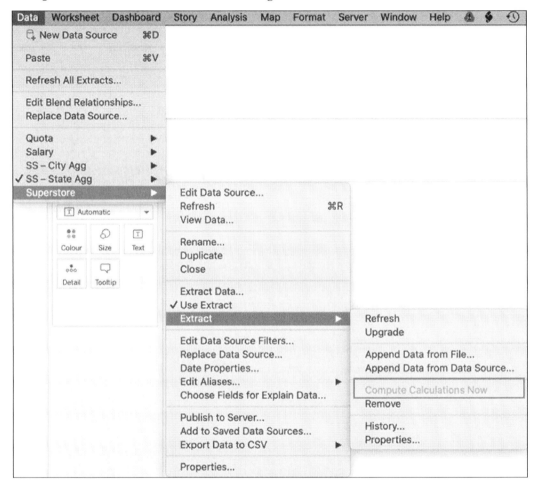

Figure 13.17: Computing calculations

If an extract is set to refresh on Tableau Server, the extract is automatically optimized for each refresh.

The following example demonstrates calculated fields that are materialized and those that are not.

Perform the following steps:

1. In Tableau, select **File | New** to create a new workbook.

2. In the new workbook, select **Connect to Data** in the upper-left corner and connect to the **Sample Superstore** dataset located in My Tableau Repository/ Datasources or in your saved data sources.

3. Connect to the **Orders** worksheet.

4. Create the following parameter:

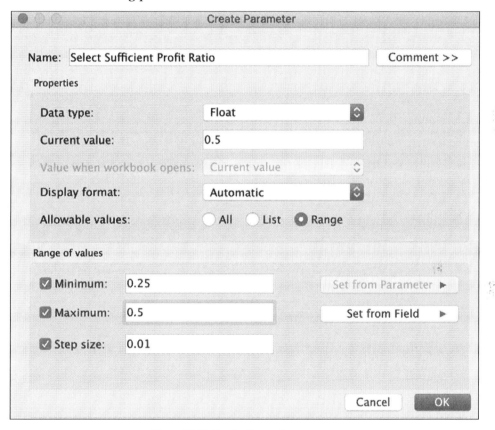

Figure 13.18: Create Parameter

The **Select Sufficient Profit Ratio** parameter shown in the preceding screenshot allows us to select a value between **0.25** and **0.5** in steps of **0.01**. This configuration is just an example; you can select any range of values that you define as a sufficient ratio.

5. Create the following calculated fields:

Name	Calculation
Profit Ratio	`SUM([Profit])/SUM([Sales])`
This Year's Profit	`IF [Profit Ratio] > [Select Sufficient Profit Ratio] THEN "Sufficient Profit" END`
Window Sum	`WINDOW_SUM(SUM([Sales]))`
Profitable?	`[Profit] > 0`

6. Right-click on the data source and select **Extract Data**.

7. Click the **Extract** button.

8. When prompted, save the resulting extract to a location of your choosing.

9. Open a new Tableau workbook, select **File | Open**, and then select the extract created in the preceding step.

10. Note the following in the data source:

    - **Profit Ratio**, an aggregate calculation, was materialized.

    - **This Year's Profit**, which references a parameter, has a value of null and was not materialized.

    - **Window Sum**, a table calculation, has an "undefined" value and was not materialized.

    - **Profitable?**, a row-level calculation, was materialized.

This exercise demonstrated that once an extract has been created and you add new calculated fields to your dashboard, they might not be included in your extract. Next time you miss a field in your extract, think back to when you did this exercise and remember that certain fields will not be materialized.

Finally, if you make use of parameters in your dashboard, check whether you can eliminate those and use calculations instead to improve performance. Also, split calculations if they can't be materialized as a whole. Put the part that can be materialized in one calculated field and the non-materialized part in another. If parts of the calculation can be calculated within the extract creation, you will gain performance.

The advantage of using extracts has now been discussed in great detail, so let's move on and see how we can make the most out of filters.

Using filters wisely

Filters generally improve performance in Tableau. For example, when using a dimension filter to view only the West region, a query is passed to the underlying data source, resulting in information returned for just that region. By reducing the amount of data returned, performance improves. This is because less data means reduced network bandwidth load, reduced database processing requirements, and reduced processing requirements for the local computer.

Filters can also negatively impact Tableau's performance. For example, using **only relevant values** causes additional queries to be sent to the underlying data source, thereby slowing down the response time. Also, creating quick filters from high-cardinality dimensions can impair performance.

Tableau's filters are executed in a specific order, so keep this in mind when using them. Refer to the Tableau help pages here: `https://help.tableau.com/current/pro/desktop/en-us/order_of_operations.htm`. The following flowchart, accessible via the preceding link, along with a link to an hour-long presentation, may help:

Figure 13.19: Filtering the order of operations

The rest of this section follows, step by step, the order of operations. By the end of it, you will be able to know which filters to use in which situation so as to achieve the best performance for your dashboard.

Extract filters

Extract filters remove data from the extracted data source. Simply put, the data isn't there. Thus, performance is enhanced by reducing the overall amount of data. Performance may also be improved since extracted data uses Tableau's proprietary, columnar dataset.

Furthermore, extracts are always flattened, which will have performance advantages over connecting to datasets using joins. To create an extract filter, begin by selecting **Data | [Data Source] | Extract Data**. In the resulting dialog box, choose to add a filter.

Data source filters

Data source filters are applied throughout the workbook. For example, if you create a data source filter that removes all members of the **Country** dimension except the USA, the **Country** dimension will only include the USA for all worksheets in the workbook.

Data source filters improve performance in the same way as dimension and measure filters; that is, data source filters cause Tableau to generate a query to the underlying data source, which will limit the data that is returned. Less returned data generally results in quicker processing and rendering. A further advantage that data source filters offer is ease of authoring. For example, if the Tableau author knows in advance that an entire workbook is going to be USA-centric, creating a data source filter saves you the trouble of applying a dimension filter to every worksheet in the workbook using that data source.

Also note that data source filters occur quite early in the process flow. All calculations (including calculations using fixed LOD expressions that are rendered before dimension and measure filters are triggered) respect data source filters.

To create a data source filter, click the **Data Source** tab located in the bottom-left corner of **Tableau Desktop**. Then, click on the **Add** link located in the top-right corner of the page:

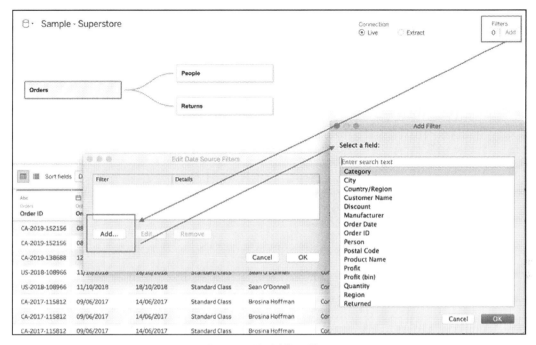

Figure 13.20: Adding filters

Context filters

A context filter is created simply by right-clicking on a field in the **Filter** shelf and selecting **Add to Context**:

Figure 13.21: Context filters

Dimension and measure filters are independent. Each filter queries the data source independently and returns results. A context filter, on the other hand, will force dimension and measure filters to depend on it. This behavior can be helpful (and necessary) for getting the right answer in some circumstances. For instance, if a Tableau author accesses the **Superstore** dataset and uses a filter on **Product Names** to return the top-10 selling product names in a single category, it will be necessary that **Category** is defined as a context filter. Otherwise, the **Product Names** filter will return the top 10 overall. Because of this, context filters improve performance.

Dimension and measure filters

Dimension and measure filters can improve performance. Since either a dimension filter or a measure filter will cause Tableau to generate a query to the underlying data source, which will limit the data that is returned, performance is improved. Simply put, the smaller the returned dataset, the better the performance.

However, dimension and measure filters can degrade performance. Since Tableau not only generates queries to the underlying data source in order to display visualizations, but also generates queries to display filters, more displayed filters will slow performance. Furthermore, displayed filters on high-cardinality dimensions can inhibit performance. (A dimension with many members is referred to as having high cardinality.) Consider the example of a filter that displays every customer in a dataset. Performance for such a filter might be slow because every customer in the underlying dataset must be located and returned, and then Tableau has to render and display each of these customers in the filter.

When using two or more dimension or measure filters on a view, a relevant filter may be used to limit the choices that display. For example, if a view includes a filter for city and postal code, the latter might be set to show **Only relevant values**:

Figure 13.22: Only relevant values

This is advantageous to the end user in that it adjusts the number of postal codes that display to reflect only those pertinent to the cities selected in the first filter. However, using relative filters will cause additional queries to be sent to the data source and thus may degrade performance.

Table calculation filters

Using table calculations as filters does not have the same corresponding performance enhancements as dimension or measure filters. As discussed above, dimension and measure filters reduce the returned dataset, while table calculation filters do not. In the Tableau process flow, table calculations are not rendered until after the data is returned from the data source. This means that table calculations cannot be used to generate queries to limit returned data. Or, to put it another way, table calculation filters cause all data related to a given dimension or measure to be returned, after which Tableau executes the filter on the returned dataset.

To demonstrate this, perform the following steps:

1. Open the workbook associated with this chapter and navigate to the **Late Filter** worksheet.

2. In the **Data** pane, select the **Superstore** data source.

3. Create a calculated field named **Cust Name Tbl Calc** with the following code:

   ```
   LOOKUP( MAX( [Customer Name] ),0 )
   ```

4. Place **Customer Name** on the **Rows** shelf.

5. Place **Cust Name Tbl Calc** on the **Filters** shelf and constrain to show only **Aaron Bergman**.

6. Place **Sales** on the **Text** shelf.

7. Right-click on **Sales** and select **Quick Table Calculation | Rank**.

In this exercise, the entire list of customers is returned to Tableau, after which Tableau deploys the filter. Essentially, using **Cust Name Tbl Calc** as a filter merely hides the underlying data. This is useful because the rank returned for **Aaron Bergman** is correct. Merely filtering on **Customer Name** would return a rank of **1** for **Aaron Bergman**. Unfortunately, the correct results come with a performance hit. Running the performance recorder on this exercise will show that the table calculation negatively impacts performance.

Fortunately, with the advent of LOD calculations, using table calculations as filters is often not necessary. LODs are calculated fields that include or exclude data independent of the current view. For more information, please refer to *Chapter 5, Table Calculations*.

Using actions instead of filters

Another way to improve performance might be to use actions instead of filters. You can develop a dashboard that shows a high-level overview first and goes into detail only once the user selects something. The mechanics are similar to the ones we showed in the *Aggregation* section; however, aggregation happens per worksheet and not on the data source itself. By selecting a mark in the high-level overview, an action will be triggered. The user can dive deeper into details, but the level of detail will only be increased step by step. Hence, less data has to be loaded at once.

 A very nice presentation regarding this topic can be found at `https://youtu.be/veLlZ1btoms`.

The next topic we will be discussing involves calculations. How can we write a calculation in the most efficient and performant way?

Efficient calculations

Calculations may be constructed differently and yet accomplish the same thing. Look, for instance, at the following example, which shows that an IF statement can be replaced by simpler code:

Scenario I	Scenario II

Create a calculated field with the following code:
 	
`IF SUM (Profit) > 0 THEN`
`'Profitable' ELSE 'Unprofitable' END`
 	
Place the calculated field on the **Colour** shelf.
	Create a calculated field with the following code:
	
	`SUM (Profit) > 0`
	
	Place the calculated field on the **Colour** shelf.
	
	Right-click on **True** and **False** in the resulting legend and rename to **Profitable** and **Unprofitable**.

Since either of these scenarios will return the desired results, which should be used? The deciding factor is performance. This section will explore what to do and what to avoid when creating calculated fields in order to maximize performance.

Prioritizing code values

Calculations that use Boolean values or numbers are more performant than those that use dates. Calculations that use dates, in turn, are more performant than those using strings. This is not only true of Tableau, but also in computer science as a whole.

Based on this information, **Scenario II** listed in the preceding table is more performant than **Scenario I**. **Scenario I** causes Tableau to create a query that requires the data source engine to handle strings for reporting profitability, whereas **Scenario II** sends only 1s and 0s to determine profitability. The third step for **Scenario II** (that is, aliasing **True** and **False** to **Profitable** and **Unprofitable**) is merely a labeling change that happens after the aggregate dataset is returned from the data source, which is quick and easy for Tableau.

Level-of-detail calculation or table calculations

In some instances, an LOD calculation might be faster than a table calculation and vice versa. If you are not sure, try both to see which one performs better. Also, if they're not really needed, use neither. Refer to the following diagram, which explains when to choose which:

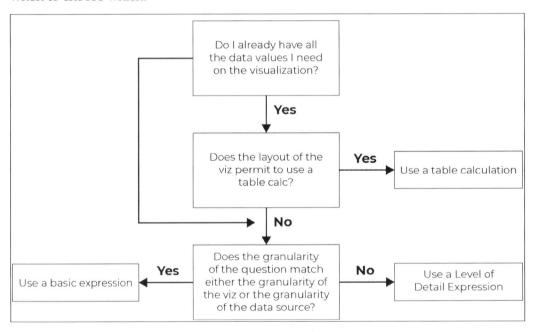

Figure 13.23: Choosing a calculation type

This diagram, along with more advice about selecting a calculation type, can be accessed at `https://www.tableau.com/about/blog/2016/4/guide-choosing-right-calculation-your-question-53667`.

Other ways to improve performance

To conclude this chapter, let's consider a few other possibilities for improving performance.

Avoid overcrowding a dashboard

Often, end users want to see everything at once on a dashboard. Although this may be perceived as beneficial, it often is not. Consider the inclusion of a large crosstab on a dashboard. Does scrolling through pages of details add to the analytical value of the dashboard? Perhaps the answer is "noo." Furthermore, an excess of information on a dashboard may obscure important insights. Diplomatically arguing for leaner dashboards may lead to better decision making as well as better performance.

Fixing dashboard sizing

Dashboards can be set to an exact size or to **Range** or **Automatic**. Exact size results in quicker performance because once Tableau Server has rendered a view for one end user, that render stays in cache and can be reused for the next end user that accesses that dashboard. **Automatic** and **Range**, on the other hand, cause Tableau Server to attempt to determine the resolution size used by each end user and render the dashboard accordingly. This means that Tableau Server does not use the instance of the dashboard stored in cache for the next end user. This, in turn, impacts performance.

Setting expectations

If an end user is expecting near-instantaneous performance, then, of course, anything less is disappointing. Explaining in advance that a complicated, detailed-oriented dashboard may not be performant can help in at least two ways. First, upon explaining the likely performance problems, a compromise may be reached that results in the creation of a less complicated dashboard that still delivers valuable information. Second, if it is absolutely necessary for the dashboard to be complicated and detail-oriented, at least the end user has been warned that patience may be needed when interfacing it.

Summary

We began this chapter with a discussion of the performance-recording dashboard. This was important because many of the subsequent exercises utilized the performance-recording dashboard to examine underlying queries. Next, we discussed hardware and on-the-fly techniques, where the intent was to communicate hardware considerations for good Tableau performance and, in the absence of optimal hardware, techniques for squeezing the best possible performance out of any computer.

Then we covered working with data sources, including joining, blending, and efficiently working with data sources. This was followed by a discussion on generating and using extracts as efficiently as possible. By focusing on data sources for these three sections, we learned best practices and what to avoid when working with either remote datasets or extracts. The next sections explored performance implications for various types of filters and calculations. Lastly, we looked at additional performance considerations, where we explored a few more thoughts regarding dashboard performance as well as setting expectations.

In the next chapter, we will turn our attention to Tableau Server. Tableau Server is a dense topic worthy of a book. Thus, our exploration will be truncated to focus on Tableau Server from the desktop author's perspective.

14

Interacting with Tableau Server/Online

Tableau Server/Online is an online solution for sharing, distributing, and collaborating on content created in Tableau Desktop. Its benefits include providing an environment where end users can securely view and explore data visualizations that are constantly updated from underlying data sources so that content is always fresh. The main difference between Tableau Server and Tableau Online is that Tableau Server needs to be maintained by you, while Tableau Online is fully hosted in the cloud by Tableau and backed up by Amazon Web Services infrastructure. For the ease of reading, we will further refer to both as Tableau Server.

The scope of this chapter is limited to the Tableau Desktop author's interaction with Tableau Server. Topics such as installation and upgrades, authentication and access, security configuration, and command-line utilities are not directly related to the Tableau Desktop author's interaction with Tableau Server and are thus are not included in this chapter. However, the help documentation is quite good. Also consider watching some videos from Tableau Software about Tableau Server (for example, `https://www.youtube.com/c/tableausoftware/search?query=Tableau%20 Server`). If you have questions related to any of the topics listed here or regarding any other Tableau Server topics, be sure to visit the online help site at `https://www. tableau.com/support/help`.

This chapter will explore the following topics:

- Publishing a data source to Tableau Server
- Web authoring
- Maintaining workbooks on Tableau Server
- More Tableau Server settings and features

Tableau Server is a great way to take your company's Tableau adoption to the next level. The most important question on your mind is probably, how can you bring Tableau dashboards from Desktop to Server? That is exactly what we are going to show you in the first section.

Publishing a data source to Tableau Server

So, you purchased Tableau Desktop, became a pro dashboard developer, and now you want to share your work with your colleagues. Do they all need a Tableau Desktop license and installation to see your vizzes? Luckily, the answer is: NO! The best way to share Tableau dashboards is on Tableau Server. This way your colleagues only need a Tableau Server viewing license, which is much cheaper than the developer license you purchased, and they can fully interact with the dashboard you built and uploaded to Server. But how do you upload your dashboard from Desktop to Server?

Note: This chapter assumes the reader has access to Tableau Server with sufficient privileges to publish data sources and edit in the web authoring environment. If you do not have access to Tableau Server but would like to work through the exercises in this chapter, consider downloading the trial version that, as of the time of writing, provides full functionality for two weeks. If you would like a longer trial, consider joining the Tableau beta program at http://www.tableau.com/getbeta, which will give you access to each beta release in which you participate.

Let's take a look at the following steps to see how we can publish a data source to Tableau Server:

1. Navigate to `https://public.tableau.com/profile/marleen.meier` to locate and download the workbook associated with this chapter.

2. Navigate to the **Publish** worksheet.

3. Make sure the data source is **My Superstore**.

4. If you have not already done so, log in to your instance of **Tableau Server** by clicking on **Server | Sign In...**:

Figure 14.1: Server—Sign in

5. In the **Data** pane, select the **My Superstore** data source.

6. Select **Server | Publish Data Source | My Superstore**:

Figure 14.2: Server—Publish Data Source

7. In the resulting dialog box, input your desired settings:

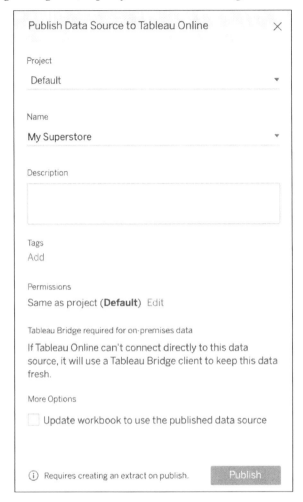

Figure 14.3: Server — Publish Data Source settings

If you have different projects on your Tableau Server, you can choose which project to publish the data source to. You can also change the name if you like or add a description, which comes in handy especially if you have lots of different data sources and you want to allow your users to look for the one they need. By adding tags, you will add a metadata layer that will allow your Tableau Server users to search for a given data source based on tags. You can also change the permissions. Your setup might be that different users are in different groups, so here you can select which group is allowed which permissions. And lastly, you can immediately upload the workbook with the data source such that both are available on Tableau Server.

Tableau file types

We will continue our discussion of Tableau Server by considering the various Tableau file types. This may seem a surprising place to continue but as you read, you will discover that a clear understanding of file types provides the Tableau Desktop author with foundational knowledge for efficiently and effectively interacting with Tableau Server.

The file types discussed previously that are relevant for understanding how to interact with Tableau Server are considered in some depth. The file types that are not relevant for understanding Tableau Server are considered only briefly. Some file types (for example, those associated with license activation) are not considered.

Tableau data source

Let's now look at the various data sources available in Tableau. Take a look at the following Tableau data file:

- **File format type**: XML.

- **What it contains**: Metadata.

- **Why it's useful**: The .tds file is important because it allows the Tableau author to define default formatting and aggregation, calculated fields, data types, field types, and more. Furthermore, the .tds file can be published to Tableau Server and thus accessed by other authors in the environment. This effectively makes a .tds file a playbook, which ensures consistency across the organization. This important feature will be explored more fully in the *Tableau Server architecture* section.

- **How it's generated**: A .tds file can be generated by right-clicking on a data source in the **Data** pane and selecting **Add to Saved Data Sources...**, followed by selecting **Tableau Data Source** in the resulting dialog box. A .tds file can also be generated when publishing to Tableau Server via **Server | Publish Data Source | [data source]**. The *Publishing a data source to Tableau Server* section demonstrates how to publish a .tds file and also a .tdsx file.

- **How to access it**: The .tds file type is usually accessed in one of two places. First, it can be stored in **My Tableau Repository | Datasources**. When stored in this directory, a .tds file will display in the left portion of the **Start Page** under the **Saved Data Sources** section. The second place a .tds file is often stored is on Tableau Server. Navigating to **Data | New Data Source** and choosing **Tableau Server** allows the Tableau author to point to the .tds and .tdsx files that have been published to Tableau Server.

Tableau packaged data source

Take a look at the following Tableau data file details:

- **File format type**: Compressed.

- **What it contains**: Metadata and a data extract.

- **Why it's useful**: The .tdsx file is useful because it can be accessed for both metadata and data. Tableau authors can access a .tdsx file located on Tableau Server as a data source, thus eliminating the need for a workbook to connect directly to an external data source. A published .tdsx file can be placed on a schedule so that it is regularly updated from the underlying data source.

- **How it's generated**: A .tdsx file can be generated by right-clicking on a data source in the **Data** pane and selecting **Add to Saved Data Sources...**, followed by selecting **Tableau Packaged Data Source** in the resulting dialog box. Like the .tds file, the .tdsx file can also be generated when publishing to Tableau Server via **Server | Publish Data Source | [data source]**. See the next exercise section for more details.

- **How to access it**: A .tdsx file is accessed the same way a .tds file is. First, it can be stored in **My Tableau Repository | Datasources**. When stored in this directory, a .tdsx file will display in the left portion of the **Start Page** under the **Saved Data Sources** section. The second place a .tdsx file is often stored is on Tableau Server. Selecting **Data | New Data Source** and choosing **Tableau Server** allows the Tableau author to point to the .tds and .tdsx files that have been published to a given instance of Tableau Server.

Tableau workbook

Next to data sources we have Tableau workbooks. Take a look at the following Tableau data file details:

- **File format type**: XML.

- **What it contains**: Metadata and schema. The schema defines the visualizations in the workbook. Note that schema, in this context, refers to the XML that defines the visual components of the workbook, including the visualizations displayed on worksheets as well as the layout of dashboards and stories.

- **Why it's useful**: The .twb file type is the file type most often used by the Tableau author. It is necessary for creating visualizations that point to a live dataset. Thus, real-time solutions will utilize this file type.

- **How it's generated**: A .twb file is created via **File | Save As**, then selecting the .twb file type in the resulting dialog box.

- **How to access it**: A .twb file can be opened via Tableau Desktop or accessed via a browser that points to an instance of Tableau Server. Since a .twb file is XML, it can be opened, viewed, and updated via a text editor.

Tableau packaged workbook

Take a look at the following Tableau data file details:

- **File format type**: Compressed.

- **What it contains**: Metadata, schema, and optionally, one or more data extracts.

- **Why it's useful**: The .twbx file type is required for use with Tableau Reader. It can also be effectively used with Tableau Server when accessing data sources to which Tableau Server does not directly connect, such as flat files, and Microsoft Excel and Access files. Drawbacks to the .twbx files will be discussed next.

- **How it's generated**: A .twbx file is created via **File | Save As**, then selecting the .twbx file type in the resulting dialog box.

- **How to access it**: A .twbx file can be opened via Tableau Desktop or accessed via a browser that points to an instance of Tableau Server. Since a .twbx file is a compressed file, it can also be unzipped via a compression utility, such as WinZip or 7-Zip.

Other file types

The remaining file types you should be familiar with are not particularly relevant for Tableau Server and will thus only be briefly discussed here. There might be some issues with the compatibility of Tableau Desktop extracts and Tableau Server versions. A full list of compatibility scenarios can be found at https://help.tableau.com/current/desktopdeploy/en-us/desktop_deploy_compatibility.htm.

Let's take a look at the following other file types:

- **Hyper**: To know more about Hyper, you can refer to https://www.tableau.com/support/hyper-resources.

- **Tableau Data Extract**: The `.tde` file can be generated via the following: if a `.twb` file is opened in Tableau Desktop, a `.tde` file can be created by right-clicking on a data source in the **Data** pane and selecting **Extract Data**. After selecting the desired options, Tableau will provide a dialog box for the author to save the `.tde` file in a given location. The extract file can be used to create a local snapshot of a data source for a quicker authoring experience. That same local snapshot is also portable and can thus be used offline. Often the data extracts compressed inside the `.twbx` and `.tdsx` files are in the `.tde`/`.hyper` format. An important clarification should be made here: often Tableau authors will refer to publishing an extract to Tableau Server. The extract that is published is not a `.tde` or `.hyper` file. Rather, it is a `.tdsx` file. Refer to *Chapter 13, Improving Performance*, for additional information about the extract file format.

- **Tableau Bookmark**: The `.tbm` file can be generated via **Window | Bookmark | Create Bookmark**. It can be useful for duplicating worksheets across multiple workbooks and also for sharing formatting across multiple workbooks.

- **Tableau Map Source**: The `.tms` file is discussed in detail in *Chapter 9, Mapping*.

- **Tableau Preferences Source**: The `.tps` file can be used to create custom color palettes. This can be helpful when an organization wishes to use its color scheme within Tableau workbooks. The `.tps` file that Tableau utilizes is called `Preferences.tps` and is located in the My Tableau Repository. Since it's an XML format, it can be altered via a text editor. Matt Francis has posted a helpful blog at `https://wannabedatarockstar.blogspot.com/` that clearly communicates how to adjust this file. You can also reference the Tableau help page.

Now that we've discussed the different file types, you will be able to recognize them as we move on to the next big technical subsection, the server architecture.

Tableau Server architecture

Now that we have reviewed the various Tableau file types, we can use that information to understand different ways to architect a Tableau Server environment. Since this is not a book dedicated to Tableau Server, this architecture discussion is presented on a high level. The intent is to help the Tableau Desktop author understand how to interact with Tableau Server so that the workbooks best serve the end user. Take a look at the following diagram:

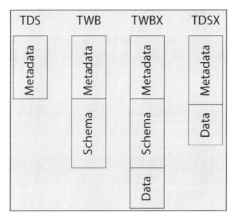

Figure 14.4: Server architecture

The preceding diagram visually represents the contents of the four previously discussed file types that are most relevant when considering how the Tableau Desktop author should interface with Tableau Server. To be clear, the previous sections of this chapter provided descriptions of the various file types. Each of these descriptions included the line *What it contains*, which is visually represented in the preceding diagram. Each of the four file types listed in the graphic includes metadata; two include data and two include schema.

Let's consider four approaches to the Tableau Server architecture and how each presents its own advantages and disadvantages that the Tableau Desktop author should be aware of. The first two approaches presented should generally be avoided. The second two approaches should generally be adopted. Of course, these four approaches do not encompass every possible approach. They do, however, provide a basic framework.

Approaches to avoid

If the following Tableau Server architecture approaches should be avoided, why mention them at all? Because they are often utilized! An administrator who hasn't had the opportunity to go to Tableau Server training may default to these approaches and may even build out a large infrastructure before realizing that it's difficult to maintain and scale.

TWB-centric

Take a look at the following diagram depicting the Tableau Server architecture:

Figure 14.5: TWB-centric server architecture

The preceding diagram shows the .twb files that have been published to Tableau Server. The diagram also communicates that, since the .twb files do not include any data, each workbook must access an external data source in order to display a visualization. Furthermore, this access will cause Tableau to return data in real time, that is, the latest data available in the external data source.

The TWB-centric approach to the Tableau Server architecture results in the following advantages:

- **Small footprint**: The small-footprint advantage stems from the small file size; the .twb files are rarely larger than a few MB. Small file size leads to fewer issues for revision history.

- **Easy revision history**: This is in contrast to the .twbx files, which can become quite large and thus unexpectedly overload a hard drive when storing many copies via revision history.

- **Real time**: The real-time advantage is as a result of .twb files always pointing to an external data source. As the data source updates, the workbook that is based on a .twb file updates. Of course, *real time* in this case should not be mistaken for something like a stock ticker; that is, updated results do not display in a worksheet unless the end user performs a manual refresh. Even when manually refreshed, a worksheet may be regenerated from the cache as opposed to making a call to the data source. This will depend on the settings in Tableau Server.

- **Added security**: In order to open a .twb file with a database connection, the user needs database credentials to do so.

The following are the disadvantages of taking a TWB-centric approach:

- **Difficult to maintain**: From one perspective, maintenance is fairly easy; that is, a .twb file can be quickly downloaded, edited, and then re-uploaded. From another perspective, the TWB-centric approach can be quite a chore. Consider a change to a single foreign key in a data source that breaks every workbook in production. Editing dozens of workbooks (or more) to rectify the issue would not be trivial.

- **Potentially poor performance**: Another disadvantage of the TWB-centric architecture is potentially poor performance. This is because it requires the .twb files to point to external data sources. Network latency and slow database servers will negatively impact workbook performance. It should be noted, however, that some data source engines (such as the **massively parallel processing** (**MPP**) systems discussed in *Chapter 6, All About Data – Data Densification, Cubes, and Big Data*) can potentially outperform the following architecture options.

To sum up, avoid the TWB-centric architecture. A TDS-centric architecture maintains all the advantages of a TWB-centric architecture and mitigates the maintenance difficulties we just discussed.

TWBX-centric

Let's take a look at the following diagram, which depicts the TWBX-centric architecture:

Figure 14.6: TWBX-centric server architecture

The preceding diagram shows .twbx files that have been published to Tableau Server. Assuming that the .twbx files contain extracts for each required data source, no call is necessary to external data to display a visualization.

The TWBX-centric approach to the Tableau Server architecture has a strong advantage:

- **Typically performant**: The TWBX-centric approach has at least one advantage: performance. Since a .twbx file can include data extracts, no calls to external data sources are required. This circumvents problems with network latency and slow database servers, thus enabling quick performance. Note that a .twbx file can be scheduled for refreshes thus ensuring that the data is never stale.

However, the following are the various TWBX-centric disadvantages:

- **Large footprint**: Unfortunately, the TWBX-centric approach has major drawbacks. The large-footprint disadvantage costs a lot of storage space and can occur as a result of large .twbx files.

- **Very difficult to maintain**: These files can be as large as several GB. Such large files are very difficult to maintain and can lead to potential problems with revision history. Large .twbx files can be difficult and time-consuming to download, update, and re-upload.

- **Potential problems with revision history**: Also, as mentioned previously, revision history on large .twbx files may unexpectedly overload a hard drive.

- **Not real time**: Furthermore, the TWBX-centric solution is not real time.

For most Tableau Server implementations, the TWBX-centric solution should be avoided. The Tableau Server administrator who observes a .twbx file in excess of 500 MB should likely contact the author who uploaded the file in order to seek a better solution. This is not to say that the .twbx files should never be used on Tableau Server. If a Tableau author uses a local spreadsheet as a data source, a .twbx file will almost certainly be used in order for the workbook to function on Tableau Server. However, this will typically not lead to large .twbx files. Thus the disadvantages we just listed would not apply.

To sum up, avoid the TWBX-centric architecture. A TDSX-centric architecture maintains all the advantages of a TWBX-centric architecture and mitigates most of the difficulties we just discussed.

Approaches to adopt

Previously, we considered two approaches to Tableau Server architecture to avoid. Now let's consider two approaches to adopt.

TDS-centric

Let's take a look at the following diagram, which depicts the TDS-centric architecture:

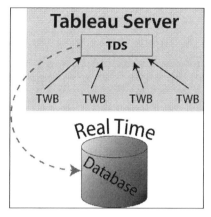

Figure 14.7: TDS-centric server architecture

The preceding diagram shows the `.twb` files that have been published to Tableau Server. The `.twb` files point to a `.tds` file as a data source. The `.tds` file points to the database.

The TDS-centric approach to Tableau Server architecture results in various advantages:

- **Small footprint**: Like the TWB-centric approach, the TDS-centric approach has the advantage of a small footprint, which stems from the small size of the `.tds` and `.twb` files.

- **Easy revision history**: These small file sizes result in fewer issues for the revision history.

- **Easy to maintain**: By using `.twb` files with their corresponding small footprints, maintenance is relatively easy since `.twb` files can be quickly downloaded, updated, and then re-uploaded. Furthermore, pointing to a `.tds` file has an additional maintenance advantage. If changes are made to the metadata in the `.tds` file (for example, a calculated field is updated), those changes will trickle down to every `.twb` file that points to the `.tds` file, thus allowing for an update in a single location to impact multiple workbooks. Previously in this chapter, we considered a scenario in which a change to a single foreign key broke every workbook in production. By utilizing the TDS-centric approach, updating the metadata in a `.tds` file to account for the change to the foreign key could instantly fix the problem for every `.twb` file that points to the `.tds` file.

- **Real time**: As with the TWB-centric approach, the TDS-centric approach provides a real-time advantage.

The following is the TWB-centric disadvantage:

- **Potentially poor performance**: Lastly, the TDS-centric architecture has a disadvantage: potentially poor performance. This is because a .tds file must point to external data sources that could, in turn, introduce network latency and slow database engines that negatively impact workbook performance.

To sum up, consider adopting the TDS-centric approach, especially when a real-time solution is required. The TDS-centric architecture maintains all the advantages of a TWB-centric architecture while providing easier maintenance.

TDSX-centric

Let's take a look at the following diagram, which depicts the TDSX-centric architecture:

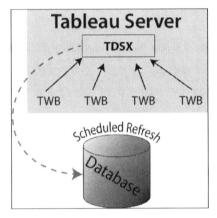

Figure 14.8: TDSX server architecture

The preceding diagram shows the .twb files that have been published to Tableau Server. The .twb files point to a .tdsx file as a data source. The .tdsx file can be scheduled to refresh regularly so that the data does not become stale. The TDSX-centric approach to the Tableau Server architecture results in various advantages:

- **Typically quick performance**: The TDSX-centric approach allows for typically quick performance. Since the .twb files point to a .tdsx file that resides on Tableau Server, problems with network latency and slow database servers are circumvented.

- **User-friendly**: The ability to add additional calculations, structures, and folders to a data source leads to a better user experience.

- **Relatively small footprint**: By using the `.twb` files with their corresponding small footprints, maintenance is relatively easy since the `.twb` files can be quickly downloaded, updated, and then re-uploaded. However, the `.tdsx` size is relative as the `.tdsx` files can become quite large even though the `.twb` files remain small.

- **Easy to maintain**: Furthermore, pointing to a `.tdsx` file has an additional maintenance advantage. If changes are made to the metadata in the `.tdsx` file (for example, a calculated field is updated), those changes will trickle down to every `.twb` file that points to the `.tdsx` file, thus allowing for an update in a single location to impact multiple workbooks.

- **Revision history-friendly**: This is revision history-friendly in that the user can always restore an older version of the workbook.

The following is the TDSX-centric disadvantage:

- **Not real-time**: Not real-time. However, this can be mitigated with frequent updates.

To sum up, in most environments, a TDSX-centric architecture should be the approach you use. Even the one disadvantage, not real-time, can be mitigated with frequent updates. That said, a TDS-centric approach should be used when a real-time solution is required or when accessing a data source engine that outperforms Tableau extracts.

As previously stated, this discussion of Tableau Server architecture is at a high level. Different environments require different approaches. Thus, some combination of these two approaches may often be appropriate. Also, there may be special cases that utilize one of the approaches to be avoided. For example, it may be advantageous in some environments to programmatically generate a `.twbx` file for different end users, thus allowing those end users to download the `.twbx` files that contain only their data.

Now that we know about the different Tableau Server setups, we will move on to the next section. Tableau Server allows you to alter dashboards even after they have been published and without using Tableau Desktop. This feature is called web authoring and will be discussed next.

Web authoring

After you have published a dashboard to Tableau Server, how do you imagine editing it? Well, Tableau offers two options. In the first option, both you and everyone else who has access and the rights to download the dashboard can download it, edit it in Tableau Desktop, and overwrite the latest version on Tableau Server with a new upload. The other option is to edit the dashboard live on Server. This feature is called **web authoring**. Web authoring is a Tableau Server feature that provides an interface for authoring that is similar to Tableau Desktop. Originally, the web authoring interface was pretty limited, but more features are introduced with each version. Thus, the capability gap between the Tableau Server web authoring environment and Tableau Desktop has shrunk. The web authoring environment provides robust capabilities for creating and applying table calculations and also provides capabilities for creating dashboards.

As of the time of writing, some features are still missing altogether in the Tableau Server web authoring environment, but the following Tableau Public dashboard will give you a complete overview of what is out there, comparing Tableau Desktop and Tableau Server web authoring functionality and even allowing you to select the versions. Thanks to Andrew Pick for creating this very helpful dashboard: `https://public.tableau.com/views/TableauDesktopvTableauWebEditing/ DesktopvsWebEdit?_fsi=yR9nQtlX&:showVizHome=no`.

The following two very brief exercises demonstrate how to access the authoring environment within Tableau Server. Keep in mind that the Tableau Server admin needs to grant access to users to do so.

Editing an existing workbook with web authoring

Let's perform the following steps to edit an existing workbook on Tableau Server:

1. Log in to an instance of Tableau Server.

2. Select the **My Superstore** data source that we uploaded in the *Publishing a data source to Tableau Server* section.

3. Select **New Workbook** to create a workbook based on the published data source:

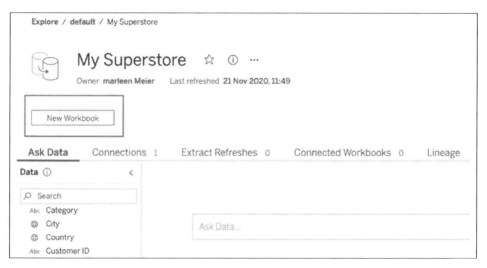

Figure 14.9: Published data source

4. Drag **Category** on to **Columns** and **Profit** on to **Rows**.

5. Now click on **File | Save** and in the popup, choose a name for the workbook, (I called mine Test) and hit **Save**.

6. If you go back now to the overview of Tableau Server you will see an additional workbook called **Test**, next to the **My Superstore** published data source:

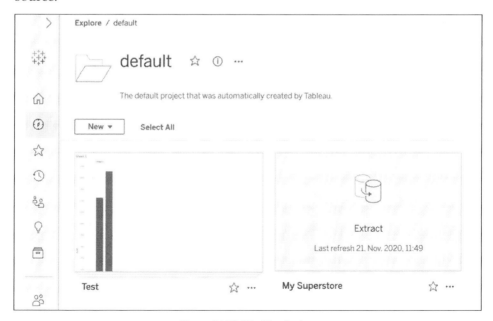

Figure 14.10: Workbook view

7. If you want to continue editing the **Test** workbook, simply open it on Tableau Server and select the **Edit** button at the top right:

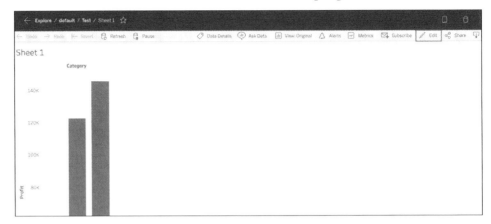

Figure 14.11: Web authoring

This is as easy as it gets.

So far, we have published a dataset, built a workbook from that dataset on Tableau Server, and maybe you edited the workbook as well. If not, we will do so in the next exercise.

Understanding the Tableau Server web authoring environment

Let's perform the following steps to understand the Tableau Server web authoring environment:

1. Access the workbook associated with this chapter and note the **Sales & Quota** worksheet:

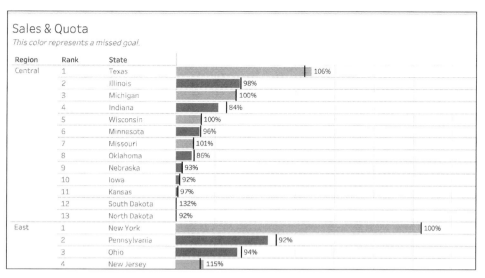

Figure 14.12: Web authoring II

2. Publish the worksheet to an instance of Tableau Server by clicking on **Server |
   Publish Workbook**. In the window that appears, rename the workbook to Sales
   & Quota and make sure that only the **Sales & Quota** worksheet will be uploaded:

Figure 14.13: Publish workbook

3. The following popup will appear:

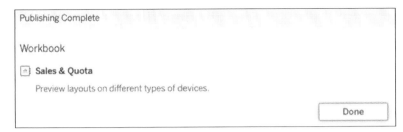

Figure 14.14: Publish workbook II

4. Open the worksheet on Tableau Server by clicking on the **Sales & Quota** published view, and click on **Edit** to access web authoring:

Figure 14.15: Accessing web authoring

5. From here you should see an interface similar to the one you are used to from Tableau Desktop. This is what web authoring is all about—you have most of the Tableau Desktop functionality online and you don't even need to open Tableau Desktop as long as your workbook has been published to Tableau Server. Let's try it!

6. The first thing you might notice is that even though we didn't publish the **Publish** sheet, it is visible in the web authoring view. You can right-click on it and press **Publish Sheet** to make this worksheet accessible for Tableau Server users that don't have access to web authoring:

Figure 14.16: Web authoring

7. Press the *Ctrl* (Windows) or *Command* (macOS) button on your keyboard and while doing so, drag the **Quota Met?** field to the **Rows** shelf:

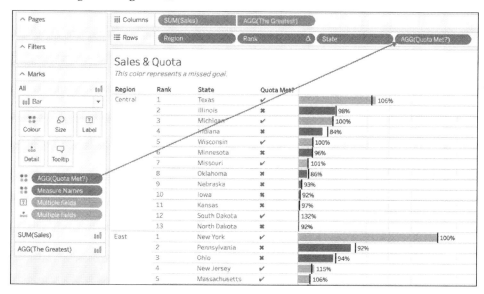

Figure 14.17: Web authoring II

8. You will see that crosses and checkmarks appear in the view. This shows us that we can not only use a color to indicate whether we met a quota, but also a mark in the view. Feel free to try out the other operations you are used to handling with ease in Tableau Desktop, including the following:

- Creating a calculated field
- Adding a filter
- Adjusting the tooltip
- Creating a new worksheet
- Creating a dashboard

After you are done with editing, you simply click on the cross in the upper-right corner and hit **Save**. Make sure you have the rights to save and thereby overwrite the dashboard in web authoring mode:

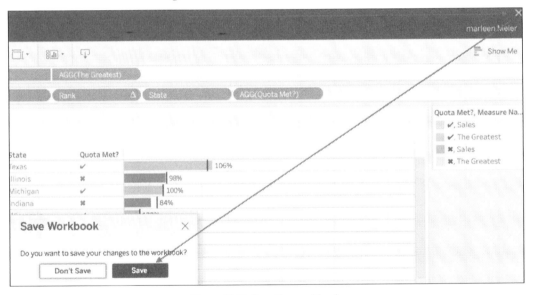

Figure 14.18: Save the workbook

You will see that the original worksheet has been changed to whatever you did in the web authoring mode.

Comparing Tableau Desktop and web authoring

By now we know that editing published dashboards can be done by downloading from Tableau Server, editing in Tableau Desktop, and then uploading again, as well as leveraging the web authoring feature that ships with Tableau Server. Web authoring is advantageous for small changes and a real time-saver because there is no need to download and upload a dashboard.

Bigger changes however are more easily executed in Tableau Desktop and some changes are not even possible in web authoring. Therefore sometimes it's unclear which individuals in an organization require a Tableau Desktop license and which only need a Tableau Server user license. For example, a technologically oriented executive with limited time to learn new software could go either way. On the one hand, they may want to delve into the details of the data, but on the other, they may not be able to invest the time necessary to learn enough about Tableau Desktop to warrant the price of an additional license. When the web authoring environment was released the features were fairly rudimentary. The busy executive may have been best served with a Tableau Desktop license. Since that time, more and more capabilities have been introduced. Today, that same executive may be reasonably content with using the web authoring environment.

The rights regarding whether you are allowed to use web authoring and to what extent are often related to your licensing model. For more information please read the following Tableau help article: `https://onlinehelp.tableau.com/current/pro/desktop/en-us/server_desktop_web_edit_differences.htm`.

Starting from Tableau 2020.4, it is also possible to use the web authoring functionality for Tableau Prep Builder. If you have a flow published to your Tableau Server, check it out!

To create a new Prep Builder project in your browser, you can select **New | Flow** on the **Start**, **Explorer**, or **Data Source** pages. More information can be found here: `https://www.tableau.com/blog/2020/12/tableau-prep-builder-now-available-browser`.

Maintaining workbooks on Tableau Server

We have now learned about the dashboard editing options, but we have not yet discussed how we can keep track of changes and make sure that we don't lose important information in the process of producing new information. This section will provide help on how to maintain workbooks on Tableau Server, starting with revision history.

Revision history

You, as a Tableau dashboard developer or maybe even a Tableau Server admin, want to make sure that your users are always looking at the right data. But then it happens: you edit a dashboard and after your edit, the dashboard displays faulty information. A user calls you and wants the old dashboard back immediately. What do you do? Use revision history!

Tableau Server ships with a revision history that ensures that the past 25 versions of each workbook and data source are retrievable. This setting can be enabled or disabled by the Tableau Server admin. In Tableau Desktop, if you attempt to upload a workbook or data source with the same name as a previously uploaded file, Tableau Desktop will display a warning such as **Data source name is already in use**:

Figure 14.19: Overwriting data source

Publishing will overwrite the existing data source. If you proceed with the upload, revision control will be activated, and the previous version of the file will remain accessible as a revision. To access the revision history for individual workbooks and data sources in Tableau Server, simply select any data source or workbook you uploaded and click on the three dots at the bottom right. In the popup, select **Revision History...**:

Figure 14.20: Revision History

This will open a dialog box where you can choose which previous version to restore:

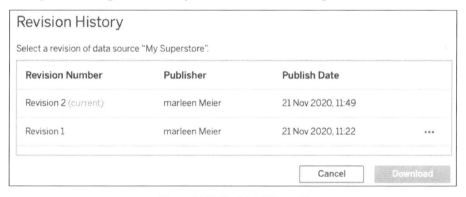

Figure 14.21: Revision History II

If you'd like to peek beneath the hood of Tableau Server to begin to understand how revision history works, do the following: on a computer with Tableau Server installed, go to the directory for revision history. By default, this is located at `C:\ProgramData\Tableau\Tableau Server\data\tabsvc\dataengine\revision`. In the `revision` directory, there are files with alphanumeric names. Simply rename one of those files by adding the appropriate extension (for example, `.twbx`) to open the file in Tableau Desktop. Renaming with an existing file name will replace the earlier version.

Revision histories are so helpful! I hope you will not have to use them often but it's always good to have options. The next question many organizations have is, how can I make sure that users only see what they are supposed to see and not just everything that has been published to Tableau Server? One solution is user filters. We will discuss this topic next!

User filters

Students often ask me something along the lines of the following question: I have sales managers over various territories. It's important that the sales managers see only their metrics; that is, not the metrics of the other sales managers. In order to accomplish this, do I have to create separate workbooks for each sales manager?

Fortunately, the answer is no. Tableau provides user filters that allow the Tableau author to make sure that each of those sales managers sees only the information for which they have clearance. To demonstrate this, take the following steps:

1. This exercise needs more than one user on Tableau Server. Therefore, go ahead and create at least one additional user on Tableau Server by clicking on **Users** | **Add Users**. I used a second email address that I own to do so:

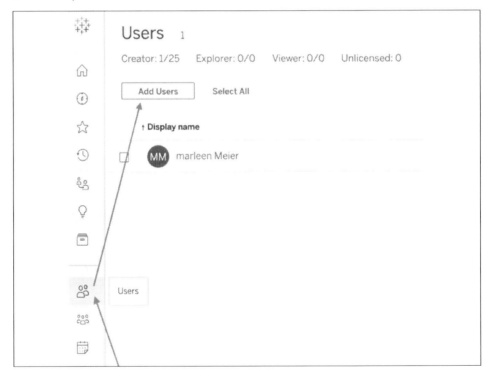

Figure 14.22: Add user

2. As an optional step, you can change an account's display name. In order to change the display name of an account, log in to `https://www.tableau.com/`, click on **User | Edit Account**, and make the desired changes to the first and last name entries. I renamed my two accounts **Marleen** and **MarleenTest** to make it easier for you to distinguish the two accounts in the following screenshots:

Figure 14.23: Add user II

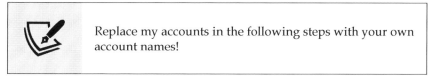

Replace my accounts in the following steps with your own account names!

3. As a second optional step, instead of assigning single users to a filter, you can also assign groups of users. In order to do so, you can create different groups as follows:

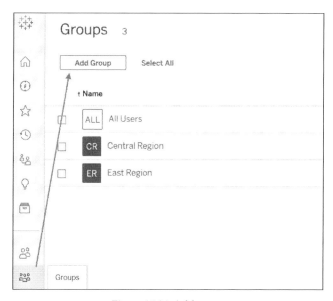

Figure 14.24: Add group

4. You can then split the users on your Tableau Server instance into **Central Region** and **East Region** by selecting a user and then **Group Membership** under **Actions**:

Figure 14.25: Add group II

5. Now, access the workbook associated with this chapter and navigate to the **View Level User Filter** worksheet. Note that the view is a field map of the USA with **State** on the **Detail** shelf, **Region** on the **Color** shelf, and **Sales** on the **Label** shelf.

6. Log in to an instance of Tableau Server via **Server | Sign In**.

7. Select **Server | Create User Filter | Region...**:

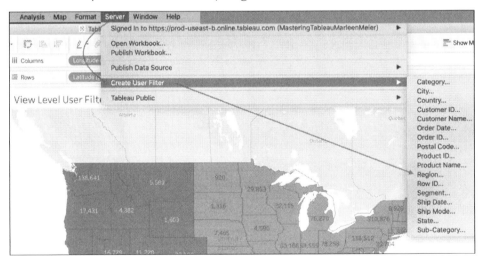

Figure 14.26: User filter

8. In the resulting **User Filter** dialog box, you can now assign either a single user or a group to a region. I will select **Marleen** and check the **Central** region. Also, I will select **MarleenTest** and check the **East** region. Name the user filter `Sales Region` and click on **OK**:

Figure 14.27: User filter II

9. Note that **Sales Region** is now actually added to the **Sets** portion of the data pane:

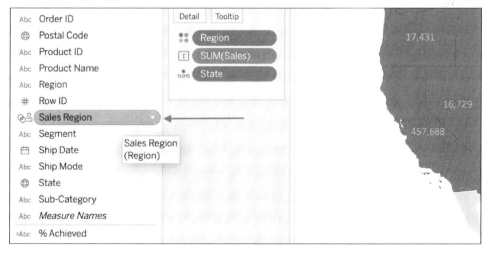

Figure 14.28: Set added

10. Place the **Sales Region** on the **Filters** shelf.

11. In the right portion of the status bar, click on the dropdown to access the user filter:

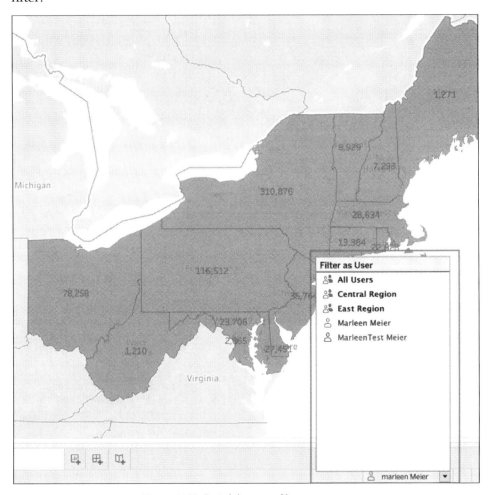

Figure 14.29: Switch between filter

12. Choose a different user and note that the results display only the region that the given user has access to:

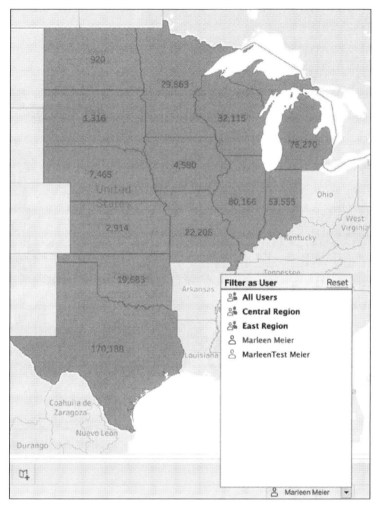

Figure 14.30: Switch between filter II

Once the workbook is published to Tableau Server, users who access the workbook will only see the information the filter allows. This can also be applied to saved data sources (published TDSX files) at the data source level.

One important thing to note is, as opposed to simply adding a dimension filter to the **Filters** shelf, you might want to consider adding the **Sales Region** to the **Data Source** filter. This is important because any user with web authoring permission can simply remove a filter from the **Filters** shelf. In the case of this exercise, the user would then be able to see metrics for every region. Data source filters, however, cannot be removed via the web authoring environment and are thus more secure. Furthermore, a data source filter is workbook-wide, which further secures the data. However, if you don't have web authoring enabled, the **Filters** shelf serves its purpose.

For more details on filters and Tableau's order of operation, please check *Chapter 13, Improving Performance*.

Performance-recording dashboard

In *Chapter 13, Improving Performance*, we explored the Performance Recording dashboard. Sometimes a workbook may perform satisfactorily on Tableau Desktop but, mysteriously, may perform poorly when published to Tableau Server. In such cases, accessing the Performance Recording dashboard on Tableau Server can be very helpful.

Note: This does not work on Tableau Online.

The following exercise provides step-by-step instructions for doing so:

1. Navigate to an instance of **Tableau Server**.
2. On the toolbar, click on **Settings**.
3. On the resulting page, locate the **Workbook Performance Metrics** section and select **Record Workbook Performance Metrics**.

4. Click on **Save**.

5. Navigate to a workbook of your choosing and open a **view**. Note that the ending portion of the URL is :iid=<n>.

6. Type :record_performance=yes& immediately before :iid=<n>. For example, http://localhost:8000/#/views/Finance/Taleof100Start-ups?:record_performance=yes&:iid=5.

7. Note that the toolbar now includes a **Performance** link:

Figure 14.31: Performance recording on Tableau Server

8. Click the **Refresh** icon on the toolbar. Click on **Performance** and observe the resulting performance-recording dashboard that is displayed, just like the one you already know from *Chapter 13, Improving Performance*.

We are getting closer to the end of this chapter and last but not least, we want to mention the small settings and features that Tableau Server offers that can really improve the user experience. The next section will be all about alerts, subscriptions, comments, and other cool stuff. Let's dive right in!

More Tableau Server settings and features

Once a dashboard has been published, users can set alerts, certify data sources, subscribe, add comments to a dashboard, and more, depending on their permissions. This section will address the different functionalities in two different places: on a worksheet and on a view. Next to those, Tableau Server has many more functionalities, especially settings for site admins, which are—unfortunately—out of the scope of this book.

Features on the worksheet level

By *features on the worksheet level*, I mean the settings that are available to you after selecting a project and a certain worksheet like so:

Figure 14.32: Tableau Server

On this level, we see six different tabs, which we will discuss over the next few pages.

Views: Views show a thumbnail of all the worksheets or dashboards that have been published within one workbook. When uploading a workbook to Tableau Server, you can select all the views that should show here:

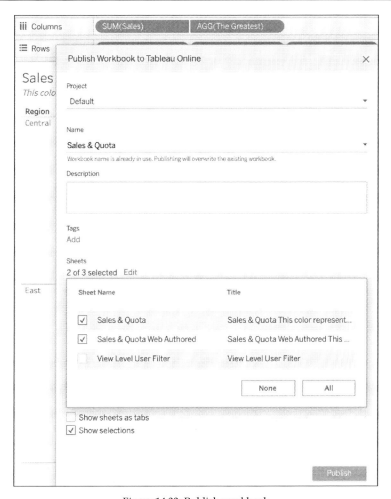

Figure 14.33: Publish workbook

By clicking on the three dots next to a view, more options will show, as can be seen in the following screenshot:

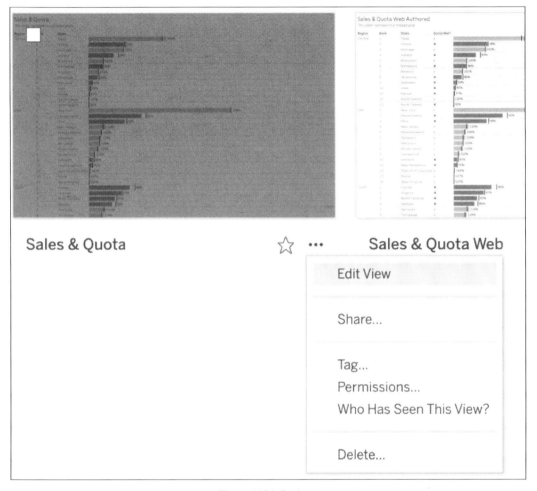

Figure 14.34: Options

The different options are self-explanatory: you can edit the view (also referred to as web authoring, which we've discussed earlier in the chapter), and you can share the view with other users, where Tableau will send an email with an image and a hyperlink to the user you shared the view with. You can also add tags that will help other users find the view, you can check which user or group has permission to open the view and who has seen this view, and lastly, you can delete it. Which of those options will display is a matter of the configuration in Tableau Server, so your admin can enable or disable the different features to show or else they might be grayed out.

Data Sources: The next tab is **Data Sources**. It will give you an overview of the data sources used to create this workbook:

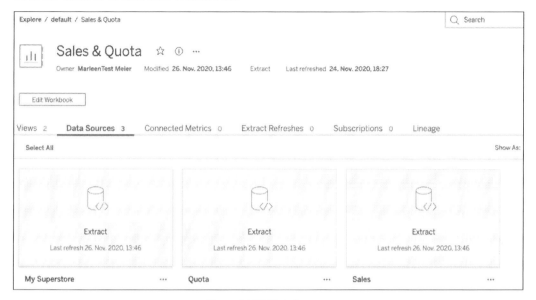

Figure 14.35: Data Sources

You will be able to see which type of data sources were used; for example, with an extract of live connections, by clicking on the three dots by each source, you will again be able to see more settings, depending on the settings of your Tableau Server:

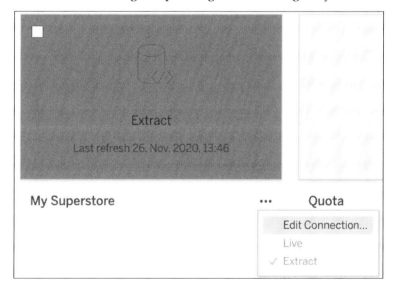

Figure 14.36: Data Sources II

Connected Metrics: Next in line are the connected metrics. This is a relatively new feature. In order to see metrics, you first have to set them up in a view. We will get to this in the second part of this section, but basically, it allows you to select pieces of different dashboards and views and combine those data points as metrics to monitor your data. Metrics make use of a specific data mark in your view. Therefore, you might need to adjust your view to show the one mark you want to use.

For example, if you have a dashboard with daily profits over the past year but your metrics should show only the last profit data point, you will have to create a new view in order to use the explicit last profit in a metric, even though the data is already part of the initial view. However, a big advantage is that you don't need to connect to different data sources, as the connections that are already set up in the different workbooks will be leveraged.

 More details regarding metrics can be found here: `https://www.tableau.com/about/blog/2020/5/introducing-metrics-headlines-your-data`.

Extract Refreshes: When using extracts as the data source, you can define a refresh schedule while uploading the workbook to Tableau Server or even after you published the workbook. The different schedules can be set by your server admin. If you set the extract refresh to run at 7 AM every day, for example, Tableau Server will access the data source, perhaps a SQL database, at 7 AM, and load the data, and you will in return see the latest data in your Tableau dashboard. Using extracts tends to perform better than a live connection, depending on the amount of data and the type of data source, but be aware that the data in the dashboard will always be as old as your latest extract.

Subscriptions: Subscriptions can be set on a view level; we will get to it in the next section. But on a workbook level, you will be able to see all subscriptions that are active for a certain workbook.

Lineage: Lineage is another rather new feature on Tableau Server. It is only available through the Data Management add-on, at additional cost, and will show you the dependencies of a data source.

For more information on Lineage, please check: `https://help.tableau.com/current/server/en-us/dm_lineage.htm`.

Lastly, please note the three dots on a workbook page, which contain more options as well as options we have seen before:

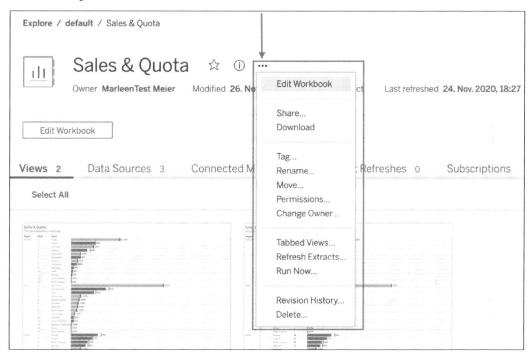

Figure 14.37: Options

Again, which ones you will be able to use is dependent on the permissions the Tableau Server admins gave you.

The available options look a little bit different when the selection is based on a published data source, like the My Superstore data source that we published to Tableau Server at the beginning of this chapter:

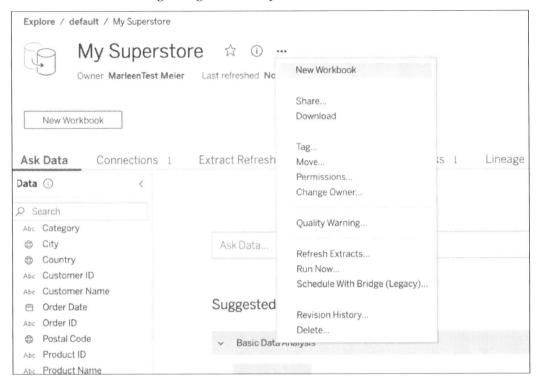

Figure 14.38: Options II

Most of the items are self-explanatory, but I want to point out **Quality Warning…**, which is available at an additional cost within the Data Management add-on. This feature will allow you to alert every user of the data or any workbook based on the data to be extra careful when using it. Depending on the settings, Tableau Server will show warnings of various types, such as **Deprecated**, **Stale data**, **Under maintenance**, and **Sensitive data**, which are selectable from a dropdown.

You can also decide whether you want to show the type on the data source only or also on the related workbooks. The following is an example on the data source only:

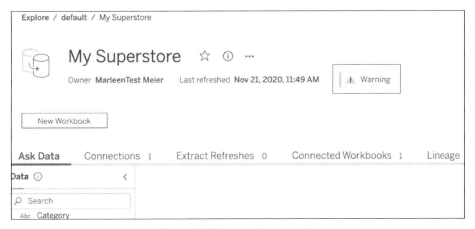

Figure 14.39: Data quality warning

And here is an example of how the warning looks on the workbook level:

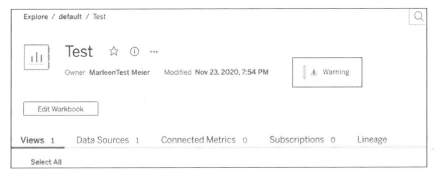

Figure 14.40: Data quality warning II

And even when opening the view:

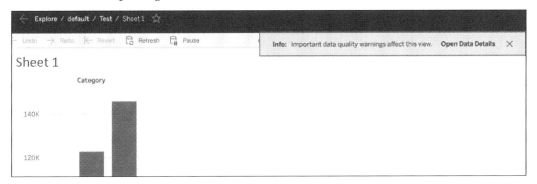

Figure 14.41: Data quality warning III

This is a very powerful feature and shows how Tableau matures more and more with each release. Data quality is the focal point for many data strategies and the base of all analytics. Tableau Server adapted to it and provides you with features that will grow along with your data strategy and quality measures.

Ask Data: The last item before we continue with the view level is **Ask Data**, which is only available for Tableau Server. To access **Ask Data**, select a published data source and click on the first tab. Now the fun part starts where Tableau Server will help you build vizzes based on **Natural Language Processing (NLP)**:

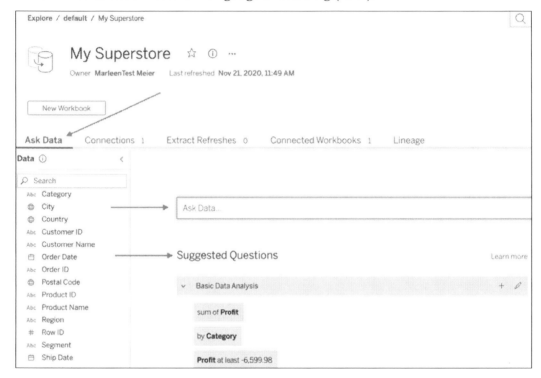

Figure 14.42: Ask Data

On the left-hand side, you see all available fields and, in the middle, you can either select one of the suggested questions that were created based on a smart algorithm, or start typing in your own question:

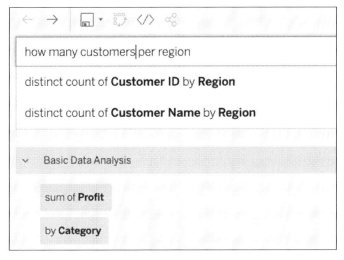

Figure 14.43: Ask Data II

You can see that I typed how many customers per region and Tableau offers me two options, translated into Tableau language, that I can choose from. I select the first one and hit *Enter*. See what happens now:

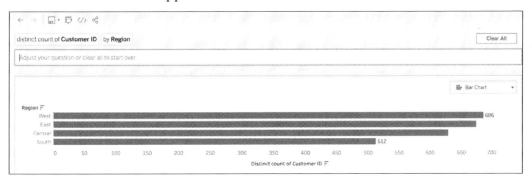

Figure 14.44: Ask Data III

Tableau Server created a view. The dropdown on the right allows me to change the view and at the top I can use the swap axis feature, known from Tableau Desktop, or save the view, or share the link to this view. Next, I hover over **Customer ID** in the left panel with all the fields and click on the pen that appears next to the name. This allows me to add a synonym to the field because I know that some other departments refer to customers as clients, therefore I add `Clients`:

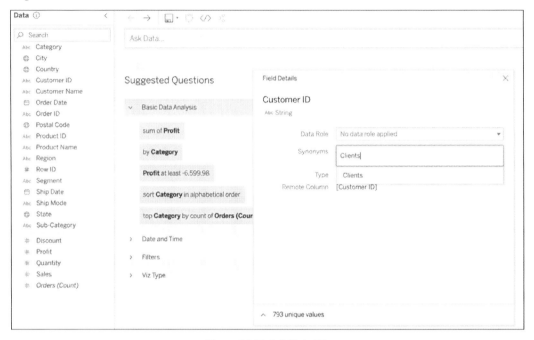

Figure 14.45: Ask Data IV

Now I am testing whether Tableau Server will pick up my synonym. My inquiry looks as follows:

Figure 14.46: Ask Data V

I click on the first option and Tableau Server creates the following graph:

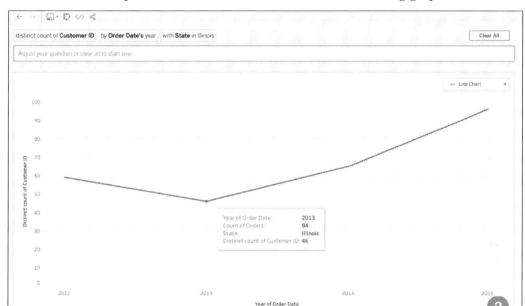

Figure 14.47: Ask Data VI

 Starting from Tableau 2021.1 your Tableau Server admin will also be able to improve the **Ask Data** suggestions, change the indexing, and analyze the string sequences entered by Tableau users. More information on how to do this can be found here: `https://help.tableau.com/current/pro/desktop/en-us/ask_data_optimize.htm`.

How cool is **Ask Data**? In my opinion, this feature is especially powerful, because even though Tableau is very intuitive, many people are not as data-savvy as you are. Providing a high-quality dataset and publishing it to Tableau Server will allow even more people to become data-driven and perform quick analysis themselves. This will help you to focus on more complex dashboards, while ad hoc questions can be answered using this feature.

Features on the view level

We have covered all settings on the workbook level, so now we will take a closer look at a lower level, the view. The view looks something like this, and the settings in the red frame are of interest for this section:

Figure 14.48: View-level features

Data Details: The **Data Details** tab will show more details regarding the data source used in the view. This feature is available at an additional cost within the Data Management add-on. The popup that will appear on the right side has three different sections: **Views of this sheet**, **Data Sources**, and **Fields in Use**:

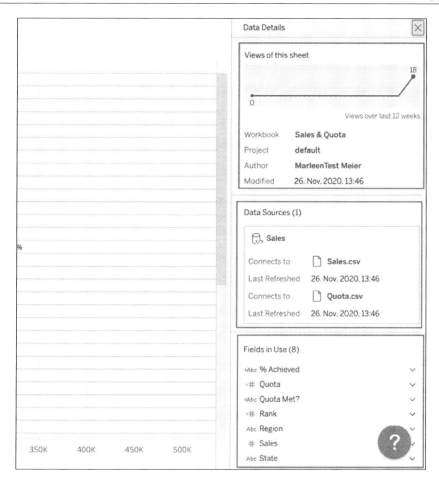

Figure 14.49: Data details

In the last section, you will have the option to open each field individually. If it is a calculated field, the calculation will show, while if it is a field from the original data source, the data type and description will be visible (if a description has been added):

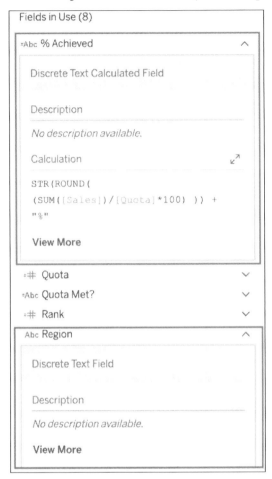

Figure 14.50: Data details II

View: The **View** tab allows you to add a view other than the default and save it. The next time you open the dashboard you can select the view you created by clicking on this tab and the saved settings will be applied all at once. Your view may contain, for example, a specific filter selection, a different parameter selection than the default view, and maybe a set that is most important to you. Instead of having to change filters, parameters, and sets every time you open the view, you can use the **View** tab:

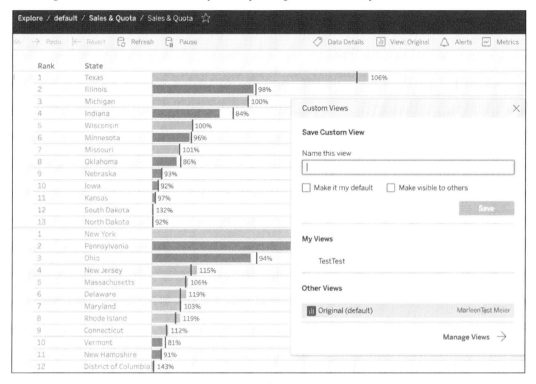

Figure 14.51: Custom views

Alerts: As of the time of writing, an alert can be set on a continuous numerical axis only. However, there are ideas being discussed on the Tableau forum that will increase the flexibility with setting alerts.

In the Tableau Ideas forum, users can write down what ideas they have for future releases and the community can vote for them. Ideas with high votes are likely to be picked up soon. You can find the forum here: https://community.tableau.com/community/ideas.

Click on the **Alerts** button and text on the right side will show:

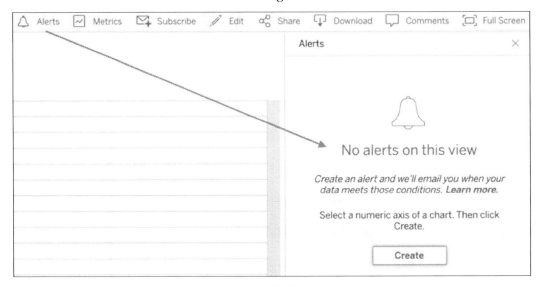

Figure 14.52: Alerts

After selecting a numeric axis (here: **Sales**), a new popup will appear in which a condition and a threshold can be entered. Also, the frequency of the threshold check can be specified:

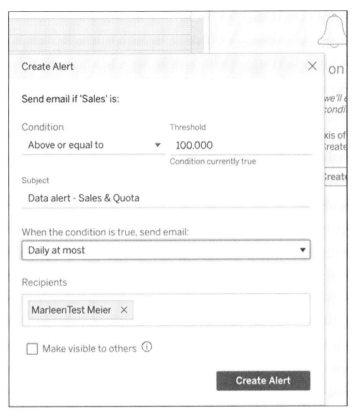

Figure 14.53: Alerts II

If an alert is set, all users and groups specified in that alert will receive an email once the threshold has been breached. The email will contain a static image and a link to the interactive version on Tableau Server.

Metrics: As mentioned before, this is a relatively new feature. In order to create a metric, select a mark in any view and click on the **Metrics** tab. The following screen opens on the right side of the view:

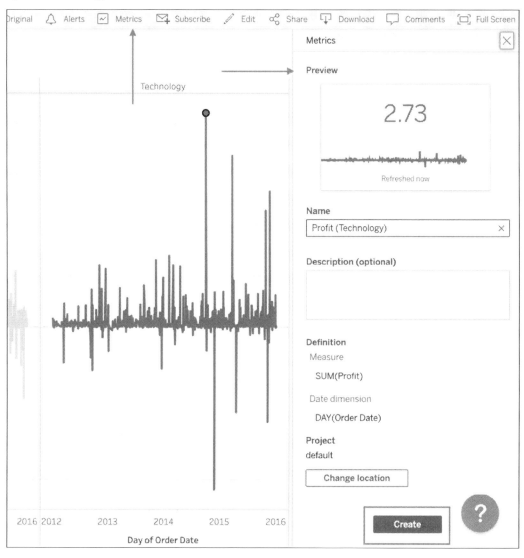

Figure 14.54: Metrics

As you can see, the metric will add a value on top of the line chart, which has a date field as the *x* axis. Especially for line plots with time on the *x* axis, metrics can add value because the metric will print the change over a given period, here from day to day. The **Metrics** feature is also very well integrated with Tableau Mobile and hence can be used to show key performance indicators to anyone, wherever they are. After clicking **Create**, the metric view can be accessed from the project it has been saved to and looks as follows:

Figure 14.55: Metrics II

The longest blue line with a date at the top (right side of the line chart) can be moved by hovering over the data points. As you move your cursor, the value and change (percentage and absolute) will automatically adjust. Metrics make use of a specific data point in your view. Therefore, you might need to adjust your view to show the metric you desire. However, a big advantage is that you don't need to connect to different data sources, as the connections that are already set up from different workbooks will be leveraged. If on that dashboard a metric has been created before, you will see it appear immediately on the right-hand side of the screen after clicking **Metric**.

Subscribe: Subscriptions can be found on Tableau Server in the upper-right corner:

Figure 14.56: Subscribe

They work in a similar way to alerts; people or groups can be subscribed and will receive an email with an overview of the relevant dashboard at a set time. The scheduling can be predefined by the administrator, for example, every morning at 7 AM.

Edit: You know this one already. **Edit** allows you to enter the web authoring environment on Tableau Server.

Share: By clicking on **Share**, a popup opens that allows you to share the URL to the view with anyone that is known to Tableau Server. That person will receive an email with the link. Make sure that that user has access to the project or else they will fail to open the view:

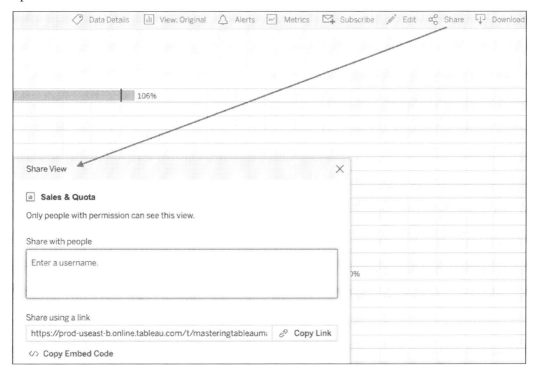

Figure 14.57: Share view

Download: Tableau Server also offers a download functionality. Depending on the configuration done by your admin, you can select between different formats for downloading purposes:

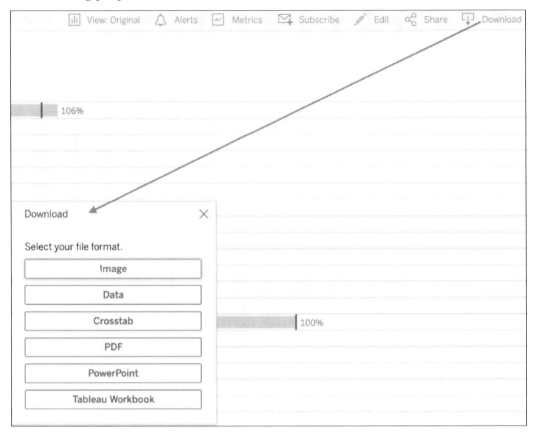

Figure 14.58: Download

Comments: Last but not least, you can comment on views—original or edited, both are possible. To do so, click on the **Comments** button in the upper-right corner:

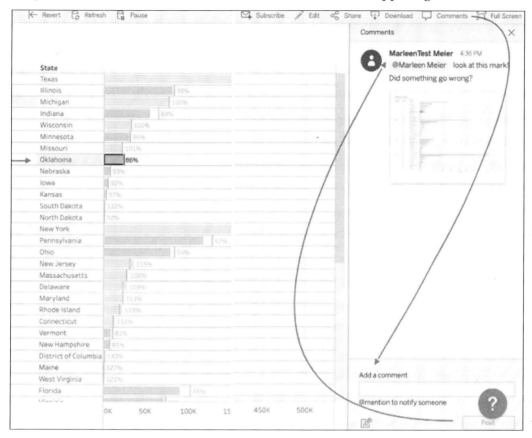

Figure 14.59: Comments

You can mention a colleague in the comment with @colleaguesname, and they will receive an email with your comment in it. It is also possible to add screenshots to your comment.

Summary

We began this chapter by considering the various Tableau file types—in particular, the .tds, .tdsx, .twb, and .twbx file types. This provided us with a foundation to understand different ways to architect a Tableau Server deployment. We considered four basic architecture scenarios and the advantages and disadvantages of each.

Next, we looked at Tableau Server revision history, where we learned that version-control features can provide a safety net against inadvertently overwriting files. This was followed by a section on the Tableau Server web authoring environment, which compared and contrasted that environment with Tableau Desktop. The primary purpose of this section was to establish a knowledge base for determining which personnel should have Tableau Desktop licenses and for whom the web authoring capabilities of Tableau Server should suffice.

Then we discussed user filters and the **Performance Recording** dashboard. User filters enable the Tableau author to ensure that users are only able to access data for which they have clearance. Although the Performance Recording dashboard was covered in *Chapter 13, Improving Performance*, in this chapter we learned how to access it with Tableau Server. And finally, we looked at some handy features, such as alerts, subscriptions, commenting, and others.

In the next and final chapter, we will branch out from the Tableau world, and will consider how to integrate it with R and Python. Knowledge of the programming integration will help the Tableau author accomplish analytics tasks that are beyond the capabilities of Tableau itself, while still using Tableau to visualize the results.

15

Programming Tool Integration

After 14 chapters full of Tableau functionality and exercises, what are we still missing? Well, we won't really know until we come across an issue. But wouldn't it be nice to know that even if we encounter a problem that can't be solved by Tableau's native capabilities, that we will still be able to write our own functions? The good news is, we can! Because we can always fall back on programming integrations. Two of them to be precise: R and Python.

Imagine the following scenario, you want to add a pricing formula to your Tableau dashboard. You look up the formula and see that you have all the required variables, like strike price, stock price, and volatility, but you also need a probability density function, which you can't find in Tableau. In this case, you can fall back to the programming integration and run the calculation in R or Python and send back the output—great, isn't it? Now imagine a second scenario: You're working on a sentiment analysis project. You could calculate the sentiment in Python outside of Tableau and then use the output as input for your model, but wouldn't it be great if you could have it all in Tableau? Well, you can by using the programming tool integration.

In this chapter, we will cover the following topics:

- Integrating programming languages
- R installation and integration
- Implementing R functionality

- Python installation and integration
- Implementing Python functionality

Integrating programming languages

How does integration empower Tableau? It happens through calculated fields. Tableau dynamically interfaces with Rserve or TabPy to pass values and receive results. And Tableau Prep Builder also has R and Python integration as we saw in *Chapter 3, Tableau Prep Builder*! So let's not waste any time and jump right in.

Basic Tableau-to-R and Tableau-to-Python integration is quite simple: The view shows data based on a calculated field, with the help of which Tableau pushes data to Rserve or TabPy respectively and then retrieves the results via a table calculation:

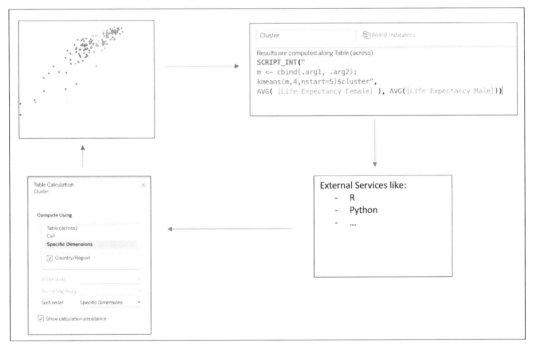

Figure 15.1: Tableau external services

Naturally, whether you are viewing a workbook on Tableau Desktop or via Tableau Server, if you wish to run R and Python calculations, then Rserve or TabPy must be accessible.

For a proper understanding of the integration, let's also look at the Tableau/R workflow as an example. Terms used in the following diagram, which you may be unfamiliar with, will be explained throughout this chapter:

Figure 15.2: Tableau/R workflow

The preceding screenshot can be used likewise for Python. Let's begin with R since it was the first available integration.

R installation and integration

In order to adequately understand how Tableau and R work together, it's important to grasp the big picture. To facilitate that understanding, we'll cover high-level concepts and information in this section before delving into calculated fields and R scripting details.

Installing R is typically not difficult, but it does involve more than simply double-clicking on an executable. In order to successfully connect Tableau with R, you will need to make sure that permissions are correctly set and that various components—some required and some just nice to have—are correctly implemented. We will cover the basics, review a couple of the typical challenges faced during installation, and provide troubleshooting guidance.

Perform the following steps to install R:

1. Download R by visiting http://www.r-project.org/ and choosing a CRAN mirror. Note that R works best in a Linux or UNIX environment; however, in order to learn R and to begin working with Tableau/R functionality to complete the exercises in this chapter, installing the Windows version is adequate.

2. Install R by double-clicking on the download executable.

3. Open R.

Various issues may arise when installing R. For example, you may experience problems due to insufficient permissions for the R working directory. This issue may first become evident when attempting to install R packages. To rectify the problem, determine the working directory in R with the getwd() function. Next, either change the working directory via setwd() or, at the operating-system level—whichever you feel more comfortable with—set the appropriate read and execute permissions for the working directory.

Issues can also arise due to firewall and port-configuration problems. By default, Tableau will connect to Rserve via port 6311. Alternatively, within Tableau, you can specify a different port when connecting to R.

The documentation at http://www.r-project.org/ provides detailed information regarding overcoming a variety of installation challenges.

Although not required, RStudio Desktop provides a better user interface than the default RGui that installs with R. RStudio includes a console that features intelligent code completion (that is, IntelliSense), a workspace browser that provides easy access to files, packages, and help, a data viewer, and much more all within a single, unified environment:

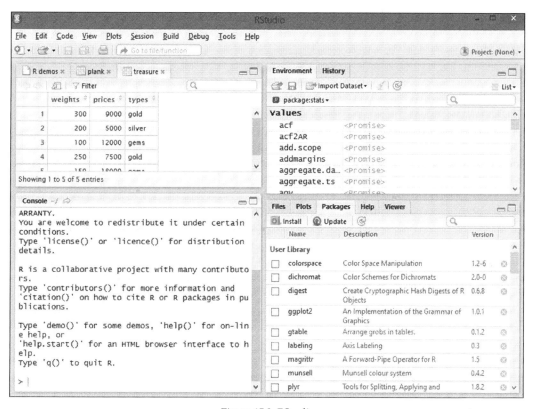

Figure 15.3: RStudio

The open source edition of RStudio is sufficient for many uses. You can download the application via `www.rstudio.com`. Just choose for yourself which one you like better out of the Desktop and RGui versions.

To start R within a Windows environment, navigate to **Start | Programs | R x64 4.0.3**. (Of course, your version of R may differ from mine.) This will open the RGui:

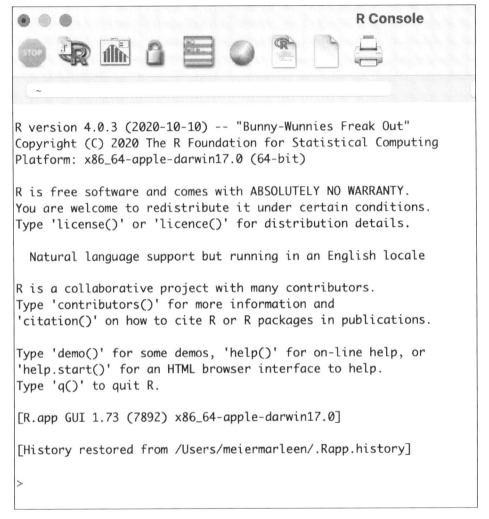

Figure 15.4: RGui

In order to establish a connection with Tableau, you will need to start Rserve. Technically, Rserve is a separate package; however, by default, it is installed with R:

- In order to make sure that the Rserve package is installed, within R, enter the following command:

```
rownames(installed.packages())
```

- Several packages should be listed including RServe. If for some reason the Rserve package did not install with your instance of R, you can do so via `install.packages("Rserve")`.

- To start `Rserve`, enter `library(Rserve); Rserve()`.

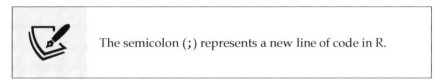 The semicolon (;) represents a new line of code in R.

Now that you have successfully installed R and started Rserve, you are ready to connect Tableau to R. Within Tableau, select **Help | Settings and Performance | Manage Analytics Extension Connection**:

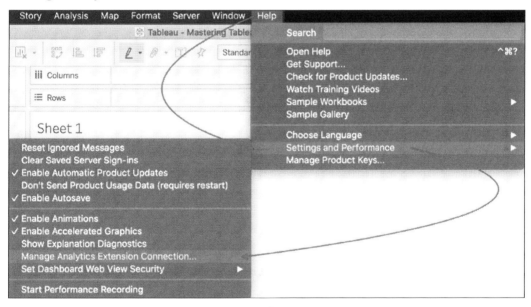

Figure 15.5: Analytics Extension

The default settings in the following screenshot will work for most local installations:

Figure 15.6: Analytics Extension Connection

While integrating Tableau with R doesn't require any interaction with an R interface, you will probably want to try out your R code in a GUI, such as RGui or RStudio, before embedding the code in Tableau. This will allow you to take advantage of useful accompanying features relevant to the R language, such as help, examples, and sample datasets tailored to R. Note that the calculated field editor in Tableau simply acts as a pass-through for R code and does not provide any support.

Implementing R functionality

Now that we have successfully connected Tableau with R, let's write some code in Tableau to invoke R. Within Tableau, open the Calculated Field Editor. Notice the class of functions beginning with SCRIPT_, as shown in the following screenshot:

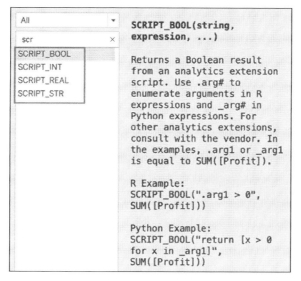

Figure 15.7: SCRIPT functions

The SCRIPT functions are used by Tableau to invoke R. The function names communicate the data type of the returned results; **SCRIPT_REAL** returns float values, **SCRIPT_BOOL** returns true or false values, and so forth.

The syntax of a SCRIPT function is represented in the following diagram:

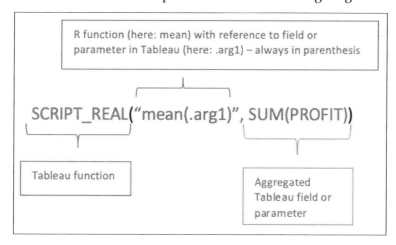

Figure 15.8: R script syntax

The preceding example code calculates the average profit, but we will get to more examples in the next sections. Let's start by reproducing Tableau functionality using the R integration and hence prove that R is working properly.

Reproducing native Tableau functionality in R

For our first exercise, we will use the AVG, MEDIAN, and STDEV functions in Tableau and compare the results with the mean, median, and sd R functions. This will allow you to practice the **SCRIPT_** functions, begin to understand R syntax, and compare results generated by Tableau with those generated by R.

Perform the following steps:

1. Navigate to `https://public.tableau.com/profile/marleen.meier/` to locate and download the workbook associated with this chapter.

2. Navigate to the **median | mean | sd** worksheet.

3. Select the **Sample - Superstore** data source.

4. Create the following Tableau-centric calculations:

   - **Tab Avg**: WINDOW_AVG(SUM(Sales))

   - **Tab Median**: WINDOW_MEDIAN(SUM(Sales))

   - **Tab Stdev**: WINDOW_STDEV(SUM(Sales))

5. Place the **Region** dimension on the **Rows** shelf and **Sales** on the **Text** shelf.

6. Double-click on **Tab Avg, Tab Median**, and **Tab Stdev**. They will now appear on the **Measures Values** shelf:

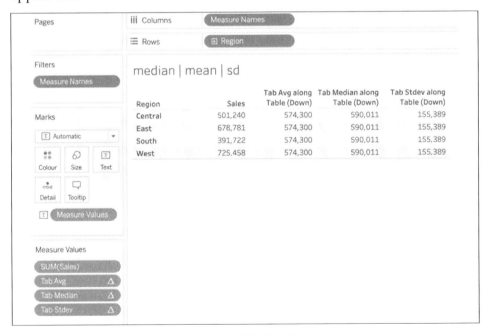

Figure 15.9: Testing R

7. Make sure R is installed, connected, and running as per the instructions in the *R installation and integration* section.

8. If you haven't installed the Rserve package yet, type `install.packages("Rserve")` into your R interface to install the Rserve package and select a CRAN mirror close to your current location:

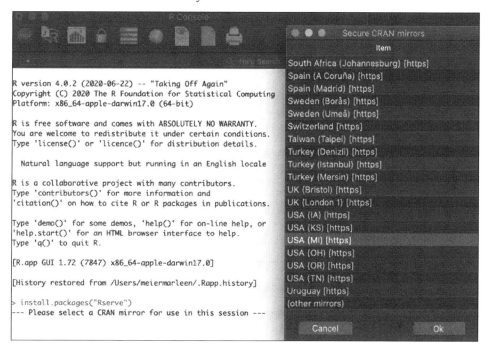

Figure 15.10: CRAN mirror

9. Next, type `library(Rserve); Rserve()` into the R interface. You may see the following error:

    ```
    Fatal error: you must specify '--save', '--no-save' or
    '--vanilla'
    ```

In this case, typing `Rserve(args = "--no-save")`. R requires you to make a choice of saving, not saving, or a combination (vanilla) after your session ends (not saving is my preferred option but the other two will work too):

```
> library(Rserve); Rserve()
Starting Rserve:
 /Library/Frameworks/R.framework/Resources/bin/R CMD /Library/Frameworks/R.framework/Versions/4.0/Resources/
library/Rserve/libs//Rserve

Fatal error: you must specify '--save', '--no-save' or '--vanilla'
>
> Rserve(args = "--no-save")
Starting Rserve:
 /Library/Frameworks/R.framework/Resources/bin/R CMD /Library/Frameworks/R.framework/Versions/4.0/Resources/
library/Rserve/libs//Rserve --no-save


R version 4.0.2 (2020-06-22) -- "Taking Off Again"
Copyright (C) 2020 The R Foundation for Statistical Computing
Platform: x86_64-apple-darwin17.0 (64-bit)

R is free software and comes with ABSOLUTELY NO WARRANTY.
You are welcome to redistribute it under certain conditions.
Type 'license()' or 'licence()' for distribution details.

  Natural language support but running in an English locale

R is a collaborative project with many contributors.
Type 'contributors()' for more information and
'citation()' on how to cite R or R packages in publications.

Type 'demo()' for some demos, 'help()' for on-line help, or
'help.start()' for an HTML browser interface to help.
Type 'q()' to quit R.

Rserv started in daemon mode.
```

Figure 15.11: Start Rserve

10. Connect R to Tableau as demonstrated in the *R installation and integration* section. After you have done so, return to Tableau and click the **Test Connection** button to see if it works:

Figure 15.12: Testing R connection

11. Click **OK** to close the windows.

12. Create the following R-centric calculations in Tableau. Note that R functions (such as mean) are case-sensitive:

- **R - mean**: SCRIPT_INT("mean(.arg1)", SUM(Sales))

- **R - median**: SCRIPT_INT("median(.arg1)", SUM(Sales))

- **R - sd**: SCRIPT_INT("sd(.arg1)", SUM(Sales))

13. Place each of the R calculated fields on the **Measure Values** shelf and arrange them in a way that the same type of calculations are next to each other but alternating Tableau and R-centric; for example **Tab Avg** then **R – mean** then **Tab Median** then **R – median** and so on. Since SCRIPT functions are categorized as table calculations (more on that later), be sure that each instance of the R calculated fields as well as the Tableau calculated fields use **Compute Using** set to **Table (down)**:

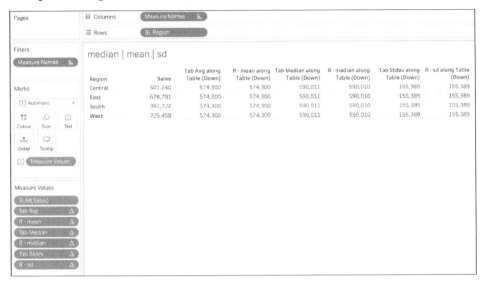

Figure 15.13: Tableau versus R output

14. Observe that, other than a slight rounding difference between **Tab Median** and **R - median**, the results of the Tableau and R functions are identical.

15. To address the rounding difference, adjust the code for **R - Median** as follows:

```
SCRIPT_REAL("median(.arg1)", SUM( [Sales] ))
```

Note that INT has now been replaced with REAL, demonstrating that, as the names suggest, SCRIPT_REAL works with float values and SCRIPT_INT works with integers.

This was our very first exercise with R integration—easy, right? The purpose of this exercise was mainly to show you that the R calculation works and therefore we compared three of the same calculations, each one calculated by Tableau as well as R. Or in other words, replicating Tableau functionality to prove that the R integration works as expected. The next exercise will be something that we can't do with Tableau's built-in functionality (as of the time of writing). We are going to calculate a regression analysis with more than two variables.

Using R for regression calculations

Succinctly stated, regression analysis is a technique for estimating variable relationships. There are various types of regression analyses, the most popular of which is linear regression. As demonstrated in the following screenshot, linear regression estimates a line that best fits the data and is a built-in function in Tableau.

You only need two measures on **Rows** and **Columns** as well as a dimension to partition the points in your view. Then you go to **Analysis** and drag the **Trend Line** onto your screen and select **Linear**:

Figure 15.14: Scatterplot

Notice that this screenshot is from Tableau. You can access it by clicking on the **Scatterplot** worksheet in the workbook associated with this chapter. It's a simple scatterplot with trend lines turned on. Trend lines, in Tableau, default to linear but also include logarithmic, exponential, and polynomial, which are all examples of regression analysis. By accessing **Worksheet | Export | Data** on a visualization utilizing a trend line, you can generate an Access database with predictions and residuals for marks on the view. But this is a tedious process and does not give a robust, dynamic solution for implementing more vigorous uses of linear regression. Using R provides much more flexibility.

Linear regression may use single or multiple variables. Single-variable equations are great for learning, but multiple-variable equations are typically necessary for real-world application. The following exercise includes multiple-variable equations. Our goal for this exercise is to determine how closely a linear regression model of **Profit** fits COUNT(Quantity), SUM(Sales), and AVG(Discount):

1. Navigate to the **Regression** worksheet.
2. Select the **Superstore** data source.
3. Build the basic layout by placing **Profit** on the **Columns** shelf, **State** on the **Rows** shelf, and filtering to **Top 10** by **Sum** of **Profit** by placing **State** on the **Filters** shelf as well:

Figure 15.15: Filter top 10

4. Create a calculated field entitled **Profit_Expected** utilizing the following code:

```
SCRIPT_REAL("
x <- lm(.arg1 ~ .arg2 + .arg3 + .arg4)
x$fitted",
SUM(Profit), COUNT(Quantity), SUM(Sales), AVG(Discount)
)
```

The details of this function will be explained shortly.

5. Create a calculated field entitled **% Diff** that calculates the percent difference between **Sum(Profit)** and **Profit_Expected**:

```
SUM(Profit)/Profit_Expected - 1
```

6. Create a calculated field entitled **Profit_Expected (residuals)** to return the difference between **Sum(Profit)** and **Profit_Expected** in terms of dollars:

```
SCRIPT_REAL("
x <- lm(.arg1 ~ .arg2 + .arg3 + .arg4)
x$residuals",
SUM(Profit),COUNT(Quantity), SUM(Sales), AVG(Discount))
```

7. Double-click **Profit_Expected**.

8. Move the instance of **Measure Names** from the **Rows** shelf and place it on the **Colour** shelf. Also, take an instance of **Measure Names** from the **Data** pane and place it on the **Size** shelf.

9. From the menu, select **Analysis | Stack Marks | Off**.

10. Drag the **calculated fields % Diff** and **Profit_Expected** to the **Label** shelf:

Figure 15.16: Expected profits

The preceding visualization shows a comparison of the actual profit, the expected profit, and the difference between the two. This calculation is especially helpful in retail markets but also in financial planning for any company.

Now that we've completed the exercise, let's take a moment to consider some of the code we used in this exercise:

`SCRIPT_REAL`	This Tableau function calls the R engine and returns a float value.
`"x <- lm(.arg1 ~ .arg2 +.arg3+.arg4); x$residuals"`	This is an R expression that houses a variable, a function, and an argument, and then returns predicted values.
`x <-`	This is the variable to be populated by the subsequent R function.
`lm(.arg1 ~ .arg2 + .arg3 +.arg4)`	This R function is used to fit linear models. It can be used to return regression based on variables provided by the argument. The information within the parentheses is referred to as an argument and is used to fit the model. Specifically, the response is to the left of the tilde ($\sim$), and the model is to the right. Thus, this is a multi-variable linear regression where `.arg1 = SUM(Profit)`, `.arg2 = COUNT(Quantity)`, `.arg3 = SUM(Sales)`, and `.arg4 = AVG(Discount)`. In English, the argument could be read as `SUM(Profit)`, and is modeled as the combined terms of `COUNT(Quantity)`, `SUM(Sales)`, and `AVG(Discount)`.
`x$fitted`	The `lm` function returns many values as part of its model object, including coefficients, residuals, rank, and fitted values. `x$fitted` is referencing the fitted values generated as a result of passing data to the model.
`", SUM(Profit), COUNT(Quantity), SUM(Sales) , AVG(Discount))`	These are the parameters used to populate the `.arg#` variables. Note that the double-quote (`"`) designates the end of the code passed to R, and the comma (`,`) designates the second half of the Tableau function, that is, the expression.

After having successfully implemented the regression, we will now look into a different statistical method that is often used to differentiate between subsets within a dataset, called clustering.

Clustering in Tableau using R

Clustering is used to select smaller subsets of data with members sharing similar characteristics from a larger dataset. As an example, consider a marketing scenario. You have a large customer base to which you plan to send advertising material; however, cost prohibits you from sending material to every customer. Performing clustering on the dataset will return groupings of customers with similar characteristics. You can then survey the results and choose a target group.

Major methods for clustering include hierarchical and *k*-means. Hierarchical clustering is more thorough and thus more time-consuming. It generates a series of models that range from *1*, which includes all data points, to *n*, where each data point is an individual model. *k*-means clustering is a quicker method in which the user or another function defines the number of clusters. For example, a user may choose to create four clusters from a dataset of a thousand members.

Clustering capabilities are included with Tableau. You can find this functionality under the **Analytics** tab. The clustering implementation in Tableau is based on four pillars:

- Solid methodology
- Repeatable results
- A quick processing time
- Ease of use

By utilizing the Howard-Harris method and the Calinski-Harabasz index within a *k*-means framework, the team succeeded on all accounts. Be sure to check out more details (https://help.tableau.com/current/pro/desktop/en-us/clustering.htm).

There are numerous ways the Tableau development team could have approached clustering. R, for instance, provides many different clustering packages that use different approaches. A Tableau author may have good reason to choose one of these different approaches. For example, clustering results are always identical when using the native Tableau clustering capabilities. But they do not have to be. By using R for clustering, the underlying data and the view may remain unchanged, yet clustering could differ with each refresh because the function will stop at the best result (local minima) before it has seen the whole dataset. The trade-off between using a so-called local minima versus a global minima for performance has been proven to be worth it. But depending on the order of numbers, the local minima can differ each time you run the function. This could be advantageous to you, looking for edge cases where marks may switch between clusters. The following example explores such a case.

Our goal in this exercise is to create four clusters out of the countries of the world based on birth rate and infant mortality rate:

1. Navigate to the **Cluster** worksheet.

2. Select the **World Indicators** data source (this dataset ships with Tableau and can be found under **Saved Data Sources**).

3. Build the initial view by placing **Infant Mortality Rate** on the **Columns** shelf, **Birth Rate** on the **Rows** shelf, and **Country/Region** on the **Details** shelf.

4. Right-click on each axis and select **Logarithmic** and deselect **Include Zero**. This will spread the data points more uniformly and will help make the visualization more aesthetically pleasing and easier to read:

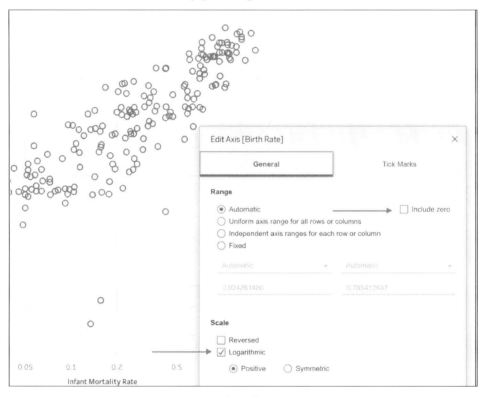

Figure 15.17: Clustering

5. Create a calculated field named **Cluster** with the following code:

```
SCRIPT_INT("
m <- cbind(.arg1, .arg2);
kmeans(m,4,nstart=5)$cluster",
AVG( [Life Expectancy Female] ), AVG([Life Expectancy Male]))
```

The details of this code will be explained at the end of this exercise.

6. Drag the **Cluster** field you just created to the **Shape** and the **Colour** shelves. Note that the Rserve engine throws an error:

Figure 15.18: Error handling

This is because nulls exist in the underlying dataset. For example, the data does not include an **Infant Mortality Rate** for *Puerto Rico*.

7. To rectify the error, drag an instance of **Infant Mortality Rate** onto the **Filters** shelf. Within the **Filter** dialog box, select the values as shown to remove all values below 0.01:

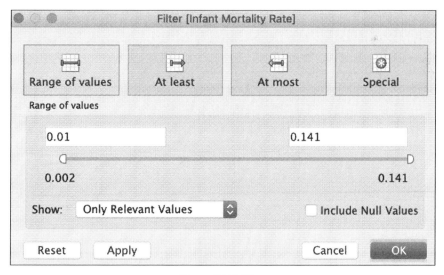

Figure 15.19: Filter

8. Make sure that you set **Cluster** to **Compute Using | Country/Region**.

9. The resulting view should look similar to the following screenshot:

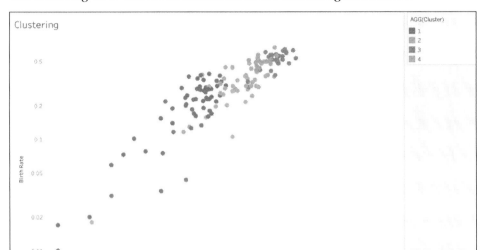

Figure 15.20: Clustering

10. Press *F5* and observe that the clustering changes with each refresh.

Now that we've completed the exercise, let's take a moment to consider some of the code we saw:

`SCRIPT_REAL`	This Tableau functions calls the R engine and returns a float value.
`"m <- cbind(.arg1, .arg2); kmeans(m,4,nstart=1)$cluster"`	This is the R expression that houses a variable, a function, and an argument, and then returns clusters.
`m <-`	This is the variable to be populated by the subsequent R function.
`cbind`	This R function combines the following `.arg#` variables into columns.

`(.arg1, .arg2)`	The variables within the parentheses are referred to as an argument. Each variable contains vector information. Specifically, `.arg1 = AVG( [Infant Mortality Rate] )` and `.arg2 = AVG([Birth Rate])`.
`kmeans(m,4,nstart=1)$cluster"`	kmeans declares the method of clustering. m contains the vector created by the cbind argument. The 4 integer declares the number of clusters. nstart declares the number of random sets.
`", AVG( [Infant Mortality Rate] ), AVG([Birth Rate]))`	These are the parameters used to populate the `.arg#` variables. Note that the double-quote (") designates the end of the code passed to R, and the comma (,) designates the second half of the Tableau function, that is, the expression.

What did we achieve? Well, we were able to categorize the countries in our dataset into four subgroups, based on life expectancy. We show the results of the clustering on a scatterplot with the two measures, infant mortality and birth rate. This way we can indirectly analyze four measures at the same time, which in this case are **Infant Mortality Rate**, **Birth Rate**, **Country/Region**, and **Life Expectancy**. The R clustering is based on a *k*-means approach, which differs from the Tableau default clustering and can be adjusted to any approach that it is possible to execute in R.

Next, we are going to check out the world of quantiles.

Introducing quantiles

Quantiles are often considered to be synonymous with quartiles. They are not. Quantiles are the sets that make up an evenly divided population of values. A quartile is a type of quantile—as is a quintile, a tercile, and a decile, for example. To understand how quantiles evenly divide a population of values, imagine multiplying a population by 1/4, 2/4, 3/4, and 4/4, and you get 4 quartiles. In order to get quintiles, you multiply the population by 1/5, 2/5, 3/5, 4/5, 5/5, and so forth.

Tableau allows you to view quantiles via right-clicking on an axis and choosing **Add Reference Line** | **Distribution** | **Computation** | **Quantiles**:

Figure 15.21: Terciles

But you can also change the number of tiles to 4, 5, or any other number to create quartiles, quintiles, and so on. The functionality of quantiles thus accessed, however, is quite limited. Primarily this is because reference lines do not generate measures that can be placed on shelves. This limits visualization options. Generating quantiles via R greatly expands those options.

Our goal for this exercise is to create *n* quantiles through R in order to view customer distribution by sales. We will further expand the exercise by creating parameters that restrict the number of members in the total dataset to a given percentile range. Finally, we will fine-tune the visualization by adding jittering.

Let's have a look at the following steps:

1. Navigate to the **Quantiles** worksheet.
2. Select the **Superstore** data source.
3. Change the view type to **Shape** on the **Marks** card.
4. Drag **Sales** to the **Rows** shelf, **Customer Name** to the **Details** shelf, and **Region** to the **Colour** shelf:

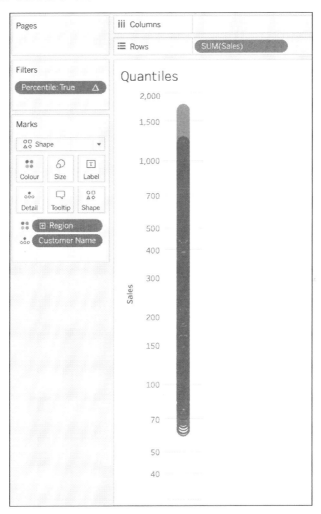

Figure 15.22: Quantiles

5. Create and display a parameter entitled **Number of quantiles** with the following settings:

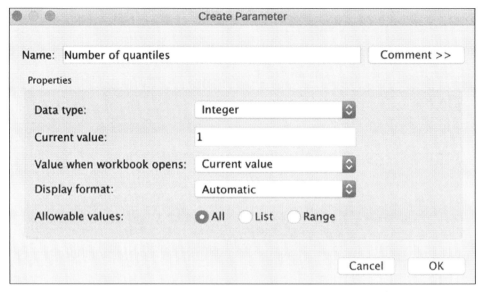

Figure 15.23: Quantile parameter

6. Right-click on the created parameter and select **Show Parameter**.

7. Create a calculated field entitled Quantiles with the following code:

```
SCRIPT_REAL("
x <- .arg1;
y <- .arg2[1];
m <- c(1:y)/y;
n <- length(x);
z <- c(1:n); for (i in c(1:n)) z[i] <- 0;
for (j in c(1:y)) for (i in c(1:n)) z[i] <- if (x[i] <=
quantile(x,m)[j] && z[i] == 0 ) j else z[i];
z;"
, SUM(Sales), [Number of quantiles])
```

The details of this code will be explained at the end of this exercise.

8. Right-click on the newly created calculated field **Quantiles** and select **Convert to Discrete**.

9. Create and display two parameters, **Select Percentile Bottom Range** and **Select Percentile Top Range**. Use the following settings for both:

Figure 15.24: Percentile parameter

10. Right-click on both newly created parameters and select **Show Parameter**.

11. Create a calculated field entitled **Percentile** with the following code:

```
RANK_PERCENTILE(SUM([Sales])) < [Select Percentile Top Range]
AND
RANK_PERCENTILE(SUM([Sales])) > [Select Percentile Bottom Range]
```

12. Drag **Quantiles** to the **Columns** shelf and set **Compute Using** to **Customer Name**.

13. Drag **Percentile** to the **Filters** shelf, click **OK**, then set **Compute Using** to **Customer Name**. Open the filter again and select the value **True**.

So, let's recapture what we have done so far. We plotted the sales values per region, then we added an R script that creates quantiles out of the sales dot cloud. We also created a parameter that lets us select how many quantiles we want to see in the view since we learned that quantiles don't always have to be quartiles but could also be terciles or quintiles, or more.

Next up we will see this view in action, and we will add jittering:

14. You may wish to add these additional steps to further enhance the visualization. To utilize jittering, create an index calculated field, Index(), and place that field on the **Columns** shelf. Set **Compute Using** to **Customer Name**. Be sure to deselect **Show Header** so **Index** does not display in the view.

15. Right-click on each axis and select **Logarithmic** and deselect **Include Zero**. You should see the following on your screen:

Figure 15.25: Quantiles dashboard

In the preceding figure, you can see that we decided to show four quantiles (utilizing the **Number of quantiles** parameter), which as such are called quartiles. By adding the Index() function to columns, we were able to divide the quantiles of each of the four components. One conclusion from this dashboard could be that, in each of the four quantiles, the West region has the highest sales figures, and the South region has the lowest. However, the Central and South regions come very close to each other in the third quantile. Based on this information, we could do some further analysis on what is going on in those regions specifically and why the Central region's sales decrease in that quantile compared to the other regions.

Now that we've completed the exercise, let's take a moment to consider some of the code we looked at in this exercise:

`SCRIPT_REAL`	This Tableau function calls the R engine and returns a float value.
`x <- .arg1;`	x is the variable on which we'll create quantiles. The variable, in this case, is [Sales].
`y <- .arg2[1];`	This variable sets the quantile count. [1] forces a single number to be set and not a vector.
`m <- c(1:y)/y;`	m distributes probabilities evenly from 1:y.
`n <- length(x);`	This sets the size of the loops. The loops are discussed below.
`z <- c(1:n); for (i in c(1:n)) z[i] = 0;`	z sets the initial response vector by setting everything to 0.
`for (j in c(1:y))    for (i in c(1:n)) z[i] = if (x[i] <= quantile(x,m)[j] && z[i] == 0 ) j else z[i];`	For each quantile, we go through the z vector, and for each entry, we test whether the value of x is less than the upper limit of that quantile. If x has previously been set, we leave it. Otherwise, z[i] = that quantile (j).

In this exercise, you saw that by using R, a Tableau default functionality such as clustering can be extended and will give your dashboard users more freedom to answer new questions that come up while using the dashboard because it will be possible for them to change, for example, parameters and see the visualization changing. Now that we've learned about a few possible R use cases, it is time to discuss something worth your attention, the performance challenges that come along by using programming integrations with Tableau.

Performance challenges

R scripts are table calculations. Like all table calculations, this means that you can only utilize fields that are on your view. Also, it's important that you set partitioning and addressing correctly otherwise you may receive unexpected results.

In the *Introducing quantiles* section, you may have noticed that the greater the number of quantiles set with the **Number of quantiles** parameter, the longer it takes the results to display. This is because R runs the loops in the **Quantile** calculated field one iteration for each quantile. For example, if the **Number of quantiles** parameter is set to **1**, the loop is instigated only once. If it is set to **2**, it runs twice, and so forth. The rule of thumb is that R code is executed once for every partition. The more partitions, the slower the performance. Therefore, when using R code, reduce the number of partitions whenever possible.

This was the R part of this chapter. I hope you enjoyed it and that it has given you the inspiration to come up with your own ideas to extend the functionality we have shared so far. We will now continue with the other very well-known programming language: Python. Lucky us, Tableau also has an integration layer with Python.

Python installation and integration

Python is an interpreted programming language and is very well known for its readability. The first release was in 1991, so quite some time ago (longer than most people would guess), and it was developed by Guido van Rossum. TabPy is an external service that will allow you to connect Python and Tableau—similar to Rserve. By using TabPy, you will be able to parse fields from your Tableau dashboard to Python, execute a calculation, and send back the result as a new calculated field to Tableau. Or you can also call functions that you implemented in Python, again in a calculated field. A more extensive article on TabPy can be found here: https://tableaumagic.com/tableau-and-python-an-introduction.

Installing Python is typically not difficult, but it does involve more than simply double-clicking on an executable. In order to successfully connect Tableau with Python, you might have to install some libraries and execute comments on the command line. The following paragraphs will guide you through this process.

The easiest way to install Python is by performing the following steps:

1. Download, for example, Anaconda with the Python 3.7 version: https://www.anaconda.com. Any other Python interpreter will work too.

    In order to integrate Python and Tableau, some additional steps are needed:

2. Open, for example, Jupyter Notebook within Anaconda and write:

    ```
    !pip install tabpy
    ```

    Alternatively, execute the following command on the command line or Terminal (for Mac) in your Python directory:

    ```
    pip install tabpy
    ```

3. Navigate to the directory where **TabPy** has been installed via the command line or Terminal (for Mac) and type tabpy into the command line or Terminal interface:

Figure 15.26: Starting TabPy

4. You will most likely see a popup window. Click **Allow**:

Figure 15.27: Allow a network connection

5. You are now connected to the `tabpy` server, which has to remain open while running Tableau and Python combined.

6. You might get error messages due to version incompatibility similar to the following: `module 'tornado.web' has no attribute 'asynchronous'`. In my case, I had a newer version of Tornado installed, therefore I had to uninstall Tornado and `pip` and install the proper version (4.2), which works just fine with TabPy. If you encounter any other issues with TabPy, a quick Google search will go a long way.

7. Open Tableau, select **Help | Settings and Performance | Manage Analytics Extension Connection**, and select **localhost** for **Server** and enter **9004** for **Port**:

Figure 15.28: Analytics Extension Connection

8. As you can see in the previous screenshot, it is possible to set up usernames and passwords and SSL if you have any security concerns or for a bigger enterprise-wide rollout.

9. Click on **Test Connection** and you should see the following popup:

Figure 15.29: Testing analytics extension

The full documentation on how to get TabPy up and running can be found at
`https://github.com/tableau/TabPy`. If you don't want to or can't install TabPy
on your machine, Tableau also offers a Docker container that will install the latest
version of TabPy. You can find more information here: `https://hub.docker.com/r/emhemh/TabPy/`.

Implementing Python functionality

Just like R, TabPy makes use of the script functions in Tableau. In the next sections,
we will practice working with TabPy and will look at multiple use cases. Tableau
calculations using TabPy look very similar to R's. For TabPy, it is important to add a
return statement in the calculated field and notice that arguments are noted with an
underscore instead of a dot:

Figure 15.30: Python TabPy syntax

This will be manifested in the next exercises; we will first look into random number
generators.

Random and random normal

Many calculations are easily accessible via the calculated fields, others via the table calculations—and then there are some hidden functions. If you tried to find the function Random for example, you wouldn't. But you can still use the Random() function as can be seen here:

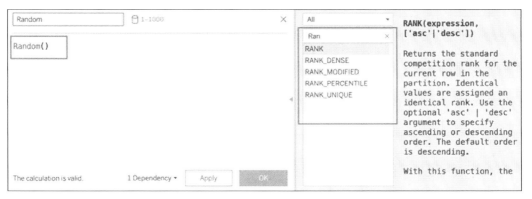

Figure 15.31: Random

Another option is, using TabPy to get the Random function. We will look at random as well as random normal with the variables mu and sigma. This will allow us to draw random numbers from a distribution, a method often used in statistics and quantitative modeling as well as other areas to simulate, reproduce, or calculate probabilities. mu and sigma are the mean and standard deviation defining the distribution.

Generating random numbers

Perform the following steps to create a dot cloud of random variables with a specific underlying distribution, defined by the mean and standard deviation:

1. Create an Excel sheet with one `Index` column and rows with the numbers 1-1,000. This is needed to have an initial dataset with the number of rows we want to use for the random number generator:

	A
1	Index
2	1
3	2
4	3
5	4
6	5
7	6
8	7
9	8
10	9
11	10
12	11
13	12

Figure 15.32: Excel sheet 1-1,000

2. Save the file and connect Tableau to this Excel sheet. You should see one imported measure called **Index** (just like the header in your Excel file).

3. Connect Tableau to Python as described in *Python installation and integration*.

4. Create a calculated field called `Random`, which should look as follows:

```
SCRIPT_REAL("
from numpy import random as rd
return rd.random(_arg1[0]).tolist()",
SIZE()
)
```

5. Drag **Index** to **Rows** and **Random** to **Columns**.

6. Disable **Aggregate Measures** on the **Analysis** tab.

7. Change the **Marks** type to **Density**:

Figure 15.33: Random visualized

In the preceding screenshot, you can see the 1,000 random data points. Let's consider some of the code used in this exercise that allowed us to generate this visualization:

`SCRIPT_REAL`	This Tableau function calls the Python engine and returns a float value.
`"from numpy import random as rd`	In this part of the code, we need the Python library numpy, and from that library, we need the module random, which we will load with the shorter name rd.
`return`	This command is simply needed to return a value.

rd.random(_arg1[0]).tolist()"	In this step, we call the module rd that we imported before. From the rd module, we retrieve the random function. The _arg1[0] is needed to activate the function given a certain value. And lastly, we put all the retrieved values in a list of values by adding .tolist().
SIZE()	This is the value that will be replacing _arg1 and _arg1 is required by the random function. We use SIZE() to fulfill the requirement because it will return the number of rows in the partition and is sufficient to get a random number back from the function.

We were able to get exactly 1,000 numbers because our initial Excel sheet had 1,000 rows. By using calculated fields, you can add columns to a data frame but no rows. Therefore, we need a data source that will provide us with the data schema. In the next section, we will learn how to specify a random number drawn from a normal distribution.

Random normal

Now, let's reproduce a random variable with a normal distribution. This technique is often used in statistical modeling to calculate probabilities. The random normal values can be used instead of or in addition to observations you already collected. Once we know how to use a normal distribution, you can extend this knowledge and create other distributions in Tableau as well:

1. Reuse the workbook from the previous exercise.
2. Create a Random Normal calculated field:

   ```
   SCRIPT_REAL("
   from numpy import random as rd
   mu, sigma = 0, 1
   return (rd.normal(mu, sigma, _arg1[0])).tolist()
   ",
   SIZE()
   )
   ```

3. Place **Random Normal** on **Columns** and **Index** on **Rows**.
4. Disable **Aggregate Measures** on the **Analysis** tab.

5. Select a **Marks** type of **Density**. You can now see a plot with the 1,000 data points normally distributed:

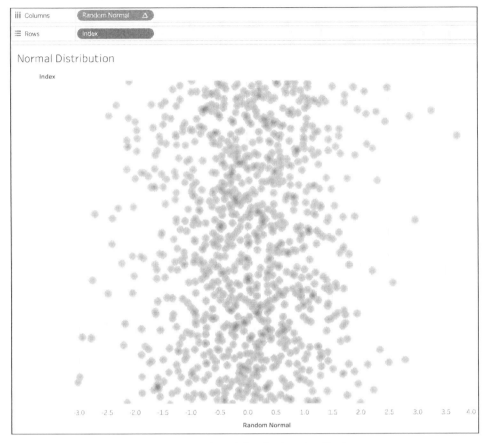

Figure 15.34: Normal distribution visualized

To give your users more flexibility, you can also add parameters to your view that interact with the Python integration. For example, create the following two parameters:

Figure 15.35: Parameters mu and sigma

Then change the **Random Normal** calculated field as shown here:

```
SCRIPT_REAL("
from numpy import random as rd
mu, sigma = _arg2, _arg3
return (rd.normal(mu, sigma, _arg1[0])).tolist()
",
SIZE(), [mu], [sigma]
)
```

Add the parameter control to your view and your users can decide which variables they want to pass to Python:

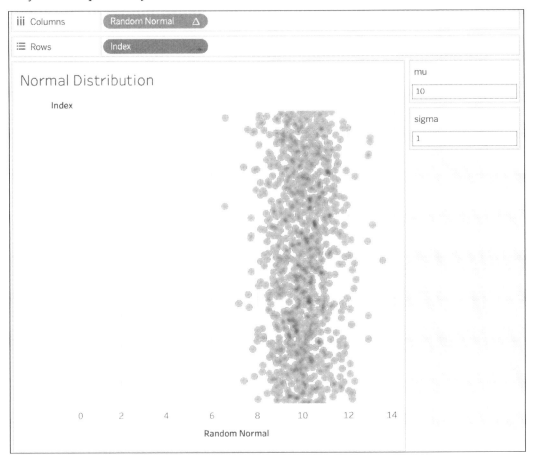

Figure 15.36: Final normal distribution worksheet

Compared to our prior visualization with the normal distribution, you can see in the preceding screenshot that by changing the mu parameter to 10, we change the mean to 10 and thus can move the whole dot cloud in any direction. With the random number being available in Tableau, you can, for example, visualize a Monte Carlo simulation.

 More information on how to calculate a Monte Carlo simulation can be found here: https://jacksontwo.com/exploring-python-tableau.

Before moving on, let's again consider some of the key lines of code that were used in this exercise:

`SCRIPT_REAL`	This Tableau function calls the Python engine and returns a float value.
`"from numpy import random as rd`	In this part of the code, we need the Python library numpy, and from that library, we need the module random, which we will load with the shorter name rd.
`mu, sigma = _arg2,_arg3`	This part defines that we will refer to mu and sigma with _arg2 and _arg3.
`return`	This command is simply needed to return a value.
`rd.normal(mu, sigma, _arg1[0])).tolist()`	In this step, we call the module rd that we imported before. From the rd module, we retrieve the random function. The _arg1[0] is needed to activate the function given a certain value. Optional values are mu and sigma. This time, we will use those two as well. And lastly, we put all the retrieved values in a list of values by adding .tolist().
`SIZE(), [mu], [sigma]`	This is the value that will be replacing _arg1, _arg2, and _arg3. Just like before, we use SIZE() to activate the function. The optional values mu and sigma will be pointing to the parameter we created before.

After finishing the first two exercises with TabPy, we learned how we can use a random number in Tableau by using the TabPy connector. Next, we changed the random number to a random number drawn from a normal distribution and added parameters to the dashboard such that the user can change mu and sigma of the normal distribution. Of course, you can change the function in TabPy to other distributions as well.

The next topic is more advanced. We will use TabPy to execute a sentiment analysis on the words that were used in Lord of the Rings.

Calculating sentiment analysis

Alongside machine learning and artificial intelligence, another term is being used more and more: **Natural Language Processing (NLP)**. This is the process of machines understanding words and their meaning. Sentiment analysis falls into this category; the technique has different flavors but one of them is to measure polarity, that is, whether the speaker has a positive or negative opinion. Use cases are, for example, datasets of reviews, tweets, comments, plots, lyrics, and so on. Let's have a look!

This exercise is based on the idea of Brit Cava, who used the Makeover Monday data from the top 100 song lyrics in order to try out the Tableau-Python integration. You can find the blog post here: https://www.tableau.com/about/blog/2016/12/using-python-sentiment-analysis-tableau-63606. Let's reproduce it with another dataset:

1. Navigate to the **Sentiment** tab in the workbook associated with the chapter.
2. Connect to the **Lord of the Rings** data source.
3. Connect Tableau to Python.
4. Create a `Sentiment Score` calculated field. The formatting, for example, indented text, is important:

```
SCRIPT_REAL("
from nltk.sentiment import SentimentIntensityAnalyzer
text = _arg1
scores = []
sid = SentimentIntensityAnalyzer()
for word in text:
    ss = sid.polarity_scores(word)
scores.append(ss['compound'])
return scores "
,ATTR([Dialog]))
```

5. Create a `Color Coding` calculated field:

```
IIF ([Sentiment Scores] >= 0, 'Positivity', 'Negativity')
```

6. Place **Character** on the **Filter** shelf and filter the top 20 characters by **Count** of **Dialog**:

Figure 15.37: Filter character

7. Put **Character** on **Rows** and **Dialog** on the **Detail** shelf. Change the **Marks** type to **Bar**.

8. Add **Sentiment Score** to **Columns** and **Color Coding** to the **Colour** shelf. Lastly, drag an average line from the analytics pane on the view (per cell):

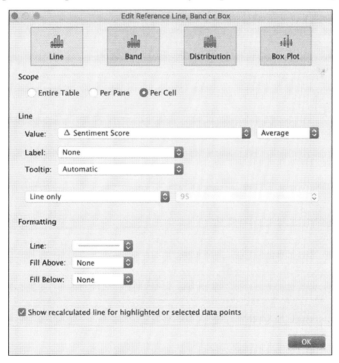

Figure 15.38: Sentiment score

This will result in the following visualization:

Figure 15.39: Worksheet

So far, we have loaded the dataset and created a Python calculation that uses a pre-trained sentiment analyzer that tells us if a person's dialog in Lord of the Rings is negative or positive. In the preceding figure, we brought everything together and you can see how much of the total dialog of any given character from those movies is positive and how much is negative. We also added an average to clearly indicate the overall sentiment for each role.

9. Rename the worksheet to **Sentiment Analysis per Character** by right-clicking on the worksheet tab and selecting **Rename**.

10. Make the **Character** filter applicable to all sheets that use this data source:

Figure 15.40: Apply filter to worksheets

11. Create a second sheet by right-clicking on the worksheet tab and selecting **Duplicate**.

12. Name the new worksheet **Sentiment Analysis per Movie** and replace **Character** with **Movie** on the **Rows** shelf:

Figure 15.41: Sentiment analysis per movie

13. Create a dashboard with the **Movie** worksheet at the top and the **Character** worksheet at the bottom, then activate the **Use as Filter** function of the two sheets:

Figure 15.42: Enable filter

14. *Et voilà*, you created a **Sentiment Analysis** of the three Lord of the Rings movies based on their tendency to use a greater number of positive or negative words:

Figure 15.43: Final dashboard

In this exercise, we were able to show that Tableau can analyze text data for its sentiment, something we have not seen before. In order to do so, we needed to connect Tableau with Python, which is possible by using the external service TabPy. Python can make use of libraries such as `nltk.sentiment` — which we used in this case. A thorough description of this package can be found here: `https://www.nltk.org/api/nltk.sentiment.html`. There are many other libraries for sentiment analysis but `nltk` is used a lot for demonstration purposes and learning. Feel free to try other libraries as well!

Let's demystify some of the new code instances we included in this exercise:

`SCRIPT_REAL`	This Tableau function calls the Python engine and returns a float value.
`from nltk.sentiment import SentimentIntensityAnalyzer`	In this part of the code, we need the Python library `nltk`, and from that library, we need the module `sentiment` from which we will load the function `SentimentIntensityAnalyzer`.

`text = _arg1`
 	
`scores = []`
 	
`sid = SentimentIntensityAnalyzer()`
 	
`ss = sid.polarity_scores(word)`
	This part defines that our `_arg1` will be called `text`, `scores` will be an empty list (and filled later in the code), `sid` will refer to the `SentimentIntensityAnalyzer` function and lastly, `ss` will be the reference to the scores per word.

`scores.append(ss['compound'])`	In this step, we will fill the empty `scores` table with the polarity scores.
`return scores`	Here, we are returning the now filled `scores` table as output to Tableau.
`ATTR([Dialog])`	Our `_arg1` is specified as the field `Dialog` from the Tableau workbook.

We have seen embedded Python code now; you create a calculated field and use fields from your dataset as input. But what if you wanted to use a large model with many lines of code and many different variables, or upfront training of your model? Would this exceed TabPy's capabilities? No! Because next to embedded code, we are also able to write Python scripts outside of Tableau.

Deploying models with TabPy

At times, your script will just be too long to be used in a calculated field, or you'll need upfront training on a different dataset or an extended dataset rather than the one you have in Tableau. In this case, we can use TabPy in a slightly different way. You can write a model outside of Tableau—in Python and deploy it to Tableau such that you can call it from within the desktop.

In the upcoming example, we will build a recommender system that predicts the likelihood of a Pima woman having diabetes when inputting 7 parameters (age, BMI, pregnancies, blood pressure, glucose, insulin, and skin thickness). The dataset is from a 1988 study by *J.W. Smith, J.E. Everhart, W.C. Dickson, W.C. Knowler, and R.S. Johannes*, accessible via the following link: https://www.ncbi.nlm.nih.gov/pmc/articles/PMC2245318/.

We will begin with the code in the Jupyter notebook. Please follow along with the next steps:

1. We start the code by importing the client, which we need to make a Python-Tableau connection:

    ```
    from tabpy.tabpy_tools.client import Client
    client = Client('http://localhost:9004/')
    ```

2. Then we import all the libraries we will need, and the data, and make sure to replace the dataset name with the full path of the file location (for example, H:/Documents/Diabetes.csv):

    ```
    import numpy as np
    import pandas as pd
    from sklearn import ensemble
    from sklearn.model_selection import train_test_split

    df = pd.read_csv("Diabetes.csv", sep = ',')
    df = df[['Pregnancies', 'Glucose', 'BloodPressure',
    'SkinThickness', 'Insulin', 'BMI', 'Age', 'Outcome']]
    ```

3. Now we split the dataset in four; two test datasets that will help us check how accurate our model is, as well as an X_train dataset and a Y_train dataset:

    ```
    X_train, X_test, y_train, y_test = train_test_split(df.
    drop(['Outcome'], axis = 'columns'),df['Outcome'], test_size =
    0.2)
    ```

If you are interested in more detail and the math behind this code, please check: https://scikit-learn.org/ stable/modules/generated/sklearn.ensemble. GradientBoostingClassifier.html.

4. Next, we will load the **GradientBoosting** model from sklearn and fit our data, then we can immediately visualize the score, which can be interpreted as the percentage of the total that our model predicted the correct value for:

```
gb = ensemble.GradientBoostingClassifier()
gb.fit(X_train, y_train)
gbscore = gb.score(X_test, y_test)

print('gradient boost: ' + str(round(gbscore*100,2)))
```

5. And this is the full code in Jupyter:

```
1   import numpy as np
2   import pandas as pd
3   from sklearn import ensemble
4   from sklearn.model_selection import train_test_split
5
6
7   #load dataset
8   df = pd.read_csv("Diabetes.csv", sep = ',')
9
10  df = df[['Pregnancies', 'Glucose', 'BloodPressure', 'SkinThickness', 'Insulin',
11        'BMI', 'Age', 'Outcome']]
12
13  #split dataset
14  X_train, X_test, y_train, y_test = train_test_split(df.drop(['Outcome'], axis = 'columns'),df['Outcome'],
15                                    test_size = 0.2)
16
17
18  #gradient boost
19  gb = ensemble.GradientBoostingClassifier()
20  gb.fit(X_train, y_train)
21  gbscore = gb.score(X_test, y_test)
22
23  print('gradient boost: ' + str(round(gbscore*100,2)))
24
25
26
gradient boost: 79.87
```

Figure 15.44: Python script

To conclude this first phase, our model predicted the right outcome in 79.87% of cases, either having diabetes or not having diabetes. This is a pretty good result. In order to further improve it, we could add more data (in terms of rows), extend our input variables (in terms of columns), or create new features like ratios between variables (hidden information could be emphasized this way). But for now, we can continue working with the model, because eventually, we want to predict a likelihood as a percentage of someone having diabetes. Let's switch over to Tableau:

6. We won't need a dataset for this exercise because all of our data lives in the Jupyter notebook. In Tableau, you can just select one randomly, as we won't use it. In a new Tableau worksheet called **Diabetes**, create the following seven parameters:

Figure 15.45: Age parameter

Figure 15.46: BloodPressure parameter

Figure 15.47: BMI parameter

Figure 15.48: Insulin parameter

Figure 15.49: SkinThickness parameter

Figure 15.50: Glucose parameter

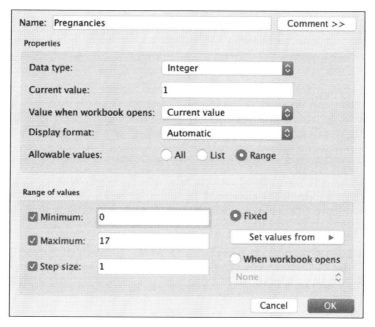

Figure 15.51: Pregnancies parameter

7. After you have created all seven parameters, select all of them and click **Show Parameter**:

Figure 15.52: Show Parameter

8. Please go back to Jupyter now and execute the two last missing pieces of code that will create a function to call our model:

    ```python
    def diabetes_predictor(_arg1, _arg2, _arg3, _arg4, _arg5,_arg6,
                        _arg7):
        import pandas as pd

        row = {'Pregnancies': _arg1, 'Glucose': _arg2, 'BloodPressure':
            _arg3, 'SkinThickness': _arg4, 'Insulin': _arg5, 'BMI':
            _arg6, 'Age': _arg7
            }
        test_data = pd.DataFrame(data = row,index=[0])
        predprob_diabetes = gb.predict_proba(test_data)
        return [probability[1] for probability in predprob_diabetes]
    ```

9. And lastly, the line that will deploy the function to TabPy:

    ```python
    client.deploy('diabetes_predictor', diabetes_predictor,'Predicts
        the chances of a Pima female having diabetes', override = True)
    ```

10. This looks as follows in Jupyter:

    ```python
    def diabetes_predictor(_arg1, _arg2, _arg3, _arg4, _arg5,
                        _arg6, _arg7):
        import pandas as pd

        row = {'Pregnancies': _arg1, 'Glucose': _arg2, 'BloodPressure': _arg3, 'SkinThickness': _arg4,
            'Insulin': _arg5, 'BMI': _arg6, 'Age': _arg7
            }
        test_data = pd.DataFrame(data = row,index=[0])
        predprob_diabetes = gb.predict_proba(test_data)
        return [probability[1] for probability in predprob_diabetes]


    client.deploy('diabetes_predictor', diabetes_predictor,
                'Predicts the chances of a Pima female having diabetes', override = True)
    ```

    Figure 15.53: Deploying the function

11. In order to check if your model has been deployed, type `https://localhost:9004/endpoints` in your browser. This will list all the models that have been deployed to TabPy on your machine:

    ```
    {"diabetes_predictor":{"description": "Predicts the chances of
    a Pima female having diabetes", "type": "model", "version": 2,
    "dependencies:[], "target": null, "creation_time": 1608445088,
    "last_modified_time": 1608445680, "schema": null, "docstring
    found in query function -"}}
    ```

12. Go back to Tableau and double-check if the connection to TabPy is still active.

13. Create a calculated field called `Diabetes predictor` like so:

```
SCRIPT_REAL("
return tabpy.query('diabetes_predictor',_arg1,_arg2,_arg3,_
arg4,_arg5,_arg6,
_arg7)['response']",
[Pregnancies], [Glucose], [BloodPressure], [SkinThickness],
[Insulin],
[BMI],[Age]
)
```

You can see here that since we did all the coding in Python, we only tell
Tableau to return a TabPy query called `diabetes_predictor`, then add all the
n references to variables that are required for the function, and lastly add
`['response']` at the end.

14. Now place the field **Diabetes predictor** on the **Text** shelf and observe the
outcome:

Figure 15.54: Interactive TabPy Diabetes worksheet

By sliding the parameters to the left and right, you will see that the likelihood of
diabetes changes. The calculated field sends the data of the parameters via TabPy to
Python where your data will be fitted to the model. And the result will be sent back,
and you can see it. Of course, you can build a whole dashboard around it. Examples
can be found on the Tableau website: `https://www.tableau.com/about/blog/2017/1/`
`building-advanced-analytics-applications-tabpy-64916`.

If you want to learn more about the Python language itself, a good source of information is, for example, `https://www.w3schools.com/python/default.asp`. The web page will, step by step, guide you through the Python syntax. But Tableau makes it even easier because a set of functions have already been written for you.

Predeployed TabPy functions

Not everyone likes to program outside of Tableau and that's why Tableau came up with a set of widely used, predeployed functions you can use out of the box. You will still need to execute one line of code, once! But that is all you need to do in Python itself. The available functions are Anova, T-test, Sentiment Analysis, and PCA but Tableau has mentioned on multiple occasions that more functions might be coming soon. You can find the documentation here: `https://tableau.github.io/TabPy/docs/tabpy-tools.html`.

But let's walk through the steps:

1. In your Jupyter notebook, execute `tabpy-deploy-models` and see that the four functions will be installed:

```
1  ! tabpy-deploy-models

Using config file at /Applications/anaconda3/lib/python3.8/site-packages/tabpy/tabpy_server/common/default.conf
Successfully deployed anova
Successfully deployed ttest
/Applications/anaconda3/bin/python3: can't find '__main__' module in '/Applications/anaconda3/lib/python3.8/site-pa
ckages/tabpy/models/scripts/__pycache__'
[nltk_data] Downloading package vader_lexicon to
[nltk_data]     /Users/meiermarleen/nltk_data...
[nltk_data]   Package vader_lexicon is already up-to-date!
[nltk_data] Downloading package punkt to
[nltk_data]     /Users/meiermarleen/nltk_data...
[nltk_data]   Package punkt is already up-to-date!
Successfully deployed Sentiment Analysis
Successfully deployed PCA
```

Figure 15.55: Deploying TabPy default models

2. You can double-check this by typing `http://localhost:9004/endpoints` in your browser, where you should see all deployed models.

And that's it, calling the function in a calculated field in Tableau is now as easy as the following (using `ttest` as an example function being called):

```
tabpy.query('ttest', _arg1, _arg2)['response']
```

From Python, you can connect directly to, for example:

- DataRobot (`https://www.tableau.com/solutions/datarobot`)

- Dataiku (`https://www.dataiku.com/partners/tableau/`)

- MATLAB (`https://www.mathworks.com/products/reference-architectures/tableau.html`)

These are all paid third-party tools that help make your data analysis easier. And if you can make a connection from Python to another external tool, you can also leverage that capability back to Tableau via TabPy. If you are interested in this type of connection or if you want to refresh the topic of deploying functions, you can check out this video: `https://youtu.be/0BN_Y2CxdYY`, in which Nathan Mannheimer, a product manager for advanced analytics at Tableau, explains everything we have discussed as well.

What are your personal goals with a programming integration? If you have a great idea, feel free to share it with the Tableau community.

Summary

This chapter just scratched the surface regarding the options of working with R and Python. After finishing this chapter, you should now be able to connect to Python and R from Tableau and recognize and write the basic syntax for both programming languages in Tableau. Most importantly, you are now skilled to leverage the power of R and Python functions in Tableau from a simple mean calculation, to regressions, all the way to implementing your own machine learning model. Although we covered installation, integration, and workflow, as well as some of the more popular functions and use cases, there is much more to explore. In fact, the possibilities of Tableau's programming integration remain largely uncharted territory in the BI community. The intrepid in data visualization are pushing the envelope, but there's much to be done. For those readers looking to enhance their career options, expertise in both packages could offer great advantages!

Now we've reached the end of the book, consider our journey, which started with loading data into Tableau, creating our first visualizations and executing our first functions. We moved on by familiarizing ourselves with level of detail and table calculations, learning about Tableau Prep Builder, Tableau Server, and general visualization best practices before our final round, in which we learned about advanced analytics and leveraging the power of Tableau programming tool integration.

This leaves me with just one question: What will be your next Tableau project? Feel free to share it on Tableau Public and don't forget to add the tag #MasteringTableau. I want to congratulate you all for participating and engaging in this learning process! Whether you have more questions, remarks or feedback, feel free to reach out to me or to the Tableau community. I wish you a lot of success with your personal Tableau career.

Happy Tableau'ing!

Share your experience

Thank you for taking the time to read this book. If you enjoyed this book, help others to find it. Leave a review at https://www.amazon.com/dp/1800561644.

packt.com

Subscribe to our online digital library for full access to over 7,000 books and videos, as well as industry leading tools to help you plan your personal development and advance your career. For more information, please visit our website.

Why subscribe?

- Spend less time learning and more time coding with practical eBooks and Videos from over 4,000 industry professionals

- Learn better with Skill Plans built especially for you

- Get a free eBook or video every month

- Fully searchable for easy access to vital information

- Copy and paste, print, and bookmark content

At www.Packt.com, you can also read a collection of free technical articles, sign up for a range of free newsletters, and receive exclusive discounts and offers on Packt books and eBooks.

Another Book You May Enjoy

If you enjoyed this book, you may be interested in this another book by Packt:

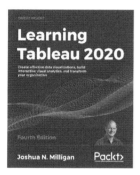

Learning Tableau 2020 - Fourth edition

Joshua N. Milligan

ISBN: 978-1-80020-036-4

- Develop stunning visualizations to explain complex data with clarity
- Explore exciting new Data Model capabilities
- Connect to various data sources to bring all your data together
- Leverage Tableau Prep Builder's amazing capabilities for data cleaning and structuring
- Create and use calculations to solve problems and enrich the analytics
- Master advanced topics such as sets, LOD calculations, and much more
- Enable smart decisions with data clustering, distribution, and forecasting
- Share your data stories to build a culture of trust and action

Index

D

dashboard
best practices, for user experience 525
creating 2, 14-18
documentation, maximizing on 499, 500
interactivity, adding 18-21
dashboard, best practices for user experience
Actions 525
Dashboard Button, exporting 543, 544
Item hierarchy 544, 545
Used In feature 545
Dashboard Button
exporting 543, 544
dashboard design 502
collapsible menu, creating 513-525
sheet swapping, utilizing 507-512
dashboard layout 503
golden ratio layout 503-505
quad layout 506
small multiple layout 506, 507
dashboard, performance
expectations, setting 641
overcrowd, avoiding 641
size, fixing 641
data
blending 150
cleaning 71-76
connecting to 84-86
densification 245
dumps 81
exporting, to mobile phone 43, 44
exporting, to other devices 43
extracting 77-81
extrapolating 66-70
mining 57
null values, establishing 62-66
preparation, focusing 61
surveying 61
Tableau, connecting to 22
database administrator (DBA) 618
Dataiku
reference link 756
DataRobot
reference link 756

dataset
generating, with grid 384, 385
data source filters 634
data sources
columns, defining as NOT NULL 619
connecting to 617, 618
foreign keys, defining 619
indexing 620
primary keys, defining 619
publishing, to Tableau Server 644-646
working with 618, 619
data structures 175
adjusting 176-183
data, Tableau Prep Builder
aggregating 107-111
joins, adding 104-106
pivoting 111-115
scripting 116-120
unions, adding 98-103
default behavior, Tableau
nested sorting 9-11
sorting 9-11
dense information
presenting 497
Department of Health and Human Services (HSS) 71
dimension 35, 36
dimension and measure filters 636
directional table calculations 188-190
discrete 39-42
distance line
adding 599-602
distance measures
used, for extending geo-spatial analytics 592-595
documentation
maximizing, on dashboard 499, 500
domain completion 245
activating, in crosstab 246-250
deploying 246
need for 251
nulls, labeling 252, 253
through, view types 250, 251
unwanted marks, removing 253-258